Microsoft®

Inside
Direct3D®

W0010421

Peter J. Kovach

Foreword by
Michael D. Anderson

PUBLISHED BY
Microsoft Press
A Division of Microsoft Corporation
One Microsoft Way
Redmond, Washington 98052-6399

Library of Congress Cataloging-in-Publication Data
Kovach, Peter J., 1961-
    Inside Direct3D / Peter J. Kovach.
    p. cm.
    Includes index.
    ISBN 0-7356-0613-7
    1. Computer graphics.   2. Direct3D.   3. Three-dimensional display systems.
    I. Title.
  T385.K69 1999
  006.6'93 21--dc21   99-045528

Printed and bound in the United States of America.

1 2 3 4 5 6 7 8 9 MLML 5 4 3 2 1 0

Distributed in Canada by Penguin Books Canada Limited.

A CIP catalogue record for this book is available from the British Library.

Microsoft Press books are available through booksellers and distributors worldwide. For further information about international editions, contact your local Microsoft Corporation office or contact Microsoft Press International directly at fax (425) 936-7329. Visit our Web site at mspress.microsoft.com.

Acquisitions Editor: Eric Stroo
Project Editor: Sally Stickney
Technical Consultant: Michael Anderson
Technical Copy Editor: Shawn Peck

To Monica and Shannon

BRIEF CONTENTS

CONTENTS

CHAPTER SIX

Rendering 3D Primitives   **141**

FOREWORD

In my favorite episode of the TV show "The Simpsons," Homer gets the job of doing the voice for a cartoon character on "The Itchy and Scratchy Show." At his first recording session, in his classic clueless manner, Homer asks whether this episode is being done live. The producer's sarcastic reply is, "No, Homer. Very few cartoons are broadcast live—it's a terrible strain on the animators' wrists." Indeed, it would be impossible for humans, but personal computers are now up to the task of generating "live" 3D animation. Real-time rendered scenes indistinguishable from photographs are not quite within reach yet, but thousands of textured polygons per frame at 60 frames per second can create a very believable world. Almost all computer systems sold today contain chips—some even more complex than the main microprocessor—dedicated to the acceleration of 3D rendering. From year to year, the graphics processors being introduced are increasing in power at a phenomenal rate. The result is that the graphics for computer games can be more dazzling than ever before.

Microsoft's Direct3D team has the challenging job of delivering an API to software developers that lets them take full advantage of this technology. Given the incredible rate of innovation by the graphics companies, this process of keeping up with the state of the art is a continuous one. Making the API easy to use—yet totally flexible and lightning fast—has always been the key goal. With each version, Direct3D gets more efficient and powerful. Sometimes adding a feature (such as automatic texture management) simply makes life easier for the programmer. Other features (such as stencil buffers) require additional understanding and code from the programmer, but the result is more freedom to create realistic, immersive game worlds.

In this book, Peter Kovach provides an excellent introduction to the Direct3D API that will help you learn how to use 3D graphics technology like a pro. He also shows how to use the related DirectX APIs for input and networking to write a complete game. Making a game that's fun to play is still up to you, but with a solid understanding of the power of Direct3D, you'll be well on your way.

Michael Anderson
DirectX SDK Team

ACKNOWLEDGMENTS

I'd first like to thank William Chin, who developed the concept for the RoadRage game and the original version of the RoadRage code that we then enhanced and used throughout this book. William is a great guy who has put an incredible amount of effort into the RoadRage code. William, I've greatly enjoyed working with you on this project and look forward to our future endeavors.

William and I and the rest of the Head Tapper Software team are currently in the process of developing a new game, RamRaider, which incorporates all the features in RoadRage and adds a great deal more. We'll release this game as shareware. To find out more information about this game and our software development company, Head Tapper Software, visit our Web site at *www.headtappersoftware.com*.

I'd also like to thank the following individuals, also members of Head Tapper Software, who have been involved in the development of the models and textures used in RoadRage: Mark Bracey, Blair Harris Burrill, James Glendenning, and Correia Emmanuel.

I'd like to extend a very special thank you to Michael Anderson of the Microsoft Direct3D SDK team. He reviewed the entire book in galleys and pages and made numerous suggestions that improved the quality of the book immeasurably.

I'd also like to thank all the other folks at Microsoft, especially those on the DirectX team and at Microsoft Press (Eric Stroo, Sally Stickney, Donnie Cameron, and Dail Magee Jr.). I also want to thank the people and companies who provided material used on the companion CD: Robert Lansdale of Okino Computer Graphics, Inc., MadOnion.com, Credo Interactive Inc., Indotek, Greg Kochaniak of Hyperionics, and Phillip Martin.

Thank you also to Dad and Mom for always supporting me and showing me that I could do anything I had the desire to do. You never know what I'll do next, do you?

Finally, and most of all, I'd like to thank my wife, Monica, and my daughter, Shannon. Thank you both so much for putting up with me writing all hours of the evening and working on code at every possible moment. Shannon, I love you tons and tons—you are the best daughter in the world; and Monica—forever + a day.

Peter Kovach
February 2000

USING THE COMPANION CD

The companion CD includes all the code from this book. Unlike most books on the market, which provide numerous simple applets showing commands working in relative isolation (for example, showing how to display a generic 3D shape but neglecting to show how to shade it, animate it, texture it, combine it, let you control it, and have it interact with other objects), this book will walk you through the development of a *complete* 3D application. Each chapter builds on the previous one, demonstrating capabilities that include the following:

- Showing you how to write the code to handle windowed and full-screen functionality
- Creating a complex 3D world containing streets and fields
- Adding 3D objects to scenes, such as buildings, street lights producing lighting for the scene, and signs
- Coloring objects within scenes
- Adding textures to scenes
- Adding animated characters to scenes
- Adding sound
- Adding keyboard, joystick, and mouse input
- Adding fog
- Adding network game play

By the end of the book, you'll have seen how to build a working 3D application in which you can create new 3D environments and then drive or walk around in them as well as shoot and see weapons fire, and play head-to-head with other players. Most important, even with all these advanced features, the game will run between 30 to 60 frames per second on a system with an inexpensive 3D accelerator.

The companion CD also contains the Microsoft DirectX 7 Software Developer's Kit (SDK), which you need to install in order to compile and run the RoadRage code discussed in this book. This SDK includes the documentation, run-time files, headers, and libraries that are part of the DirectX distribution. It also includes many example projects that the DirectX team developed. These are a standard part of the CD-based distribution that provides examples of how to implement code using DirectX functionality.

In addition to the code and the DirectX 7 SDK, you'll find a number of third-party programs and 3D objects that will help you get the most out of the RoadRage code and DirectX:

- Quake 2 Modeller
- 3DMark 2000
- Render It 3D! 3.02 (evaluation version)
- LifeForms 3 demo, animated human model, and animated model by Credo Interactive
- PolyTrans, by Okino Computer Graphics

Finally, a complete electronic version of this book is also available on the CD. The electronic version features hot links and full search capabilities.

How the Code Is Organized

The setup program on the companion CD installs the sample code in the \RoadRage directory on your hard drive. The code for each chapter, which demonstrates the Direct3D (and other DirectX) functionality discussed up to that point, is stored in a subdirectory under the main tutorial directory (for example, \RoadRage\Chap4). You can load the main makefile for all projects in Microsoft Visual C++ by selecting Open Workspace from the File menu and selecting the file roadrage.dsw from the top-level tutorial directory. Once this file is loaded, you can select a particular chapter to compile by right-clicking on it in the FileView window and selecting Set As Active Project. To compile the chapter's code, just select Rebuild All from the Build menu.

Before starting to read this book, please install the code from the CD. By having the code handy as you read, you'll be ready to compile the projects for each chapter as you complete reading that chapter. I feel that the best way to learn is to immediately implement what you've read, and by loading and working with the code for each chapter, you'll be able to use the code before you forget it. This immediate reinforcement will help ingrain the ideas presented, benefiting you as you progress through the book as well as in your development efforts. Not every line of code in the projects on the CD is shown in the book. I discuss all code that is important to learning Direct3D Immediate Mode and integrating the other DirectX APIs into your code. Don't attempt to type in the code from the book and expect it to run as is. Although all critical routines are listed and discussed in this book, various auxiliary routines for Windows/ full-screen handling, basic object handling, and so on are provided in the projects on the CD but not in the text. These additional routines are required to make the code run, but listing them in the book would have added hundreds of pages to the book at little value.

System Requirements

To use this book effectively, you should have Microsoft Windows 98 (although Microsoft Windows 95 will work fine) and a PC with a 3D accelerator (or at least a Pentium II–based machine). You can also use Microsoft Windows 2000, which has DirectX 7 integrated into its environment. I use the C++ notation for everything in this book, so you should own or purchase Microsoft Visual C++. (I used Visual C++ 6 for the projects on the CD.)

I don't attempt to teach you how to use your compiler. I assume that you have a working knowledge of it and can comfortably load and build projects. I also assume that you understand C (and a little C++ since I do use this notation exclusively throughout the book and the code on the CD).

INTRODUCTION

With the introduction of Microsoft Windows 95, game developers had the opportunity to develop Windows-based games that were far more powerful than was possible with earlier versions of Windows. Even with this capability, however, accessing the multimedia hardware consistently and efficiently was no easy task—that is, until Microsoft introduced DirectX. DirectX not only provides fast access to the hardware and therefore incredibly speedy performance, but it also makes it much easier for hardware developers to produce new devices that work well in the Windows environment. The DirectX APIs take away the necessity of writing your own low-level, device-specific code to access hardware such as the display adapter and network card, making it much easier for you to write programs that take full advantage of the computer's multimedia capabilities.

In this book, I focus on the Direct3D Immediate Mode API of DirectX. Immediate Mode provides a very fast 3D development library that works hand in hand with the other DirectX APIs, which implement sound, device input, network play, and display device handling. To teach you how to develop a *real* application supporting all these capabilities, I also show how you to develop code that uses and integrates the other DirectX APIs. By the end of the book, you'll see how to implement a complex 3D game with detailed 3D graphics, animated characters, multiple input device support (including easy enhancement to force feedback support), sound, and multiplayer support via modem, network, or direct serial connection.

I wrote this book because even though several books have been written on the DirectX APIs, including Direct3D Retained Mode, to date very little has been written on Direct3D Immediate Mode. The main reason for this lack of books about Immediate Mode is that unlike Retained Mode, which provides a library of high-level, easy-to-use commands, Immediate Mode provides a much more challenging—but much more efficient—API that most game developers have adopted for their professional games and engines. Because of this, most individuals have chosen to take the code they have developed using DirectX Immediate Mode—and the lessons learned from it—and keep it proprietary. William Chin (who originally developed the RoadRage game) and I chose to provide our game engine free with this book as a way of helping people move into a software market that has typically been difficult to penetrate because of the complexities of developing a commerically viable engine. I've seen many people struggle with trying to determine how to use the commands of the DirectX APIs together to create a functional 3D application. Although the Direct3D API might seem daunting at first, I believe that by the end of this book, you'll thoroughly understand the power of the DirectX APIs and know how to make them work together in a very powerful and sensible manner.

Armed with this understanding, you'll be able to move forward, comfortably using Direct3D for your game development efforts. In demonstrating in detail how to build a real-world application in Direct3D, I hope to give you the background and confidence you need to create your own Direct3D applications. With this background, any initial trepidation toward developing an Immediate Mode application should, I hope, be erased. Using Immediate Mode and the code framework presented in this book, you should be able to build powerful and fast commercial-quality applications. There's a reason that all commercial game developers use Immediate Mode rather than other APIs, and when you've completed this book, I'm sure you'll choose this path as well.

With that, let's get on to learning about Direct3D!

CHAPTER ONE

DirectX Fundamentals

The Microsoft DirectX application programming interface (API) was developed to provide a set of interfaces that provide extremely efficient control of multimedia hardware on a computer running Microsoft Windows. DirectX lets programmers work with commands and data structures that are very close to those that the hardware can natively process, without being so low level that code has to be written differently for each device. By writing device-independent code, programmers can create software that will always perform at its best—even as users enhance their systems with new and improv 3D graphics accelerators, sound cards, input devices, and so on.

DirectX was designed to give developers an environment similar in performance to MS-DOS, which was historically much faster than Windows-based code because of the overhead imposed by earlier Windows multimedia APIs. By supporting all hardware features as they become available, however, DirectX code runs faster than would be possible in most MS-DOS applications. The DirectX API is built on a *hardware abstraction layer* (HAL) that hides the device-specific dependencies of the hardware. Because it is designed for future extensibility, DirectX defines a number of hardware acceleration support features that aren't available on much of the hardware built today. Such features are emulated through the *hardware emulation layer* (HEL) or ignored if the HEL doesn't support them either. When a device that accelerates a DirectX feature (such as advanced texturing) is introduced, you can replace your old device with the new one. The software you wrote with such great foresight will instantly use the acceleration features this new hardware supplies.

Whenever you create a DirectX object for a device, DirectX queries the hardware, which the HAL represents, for information on the device. This information is then used to fill up a table of cap bits. (The term *cap bits* is shorthand for *capability bits*.) The information in the cap bits is used to determine whether the hardware is capable of performing a particular operation or whether a HEL function must be used to emulate it.

Given that Microsoft has provided cap bits so that you can determine what features are provided in the hardware (the HAL) versus what features are only emulated through software (the HEL), you should decide what system configuration is the minimum acceptable setup and optimize your code to run as effectively as possible on this system. In other words, although you should avoid using the HEL except as a last resort, you still need to write your application assuming the HEL is the least common denominator. Then, by using any advanced features supported on target systems with more capable hardware than this minimum configuration, you can provide enhanced features in your games, such as advanced texturing, higher polygon complexity, or dynamic lighting, for users who have more powerful systems. Make sure your design takes advantage of as many advanced features as possible. Hardware capabilities are increasing rapidly, and gaming aficionados update their systems as often as they can afford to. If you design your software without looking ahead, you'll lose untold potential sales.

The DirectX APIs

DirectX is composed of several APIs that are designed to work together to help you develop 3D multimedia games and simulations (as well as many other non-3D applications). It provides libraries of functions to perform 2D and 3D rendering; standard and 3D sound; music; support for keyboards, joysticks, and many other types of input devices, including force-feedback-capable hardware; and network game play. These interfaces mesh to provide you with a powerful, integrated library of commands that you can use to efficiently create superb games and simulations.

The APIs currently implemented in DirectX are DirectDraw, Direct3D, DirectMusic, DirectSound, DirectPlay, DirectInput, and DirectSetup. Throughout this book and in the code on the companion CD, I show you how to integrate several of these APIs—DirectDraw, Direct3D, DirectSound, DirectPlay, and DirectInput—into a 3D application aimed at the first-person-perspective 3D gaming market.

DirectDraw

The DirectDraw API provides display device handling, control of bitmap data and off-screen memory, and fast access to other hardware features such as blitting and page flipping. It is also the foundation on which Direct3D is built. In Chapter 3, I'll be covering all the aspects of DirectDraw that you need to understand to create a Direct3D application. You can use the code there as the basis for all your 3D games. If you want to, you can also use DirectDraw by itself to develop 2D games; however, I won't be describing how to use DirectDraw for 2D games in this book since the focus is on developing 3D games.

Direct3D

Direct3D, the main focus of this book, is an API that can be used to write programs that use 3D graphics and take advantage of hardware acceleration of 3D operations. Almost all graphics cards now being sold support 3D acceleration, and the innovation taking place in the field of 3D graphics on PCs is tremendous. Most 3D games now available for Windows were implemented using Direct3D.

When Direct3D was first introduced, it provided two APIs: Immediate Mode and Retained Mode. Immediate Mode (so named because rendering of objects took place immediately upon the programmer's request) was difficult to use, but it was the most flexible, low-level API for writing games that ran as efficiently as possible. Retained Mode (so named because the API retained the scene database and rendered it all at once) was built as a layer on top of Immediate Mode that provided additional services, such as texture management, object file loading, a frame hierarchy, and animation. Retained Mode was easier to learn and use than Immediate Mode, but ultimately, programmers wanted the added performance and flexibility that Immediate Mode provided. Development of the Retained Mode API stopped with the release of DirectX 6, and the Direct3D team has focused on improving both the power and the ease of use of the Immediate Mode API. Retained Mode doesn't support important new technologies such as multitexturing, bump mapping, or hardware transformation and lighting. All future 3D programs should be written using Immediate Mode, and this book is exclusively devoted to the Immediate Mode API. By the time you've finished reading this book, you'll have a solid understanding of the nuances of Immediate Mode and you'll know how to integrate it with the other portions of DirectX to create powerful 3D games.

DirectMusic

This API of DirectX works with message-based musical data that is converted to wave samples using a hardware or software synthesizer. The default software implementation uses the Microsoft Software Synthesizer to create wave samples that are streamed to DirectSound. The instrument voices used are synthesized from samples according to the Downloadable Sounds (DLS) Standard. DirectMusic also has a composition engine that can compose music on the fly based on certain rules that you provide.

DirectSound

This API provides efficient stereo and 3D sound handling, including memory management and hardware sound mixing. DirectSound is designed to take advantage of whatever hardware is on the target system. Integrating 3D sound into any game or simulation you develop is a good idea because of the level of realism it adds to your applications. Hearing sounds coming from your left, your right, above you—essentially from all over—can make an environment much more intriguing, especially when you're playing against an opponent using DirectPlay.

DirectPlay

DirectPlay launches multiplayer games and enables transport-independent connection and messaging services. Gamers have begun to expect that any good first-person-perspective game will support network play, modem play, or both. Many of the most popular games today provide these features, and gamers have realized that multiplayer gaming (head-to-head play) is much more fun than playing alone or against the computer. (Many businesses have learned this fact the hard way—after their networks became tied up and they had to introduce policies forbidding people to play these games at the office!) I recommend that you implement network play for any first-person-perspective game you design if you want it to compete successfully in the gaming market. In Chapter 15, I'll show you all the DirectPlay code that a game needs to connect to a host via the network, over the Internet, or using a modem.

DirectInput

This DirectX API supplies low-latency input support for almost every input device. DirectX 7 integrates force-feedback support for every type of device, including steering wheels and joysticks. Force-feedback devices can simulate sensations such as bumps in the road, gun recoil when firing, wind shear when flying, and wave motion on a boat.

DirectSetup

This API handles the automated installation of DirectX. Most systems today have DirectX installed, but for those that don't, DirectSetup provides an automated way to install the DirectX run-time components that an application needs. Because Microsoft allows DirectX to be distributed free of charge, developers can configure their software to always install DirectX if it isn't present or if it's an older version.

Microsoft provides the DirectX run-time components in the DXF\redist directory of the DirectX 7 SDK, which is included on the companion CD for this book. Also be aware that the DirectX run-time components are subject to the End-User License Agreement terms found in DXF\redist\license\directx end user eula.txt.

How Direct3D Works as a DirectX API

Direct3D first appeared in DirectX 2.0, which came out in 1996. In the short time since its introduction, Direct3D has become the most popular 3D API on the market. Many games and simulations use it, and almost every 3D graphics accelerator produced supports it. The hardware accelerators now being developed can achieve multimillion-polygon-per-second performance on graphic cards that cost between $100 and $200. Until recently, this speed was possible only on hardware costing tens of thousands of dollars. These accelerators used in conjunction with Direct3D have dramatically increased the speed and drastically reduced the cost of 3D applications; no longer does high performance necessitate high cost.

Like all the DirectX APIs, Direct3D was designed not only to provide developers with a common API for game development that was extensible for the future but also to allow for complete backward compatibility. All games developed in early versions of DirectX are guaranteed to run in future versions of DirectX.

Direct3D applications work with graphics acceleration hardware similarly in both Retained Mode and Immediate Mode. As mentioned earlier, they use hardware through the HAL, if it's available—otherwise, they use the HEL. Because Direct3D is an interface to a DirectDraw object, Microsoft refers to this HAL as the DirectDraw/Direct3D HAL.

Figure 1-1 illustrates how Direct3D works with the Microsoft Win32 environment and the available hardware accelerators.

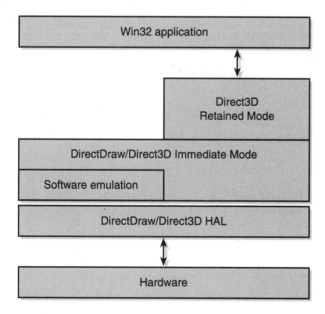

Figure 1-1
The relationship of Direct3D to the DirectX environment and to the system

What You Need to Know to Use a DirectX API

To use a DirectX API effectively, you need to understand several key concepts: using Component Object Model (COM) objects, using the *AddRef* and *Release* methods, knowing the difference between calling DirectX methods with C and C++, and handling the DirectX return codes. We'll cover these topics in the remainder of this chapter.

What Is a COM Object?

A COM interface is similar to an abstract class in C++. Just as a C++ abstract code class has no code associated with it, a COM interface describes a set of signatures and semantics but not the implementation. Both COM interfaces and pure virtual functions use a device known as a *vtable,* which holds the addresses of the functions (also known as *methods*) used to implement the interface.

To have an object use the methods of a COM interface, you call the *Query-Interface* method to make sure an interface exists for the object and to acquire a pointer to the interface. You can call the interface methods the object implements by using the pointer to the vtable received from the call to the *QueryInterface* method.

Programmers access the DirectX features through several COM objects. Each interface to an object that represents a device, such as *IDirectDraw7*, is derived directly from the *IUnknown* COM interface. These objects are created through the use of functions in the dynamic-link library (DLL) for each object. In some cases, the interface to the base-level object is acquired through a function such as *DirectDrawCreateEx.* In other cases, the standard COM *CoCreateInstance* function is used to initialize the object and return a pointer to its interface.

The DirectX object model supplies one main object for each device, and other support objects are created from this object. For DirectDraw, the main object represents the display adapter. You use this object to find out what capabilities, such as color depth and supported screen sizes, exist on the hardware device. You also use it to create other objects and acquire their interfaces, such as an *IDirectDrawPalette* object, which represents a hardware palette, and an *IDirectDrawSurface7* object, which represents display memory.

The capabilities of COM objects are updated by creating new interfaces that provide new features rather than by changing the methods within the existing interfaces. COM was designed to make sure that all software and objects written for a COM-based application would be completely compatible with any new version of that software. To access the features a new DirectX interface provides, you might need to call the object's *QueryInterface* method, using the globally unique identifier (GUID) of the interface you want to acquire (for example, *IID_IDirectDraw7*). If your application doesn't need the new features provided in newer versions of the interface, it doesn't need to retrieve these newer interfaces.

Since its inception, DirectX has used the COM style of interface design. As an example, DirectDraw provides five interfaces for accessing a *DirectDrawSurface* object: *IDirectDrawSurface*, *IDirectDrawSurface2*, *IDirectDrawSurface3*, *IDirect-DrawSurface4*, and *IDirectDrawSurface7*. Even if DirectX eventually offers *IDirectDrawSurface29*, you can be certain that your applications' calls to *IDirect-DrawSurface7* will still work.

What Are the *AddRef* and *Release* Methods For?

In addition to the *QueryInterface* method, all COM interfaces supply two other methods: *AddRef* and *Release*. These methods maintain an object's reference count. Reference counting is a technique by which multiple pieces of code can make use of a resource while handling deallocation properly. The *AddRef* method increases an object's reference count by one, and *Release* decreases the object's reference count by one. Whenever a function returns a pointer to an interface for an object (for example, when you create an instance of the object) that function must call *AddRef* through that pointer to increment the reference count. You must match each call to *AddRef* with a call to *Release* through the same pointer. You must call *Release* through the pointer before the pointer can be destroyed. When the object's reference count hits 0, the object is destroyed and all interfaces to it are no longer valid.

So, when *QueryInterface* returns a pointer to an interface, it calls *AddRef* to increment the reference count. Because of this, you must make sure that you call *Release* to decrement the reference count before destroying the pointer to the interface. The same rule applies when you call any DirectX API that gives back a pointer to an interface, such as *IDirectDrawSurface7::GetAttachedSurface*.

How C and C++ Calls to DirectX Methods Differ

DirectX works with C-based, C++-based, or Microsoft Visual Basic–based applications. In this book, the focus is on using DirectX with C++. When you're deciding whether to develop your code in C or C++, you need to consider a few issues.

For a DirectX method, the first parameter is the pointer to the interface or class (the object invoking the method), which is basically the same as the *this* argument in C++. COM objects and C++ objects are binary compatible, so compilers handle COM interfaces and C++ abstract classes in the same way.

In C, you call COM interface methods by passing the *this* pointer as the first parameter of the method and reference the interface's method by using a pointer to the interface object's vtable. As an example, we create a surface for our 3D application using the following line of C code.

```
hr = lpdd->lpVtbl->CreateSurface(lpdd, &ddsd, &lpdds, NULL);
```

The first argument (*lpdd*) is a pointer to the DirectDraw object that controls the display. The second argument (*ddsd*) is a DDSURFACEDESC2 structure that contains information about the surface we want to create. The third argument (*lpdds*) is an address to be filled with a pointer to the *IDirectDrawSurface7* object that is created. The final argument is NULL because it is a variable used for future compatibility with COM aggregation features; if you set it to anything other than NULL, an error will occur.

In C++, the *lpVtbl* pointer is implicitly dereferenced and the *this* parameter is implicitly passed. Thus, the call would look like this instead:

```
hr = lpdd->CreateSurface(&ddsd, &lpdds, NULL);
```

Other than these issues, coding in either language should be fairly similar. I prefer C++ because I use its object-oriented capabilities in my applications. I find that the ability to define things ranging from textures to characters as objects is the most logical approach, especially when I write code to simulate real-world objects, which most first-person-perspective games require.

Return Codes

Any code you produce with DirectX should be written to handle the return codes received when you make a call to a DirectX method. A *return code* is the value returned when the method completes, indicating the success or failure of the call. All return codes from DirectX methods are of the type HRESULT. An HRESULT is a 32-bit number that indicates two things: (1) whether the call succeeded or failed, and (2) why the call succeeded or failed. The SUCCEEDED() and FAILED() macros take an HRESULT as an argument and return whether it indicates a success code or a failure code, respectively. (SUCCEEDED() is the same as !FAILED(), so use whichever macro makes your code clearer.) Sometimes programmers try to check for failure by comparing the HRESULT against S_OK. This is a bad idea because some functions return success codes other than S_OK (for example, a function might return S_FALSE to indicate that it did nothing because there was no need to do it). On the other hand, it's okay to compare an HRESULT against a specific error code and respond accordingly, as long as you don't ignore other types of failures.

DirectX functions can return failure codes for a variety of reasons. A common reason for failure when writing new code is when you've passed invalid input to a function or when you call a function on an object that you haven't fully initialized yet. When you get this sort of failure, the best way to have the program react (assuming you haven't released the program yet) is to halt the program and report the file, line, and error code so that you can fix the bug. In other cases, DirectX returns a failure code to indicate that it can't perform an operation, but you might be able to do something different instead. For example, if you try to create a surface in video memory and DirectDraw returns DDERR_OUTOFVIDEOMEMORY, you might want to try to create the surface in system memory instead. Or a failure can indicate that a resource is busy, in which case you should try the operation again a bit later. Most of the time, however, a DirectX failure means that something unexpected has happened (such as running out of memory) or an operation that you need to take place just can't happen (such as when you really need a feature that isn't available). In these cases, you need to have your program interpret the error code as well as possible, report the situation to the user in plain English, and exit.

Because every DirectX function returns an HRESULT, you need to make a significant effort to structure your code to check for and handle all these potential errors. This work is frustrating at first, but it soon becomes second nature. The result of this work is that your program will be much more resistant to crashing unexpectedly.

The Direct3D Framework

On the DirectX Software Developer's Kit (SDK), the DirectX team has provided some code known as the *Direct3D Framework*. This code isn't part of the Direct3D API itself but is "helper code" that performs common tasks such as initialization, texture management, vector and matrix math, and mode switching. The code was written to provide a common foundation for most of the Direct3D sample programs in the SDK, but you're free to use this code in your own programs as well. I think you'll find that using the Direct3D Framework will save you a lot of programming effort. RoadRage, the game on which this book is based, is built on the Direct3D Framework, and I'll be walking you through much of this code as I explain several aspects of Direct3D programming. The classes *CD3DFramework7* and *CD3DApplication* are part of the Direct3D Framework, as are all functions that begin with *D3DEnum, D3DMath, D3DUtil,* and *D3DTextr.* Note that you only have to use the parts of the framework that you need. For example, you could write your own texture management code while still using the Direct3D Framework's initialization and utility functions.

Conclusion

This chapter covered all the basics of DirectX and its design. It described how DirectX technology provides developers with easy access to advanced features of multimedia hardware, and how the technology allows developers to create applications using device-independent code. You've seen that Direct3D is one of several APIs that DirectX comprises (this chapter briefly described each API), and you've learned how the COM model is used to implement all of DirectX.

So now that you understand the basics of DirectX and Direct3D, let's move on to the specifics of using Direct3D Immediate Mode to create great DirectX applications!

CHAPTER TWO

Windows Code for Direct3D Programs

Microsoft Direct3D programs can be designed to run in full-screen mode or in windowed mode—or both. Full-screen mode, in which the program takes over the entire screen, is popular for many reasons. It gives your program the opportunity to switch to the screen resolution and color depth that makes the program work best on the current hardware. It provides a more immersive experience for the user. And by allowing page flipping and by removing the need to update the graphics of any other programs, it can usually provide the fastest performance. On the other hand, sometimes it's more appropriate to run a Direct3D program in windowed mode—generally when the user might want to see the output of other programs on the screen.

I've found that it's best to develop code for both windowed and full-screen execution and to allow the user to switch between modes. Although developing for both modes adds some time and complexity to your development efforts, it allows those who use your application to choose the environment they want to run in. More important, it allows for the fastest execution of your application on the widest range of acceleration hardware. If a user is running a system with two accelerators—one that supports windowed applications and one that supports full-screen mode only—your software can determine the capabilities of each accelerator and offer the user the choice of extra speed versus extra functionality. In addition, debugging is far easier in windowed mode. To debug effectively in full-screen mode, you need to have a second monitor attached or use a remote debugger.

You'll be much better off if you understand Microsoft Windows code development before you attempt to develop a Direct3D application. This chapter presents the Windows portion of the code necessary to produce a Direct3D application named RoadRage. RoadRage uses the Direct3D Framework described in

Chapter 1 and supports both windowed mode and full-screen mode. You'll find the actual code for this chapter in the Chap2 subproject of the RoadRage workspace file, roadrage.dsw, on the companion CD. This code is encapsulated in the main *CMyD3DApplication* class as well as in several other C++ classes. It shows how to produce a window and its associated menu to control Direct3D parameters (such as fog and shading) for a Direct3D application. Throughout this book, you'll build on the RoadRage application. In Chapter 3, you'll add DirectDraw-based code that determines the target system's 2D capabilities and that lets you switch this application between windowed and full-screen mode (at various resolutions). In the remaining chapters, you'll add the code to enable the features provided in the menus (such as fog and textures) and to supply many other capabilities, including animated characters and network game play.

How to Structure Your Windows Code

The Windows portion of the code for a typical application consists of the following code blocks:

- Code to specify include files and to define globally unique identifiers (GUIDs)

- *WinMain*, the function that sets up the main window and message handling

- Code that defines the appearance of the main window (In RoadRage, this is performed by code in the *CMyD3DApplication* and *CD3D-Application* classes.)

- A main window message handling function (In RoadRage, this is *WndProc* in d3dapp.cpp, which passes the messages to *CMyD3D-Application::MsgProc* and *CD3DApplication::MsgProc*.)

Let's walk through the implementation of each of these components of our Windows-related code. If you installed the sample code from the companion CD and want to follow the code that this chapter discusses, select Open Workspace from the File menu in Microsoft Visual C++, find and select roadrage.dsw, and click Open. Roadrage.dsw is the workspace for the entire book. To make Chapter 2's code the active project, select the FileView tab in the Workspace window, right-click Chap2 Files, and select Set As Active Project from the context menu.

Code to Specify Include Files and to Define GUIDs

Programs that use DirectX need certain GUIDs (globally unique IDs, such as *IID_IDirectDraw7*) to be defined so that they can compile successfully. GUIDs are global variables rather than constants, so you must define storage for them. One way to incorporate the required GUIDs into your program is to include dxguid.lib in your libraries when building the project. If you prefer, you can instead define the symbol INITGUID as follows in *one* of your source modules before you include the header files windows.h, ddraw.h, or d3d.h, and before you use any other #*define* directives:

```
#define INITGUID
```

If you forget to define INITGUID or include the dxguid.lib library, you'll be deluged with errors when you attempt to compile your DirectX code.

> **TIP** To compile a program that uses DirectX, you need to have your compiler use the directories containing the latest DirectX include and library files. To verify that Visual C++ is configured correctly, choose Options from the Tools menu and then click the Directories tab. Make sure that the path to the DirectX include files (something like C:\mssdk\ include) is at the top of the directory list. Then use the Show Directories For control to switch to the Library Files section and make sure that the path to the DirectX library files (something like C:\mssdk\lib) is at the top of the directory list. If you don't do this, Visual C++ will use the DirectX header files and library files that shipped with Visual C++, which will usually be the wrong version.

The include files are specified at the top of the roadrage.cpp file (as they are in any C++ module). You can find the header files resource.h, d3dapp.h, and roadrage.hpp in this chapter's project directory. Resource.h defines the Windows resources that the RoadRage program uses. D3dapp.h is the header file for the d3dapp.cpp file that contains most of the code presented in this chapter and that will contain the main-event-handling code and rendering-related code added to RoadRage in later chapters.

The class *CMyD3DApplication,* defined in roadrage.hpp, will encapsulate the RoadRage code that handles all the main tasks, including 3D world creation and rendering as well as user control of the 3D world, sound, and multiplayer game play. *CMyD3DApplication* uses the DirectInput, DirectSound, and DirectPlay components of DirectX and inherits its basic attributes from the *CD3DApplication* class.

The *CMyD3DApplication* and *CD3DApplication* Classes

The following code (from roadrage.hpp and roadrage.cpp) defines the *CMyD3D-Application* class, a default constructor for the class, and the *WinMain* function (the main entry point for the application).

```
#ifndef __ROADRAGE_H
#define __ROADRAGE_H


//-------------------------------------------------------------------
// Name: class CMyD3DApplication
// Desc: Application class. The base class provides just about all
//          the functionality we want, so we're just supplying stubs to
//          interface with the non-C++ functions of the application.
//-------------------------------------------------------------------

class CMyD3DApplication : public CD3DApplication
{

public:

    CMyD3DApplication();

    void      DisplayCredits(HWND hwnd);
    void      DisplayRRStats(HWND hwnd);
    void      DisplayLegalInfo(HWND hwnd);

    LRESULT MsgProc( HWND hWnd, UINT uMsg, WPARAM wParam,
                                    LPARAM lParam );

    static HRESULT hr;

    HINSTANCE hInstApp;
};

#endif //__ROADRAGE_H



///------------------------------------------------------------------
// File: RoadRage.cpp
//
// Desc: The main RoadRage code. The CMyD3DApplication class handles
//          most of the RoadRage functionality.
//
// Copyright (c) 1999 William Chin and Peter Kovach. All rights
```

```
// reserved.
//---------------------------------------------------------------------
#define STRICT
#define D3D_OVERLOADS
#include <math.h>
#include <time.h>
#include <stdio.h>
#include "D3DApp.h"


//---------------------------------------------------------------------
// Name: WinMain
// Desc: Entry point to the program. Initializes everything, and goes
//       into a message-processing loop. Idle time is used to render
//       the scene.
//---------------------------------------------------------------------
INT WINAPI WinMain( HINSTANCE hInst, HINSTANCE,
                        LPSTR strCmdLine, INT )
{

    CMyD3DApplication d3dApp;

    d3dApp.hInstApp = hInst;

    if( FAILED( d3dApp.Create( hInst, strCmdLine ) ) )
        return 0;

    d3dApp.Run();

    CoUninitialize();
    return TRUE;
}


//---------------------------------------------------------------------
// Name: CMyD3DApplication
// Desc: Application constructor. Sets attributes for the
//       application.
//---------------------------------------------------------------------
CMyD3DApplication::CMyD3DApplication()
{
    m_strWindowTitle  = TEXT( "Chapter 2" );

    pCMyApp = this;
}
```

The *CD3DApplication* class from which the *CMyD3DApplication* class is derived is part of the Direct3D Framework and provides several member variables we'll use. *CD3DApplication* also supplies methods for creating the new application and handling many of the Windows messages the application will receive. In this chapter, we'll use a simplified version of the *CD3DApplication* class rather than the full version as specified in the standard Direct3D Framework. The *CD3D-Application* class is defined in file d3dapp.h, which you'll find in this chapter's project folder, as follows:

```
//------------------------------------------------------------------
// File: D3DApp.h
//
// Desc: Application class for the Direct3D samples framework
//       library
//
//------------------------------------------------------------------
#ifndef  D3DAPP_H
#define  D3DAPP_H
#define  D3D_OVERLOADS
#include <d3d.h>


//------------------------------------------------------------------
// Name: Class CD3DApplication
// Desc:
//------------------------------------------------------------------
class CD3DApplication
{
    // Internal variables and member functions

    BOOL            m_bActive;
    BOOL            m_bReady;

protected:
    HWND            m_hWnd;

    // Overridable variables for the application
    TCHAR*          m_strWindowTitle;

    // Overridable power management (APM) functions
    virtual LRESULT OnQuerySuspend( DWORD dwFlags );
    virtual LRESULT OnResumeSuspend( DWORD dwData );

public:
    // Functions to create, run, pause, and clean up the application
    virtual HRESULT Create( HINSTANCE, LPSTR );
    virtual INT    Run();
```

```
virtual LRESULT MsgProc( HWND hWnd,
                         UINT uMsg,
                         WPARAM wParam,
                         LPARAM lParam );

// Accessor functions
HWND Get_hWnd()              { return m_hWnd; };
BOOL GetbActive()           { return m_bActive; };
BOOL GetbReady()            { return m_bReady; };
VOID SetbReady(BOOL val)    { m_bReady = val; };
VOID SetbActive(BOOL val) { m_bActive = val; };

// Class constructor
    CD3DApplication();
};

#endif // D3DAPP_H
```

Setting Up the Main Window and Message Handling

The *WinMain* routine is always the main function of a Windows-based application. The system calls this function as the initial entry point of the application.

Our implementation of *WinMain* uses *CMyD3DApplication*'s default constructor to create the application's instance of the *CMyD3DApplication* class and then calls the class's *Create* method to generate an instance of the application's main window. *CMyD3DApplication* inherits its *Create* method from *CD3DApplication* and uses *CD3DApplication*'s constructor. Here's the constructor for the *CD3D-Application* class:

```
//---------------------------------------------------------------
// Name: CD3DApplication
// Desc: Constructor for class CD3DApplication
//---------------------------------------------------------------
    CD3DApplication::CD3DApplication()
{
    m_hWnd          = NULL;

    m_bActive       = FALSE;
    m_bReady        = FALSE;

    m_strWindowTitle = _T( "Direct3D Application" );

    g_pD3DApp = this;
}
```

This constructor initializes the member variables for our application whenever we create an instance of this class.

The *CD3DApplication::Create* method is defined as follows:

```
//-------------------------------------------------------------------
// Name: Create
// Desc: Creates the application's main window
//-------------------------------------------------------------------
HRESULT CD3DApplication::Create( HINSTANCE hInst, CHAR* strCmdLine )
{
    // Register the window class.
    WNDCLASS wndClass = { 0, WndProc, 0, 0, hInst,
                          LoadIcon( hInst,
                              MAKEINTRESOURCE(IDI_MAIN_ICON) ),
                          LoadCursor( NULL, IDC_ARROW ),
                          (HBRUSH)GetStockObject(WHITE_BRUSH),
                          NULL, _T("D3D Window") };
    RegisterClass( &wndClass );

    // Create the render window.
    m_hWnd = CreateWindow( _T("D3D Window"), m_strWindowTitle,
                          WS_OVERLAPPEDWINDOW|WS_VISIBLE,
                          CW_USEDEFAULT,CW_USEDEFAULT, 640, 480, 0L,
                          LoadMenu(hInst,MAKEINTRESOURCE(IDR_MENU)),
                          hInst, 0L );

    if (!m_hWnd)
    {
        LPVOID lpMsgBuf;
        FormatMessage(
            FORMAT_MESSAGE_ALLOCATE_BUFFER |
            FORMAT_MESSAGE_FROM_SYSTEM |
            FORMAT_MESSAGE_IGNORE_INSERTS,
            NULL,
            GetLastError(),
        // Default language
            MAKELANGID(LANG_NEUTRAL, SUBLANG_DEFAULT),
                (LPTSTR) &lpMsgBuf,
            0,
            NULL);
        //
        // Process any inserts in lpMsgBuf.
        // ...
        // Display the string.
        //
        MessageBox( NULL, (LPCTSTR)lpMsgBuf, "Error",
                    MB_OK | MB_ICONINFORMATION );
```

```
        // Free the buffer.
        LocalFree( lpMsgBuf );
    }

    UpdateWindow( m_hWnd );

    // The application is ready to go.
    m_bReady = TRUE;

    return S_OK;
}
```

This *Create* method uses the WNDCLASS type to create a window class, specifies attributes for the window class, uses the *RegisterClass* function to register the window class, and creates a window based on the registered window class by using the *CreateWindow* function. The window class's attributes include items such as the window's cursor, its icon, and its menu. *CD3DApplication::Create* uses the following functions to fill in and register the WNDCLASS structure:

- The *LoadIcon* function loads the icon, named IDI_MAIN_ICON, associated with the application.

- The *LoadCursor* function loads the cursor. In this project, the standard arrow cursor is sufficient.

- The *GetStockObject* function is called to acquire a handle to one of the predefined stock pens, palettes, brushes, and fonts. In this segment, we're requesting a white brush.

TIP You don't need to delete stock objects using a call to *DeleteObject*, but if you do, no error will occur. Also keep in mind that you can't adjust stock brush origins and that NULL_BRUSH and HOLLOW_BRUSH objects are the same.

With the window class defined, the next step is to create the window. Creating a window is fairly straightforward, though the creation command includes a variety of parameters. *CD3DApplication::Create* uses the Windows function *CreateWindow* to create the main window. The *CreateWindow* function is defined as follows:

```
HWND CreateWindow(
    LPCTSTR lpClassName,
    LPCTSTR lpWindowName,
    DWORD dwStyle,
```

(continued)

19

```
    int x,
    int y,
    int nWidth,
    int nHeight,
    HWND hWndParent,
    HMENU hMenu,
    HINSTANCE hInstance,
    LPVOID lpParam
);
```

Parameter	Description
lpClassName	Pointer to a null-terminated string containing a registered class name
lpWindowName	Pointer to a null-terminated string containing the window name
dwStyle	Window style
x	Horizontal position of window
y	Vertical position of window
nWidth	Window width
nHeight	Window height
hWndParent	Handle to parent or owner window
hMenu	Menu handle or child identifier
hInstance	Handle to application instance (ignored in Windows 2000)
lpParam	Window-creation data

Setting Up the Message-Processing Loop

In any Windows-based application, you need to define the message-processing loop that the application uses to process any Windows-based messages it receives. The routine that does this processing for RoadRage, *CD3DApplication::Run*, follows:

```
//-----------------------------------------------------------------
// Name: Run
// Desc: Message-processing loop. Uses idle time to render the scene.
//-----------------------------------------------------------------
INT CD3DApplication::Run()
{
    // Load keyboard accelerators.
    HACCEL hAccel = LoadAccelerators( NULL,
        MAKEINTRESOURCE( IDR_MAIN_ACCEL ) );
```

```
    // Now we're ready to receive and process Windows messages.
    BOOL bGotMsg;
    MSG  msg;
    PeekMessage( &msg, NULL, 0U, 0U, PM_NOREMOVE );

    while( WM_QUIT != msg.message  )
    {
        // Use PeekMessage if the application is active so that we
        // can use idle time to render the scene. If the application
        // isn't active, use GetMessage to avoid eating CPU time.
        if( m_bActive )
            bGotMsg = PeekMessage( &msg, NULL, 0U, 0U, PM_REMOVE );
        else
            bGotMsg = GetMessage( &msg, NULL, 0U, 0U );

        if( bGotMsg )
        {
            // Translate and dispatch the message.
            if( 0 == TranslateAccelerator( m_hWnd, hAccel, &msg ) )
            {
                TranslateMessage( &msg );
                DispatchMessage( &msg );
            }
        }
    }

    return msg.wParam;
}
```

The first call in this routine, made before entering the message-processing loop, is to *LoadAccelerators*. Here's the function declaration for *LoadAccelators*:

```
HACCEL LoadAccelerators(
    HINSTANCE hInstance,
    LPCTSTR lpTableName
);
```

Parameter	Description
hInstance	The handle of the application instance
lpTableName	The address of the table name string

This routine is used to load the application's *accelerator table*. In Windows, an accelerator table defines the shortcuts used to access the various menu options.

Figure 2-1 shows the Microsoft Visual C++ resource editor window presented when you're constructing a menu.

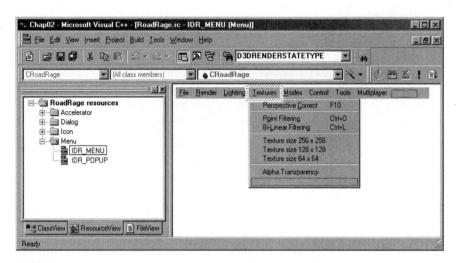

Figure 2-1
Building the application's menu

To add a new menu in Visual C++, select Resource from the Insert menu; the Insert Resource dialog box shown in Figure 2-2 appears. In the Insert Resource dialog box, select Menu from the Resource Type control and click the New button. You can name the menu whatever you want.

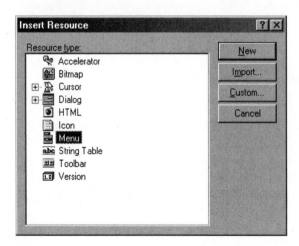

Figure 2-2
Inserting a menu resource into an application's menu

Figure 2-3 shows the Visual C++ resource editor displaying the accelerator table defined for the RoadRage application. You can add or modify these entries if you want to. In the right pane, the ID field displays the names of the menu items that can be activated, the Key field shows the keystroke sequence for the short-cut, and the Type field displays the key type (either ASCII or VIRTKEY).

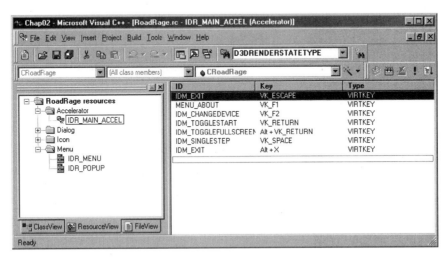

Figure 2-3
Setting the menu's shortcuts

After you've created the menu, you need to define how to handle the messages that this menu and the various window objects generate. The message retrieval and dispatch loop, which acts on each event that occurs, is the heart of the program. When the system receives the WM_QUIT message, it terminates the program, with *WinMain* returning the value passed in the message's *wParam* parameter. If the application terminates before entering the message loop, it returns a value of FALSE.

Once you've defined the accelerator table, you can begin the message-handling loop, which consists of the following steps:

1. Call *PeekMessage* to see whether a message was received. Or, if the application isn't active, call *GetMessage* to wait until a message arrives.

2. If a message was received, retrieve it, translate it, and dispatch it using *TranslateAccelerator*, *TranslateMessage*, and *DispatchMessage*.

Let's look at each of these commands individually to make sure that you understand their usage and the reason they're executed in this sequence.

PeekMessage

The *PeekMessage* function is declared as follows:

```
BOOL PeekMessage(
    LPMSG lpMsg,
    HWND hWnd,
    UINT wMsgFilterMin,
    UINT wMsgFilterMax,
    UINT wRemoveMsg
);
```

Parameter	Description
lpMsg	A pointer from the message queue to the message's structure.
hWnd	The handle to the window whose message you want.
wMsgFilterMin	The value of the first message in the range of messages you want to examine.
wMsgFilterMax	The value of the last message in the range of messages you want to examine.
wRemoveMsg	The removal flag: PM_NOREMOVE indicates that the message shouldn't be removed after the call to Peek-Message, and PM_REMOVE indicates that it should be removed.

PeekMessage is used to acquire a message from the message queue. The one argument that might need a bit of extra explanation is the final *wRemoveMsg* parameter. For nearly every application, you'll use the PM_REMOVE flag, which requests that the message be removed once it's handled. This flag is used to make sure that once a message is handled, it's removed from the queue so that the next message can be received. You'd rarely choose not to have the handled message removed. However, imagine that you've written an application such that when the code determines that it can't immediately process a message, but expects to be able to process the message within a short period of time, the code doesn't remove the message from the queue and simply tries to process the message again later (in a few milliseconds). That code would need to use the PM_NOREMOVE flag. *GetMessage* is just like *PeekMessage* except that if no messages are in the queue the function waits until a message appears. The reasoning for using both functions in this way will become clear in later chapters.

TranslateAccelerator, *TranslateMessage*, and *DispatchMessage*

The *TranslateAccelerator* function declaration follows:

```
int TranslateAccelerator(
    HWND hWnd,
    HACCEL hAccTable,
    LPMSG lpMsg
);
```

Parameter	Description
hWnd	The window whose message will be translated
hAccTable	The handle of the accelerator table loaded with *LoadAccelerators*
lpMsg	Pointer to the MSG structure that holds the message acquired from the calling thread's message queue using *PeekMessage* (or *GetMessage*)

This function processes the accelerator keys for the menu commands. *TranslateAccelerator* translates a WM_KEYDOWN or WM_SYSKEYDOWN message to a WM_COMMAND or WM_SYSCOMMAND message if an entry in the accelerator table indicates that this action should be taken. *TranslateAccelerator* then passes this translated message to the appropriate window procedure.

The function declaration for *TranslateMessage* follows:

```
BOOL TranslateMessage(
    CONST MSG * lpMsg
);
```

This function is used to translate the virtual-key messages into character messages. These character messages are then posted to the calling thread's message queue, which is read the next time the thread calls *PeekMessage* or *GetMessage*. If the message is translated (so that a character message is posted to the thread's message queue), the function's return value will be nonzero; if it isn't translated, the return value will be 0. If the message is WM_KEYDOWN, WM_KEYUP, WM_SYSKEYDOWN, or WM_SYSKEYUP, the return value will be 0 no matter what the translation is. When *TranslateAccelerator* returns a nonzero value, indicating that the message passed to it in the *lpMsg* parameter was processed, your application shouldn't process the message again with *TranslateMessage*.

The *DispatchMessage* function has a single parameter, *lpMsg*, which is a pointer to the MSG structure that holds the message acquired from the calling thread's message queue.

```
LONG DispatchMessage(
    CONST MSG * lpMsg
);
```

This function dispatches the translated message to the window procedure. The return value of this function is the value the window procedure returns.

Setting Up the Application's Window Procedure

When creating the WNDCLASS structure, you specify a pointer to a window procedure in the structure's *lpfnWndProc* member. This procedure, which is named *WndProc* in our application (Microsoft documents it as *WindowProc*), is an application-defined callback function that processes messages sent to the window. The *WindowProc* function is declared as follows:

```
LRESULT CALLBACK WindowProc(
    HWND hWnd,
    UINT uMsg,
    WPARAM wParam,
    LPARAM lParam
);
```

Parameter	Description
hWnd	The handle to the window
uMsg	The message identifier
wParam	The first message parameter
lParam	The second message parameter

D3dapp.cpp has a short *WndProc* function. It simply calls into *g_pD3DApp->MsgProc* to handle the message:

```
//-------------------------------------------------------------------
// Name: WndProc
// Desc: Static message handler that passes messages to the
//       application class
//-------------------------------------------------------------------
LRESULT CALLBACK WndProc( HWND hWnd,
                          UINT uMsg,
                          WPARAM wParam,
                          LPARAM lParam )
{
    if( g_pD3DApp )
        return g_pD3DApp->MsgProc( hWnd, uMsg, wParam, lParam );
```

```
    return DefWindowProc( hWnd, uMsg, wParam, lParam );
}
```

Since g_pD3DApp is of type *CD3DApplication*, you might think that this code would call *CD3DApplication::MsgProc*. But *CMyD3DApplication* has overridden the virtual function *MsgProc*, so *CMyD3DApplication::MsgProc* (in roadrage.cpp) gets called instead. *CMyD3DApplication::MsgProc* handles a few messages that are particular to RoadRage and passes the rest to *CD3DApplication::MsgProc*, which handles messages that are common to all programs that use the Direct3D Framework. Here's *CMyD3DApplication::MsgProc*:

```
LRESULT CMyD3DApplication::MsgProc( HWND hWnd, UINT uMsg,
                                    WPARAM wParam, LPARAM lParam )
{
    HMENU hMenu;

    m_hWnd = hWnd;

    hMenu = GetMenu( hWnd );

    switch( uMsg )
    {
        case WM_COMMAND:
            switch( LOWORD(wParam) )
            {
                case MENU_ABOUT:
                    DialogBox(hInstApp, MAKEINTRESOURCE(IDD_ABOUT),
                            hWnd, (DLGPROC)AppAbout);
                    break;

                case IDM_EXIT:
                    SendMessage( hWnd, WM_CLOSE, 0, 0 );
                    DestroyWindow( hWnd );
                    PostQuitMessage(0);
                    exit(0);

                default:
                    return CD3DApplication::MsgProc( hWnd, uMsg,
                                                     wParam, lParam );

            }
            break;

        case WM_GETMINMAXINFO:
            ((MINMAXINFO*)lParam)->ptMinTrackSize.x = 100;
```

(continued)

```
            ((MINMAXINFO*)lParam)->ptMinTrackSize.y = 100;
            break;

        case WM_CLOSE:
            DestroyWindow( hWnd );
            PostQuitMessage(0);
            return 0;

        default:
            return CD3DApplication::MsgProc( hWnd, uMsg, wParam,
                                              lParam );
    }

    return DefWindowProc( hWnd, uMsg, wParam, lParam );
}
```

The *CD3DApplication::MsgProc* method is defined as shown here:

```
//-------------------------------------------------------------------
// Name: MsgProc
// Desc: Message-handling function
//-------------------------------------------------------------------
LRESULT CD3DApplication::MsgProc( HWND hWnd, UINT uMsg,
                                  WPARAM wParam, LPARAM lParam )
{
    HRESULT hr;

    switch( uMsg )
    {
        case WM_PAINT:
            // Handle paint messages when the application isn't
            // ready.
            break;

        case WM_MOVE:
            // If in windowed mode, move the Direct3D Framework's
            // window.
            break;

        case WM_SIZE:
            // Check to see whether you're losing the window.
            if( SIZE_MAXHIDE==wParam || SIZE_MINIMIZED==wParam )
                m_bActive = FALSE;
            else
                m_bActive = TRUE;

            // A new window size requires a new back-buffer size,
            // so you must change the 3D structures accordingly.
            break;
```

```
case WM_SETCURSOR:
    // Prevent a cursor in full-screen mode.
    break;

case WM_ENTERMENULOOP:
    // Pause the application when menus are displayed.
    Pause(TRUE);
    break;

case WM_EXITMENULOOP:
    Pause(FALSE);
    break;

case WM_ENTERSIZEMOVE:
    // Halt frame movement while the application is sizing
    // or moving.
    if( m_bFrameMoving )
        m_dwStopTime = timeGetTime();
    break;

case WM_EXITSIZEMOVE:
    if( m_bFrameMoving )
        m_dwBaseTime += timeGetTime() - m_dwStopTime;
    break;

case WM_CONTEXTMENU:
    // Handle the application's context menu (via a right
    // mouse click).
    TrackPopupMenuEx(
            GetSubMenu(
                LoadMenu( 0, MAKEINTRESOURCE(IDR_POPUP) ),
                0 ),
            TPM_VERTICAL, LOWORD(lParam), HIWORD(lParam),
            hWnd, NULL );
    break;

case WM_NCHITTEST:
    // Prevent the user from selecting the menu in
    // full-screen mode.
    break;

case WM_POWERBROADCAST:
    switch( wParam )
    {
```

(continued)

```
                    case PBT_APMQUERYSUSPEND:
                        // At this point, the application should save any
                        // data for open network connections, files, and
                        // so on and prepare to go into suspended mode.
                        return OnQuerySuspend( (DWORD)lParam );

                    case PBT_APMRESUMESUSPEND:
                        // At this point, the application should recover
                        // any data, network connections, files, and so
                        // on and resume running from the point at which
                        // the application was suspended.
                        return OnResumeSuspend( (DWORD)lParam );
                }
                break;

        case WM_SYSCOMMAND:
            // Prevent moving or sizing and power loss in
            // full-screen mode.
            switch( wParam )
            {
                case SC_MOVE:
                case SC_SIZE:
                case SC_MAXIMIZE:
                case SC_MONITORPOWER:
                    // If not in windowed mode, return 1.
                    break;
            }
            break;

        case WM_COMMAND:
            switch( LOWORD(wParam) )
            {
                case IDM_TOGGLESTART:
                    // Toggle frame movement.
                    break;

                case IDM_SINGLESTEP:
                    // Single-step frame movement.
                    break;

                case IDM_CHANGEDEVICE:
                    // Display the device-selection dialog box.
                    return 0;

                case IDM_TOGGLEFULLSCREEN:
                    // Toggle between full-screen and windowed mode.
                    return 0;
```

```
        case IDM_ABOUT:
            // Display the About dialog box.
            Pause(TRUE);
            DialogBox( (HINSTANCE)GetWindowLong( hWnd,
                                            GWL_HINSTANCE ),
                    MAKEINTRESOURCE(IDD_ABOUT), hWnd,
                    AboutProc );
            Pause(FALSE);
            return 0;

        case IDM_EXIT:
            // Received key/menu command to exit application
            SendMessage( hWnd, WM_CLOSE, 0, 0 );
            return 0;
        }
        break;

    case WM_GETMINMAXINFO:
        ((MINMAXINFO*)lParam)->ptMinTrackSize.x = 100;
        ((MINMAXINFO*)lParam)->ptMinTrackSize.y = 100;
        break;

    // Close the window.
    case WM_CLOSE:
        DestroyWindow( hWnd );
        return 0;

    // The WM_DESTROY message is sent to the window procedure
    // of the window being destroyed after the window is removed
    // from the screen.
    //
    // This message is sent first to the window being destroyed
    // and then to the child windows (if any) as they are
    // destroyed. You can assume that while  the message is being
    // processed, all child windows still exist.
    case WM_DESTROY:
        // Clean up 3D environment stuff here.
        PostQuitMessage(0);
        return 0;
}
//
// The DefWindowProc function calls the default window procedure
// to provide default processing for any window messages that an
// application doesn't process. This function ensures that every
// message is processed. DefWindowProc is called with the same
// parameters received by the window procedure.
```

(continued)

```
        return DefWindowProc( hWnd, uMsg, wParam, lParam );
}
```

The *CD3DApplication::MsgProc* arguments describe the window (*hWnd*), the message received (*uMsg*), and any parameters associated with the message (*wParam* and *lParam*). The messages that follow are a few of the messages that the *MsgProc* method handles:

- **WM_SIZE**   Sent to the window after its size has been changed.

- **WM_MOVE**   Sent to the window after the window has been moved.

- **WM_SETCURSOR**   Sent to the window if the mouse causes the cursor to move within the window and mouse input isn't captured.

- **WM_PAINT**   Sent to the application when Windows or another program requests that the application repaint a portion of its window. This message is sent when the *UpdateWindow* and *RedrawWindow* functions are called.

- **WM_CLOSE**   Sent to the application when the user closes the application's window. *WndProc* processes this message by calling the *DestroyWindow* function.

- **WM_ENTERMENULOOP and WM_EXITMENULOOP**   Received when the menu modal loop has been entered or exited (when the user moves the pointer into or out of the menu).

- **WM_ENTERSIZEMOVE and WM_EXITSIZEMOVE**   Received when the user needs to halt the movement of objects in the 3D world when the application is resizing or moving.

- **WM_COMMAND**   Sent when the user selects an item from the menu, when one of the controls sends a message to its parent window, or when a user's accelerator keystroke is translated. A nested *switch* statement checks for each menu item. For now, handle only the Exit and About menu options. When the user selects the About menu item, the window shown in Figure 2-4 is displayed. When the user selects the Exit option, a WM_CLOSE message is sent to the application to close it.

The last step in the *CD3DApplication*'s *MsgProc* method is to perform default processing of any window message that the application doesn't process. *MsgProc* calls *DefWindowProc* (with the same parameters that *MsgProc* received) for this default processing.

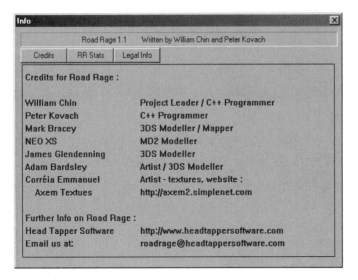

Figure 2-4
The About dialog box

DestroyWindow

The final step is to destroy the window when the code is complete, which usually occurs when the user selects Escape from the menu. To destroy the window, the *DestroyWindow* command is called. This command has one parameter, *hWnd*, which is the handle to the window to be destroyed. The *DestroyWindow* command is defined as follows:

```
BOOL DestroyWindow(
    HWND hWnd
);
```

DestroyWindow does what it sounds like: destroys the window you pass to it. It also sends a WM_DESTROY message to the window procedure, so your application can destroy any resources that depend on the window.

The Code So Far

We now have the code we need to present the user with a window ready for the addition of DirectDraw and Direct3D capabilities. If you installed the sample code and you want to test the code presented so far, open the RoadRage workspace and make the Chap2 project the active project. Start the program and you'll see a window like the one shown in Figure 2-5.

Figure 2-5
The screen from this chapter's code

This screen is blank because no content has been defined yet. In subsequent chapters, as we get into DirectDraw and Direct3D code, we'll begin filling this window with fun 3D content!

Conclusion

In this chapter, you've seen all the basic Windows code you'll need to create a DirectX application. This code should handle any messages you typically need to be concerned about. If you choose to, you can dig further into Windows programming by picking up a book focused specifically on that topic, such as *Programming Windows,* by Charles Petzold (5th ed., Microsoft Press, 1999) and *Programming Applications for Microsoft Windows,* by Jeffrey Richter (4th ed., Microsoft Press, 1999). But you should now have all you need to start concentrating on the code for 3D applications.

In Chapter 3, I'll explain the first aspect of DirectX you'll need to deal with to create a Direct3D-based application: DirectDraw. As you read in Chapter 1, DirectDraw is used for a number of critical things such as handling the primary and secondary display devices, page flipping, and so on. In Chapter 3, we'll walk through all the code necessary to use DirectDraw in your application. You'll then be ready to begin creating your 3D scene for viewing and animation.

CHAPTER THREE

Setting Up DirectDraw for a Direct3D Program

DirectDraw is a Microsoft DirectX API that lets you directly control display-device features such as the following:

- The primary surface, which is the memory that represents what you see on your screen

- Off-screen surfaces, which store images that can be transferred to the visible display area (includes texture maps in 3D programs)

- Hardware overlay support, which allows the display of a 2D image that is shown "in front of" the display without disturbing the contents of the primary surface

- Depth buffers, which are used to store depth information when rendering a 3D scene

- The hardware blitter, which is used for *blitting,* the process of copying 2D data from one location to another

- Flipping-surface support (page flipping), which is used to switch between one or more rendered views in memory (back buffers) and the main, visible display surface to keep the screen from tearing (described later in the chapter) or otherwise flickering from frame to frame

- Stereo support, in which one image is shown to the left eye and a different image is shown to the right eye

- Clipping for windowed or full-screen programs

Overall, DirectDraw provides a device-independent approach for accessing display devices and is the DirectX API used for all 2D drawing operations. It is also the foundation for Direct3D, so even "3D-only" programs need to use DirectDraw.

DirectDraw manages all the objects it creates and tracks the resources that have (or haven't) been allocated. It also handles the following features:

- The default color key, which is used to create transparent areas as blue screening in movies does

- The hardware display mode, which is the resolution, color depth, and refresh rate the system is using

- The default palette (the set of colors available) if the primary surface is in 8-bits-per-pixel mode

DirectDraw allows you to enumerate the capabilities of the underlying hardware and use the supported hardware-accelerated features.

DirectDraw works with many types of display hardware, including standard SVGA monitors; head-mounted displays; and new, more advanced systems capable of handling clipping, color formats other than RGB, and stretching. Like the other DirectX APIs, DirectDraw is designed to emulate any feature the host system's hardware doesn't provide, when possible.

DirectDraw and Direct3D enumerate the hardware capabilities of any target platform to determine which support hardware acceleration of various features. You should write your software to require only those abilities necessary for the program to execute efficiently but to check for and use any other capabilities if they are available. For example, only newer hardware supports single-pass multitexturing, so requiring this feature in your application would lock out users who have older systems; on the other hand, users who have the latest and greatest hardware will expect the games they buy to include support for such advanced features.

DirectDraw and Multiple Monitors

Microsoft Windows 98 introduced the capability to support multiple display devices and monitors on one computer. This capability, sometimes referred to as *multimon*, allows Windows to use the display areas of two or more monitors as one logical desktop. On a multimon system, you can move windows from one monitor to the next or have a program, through DirectDraw, use multiple display devices. One powerful feature of DirectX is that you can create more than one instance of a DirectDraw object at a time when you have more than one display card installed on your system. Even on computers with operating systems that don't support multiple monitors on their own, such as Microsoft Windows 95 and Microsoft Windows NT 4 (or earlier), you can create a DirectDraw object for each desired display device. When enumerating and creating display devices in DirectDraw, the term *DirectDraw device* (or sometimes *DirectDraw driver*) is used to refer to a display device that supports DirectDraw.

The primary display device that Windows uses is also the one that DirectX uses when you create an instance of the default DirectDraw object (the one with a GUID pointer of NULL). You can address the second display device, if it exists, by using its GUID to create a second DirectDraw object. You can acquire this GUID by using the *DirectDrawEnumerateEx* function, which I'll describe later in this chapter.

One or more of the display cards that are installed might support hardware 3D acceleration. You choose whether to use 3D acceleration on a given DirectDraw device by enumerating its Direct3D devices and then selecting one. A *Direct3D device,* as we'll discuss further in Chapter 4, is a Direct3D object that holds rendering state information and represents a way to render 3D scenes. Unlike a DirectDraw device, a Direct3D device doesn't necessarily represent a physical piece of hardware—it can be either a software-based renderer or a hardware-accelerated renderer.

Figure 3-1 shows an example system with multiple DirectDraw devices and multiple Direct3D devices available on each DirectDraw device.

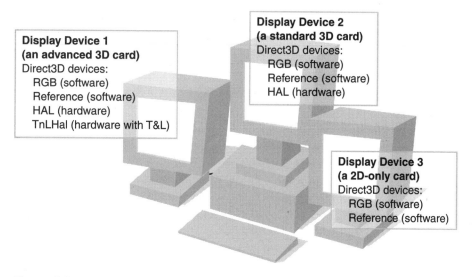

Figure 3-1
Multiple display cards connected to multiple monitors

Before doing any 3D rendering, you have to make two choices: first, which display device do you want to use? And second, for a given display device, which 3D renderer do you want to use? A Direct3D program should pick reasonable defaults for the display device and renderer but also allow users to change to a different display device and renderer if they don't like the default choice. After reading this chapter and the next one, you'll see how to implement this functionality.

Setting Up DirectDraw

Now that you've had a quick overview of DirectDraw, let's get to the meat of the chapter: setting up DirectDraw for our Direct3D Immediate Mode program. (Although this chapter focuses mainly on DirectDraw, you'll see some Direct3D enumeration code here because a 3D program needs to get some Direct3D information before completely initializing DirectDraw.) This process involves the following steps:

1. Create a structure to hold the Direct3D devices we enumerate.
2. Enumerate all the available DirectDraw devices installed on the system; then perform steps 3 through 5 on each DirectDraw device:
3. Create a DirectDraw object.
4. Enumerate the display modes.
5. Enumerate the Direct3D devices.
6. Pick a display device and a Direct3D device.
7. Initialize DirectDraw, which includes setting the cooperative level, creating the front and back buffers, and attaching a clipper.

In the following sections, I'll describe each step and explain how to implement it. We'll be looking at some code from the Direct3D framework, which does all these steps. d3denum.cpp contains the code to do steps 1-6, and d3dframe.cpp contains the code to do step 7. Code in d3dapp.cpp directs the whole process by calling into code in these other two files. By the end of the chapter, you'll see how to create the foundation of a Direct3D application. You can reuse this code for all your future Direct3D applications, so make sure you remember this sequence of steps and the basic tasks involved.

Creating a Structure to Hold the Enumerated Devices

The first step in setting up DirectDraw and Direct3D for the RoadRage application is to define a structure that we'll use to hold all the information about the Direct3D devices we enumerate on the host system. By retaining this information in our own data structure, we can easily present a dialog box to users that will show them what devices and modes are available and let them switch between them. The structure we'll use holds the Direct3D device information, the Direct-Draw device information, and the DirectDraw mode information. The *D3DEnum_DeviceInfo* structure, which works well for this purpose, is defined in d3denum.h as follows:

```
//------------------------------------------------------------------
// Name: Structure D3DEnum_DeviceInfo
// Desc: Structure to hold information about the enumerated
//       Direct3D devices
//------------------------------------------------------------------
struct D3DEnum_DeviceInfo
{
    // Direct3D device information
    CHAR            strDesc[40];
    GUID*           pDeviceGUID;
    D3DDEVICEDESC7  ddDeviceDesc;
    BOOL            bHardware;

    // DirectDraw driver information
    GUID*           pDriverGUID;
    DDCAPS          ddDriverCaps;
    DDCAPS          ddHELCaps;

    // DirectDraw mode information
    DDSURFACEDESC2  ddsdFullscreenMode;
    BOOL            bWindowed;
    BOOL            bStereo;

    // For internal use (Applications shouldn't need these members.)
    GUID            guidDevice;
    GUID            guidDriver;
    DDSURFACEDESC2* pddsdModes;
    DWORD           dwNumModes;
    DWORD           dwCurrentMode;
    BOOL            bDesktopCompatible;
    BOOL            bStereoCompatible;
};
```

We'll be filling up this structure with the information we determine about the system hardware capabilities by using the routines covered in this chapter.

Enumerating the DirectDraw Devices

In DirectX, enumeration functions such as *DirectDrawEnumerateEx* are used to list elements of a particular set by triggering a *callback* function for each element in the list. The callback function determines whether the current list item meets the criteria for the object you're attempting to create. In the RoadRage code, we'll be creating a list of all the available Direct3D devices that meet our program's criteria. As mentioned above, the code needs to enumerate the DirectDraw devices, and for each DirectDraw device, it needs to enumerate the available Direct3D devices.

By passing the flags DDENUM_ATTACHEDSECONDARYDEVICES, DDENUM_DETACHEDSECONDARYDEVICES, and DDENUM_NON-DISPLAYDEVICES to the *DirectDrawEnumerateEx* routine, we request that these types of devices be enumerated (and thus added to the list of available devices).

The *DirectDrawEnumerateEx* function, which uses these flags, is declared as follows:

```
HRESULT WINAPI DirectDrawEnumerateEx(
    LPDDENUMCALLBACK lpCallback,
    LPVOID lpContext,
    DWORD dwFlags
);
```

Parameter	Description
lpCallback	The address of a callback function that will be called with a description of each DirectDraw-enabled HAL installed in the target system.
lpContext	The address of an application-defined context that is passed to the enumeration callback function each time it is called.
dwFlags	Flags specifying the enumeration scope. If the value is 0, the function will enumerate only the primary display device. This parameter can also be a combination of the following flags: **DDENUM_ATTACHEDSECONDARYDEVICES** Enumerate the primary device and any display devices that are attached to the desktop. **DDENUM_DETACHEDSECONDARYDEVICES** Enumerate the primary device and any display devices that are not attached to the desktop. **DDENUM_NONDISPLAYDEVICES** Enumerate the primary device and any nondisplay devices, such as 3D accelerators that have no 2D capabilities.

In the Direct3D Framework, enumeration begins with *D3DEnum_Enumerate-Devices*, a function in d3denum.cpp. The code for this routine follows:

```
//-----------------------------------------------------------------
// Name: D3DEnum_EnumerateDevices
// Desc: Enumerates all drivers, devices, and modes. The callback
//       function is called for each device to confirm that the
//       device supports the feature set the application requires.
//-----------------------------------------------------------------
HRESULT D3DEnum_EnumerateDevices( HRESULT
                    (*AppConfirmFn)(DDCAPS*, D3DDEVICEDESC7*) )
{
    // Store the device enumeration callback function.
    g_fnAppConfirmFn = AppConfirmFn;

    // Enumerate drivers, devices, and modes.
    DirectDrawEnumerateEx( DriverEnumCallback, NULL,
                    DDENUM_ATTACHEDSECONDARYDEVICES |
                    DDENUM_DETACHEDSECONDARYDEVICES |
                    DDENUM_NONDISPLAYDEVICES );

    // Make sure that devices were enumerated.
    if( 0 == g_dwNumDevicesEnumerated )
    {
        DEBUG_MSG( _T("No devices and/or modes were enumerated!") );
        return D3DENUMERR_ENUMERATIONFAILED;
    }
    if( 0 == g_dwNumDevices )
    {
        DEBUG_MSG( _T("No enumerated devices were accepted!") );
        DEBUG_MSG( _T("Try enabling the D3D Reference Rasterizer.") );
        return D3DENUMERR_SUGGESTREFRAST;
    }

    return S_OK;
}
```

The parameter *AppConfirmFn* that is passed into *D3DEnum_EnumerateDevices* is a function pointer that can be used to filter out Direct3D devices that are unsuitable for the program and will be described in greater detail later in this chapter.

DirectDrawEnumerateEx takes a function pointer as its first parameter. This should be a pointer to the application-defined callback function. In this code, it is set to the *DriverEnumCallback* routine. The function must be of the following form:

```
BOOL WINPAPI DDEnumCallbackEx(
    GUID FAR *lpGUID,
```

(continued)

41

```
        LPSTR lpDriverDescription,
        LPSTR lpDriverName,
        LPVOID lpContext
        HMONITOR hm
);
```

Parameter	Description
lpGUID	The address of a globally unique identifier for the device
lpDriverDescription	The address of the device's description
lpDriverName	The address of the device's name
lpContext	The address of the user-defined data context that was passed to *DirectDrawEnumerateEx*
hm	The handle to the monitor associated with the enumerated DirectDraw object. This parameter will be NULL when the enumerated DirectDraw object is for the primary device, a nondisplay device (such as a 3D accelerator with no 2D capabilities), and devices that aren't attached to the desktop.

The *DriverEnumCallback* function is defined in d3denum.cpp as follows:

```
//-----------------------------------------------------------------
// Name: DriverEnumCallback
// Desc: Callback function for enumerating drivers
//-----------------------------------------------------------------
static BOOL WINAPI DriverEnumCallback( GUID* pGUID, TCHAR* strDesc,
                                       TCHAR* strName, VOID*,
                                       HMONITOR )
{
    D3DEnum_DeviceInfo d3dDeviceInfo;
    LPDIRECTDRAW7      pDD;
    LPDIRECT3D7        pD3D;
    HRESULT            hr;
    //
    // STEP 1
    // Use the GUID to create the DirectDraw object.
    //
    hr = DirectDrawCreateEx( pGUID, (VOID**)&pDD, IID_IDirectDraw7,
                             NULL );
    if( FAILED(hr) )
```

```
{
    DEBUG_MSG( _T("Can't create DDraw during enumeration!") );
    return D3DENUMRET_OK;
}
//
// STEP 2
// Create a Direct3D object to enumerate the d3d devices.
//
hr = pDD->QueryInterface( IID_IDirect3D7, (VOID**)&pD3D );
if( FAILED(hr) )
{
    pDD->Release();
    DEBUG_MSG( _T("Can't query IDirect3D7 during enumeration!") );
    return D3DENUMRET_OK;
}
//
// STEP 3
//
// Copy data to a device information structure.
ZeroMemory( &d3dDeviceInfo, sizeof(d3dDeviceInfo) );
lstrcpyn( d3dDeviceInfo.strDesc, strDesc, 39 );
d3dDeviceInfo.ddDriverCaps.dwSize = sizeof(DDCAPS);
d3dDeviceInfo.ddHELCaps.dwSize    = sizeof(DDCAPS);
pDD->GetCaps( &d3dDeviceInfo.ddDriverCaps,
              &d3dDeviceInfo.ddHELCaps );
if( pGUID )
{
    d3dDeviceInfo.guidDriver = (*pGUID);
    d3dDeviceInfo.pDriverGUID = &d3dDeviceInfo.guidDriver;
}

strcpy(D3Ddevicename, d3dDeviceInfo.strDesc);

// Record whether the device can render into a desktop window.
if( d3dDeviceInfo.ddDriverCaps.dwCaps2
    & DDCAPS2_CANRENDERWINDOWED )
    if( NULL == d3dDeviceInfo.pDriverGUID )
        d3dDeviceInfo.bDesktopCompatible = TRUE;
//
// STEP 4
// Enumerate the full-screen display modes.
//
pDD->EnumDisplayModes( 0, NULL, &d3dDeviceInfo,
                       ModeEnumCallback );
```

(continued)

```
// Sort the list of display modes.
qsort( d3dDeviceInfo.pddsdModes, d3dDeviceInfo.dwNumModes,
       sizeof(DDSURFACEDESC2), SortModesCallback );

// Now enumerate all the 3D devices.
pD3D->EnumDevices( DeviceEnumCallback, &d3dDeviceInfo );

// Clean up and return.
SAFE_DELETE( d3dDeviceInfo.pddsdModes );
pD3D->Release();
pDD->Release();

return DDENUMRET_OK;
}
```

As each DirectDraw device is enumerated, *DriverEnumCallback* gets called by DirectX, with the appropriate GUID, description, name, and monitor handle for each device. As you can see, the first thing *DriverEnumCallback* does with this information is to create a DirectDraw object for each device.

Creating a DirectDraw Object

The DirectDraw object is the object you'll use to operate on a particular display device. If any of the available display devices support hardware acceleration, the DirectDraw object can use this acceleration. You can use each of the unique DirectDraw objects available on the target system to manipulate the display device and to create clipper objects, surfaces, palettes, and so on for them.

In the first section (labeled STEP 1) of the *DriverEnumCallback* function shown above, the call to the *DirectDrawCreateEx* routine attempts to create the DirectDraw device. This function returns only the new *IDirectDraw7* interface. If you want to use any of the earlier interfaces, you need to create the object by using *DirectDrawCreate* and querying for the interface you want to use. When you're developing new games, you should always use the newest interfaces; I recommend using *DirectDrawCreateEx* for all your new code. This function is declared as follows:

```
HRESULT WINAPI DirectDrawCreateEx
    GUID FAR *lpGUID,
    LPDIRECTDRAW FAR *lplpDD,
    REFIID iid,
    IUnknown FAR *pUnkOuter
);
```

Parameter	Description
lpGUID	Either the address of a globally unique identifier for the DirectDraw device to be used or one of the following values:
	NULL Use the primary device (the active display driver).
	DDCREATE_EMULATIONONLY Use the HEL device (for testing or debugging).
	DDCREATE_HARDWAREONLY Use the HAL only with the default device (for testing and debugging).
lplpDD	The address of a variable to be initialized with a valid *IDirectDraw7* interface pointer upon success of the call.
iid	Must be set to *IID_IDirectDraw7*; any other value will cause the function to fail.
pUnkOuter	Must be set to NULL; provided for future compatibility with COM aggregation features.

If the call to *DirectDrawCreateEx* fails, the *DriverEnumCallback* routine returns immediately and waits to be called again to determine whether another DirectDraw hardware device found during enumeration is available and might work. If the *DirectDrawCreateEx* call succeeds, you can query the object to see what capabilities it supports by using the DirectDraw method *GetCaps* (STEP 3 in the preceding code). The *GetCaps* method returns the cap bits that define which features the target system's hardware supports and which it only emulates. Note that this function only gets DirectDraw capabilities, not Direct3D capabilities (which are examined later). If the display device lacks the DirectDraw capabilities you need, you can decide not to use it for your application. Here's the declaration for *GetCaps*:

```
HRESULT GetCaps(
    LPDDCAPS lpDDDriverCaps,
    LPDDCAPS lpDDHELCaps
);
```

Parameter	Description
lpDDDriverCaps	The address of a DDCAPS structure to be filled with the device's hardware capabilities
lpDDHELCaps	The address of a DDCAPS structure to be filled with the HEL capabilities

You need to determine which features your code requires and which are just nice to have. Many display devices currently on the market don't support capabilities such as overlays, so you'd be wise to consider not requiring this feature. Your code should run on state-of-the-art accelerators and use whatever capabilities are available, but it should also be flexible enough to gracefully degrade the appearance of your 3D world while still running efficiently if some of these features aren't available.

Enumerating the Display Modes

The next step in the *DriverEnumCallback* routine, labeled STEP 4, is to enumerate the available display modes on the current DirectDraw device. DirectDraw supports capabilities such as palette register handling (setting palette information) and blitting (copying 2D graphic data) automatically, so you don't need to handle each hardware type independently. However, you should be sure to use *IDirectDraw7:: EnumDisplayModes*, as is done in the *DriverEnumCallback* routine, to determine what display modes the currently installed monitor supports. A *display mode* is a combination of pixel resolution (for example, 1024 × 768), pixel color depth (for example, 32-bit color), and refresh rate (for example, 85 Hz). DirectDraw will compare the monitor's capabilities with the available display modes, and if the monitor doesn't support the desired mode, *IDirectDraw7::SetDisplayMode* will fail. By determining the monitor's abilities through enumeration, you won't have to worry about the call failing because you'll know ahead of time what modes are available.

The *IDirectDraw7::EnumDisplayModes* method is declared as follows:

```
HRESULT EnumDisplayModes(
    DWORD dwFlags,
    LPDDSURFACEDESC2 lpDDSurfaceDesc2,
    LPVOID lpContext,
    LPDDENUMMODESCALLBACK2 lpEnumModesCallback
);
```

Parameter	Description
dwFlags	One of the following flags: **DDEDM_REFRESHRATES** Enumerates the modes with different refresh rates. *IDirectDraw7::EnumDisplayModes* guarantees that a particular mode will be enumerated only once. This flag indicates whether the refresh rate is used when determining whether a mode is unique.

(continued)

Parameter	Description
	DDEDM_STANDARDVGAMODES Enumerates Mode 13 in addition to the 320 × 200 × 8 Mode X mode.
lpDDSurfaceDesc2	The address of a DDSURFACEDESC2 structure to be checked against available modes. If this parameter is NULL, all modes will be enumerated.
lpContext	The address of an application-defined structure that will be passed to each enumeration member.
lpEnumModesCallback	The address of the *EnumModesCallback2* function that the enumeration procedure will call each time a match is found.

The code to enumerate the display modes is shown below. The main routine used to enumerate the display modes is the *ModeEnumCallback* function. This routine will build a list of the available display modes. This list is stored in the *pDevice->pddsdModes* array.

```
//-------------------------------------------------------------------
// Name: ModeEnumCallback
// Desc: Callback function for enumerating display modes
//-------------------------------------------------------------------
static HRESULT WINAPI ModeEnumCallback( DDSURFACEDESC2* pddsd,
                                        VOID* pParentInfo )
{
    D3DEnum_DeviceInfo* pDevice = (D3DEnum_DeviceInfo*)pParentInfo;

    // Reallocate storage for the modes.
    DDSURFACEDESC2* pddsdNewModes =
        new DDSURFACEDESC2[pDevice->dwNumModes+1];
    memcpy( pddsdNewModes, pDevice->pddsdModes,
            pDevice->dwNumModes * sizeof(DDSURFACEDESC2) );
    delete pDevice->pddsdModes;
    pDevice->pddsdModes = pddsdNewModes;

    // Add the new mode.
    pDevice->pddsdModes[pDevice->dwNumModes++] = (*pddsd);

    return DDENUMRET_OK;
}
```

Enumerating the Direct3D Devices

The last step of the *DriverEnumCallback* routine is to call *IDirect3D7::EnumDevices* to enumerate all the Direct3D devices for the current DirectDraw device. Since this is a Direct3D method, we first need to get an *IDirect3D7* interface pointer. This pointer is acquired in Step 2 of *DriverEnumCallback* by calling *QueryInterface* on the *IDirectDraw7* object. The *IDirect3D7::EnumDevices* method is defined as follows:

```
HRESULT EnumDevices(
  LPD3DENUMDEVICESCALLBACK7 lpEnumDevicesCallback,
  LPVOID lpUserArg
);
```

Parameter	Description
lpEnumDevicesCallback	Address of the *D3DEnumDevicesCallback7* callback function that the enumeration procedure will call every time a match is found
LpUserArg	Address of application-defined data passed to the callback function

In a similar technique to *DirectDrawEnumerateEx* and *IDirectDraw7:: EnumDisplayModes*, *IDirect3D7::EnumDevices* calls a user-specified callback function for each Direct3D device. The Direct3D Framework's Direct3D device callback routine (in d3denum.cpp) is called *DeviceEnumCallback*. This function is defined as follows:

```
//------------------------------------------------------------------
// Name: DeviceEnumCallback
// Desc: Callback function for enumerating devices
//------------------------------------------------------------------
static HRESULT WINAPI DeviceEnumCallback( TCHAR* strDesc,
                                          TCHAR* strName,
                                          D3DDEVICEDESC7* pDesc,
                                          VOID* pParentInfo )
{
    // Keep track of the number of devices that were enumerated.
    g_dwNumDevicesEnumerated++;

    D3DEnum_DeviceInfo* pDriverInfo =
        (D3DEnum_DeviceInfo*)pParentInfo;
```

```
D3DEnum_DeviceInfo* pDeviceInfo = &g_pDeviceList[g_dwNumDevices];
ZeroMemory( pDeviceInfo, sizeof(D3DEnum_DeviceInfo) );

// Select either the HAL or the HEL device desc:
pDeviceInfo->bHardware =
    pDesc->dwDevCaps & D3DDEVCAPS_HWRASTERIZATION;
memcpy( &pDeviceInfo->ddDeviceDesc, pDesc,
        sizeof(D3DDEVICEDESC7) );

// Set up device information for this device.
pDeviceInfo->bDesktopCompatible = pDriverInfo->bDesktopCompatible;
pDeviceInfo->ddDriverCaps       = pDriverInfo->ddDriverCaps;
pDeviceInfo->ddHELCaps          = pDriverInfo->ddHELCaps;
pDeviceInfo->guidDevice         = pDesc->deviceGUID;
pDeviceInfo->pDeviceGUID        = &pDeviceInfo->guidDevice;
pDeviceInfo->pddsdModes         =
    new DDSURFACEDESC2[pDriverInfo->dwNumModes];

// Copy the driver GUID and description for the device.
if( pDriverInfo->pDriverGUID )
{
    pDeviceInfo->guidDriver  = pDriverInfo->guidDriver;
    pDeviceInfo->pDriverGUID = &pDeviceInfo->guidDriver;
    lstrcpyn( pDeviceInfo->strDesc, pDriverInfo->strDesc, 39 );
}
else
{
    pDeviceInfo->pDriverGUID = NULL;
    lstrcpyn( pDeviceInfo->strDesc, strName, 39 );
}

// Avoid duplicates: enumerate hardware devices only for
// secondary DirectDraw drivers.
if( NULL != pDeviceInfo->pDriverGUID &&
    FALSE == pDeviceInfo->bHardware )
        return D3DENUMRET_OK;

// Give the application a chance to accept or reject this device.
if( g_fnAppConfirmFn )
    if( FAILED( g_fnAppConfirmFn( &pDeviceInfo->ddDriverCaps,
                                  &pDeviceInfo->ddDeviceDesc ) ) )
        return D3DENUMRET_OK;

// Build a list of supported modes for the device.
```

(continued)

```
for( DWORD i=0; i<pDriverInfo->dwNumModes; i++ )
{
    DDSURFACEDESC2 ddsdMode = pDriverInfo->pddsdModes[i];
    DWORD dwRenderDepths =
        pDeviceInfo->ddDeviceDesc.dwDeviceRenderBitDepth;
    DWORD dwDepth =
        ddsdMode.ddpfPixelFormat.dwRGBBitCount;

    // Accept modes that are compatible with the device.
    if( ( ( dwDepth == 32 ) && ( dwRenderDepths & DDBD_32 ) ) ||
        ( ( dwDepth == 24 ) && ( dwRenderDepths & DDBD_24 ) ) ||
        ( ( dwDepth == 16 ) && ( dwRenderDepths & DDBD_16 ) ) )
    {
        // Copy compatible modes to the list of device-supported
        // modes.
        pDeviceInfo->pddsdModes[pDeviceInfo->dwNumModes++] =
            ddsdMode;

        // Record whether the device has any stereo modes.
        if( ddsdMode.ddsCaps.dwCaps2 &
            DDSCAPS2_STEREOSURFACELEFT )
            pDeviceInfo->bStereoCompatible = TRUE;
    }
}

// Bail if the device has no supported modes.
if( 0 == pDeviceInfo->dwNumModes )
    return D3DENUMRET_OK;

// Find a 640 x 480 x 16 mode for the default full-screen mode.
for( i=0; i<pDeviceInfo->dwNumModes; i++ )
{
    if( ( pDeviceInfo->pddsdModes[i].dwWidth == 640 ) &&
        ( pDeviceInfo->pddsdModes[i].dwHeight == 480 ) &&
        ( pDeviceInfo->
            pddsdModes[i].ddpfPixelFormat.dwRGBBitCount == 16 ) )
    {
        pDeviceInfo->ddsdFullscreenMode =
            pDeviceInfo->pddsdModes[i];
        pDeviceInfo->dwCurrentMode      = i;
    }
}

// Select whether the device is initially windowed.
pDeviceInfo->bWindowed = pDeviceInfo->bDesktopCompatible;
```

```
    // Accept the device and return.
    g_dwNumDevices++;

    return D3DENUMRET_OK;
}
```

This code is basically doing two things. First, it gives the application a chance to reject the device if it is not adequate for the program's needs. Second, it stores the information about the Direct3D device in its data structure.

Remember *AppConfirmFn*, the parameter passed to *D3DEnum_Enumerate-Devices*? If you pass a pointer to a device confirmation function as this parameter, *DeviceEnumCallback* will call that function for each Direct3D device that it enumerates. Your device confirmation function can decide whether the Direct3D device is suitable for your program. If you decide that it isn't a good device, you can have your device confirmation function return a failure code, and *DeviceEnumCallback* will not add the Direct3D device to its list of devices.

The class CD3DApplication defines a member variable, *m_fnConfirmDevice*, which can point to your confirmation function. CMyD3DApplication inherits this member variable because CMyD3DApplication is derived from CD3DApplication. So you can provide a device confirmation function in CMyD3DApplication and then set *m_fnConfirmDevice* to its address in CMyD3DApplication's constructor. In the RoadRage code, we're not requesting any special features such as mipmapping, so we can set *m_fnConfirmDevice* to NULL.

Here's how you would specify special capabilities during enumeration, such as multitexturing:

```
m_fnConfirmDevice = ConfirmDevice;
```

And this is what the *ConfirmDevice* function definition would look like:

```
//------------------------------------------------------------------
// Name: ConfirmDevice
// Desc: Called during device initialization, this code checks the
//       device for some minimum set of capabilities.
//------------------------------------------------------------------
HRESULT CMyD3DApplication::ConfirmDevice( DDCAPS* pddDriverCaps,
                               D3DDEVICEDESC7* pd3dDeviceDesc )
{
    // Accept devices that support multiple textures. If no device,
    // support multiple textures, accept devices that support alpha
    // blending to emulate multitexturing with multipass rendering.
    if( pd3dDeviceDesc->wMaxSimultaneousTextures > 1 )
        return S_OK;
```

(continued)

51

```
        if( pd3dDeviceDesc->dpcTriCaps.dwDestBlendCaps
            & D3DPBLENDCAPS_SRCCOLOR )
            if( pd3dDeviceDesc->dpcTriCaps.dwSrcBlendCaps
                & D3DPBLENDCAPS_ZERO )
                return S_OK;

        return E_FAIL;
}
```

Picking a Direct3D Device

After all that enumeration, it's finally time to decide which Direct3D device to use. If you're using the enumeration code in the Direct3D Framework, this is easy: just call *D3DEnum_SelectDefaultDevice*. It looks for a Direct3D device that supports windowed mode and as much hardware acceleration as possible (and hasn't been rejected by your device confirmation function). Here's its code:

```
//------------------------------------------------------------------
// Name: D3DEnum_SelectDefaultDevice
// Desc: Picks a default device, preferably hardware and desktop
//       compatible
//------------------------------------------------------------------
HRESULT D3DEnum_SelectDefaultDevice( D3DEnum_DeviceInfo** ppDevice,
                                     DWORD dwFlags )
{
    // Check arguments.
    if( NULL == ppDevice )
        return E_INVALIDARG;

    // Get access to the enumerated device list.
    D3DEnum_DeviceInfo* pDeviceList;
    DWORD               dwNumDevices;
    D3DEnum_GetDevices( &pDeviceList, &dwNumDevices );

    // Look for windowable software, hardware, and hardware
    // TnL devices.
    D3DEnum_DeviceInfo* pRefRastDevice      = NULL;
    D3DEnum_DeviceInfo* pSoftwareDevice     = NULL;
    D3DEnum_DeviceInfo* pHardwareDevice     = NULL;
    D3DEnum_DeviceInfo* pHardwareTnLDevice  = NULL;

    for( DWORD i=0; i<dwNumDevices; i++ )
    {
        if( pDeviceList[i].bDesktopCompatible )
        {
```

```
        if( pDeviceList[i].bHardware )
        {
            if( (*pDeviceList[i].pDeviceGUID) ==
                IID_IDirect3DTnLHalDevice )
                pHardwareTnLDevice = &pDeviceList[i];
            else
                pHardwareDevice = &pDeviceList[i];
        }
        else
        {
            if( (*pDeviceList[i].pDeviceGUID) ==
                IID_IDirect3DRefDevice )
                pRefRastDevice = &pDeviceList[i];
            else
                pSoftwareDevice = &pDeviceList[i];
        }
    }
}

// Prefer a hardware TnL device first, then a non-TnL hardware
// device, and finally, a software device.
if( 0 == ( dwFlags & D3DENUM_SOFTWAREONLY ) &&
        pHardwareTnLDevice )
    (*ppDevice) = pHardwareTnLDevice;
else if( 0 == ( dwFlags & D3DENUM_SOFTWAREONLY ) &&
            pHardwareDevice )
    (*ppDevice) = pHardwareDevice;
else if( pSoftwareDevice )
    (*ppDevice) = pSoftwareDevice;
else if( pRefRastDevice )
    (*ppDevice) = pRefRastDevice;
else
    return D3DENUMERR_NOCOMPATIBLEDEVICES;

// Set the windowed state of the newly selected device.
(*ppDevice)->bWindowed = TRUE;

return S_OK;
}
```

Your program might have different requirements or preferences for the default Direct3D device. For example, you might want to always default to a full-screen configuration. If this is the case, you can write your own device-selection function.

Initializing DirectDraw with the *CD3DFramework7* Object

With everything enumerated, we can now initialize the DirectDraw device that we want to use and create some of its main objects. When using the Direct3D Framework, the class *CD3DFramework7* is used to manage these main objects: the main window handle, the front and back buffers, and various state information. This chapter uses a slimmed-down version of the *CD3DFramework7* class that focuses on DirectDraw and omits some of the Direct3D-related member variables and functions. The full version of *CD3DFramework7* (which we'll use in later chapters) also manages the IDirect3D7 interface pointer, the IDirect3DDevice7 interface pointer, and the depth buffer. The slimmed-down *CD3DFramework7* class is defined as follows:

```
//-------------------------------------------------------------------
// Name: CD3DFramework7
// Desc: The Direct3D sample framework class for DirectX7. Maintains
//       the Direct3D surfaces and device used for 3D rendering.
//-------------------------------------------------------------------
class CD3DFramework7
{
    // Internal variables for the framework class
    HWND                  m_hWnd;                    // The window object
    BOOL                  m_bIsFullscreen;           // Full-screen vs.
                                                     // windowed
    BOOL                  m_bIsStereo;               // Stereo view mode
    DWORD                 m_dwRenderWidth;           // Dimensions of the
                                                     // render target
    DWORD                 m_dwRenderHeight;
    RECT                  m_rcScreenRect;            // Screen rectangle
                                                     // for window
    LPDIRECTDRAW7         m_pDD;                     // DirectDraw object
    LPDIRECTDRAWSURFACE7  m_pddsFrontBuffer;         // Primary surface
    LPDIRECTDRAWSURFACE7  m_pddsBackBuffer;          // Back-buffer surface
    LPDIRECTDRAWSURFACE7  m_pddsBackBufferLeft;      // For stereo modes
    DWORD                 m_dwDeviceMemType;
    DDPIXELFORMAT         m_ddpfBackBufferPixelFormat;

    // Internal functions for the framework class
    HRESULT CreateFullscreenBuffers( DDSURFACEDESC2* );
    HRESULT CreateWindowedBuffers();
```

```
        HRESULT CreateDirectDraw( GUID*, DWORD );
        HRESULT CreateEnvironment( GUID*, GUID*, DDSURFACEDESC2*, DWORD );

public:
    // Access functions for DirectX objects
    LPDIRECTDRAW7       GetDirectDraw()
                                    { return m_pDD; }
    LPDIRECTDRAWSURFACE7 GetFrontBuffer()
                                    { return m_pddsFrontBuffer; }
    LPDIRECTDRAWSURFACE7 GetBackBuffer()
                                    { return m_pddsBackBuffer; }
    LPDIRECTDRAWSURFACE7 GetRenderSurface()
                                    { return m_pddsBackBuffer; }
    LPDIRECTDRAWSURFACE7 GetRenderSurfaceLeft()
                                    { return m_pddsBackBufferLeft; }
    // Dimensions of the render target
    DWORD               GetRenderWidth()
                                    { return m_dwRenderWidth; }
    DWORD               GetRenderHeight()
                                    { return m_dwRenderHeight; }
    // Functions to aid rendering
    HRESULT RestoreSurfaces();
    HRESULT ShowFrame();
    HRESULT FlipToGDISurface( BOOL bDrawFrame = FALSE );

    // Functions for managing screen and viewport bounds
    BOOL    IsFullscreen()                  { return m_bIsFullscreen; }
    BOOL    IsStereo()                      { return m_bIsStereo; }
    VOID    Move( INT x, INT y );

    // Creates the framework
    HRESULT Initialize( HWND hWnd, GUID* pDriverGUID,
                        GUID* pDeviceGUID, DDSURFACEDESC2* pddsd,
                        DWORD dwFlags );
    HRESULT DestroyObjects();

            CD3DFramework7();
            ~CD3DFramework7();
};
```

After calling *D3DEnum_EnumerateDevices* and *D3DEnum_SelectDefault-Device*, *CD3DApplication::Create* calls *CD3DApplication::Initialize3DEnvironment*. This member function initializes the framework and sets up either full-screen or windowed mode. The *CD3DApplication::Initialize3DEnvironment* function is defined as follows:

```
//-------------------------------------------------------------------
// Name: Initialize3DEnvironment
// Desc: Initializes the sample framework and then calls the
//       application-specific function to initialize device-specific
//       objects. This code is structured to handle any errors that
//       might occur during initialization.
//-------------------------------------------------------------------
HRESULT CD3DApplication::Initialize3DEnvironment()
{
    HRESULT hr;
    DWORD   dwFrameworkFlags = 0L;
    dwFrameworkFlags |=
        ( !m_pDeviceInfo->bWindowed ? D3DFW_FULLSCREEN : 0L );
    dwFrameworkFlags |=
        ( m_pDeviceInfo->bStereo   ? D3DFW_STEREO    : 0L );
    dwFrameworkFlags |=
        ( m_bAppUseZBuffer         ? D3DFW_ZBUFFER   : 0L );

    // Initialize the Direct3D Framework.
    if( SUCCEEDED( hr = m_pFramework->Initialize( m_hWnd,
                    m_pDeviceInfo->pDriverGUID,
                    m_pDeviceInfo->pDeviceGUID,
                    &m_pDeviceInfo->ddsdFullscreenMode,
                    dwFrameworkFlags ) ) )
    {
        m_pDD        = m_pFramework->GetDirectDraw();
        m_pD3D       = m_pFramework->GetDirect3D();
        m_pd3dDevice = m_pFramework->GetD3DDevice();

        m_pddsRenderTarget     = m_pFramework->GetRenderSurface();
        m_pddsRenderTargetLeft = m_pFramework->GetRenderSurfaceLeft(.);
        m_ddsdRenderTarget.dwSize = sizeof(m_ddsdRenderTarget);
        m_pddsRenderTarget->GetSurfaceDesc( &m_ddsdRenderTarget );

        // Let the application run its startup code, which creates
        // the 3D scene.
        if( SUCCEEDED( hr = InitDeviceObjects() ) )
            return S_OK;
         else
        {
            DeleteDeviceObjects();
```

```
            m_pFramework->DestroyObjects();
        }
    }

    // If you get here, the first initialization pass failed. If
    // that was with a hardware device, try again using a software
    // rasterizer instead.
    if( m_pDeviceInfo->bHardware )
    {
        // Try again with a software rasterizer.
        DisplayFrameworkError( hr, MSGWARN_SWITCHEDTOSOFTWARE );
        D3DEnum_SelectDefaultDevice( &m_pDeviceInfo,
                                     D3DENUM_SOFTWAREONLY );
        return Initialize3DEnvironment();
    }

    return hr;
}
```

The *CD3DFramework7::Initialize* member function sets up some framework member variables and then calls *CD3DFramework7::CreateEnvironment* to create the essential DirectX objects to be used in the game or application.

```
//-----------------------------------------------------------------
// Name: Initialize
// Desc: Creates the internal objects for the framework
//-----------------------------------------------------------------
HRESULT CD3DFramework7::Initialize( HWND hWnd, GUID* pDriverGUID,
                                    GUID* pDeviceGUID,
                                    DDSURFACEDESC2* pMode,
                                    DWORD dwFlags )
{
    HRESULT hr;

    // Check parameters. A NULL mode is valid only for windowed modes.
    if( ( NULL==hWnd ) || ( NULL==pDeviceGUID ) ||
        ( NULL==pMode && (dwFlags&D3DFW_FULLSCREEN) ) )
        return E_INVALIDARG;

    // Set up state for windowed/full-screen mode.
    m_hWnd         = hWnd;
    m_bIsStereo    = FALSE;
    m_bIsFullscreen = ( dwFlags & D3DFW_FULLSCREEN ) ? TRUE : FALSE;
```

(continued)

```
        // Support stereoscopic viewing for full-screen modes that
        // support it.
        if( ( dwFlags & D3DFW_STEREO ) && ( dwFlags & D3DFW_FULLSCREEN ) )
            if( pMode->ddsCaps.dwCaps2 & DDSCAPS2_STEREOSURFACELEFT )
                m_bIsStereo = TRUE;

        // Create the D3D rendering environment (surfaces, device,
        // viewport, and so forth).
        if( FAILED( hr = CreateEnvironment( pDriverGUID, pDeviceGUID,
                                            pMode, dwFlags ) ) )
        {
            DestroyObjects();
            return hr;
        }

        return S_OK;
    }
```

The *CD3DFramework7::CreateEnvironment* member function lets you create the internal objects you'll be defining for your framework. It first chooses the display memory type you've selected. If you're running with a HAL device, choose video memory; otherwise, use system memory. Video memory is faster, but you're stuck with system memory if no accelerator is available on the target system.

You then call the routines to create the main DirectDraw object as well as the full-screen buffers if you're in full-screen mode or the windowed buffers if you're in windowed mode. The full version of *CreateEnvironment* also creates the Direct3D object, the Direct3D device, and the depth buffer.

```
//--------------------------------------------------------------------
// Name: CreateEnvironment
// Desc: Creates the internal objects for the framework
//--------------------------------------------------------------------
HRESULT CD3DFramework7::CreateEnvironment( GUID* pDriverGUID,
                                           GUID* pDeviceGUID,
                                           DDSURFACEDESC2* pMode,
                                           DWORD dwFlags )
{
    HRESULT hr;

    // Select the default memory type, depending on whether the
    // device is hardware or software.
    if( IsEqualIID( *pDeviceGUID, IID_IDirect3DHALDevice) )
        m_dwDeviceMemType = DDSCAPS_VIDEOMEMORY;
    else if( IsEqualIID( *pDeviceGUID, IID_IDirect3DTnLHalDevice) )
        m_dwDeviceMemType = DDSCAPS_VIDEOMEMORY;
```

```
    else
        m_dwDeviceMemType = DDSCAPS_SYSTEMMEMORY;

    // Create the DirectDraw object.
    hr = CreateDirectDraw( pDriverGUID, dwFlags );
    if( FAILED( hr ) )
        return hr;

    // Create the front and back buffers, and attach a clipper.
    if( dwFlags & D3DFW_FULLSCREEN )
        hr = CreateFullscreenBuffers( pMode );
    else
        hr = CreateWindowedBuffers();
    if( FAILED( hr ) )
        return hr;

    return S_OK;
}
```

The first call is to the *CD3DFramework7::CreateDirectDraw* function, which calls *DirectDrawCreateEx* to create the DirectDraw interface using the *IID_IDirectDraw7* interface. *CD3DFramework7::CreateDirectDraw* also sets the Windows cooperative level. (I'll explain how in the next section.) Finally, because the Direct3D Framework doesn't use palettes, you need to verify that you're not running in palettized mode. This routine is defined as follows:

```
//-----------------------------------------------------------------
// Name: CreateDirectDraw
// Desc: Creates the DirectDraw interface
//-----------------------------------------------------------------
HRESULT CD3DFramework7::CreateDirectDraw( GUID* pDriverGUID,
                                          DWORD dwFlags )
{
    // Create the DirectDraw interface.
    if( FAILED( DirectDrawCreateEx( pDriverGUID, (VOID**)&m_pDD,
                                    IID_IDirectDraw7, NULL ) ) )
    {
        DEBUG_MSG( _T("Could not create DirectDraw") );
        return D3DFWERR_NODIRECTDRAW;
    }

    // Set the Windows cooperative level.
    DWORD dwCoopFlags = DDSCL_NORMAL;
```

(continued)

```
        if( m_bIsFullscreen )
            dwCoopFlags = DDSCL_ALLOWREBOOT|DDSCL_EXCLUSIVE|
                            DDSCL_FULLSCREEN;

        // By default, the flag is set to allow Direct3D to optimize
        // floating-point calculations.
        if( 0L == ( dwFlags & D3DFW_NO_FPUSETUP ) )
            dwCoopFlags |= DDSCL_FPUSETUP;

        if( FAILED( m_pDD->SetCooperativeLevel( m_hWnd, dwCoopFlags ) ) )
        {
            DEBUG_MSG( _T("Couldn't set coop level") );
            return D3DFWERR_COULDNTSETCOOPLEVEL;
        }

        // Check that the display is not palettized. That case will fail
        // because the Direct3D Framework doesn't use palettes.
        DDSURFACEDESC2 ddsd;
        ddsd.dwSize = sizeof(ddsd);
        m_pDD->GetDisplayMode( &ddsd );
        if( ddsd.ddpfPixelFormat.dwRGBBitCount <= 8 )
            return D3DFWERR_INVALIDMODE;

        return S_OK;
    }
```

Setting the Cooperative Level

Once a DirectDraw device is created, you need to set the *cooperative level*. The cooperative level, which is used for DirectDraw, DirectSound, and DirectInput, specifies how your code will work with the system and other applications. You must set the cooperative level before you call other DirectDraw methods or they might fail, depending on what the other applications are doing.

In DirectDraw, cooperative levels are used mainly to determine whether an application is running as a windowed application or a full-screen program with exclusive access to the display. In DirectX 7, you use the *IDirectDraw7::Set-CooperativeLevel* method to set the cooperative level of DirectDraw. The standard cooperative level places DirectDraw in a windowed mode that doesn't allow you to change the primary surface's palette or perform page flipping. For most game development, this restriction wouldn't be acceptable because the palette sometimes needs to change and page flipping is definitely required for realistic 3D. I'll explain page flipping in detail later in this chapter, when we get to that segment of code.

For now, just remember that you often need to set the cooperative level to acquire exclusive, full-screen access rather than to run in windowed mode.

DirectDraw cooperative levels can also be used to do the following:

- Prevent DirectDraw from rebooting if the user presses Ctrl+Alt+Del and from releasing exclusive control of the display

- Enable the use of Mode X resolutions

- Allow DirectDraw to maximize or minimize the application (when in windowed mode)

- Indicate whether the palette will be manipulated

DirectDraw controls window activation events when in exclusive, full-screen mode. (No other applications will be fighting for display resources.) WM_ ACTIVATEAPP messages are sent as needed to the window handle registered using the *SetCooperativeLevel* method. Because of this, since DirectDraw sends activation events to the top-level window only, you must subclass any child windows your application creates that require activation event messages.

The *IDirectDraw7::SetCooperativeLevel* method is declared as follows:

```
HRESULT SetCooperativeLevel(
    HWND hWnd,
    DWORD dwFlags
);
```

Parameter	Description
hWnd	The window handle used for the application. This parameter is set to the calling application's top-level window. It can be NULL when the DDSCL_NORMAL flag is specified in the *dwFlags* parameter.
dwFlags	One or more of the following flags:
	DDSCL_ALLOWMODEX Enables the use of Mode X display modes. This flag can be used if the DDSCL_EXCLUSIVE and DDSCL_FULLSCREEN flags are present.
	DDSCL_ALLOWREBOOT Enables Ctrl+Alt+Del to function while in exclusive, full-screen mode.

(continued)

Parameter	Description
	DDSCL_CREATEDEVICEWINDOW Supported only in Windows 98 and Windows 2000. This flag indicates that DirectDraw is to create and manage a default device window for this DirectDraw object.
	DDSCL_EXCLUSIVE Requests the exclusive level. This flag must be used with the DDSCL_FULLSCREEN flag.
	DDSCL_FPUPRESERVE Indicates that the calling application cares about the floating-point unit (FPU) state and doesn't want Direct3D to modify it in ways visible to the application. This flag causes Direct3D to save and restore the state of the FPU whenever it modifies the FPU state.
	DDSCL_FPUSETUP The system will attempt to keep the FPU set up for optimal Direct3D performance with single precision and exceptions disabled so that Direct3D won't need to set the FPU each time.
	DDSCL_FULLSCREEN Indicates that the exclusive-mode owner will be responsible for the entire primary surface. The graphics device interface (GDI) can be ignored. This flag must be used with the DDSCL_EXCLUSIVE flag.
	DDSCL_MULTITHREADED Requests multithread-safe DirectDraw behavior. This flag causes Direct3D to take the global critical section more frequently.
	DDSCL_NORMAL Indicates that the application will function as a regular Windows application. This flag can't be used with the DDSCL_ALLOWMODEX, DDSCL_EXCLUSIVE, or DDSCL_FULLSCREEN flag.
	DDSCL_NOWINDOWCHANGES Specifies that DirectDraw isn't allowed to minimize or restore the application window on activation.
	DDSCL_SETDEVICEWINDOW Supported only in Windows 98 and Windows 2000. This flag indicates that the *hWnd* parameter is the window handle of the device window for this DirectDraw object. This flag can't be used with the DDSCL_SETFOCUSWINDOW flag.
	DDSCL_SETFOCUSWINDOW Supported only in Windows 98 and Windows 2000. This flag indicates that the *hWnd* parameter is the window handle of the focus window for this DirectDraw object. This flag can't be used with the DDSCL_SETDEVICEWINDOW flag.

If you use the DDSCL_NORMAL flag, have multiple DirectDraw windows, and pass NULL as the window handle, the *IDirectDraw7::SetCooperativeLevel* method will allow all the windows to be used at the same time in normal windowed mode.

By using the exclusive, full-screen cooperative level, you can use the accelerator hardware on the system to its greatest advantage, which is one reason so many developers create games using full-screen mode. This mode allows page flipping, dynamic or custom palettes, and changing display resolutions. You need to keep in mind that in exclusive, full-screen mode, other applications can allocate surfaces and use DirectDraw, but only the application with exclusive access can change the display mode or palette.

Creating Surfaces

A surface controlled by the *IDirectDrawSurface7* interface represents a rectangular area of display memory. You use this surface for items such as the primary display surface presented to the user on the screen or the textures applied to 3D surfaces. You can use either video memory or system memory for your surfaces. If you don't specify a particular memory type, DirectDraw places the DirectDrawSurface7 object into whatever memory allows for the best performance.

To create a surface, just call the *IDirectDraw7::CreateSurface* method, which is declared as shown here:

```
HRESULT CreateSurface(
    LPDDSURFACEDESC2 lpDDSurfaceDesc2,
    LPDIRECTDRAWSURFACE7 FAR *lplpDDSurface,
    IUnknown FAR *pUnkOuter
);
```

Parameter	Description
lpDDSurfaceDesc2	The address of a DDSURFACEDESC2 structure that describes the requested surface. Before calling this method, set any unused members of the DDSURFACEDESC2 structure to 0. A DDSCAPS2 structure is a member of DDSURFACEDESC2.
lplpDDSurface	The address of a variable that will be set to a valid *IDirectDrawSurface7* interface pointer if the call succeeds.
pUnkOuter	Allows for compatibility with future COM aggregation features. The *IDirectDraw7::CreateSurface* currently returns an error if this parameter is set to anything other than NULL.

You can use the *IDirectDraw7::CreateSurface* method to create a single surface object, a complex surface-flipping chain, or a three-dimensional surface. The *IDirectDrawSurface7::Lock* method lets you directly access display memory by locking the display memory and retrieving the address for that surface. This address can point to visible frame buffer memory, such as the primary surface, or to nonvisible buffers, such as overlay or off-screen surfaces.

The Front Buffer, Back Buffers, and Clipper

The primary surface, also known as the front buffer, is the surface that is visible on the monitor. Each DirectDraw object can have only one primary surface, which is identified by the DDSCAPS_PRIMARYSURFACE flag.

When the primary surface is created, its dimensions and pixel format match the current display mode, so you don't need to declare them. Accidentally specifying them will cause the call to fail.

Full-Screen Buffers

The following code shows the entire *CreateFullScreenBuffers* routine. This routine is used to create the front and back buffers. (You don't need a clipper object because you're not in windowed mode.) In the paragraphs following the code, each segment is described in detail, in the order in which it should be performed.

```
//-------------------------------------------------------------------
// Name: CreateFullscreenBuffers
// Desc: Creates the primary surface and (optional) back buffer for
//       rendering. Windowed mode and full-screen mode are handled
//       differently.
//-------------------------------------------------------------------
HRESULT CD3DFramework7::CreateFullscreenBuffers(
                                DDSURFACEDESC2* pddsd )
{
    HRESULT hr;

    // STEP 1 - Full-Screen Mode
    // Get the dimensions of the screen bounds.
    // Store the rectangle that contains the renderer.
    SetRect( &m_rcScreenRect, 0, 0, pddsd->dwWidth, pddsd->dwHeight );
    m_dwRenderWidth  = m_rcScreenRect.right  - m_rcScreenRect.left;
    m_dwRenderHeight = m_rcScreenRect.bottom - m_rcScreenRect.top;

    // STEP 2 - Full-Screen Mode
    // Set the display mode to the requested dimensions. Check for
    // 320 x 200 x 8 modes, and set the flag to avoid using Mode X.
    DWORD dwModeFlags = 0;
```

```
if( (320==m_dwRenderWidth) && (200==m_dwRenderHeight) &&
    (8==pddsd->ddpfPixelFormat.dwRGBBitCount) )
    dwModeFlags |= DDSDM_STANDARDVGAMODE;

if( FAILED( m_pDD->SetDisplayMode( m_dwRenderWidth,
                                   m_dwRenderHeight,
                                   pddsd->ddpfPixelFormat.dwRGBBitCount,
                                   pddsd->dwRefreshRate,
                                   dwModeFlags ) ) )
{
    DEBUG_MSG( _T("Can't set display mode") );
    return D3DFWERR_BADDISPLAYMODE;
}

// STEP 3 - Full-Screen Mode
// Set up to create the primary surface with a back buffer.
DDSURFACEDESC2 ddsd;
ZeroMemory( &ddsd, sizeof(ddsd) );
ddsd.dwSize           = sizeof(ddsd);
ddsd.dwFlags          = DDSD_CAPS|DDSD_BACKBUFFERCOUNT;
ddsd.ddsCaps.dwCaps   = DDSCAPS_PRIMARYSURFACE | DDSCAPS_3DDEVICE |
                        DDSCAPS_FLIP | DDSCAPS_COMPLEX;
ddsd.dwBackBufferCount = 1;

// Support for stereoscopic viewing
if( m_bIsStereo )
{
    ddsd.ddsCaps.dwCaps  |= DDSCAPS_VIDEOMEMORY;
    ddsd.ddsCaps.dwCaps2 |= DDSCAPS2_STEREOSURFACELEFT;
}

// STEP 4 - Full-Screen Mode
// Create the primary surface.
if( FAILED( hr = m_pDD->CreateSurface( &ddsd, &m_pddsFrontBuffer,
                                       NULL ) ) )
{
    DEBUG_MSG( _T("Error: Can't create primary surface") );
    if( hr != DDERR_OUTOFVIDEOMEMORY )
        return D3DFWERR_NOPRIMARY;
    DEBUG_MSG( _T("Error: Out of video memory") );
    return DDERR_OUTOFVIDEOMEMORY;
}

// STEP 5 - Full-Screen Mode
// Get the back buffer, which was created along with the primary
// surface.
```

(continued)

65

```
DDSCAPS2 ddscaps = { DDSCAPS_BACKBUFFER, 0, 0, 0 };
if( FAILED( hr = m_pddsFrontBuffer->GetAttachedSurface( &ddscaps,
                                            &m_pddsBackBuffer ) ) )
{
    DEBUG_ERR( hr, _T("Error: Can't get the back buffer") );
    return D3DFWERR_NOBACKBUFFER;
}

// Increment the back-buffer count (for consistency with
// windowed mode).
m_pddsBackBuffer->AddRef();

// STEP 6 - Full-Screen Mode
// Support for stereoscopic viewing
if( m_bIsStereo )
{
    // Get the left back buffer, which was created along with the
    // primary surface.
    DDSCAPS2 ddscaps = { 0, DDSCAPS2_STEREOSURFACELEFT, 0, 0 };
    if( FAILED( hr =
            m_pddsBackBuffer->GetAttachedSurface( &ddscaps,
                                        &m_pddsBackBufferLeft ) ) )
    {
        DEBUG_ERR( hr,
            _T("Error: Can't get the left back buffer") );
        return D3DFWERR_NOBACKBUFFER;
    }
    m_pddsBackBufferLeft->AddRef();
}

FILE *fplog = fopen("rrlogfile.txt","a");

ZeroMemory(&m_ddpfBackBufferPixelFormat, sizeof(DDPIXELFORMAT));
m_ddpfBackBufferPixelFormat.dwSize = sizeof(DDPIXELFORMAT);
hr = m_pddsBackBuffer->
        GetPixelFormat(&m_ddpfBackBufferPixelFormat);

if(hr == DD_OK)
{
    fprintf( fplog, "Backbuffer Pixelformat RGB bits  = : ");
    fprintf( fplog, "%d\n",
            m_ddpfBackBufferPixelFormat.dwRGBBitCount);

    fprintf( fplog, "Backbuffer Pixelformat RGB masks = : ");
    fprintf( fplog, "%d %d %d\n\n",
    m_ddpfBackBufferPixelFormat.dwRBitMask,
```

```
        m_ddpfBackBufferPixelFormat.dwGBitMask,
        m_ddpfBackBufferPixelFormat.dwBBitMask);
    }
    else
        fprintf( fplog, "Check on back-buffer pixel format FAILED ");


    hr = m_pddsBackBuffer->GetSurfaceDesc( &ddsd );

    fclose(fplog);

    return S_OK;
}
```

In STEP 1 of the *CD3DFramework7::CreateFullscreenBuffers* routine, *m_rc-ScreenRect* is filled with the rectangle defining the screen resolution information (for example, 640 × 480, 800 × 600, and so on). The *m_dwRenderWidth* and *m_dwRenderHeight* member variables are also set to the computed width and height of the screen.

In STEP 2, the code calls *IDirectDraw7::SetDisplayMode,* making sure to skip using the Mode X mode. The *IDirectDraw7::SetDisplayMode* method sets the mode of the display-device hardware. This method is defined as follows:

```
HRESULT SetDisplayMode (
    DWORD dwWidth,
    DWORD dwHeight,
    DWORD dwBPP,
    DWORD dwRefreshRate,
    DWORD dwFlags
);
```

Parameter	Description
dwWidth and *dwHeight*	Width and height of the new mode.
dwBPP	Bits per pixel (bpp) of the new mode.
dwRefreshRate	Refresh rate of the new mode. Set this value to 0 to request the default refresh rate for the driver.
dwFlags	Flags describing additional options. Currently, the only valid flag is DDSDM_STANDARDVGA-MODE, which causes the method to set Mode 13 instead of Mode X 320 × 200 × 8 mode. If you're setting another resolution, bit depth, or a Mode X mode, don't use this flag and set the parameter to 0.

If the display mode is successfully set, you next create the primary surface and back buffer.

STEP 3 sets up a DDSURFACEDESC2 structure specifying the following flags:

- **DDSD_CAPS** This member states that the *ddsCaps* member is valid in this type.

- **DDSD_BACKBUFFERCOUNT** Indicates that you want to create a back buffer.

- **DDSCAPS_PRIMARYSURFACE** Specifies that the type description is for a primary surface.

- **DDSCAPS_3DDEVICE** The surface can be used for 3D rendering.

- **DDSCAPS_FLIP** The surface is part of a surface flipping structure.

- **DDSCAPS_COMPLEX** Indicates that a complex surface is being described. A complex surface will cause more than one surface to be created, where the extra surfaces are attached to the root surface.

If you're running in stereo video mode, you also need to specify these two flags:

- **DDSCAPS_VIDEOMEMORY** The surface exists in display memory.

- **DDSCAPS2_ STEREOSURFACELEFT** This surface is part of a stereo flipping chain. When this flag is set during an *IDirectDraw7:: CreateSurface* call, a pair of stereo surfaces is created for each buffer in the primary flipping chain. You must create a complex flipping chain (with back buffers). You can't create a single set of stereo surfaces. The *IDirectDrawSurface7::Flip* method requires back buffers, so you must create at least four surfaces. When this flag is set in a DDSURFACE-DESC2 structure as the result of an *IDirectDraw7::EnumDisplayModes* or *IDirectDraw7::GetDisplayMode* call, it indicates support for stereo in that mode.

Because we've specified that we want a complex flipping surface, we need to specify how many back buffers we want. To do this, we set the *dwBackBufferCount* member to 1 to indicate that we want just one back buffer.

In STEP 4, we use the *IDirectDraw7::CreateSurface* method to create the front buffer, using the flags set in the *ddsd* structure, and store the new surface in the *m_pddsFrontBuffer* variable.

In STEP 5, we call the *IDirectDraw7::GetAttachedSurface* method to get the back buffer. This method acquires the attached surface that has the requested capabilities (in this case, the back buffer). This method is defined as follows:

```
HRESULT GetAttachedSurface (
    LPDDSCAPS2 lpDDSCaps,
    LPDIRECTDRAWSURFACE7 FAR *lplpDDAttachedSurface
);
```

Parameter	Description
lpDDSCaps	Address of a DDSCAPS2 structure that contains the hardware capabilities of the surface.
lplpDDAttachedSurface	Address of a variable that will contain a pointer to the retrieved surface's *IDirectDrawSurface7* interface. The retrieved surface is the one that matches the description according to the *lpDDSCaps* parameter.

Finally, in STEP 6, you get a pointer to the second back buffer if you're running in a stereo video mode. If you want this mode, call the *IDirectDraw7:: GetAttachedSurface* method with the second back buffer (for the left image, since we'll use the first back buffer for the right image).

At this point, we're ready to render to these surfaces in full-screen mode.

Windowed Mode Buffers

If you want the program to run in windowed mode rather than full-screen mode, you need to modify some of the settings. Here's the code to handle running in windowed mode:

```
//--------------------------------------------------------------
// Name: CreateWindowedBuffers
// Desc: Creates the primary surface and (optional) back buffer for
//       rendering. Windowed mode and full-screen mode are handled
//       differently.
//--------------------------------------------------------------
HRESULT CD3DFramework7::CreateWindowedBuffers()
{
    HRESULT hr;
```

(continued)

```
// STEP 1 - Windowed Mode
// Get the dimensions of the viewport and screen bounds.
GetClientRect( m_hWnd, &m_rcScreenRect );
ClientToScreen( m_hWnd, (POINT*)&m_rcScreenRect.left );
ClientToScreen( m_hWnd, (POINT*)&m_rcScreenRect.right );
m_dwRenderWidth  = m_rcScreenRect.right  - m_rcScreenRect.left;
m_dwRenderHeight = m_rcScreenRect.bottom - m_rcScreenRect.top;

// STEP 2 - Windowed Mode
// Create the primary surface.
DDSURFACEDESC2 ddsd;
ZeroMemory( &ddsd, sizeof(ddsd) );
ddsd.dwSize          = sizeof(ddsd);
ddsd.dwFlags         = DDSD_CAPS;
ddsd.ddsCaps.dwCaps = DDSCAPS_PRIMARYSURFACE;

// STEP 3 - Windowed Mode
if( FAILED( hr = m_pDD->CreateSurface( &ddsd,
                                       &m_pddsFrontBuffer,
                                       NULL ) ) )
{
    DEBUG_MSG( _T("Error: Can't create primary surface") );
    if( hr != DDERR_OUTOFVIDEOMEMORY )
        return D3DFWERR_NOPRIMARY;
    DEBUG_MSG( _T("Error: Out of video memory") );
    return DDERR_OUTOFVIDEOMEMORY;
}

// STEP 4 - Windowed Mode
// If in windowed mode, create a clipper object.
LPDIRECTDRAWCLIPPER pcClipper;
if( FAILED( hr = m_pDD->CreateClipper( 0, &pcClipper, NULL ) ) )
{
    DEBUG_MSG( _T("Error: Couldn't create clipper") );
    return D3DFWERR_NOCLIPPER;
}
// STEP 5 - Windowed Mode
// Associate the clipper with the window.
pcClipper->SetHWnd( 0, m_hWnd );
m_pddsFrontBuffer->SetClipper( pcClipper );
SAFE_RELEASE( pcClipper );

// STEP 6 - Windowed Mode
// Create a back buffer.
ddsd.dwFlags         = DDSD_WIDTH | DDSD_HEIGHT | DDSD_CAPS;
```

```
ddsd.dwWidth         = m_dwRenderWidth;
ddsd.dwHeight        = m_dwRenderHeight;
ddsd.ddsCaps.dwCaps  = DDSCAPS_OFFSCREENPLAIN | DDSCAPS_3DDEVICE;

if( FAILED( hr = m_pDD->CreateSurface( &ddsd,
                                       &m_pddsBackBuffer,
                                       NULL ) ) )
{
    DEBUG_ERR( hr, _T("Error: Couldn't create the backbuffer") );
    if( hr != DDERR_OUTOFVIDEOMEMORY )
        return D3DFWERR_NOBACKBUFFER;
    DEBUG_MSG( _T("Error: Out of video memory") );
    return DDERR_OUTOFVIDEOMEMORY;
}

ZeroMemory(&m_ddpfBackBufferPixelFormat, sizeof(DDPIXELFORMAT));
m_ddpfBackBufferPixelFormat.dwSize = sizeof(DDPIXELFORMAT);
hr = m_pddsBackBuffer->
    GetPixelFormat(&m_ddpfBackBufferPixelFormat);
hr = m_pddsBackBuffer->GetSurfaceDesc( &ddsd );

return S_OK;
}
```

In STEP 1, we acquire the bounding rectangle of the window using the window's *GetClientRect* routine. This routine returns the window's bounding rectangle in the *m_rcScreenRect* parameter. We then use the *ClientToScreen* routine to convert the display coordinates of the left and right back buffers to screen coordinates. This routine replaces the client coordinates in the *m_rcScreenRect* structure with the equivalent screen coordinates. These newly computed screen coordinates are relative to the upper left corner of the system display. In the last two lines, the screen width and height are computed.

In STEP 2, a DDSURFACEDESC2 structure is created and the DDSCAPS_ PRIMARYSURFACE flag is specified to indicate that we want to create the primary surface.

In STEP 3, we call the *IDirectDraw7::CreateSurface* method to create the front buffer using video memory and place it in the *m_pddsFrontBuffer* variable.

In STEP 4, we create a clipper object. Although a clipper isn't needed when a program is running in full-screen mode, one is required in windowed mode to handle cases in which the window is partially obscured by other windows or partially outside the display area. This clipper prevents the accidental rendering outside a window and onto other windows or the desktop.

In STEP 5, we call *IDirectDrawClipper::SetHWnd* to set the window handle that the clipper object will use to obtain clipping information. This method is defined as follows:

```
HRESULT SetHWnd(
    DWORD dwFlags,
    HWND hWnd
);
```

Parameter	Description
dwFlags	This parameter is currently not used and must be set to 0.
hWnd	The window handle that obtains the clipping information.

We then call *IDirectDrawSurface7::SetClipper* to attach the clipper object to the surface. This method is defined as follows:

```
HRESULT SetClipper (
  LPDIRECTDRAWCLIPPER lpDDClipper
);
```

The *IDirectDrawSurface7::SetClipper* has one parameter, *lpDDClipper*, which is the address of the *IDirectDrawClipper* interface for the DirectDrawClipper object that will be attached to the DirectDrawSurface object. If this parameter is NULL, the current DirectDrawClipper object will be detached.

Finally, in STEP 6, we use *IDirectDraw7::CreateSurface* to create the actual back buffer. At this point, the application is ready to run in either full-screen or windowed mode.

Flipping the Surfaces

Page flipping is an important capability that enhances the look of graphics applications. The hidden surface on which writing occurs is known as the *back buffer*. The process of switching the view from the currently displayed buffer (what shows on the screen) to the view rendered (drawn) to the back buffer is known as *page flipping*. Page flipping uses multiple surfaces to render on one surface while displaying another. By using multiple buffers in this way, you'll ensure that the transitions between frames are smooth, with no tearing. Tearing occurs when an animated image is being changed as it's drawn.

Figure 3-2 shows what happens visually in tearing. To the eye, it looks as if the top part of the square was rendered and then the lower part was rendered offset to the right. However, the programmer was attempting to render three complete images of the square to make it appear to move across the screen.

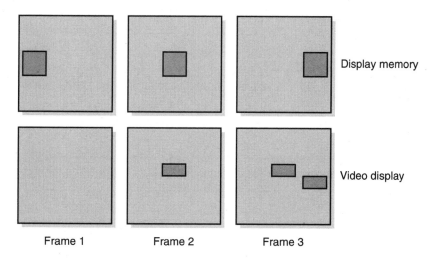

Frame 1   Frame 2   Frame 3

Figure 3-2
Tearing (frames 1–3)

Although no simple scene like this would be a problem with today's display hardware, if you want to render complex 3D scenes this effect can definitely be visually disconcerting. To prevent tearing, all you need to do is not update the display buffer while the image is being drawn to the display. By making your changes during the display's vertical blanking interval (the time it takes the beam to move from the bottom to the top of the display after drawing a frame), you can guarantee that a complete frame has been drawn. During this short interval, you can change the complete memory without worrying about tearing since the electron guns in the display are turned off and being repositioned to the top for the next frame.

The vertical blanking interval lasts only a few milliseconds, but by using the double buffering mode, you can copy the entire back buffer to the front buffer (the display the user sees) so that it can be scanned. This process requires changing only a few registers on the display card, so it can be performed during the vertical blanking interval. Again, no tearing will occur if you use this technique.

DirectDraw Complex Surfaces and Flipping Chains

DirectDraw flipping surfaces are called *complex surfaces.* A complex surface is a set of surfaces that can be created with a single call to the *IDirectDraw7::CreateSurface* method.

You can call *IDirectDraw7::CreateSurface* to create front and back buffers, which are the minimum flipping structures needed to flip pages. Using the *IDirectDraw7::Flip* method of the front buffer surface rotates the memory of all

73

the surfaces. This rotation ensures that the memory used for the back buffer is associated with the front buffer and the memory associated with the front buffer is moved to the back buffer. Rather than rely on just a front buffer and a back buffer, you can create other intermediate buffers and use them to create a "ring," or a set of multiple buffers to be cycled through.

The DDSCAPS_FLIP flag indicates that a surface is part of a flipping chain. Using the DDSCAPS_FLIP flag requires that you also include the DDSCAPS_ COMPLEX flag.

If you specify 2 for the value of the *dwBackBufferCount* member of the DDSURFACEDESC2 structure, two back buffers are created, and each call to the *IDirectDraw7::Flip* method rotates the surfaces in a circular pattern, providing a triple-buffered flipping environment. This rotation requires more memory but avoids the situation that double-buffered programs can encounter, in which the program is briefly stalled because both buffers are busy.

The code used to flip from the front to the back buffer is illustrated in the *CD3DFramework7::ShowFrame* function below. This routine handles flipping for a full-screen mono mode, a full-screen stereo mode (for 3D head-mounted displays or 3D-capable monitor presentations), and a windowed mode. For either full-screen mono or stereo mode, we use the *IDirectDrawSurface7::Flip* method to switch between surfaces. For rendering to a window, we use the *IDirectDraw-Surface7::Blt* method and pass the variable *m_rcScreenRect* defining the rectangular screen area (the window's interior) we'll be blitting to and the variable *m_pddsBackBuffer* to define the back buffer we rendered to and want to flip to the front for viewing.

```
//-----------------------------------------------------------------
// Name: ShowFrame
// Desc: Shows the frame on the primary surface, via a blit or a flip
//-----------------------------------------------------------------
HRESULT CD3DFramework7::ShowFrame()
{
    if( NULL == m_pddsFrontBuffer )
        return D3DFWERR_NOTINITIALIZED;

    if( m_bIsFullscreen )
    {
        // We're in full-screen mode, so perform a flip.
        if (m_bIsStereo)
        {
            return m_pddsFrontBuffer->Flip( NULL,
```

```
                                        DDFLIP_WAIT |
                                        DDFLIP_STEREO);
        }
        else
        {
            return m_pddsFrontBuffer->Flip( NULL, DDFLIP_WAIT );
        }
    }
    else
    {
        // We're in windowed mode, so perform a blit.
        return m_pddsFrontBuffer->Blt( &m_rcScreenRect,
                                        m_pddsBackBuffer,
                                        NULL, DDBLT_WAIT, NULL );
    }
}
```

The Code So Far

At this point, you can compile and execute the code for Chapter 3. As you can see when you execute the code, the screen (shown in Figure 3-3) looks similar to the sample in Chapter 2. However, the screen now has full DirectDraw support for rendering 2D scenes.

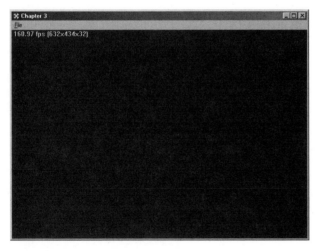

Figure 3-3
The screen from this chapter's code

Conclusion

In this chapter, we covered all the DirectDraw functionality you need to understand to set up standard Direct3D-based applications. I realize the chapter includes a great deal of code, but you can use this code for all the DirectDraw and Direct3D applications you develop in the future. You'll be in good shape if you remember the steps involved in setting up a DirectDraw-based program. You'll still need to know a lot more about DirectDraw if you want to create textures for 3D objects, support AVI (a video file can be played on a DirectDraw surface), or offer a multitude of other capabilities, but this chapter has given you a good foundation on which to build. We'll get to many of the DirectDraw's advanced features in later chapters.

In Chapter 4, you'll see all the code you'll need to set up your first basic 3D application. So let's dig into Direct3D, the reason you're reading this book!

CHAPTER FOUR

Direct3D for DirectX Applications

Now for the start of the fun stuff! At this point, we're ready to start creating the Microsoft Direct3D Immediate Mode portion of our program. In this chapter, we'll first examine the objects and interfaces available in Immediate Mode, and then we'll walk through the steps involved in creating the framework of an Immediate Mode application. After reading Chapter 3, you should feel comfortable with DirectDraw setup code. Just be sure to keep in mind that Direct3D is implemented as a COM interface to a DirectDraw object. Because of this, Microsoft calls the hardware abstraction layer (HAL) the DirectDraw/Direct3D HAL. In addition, Direct3D uses DirectDraw surfaces as the front and back buffers for displaying the 3D scene and as the z-buffer for rendering the 3D scene. Additionally, Direct3D textures are composed of DirectDraw surfaces and can use DirectDraw palettes.

Direct3D Immediate Mode Objects and Interfaces

Direct3D Immediate Mode is composed of a number of COM objects and interfaces to these objects that you can use to construct and control your application's 3D world. In this section, we'll examine the objects and their interfaces (along with some DirectDraw objects and interfaces).

DirectDraw Object

As you saw in Chapter 3, you create DirectDraw objects by using the *Direct-DrawCreateEx* function. The *DirectDrawCreateEx* function exposes the newest DirectDraw and Direct3D interfaces of DirectX 7. The DirectDraw object is the first object you create in any Direct3D application because it represents and provides access to the display device, which implements many Direct3D features. *IDirectDraw7* is the newest interface to the DirectDraw object in DirectX 7, and it's very different from the previous interfaces. It is also the one we'll be using in this book.

DirectDrawSurface Object

In a Direct3D program, the DirectDrawSurface (the *IDirectDrawSurface7* interface) object is used to create the front buffer, back buffer, texture maps, and depth buffer. A surface represents an area of memory either in one of your video cards or in the standard system memory of your computer.

If you create a DirectDrawSurface object using the DDSCAPS_3DDEVICE capability flag, you can then use *IDirect3D7::CreateDevice* with the surface to create a Direct3D device object that uses the surface as its rendering target. This is generally what you do when creating the back buffer. You can also create a DirectDrawSurface object with texture map capabilities by using the *IDirectDraw7::CreateSurface* method and the DDSCAPS_TEXTURE flag. It can then be filled with the bitmap you want to use for texturing an object in your scene.

Direct3DDevice Object

The Direct3DDevice object is the rendering component of Direct3D. It encapsulates and stores the *rendering state* for an Immediate Mode application and a method to render primitives using that state. A rendering state defines the parameters used for rendering, which can include information such as texturing, shading, color, and fog. With DirectX 7, a device-object model supplied by the *IDirect3DDevice7* interface is provided.

You create the Direct3D device object by using the *IDirect3D7::CreateDevice* method. This call lets you acquire an *IDirect3DDevice7* interface. Unlike in previous versions of DirectX, the *IDirect3DDevice7* interface doesn't use separate COM objects for materials, lights, and viewports. With DirectX 7, this new interface includes methods that supply these capabilities as a part of the Direct3D device's internal data structures.

Several types of Direct3D devices can be created on the target system:

- HAL device
- TnLHAL device
- RGB device
- Reference rasterizer device

Two others that were available in prior versions of DirectX, the MMX device and the Ramp device, are not present in DirectX 7.

The HAL device is a 3D renderer that supports Direct3D by implementing rasterization, but not transformation and lighting, in hardware. (Transformation, lighting, and rasterization are explained in more detail in the next two chapters). If a HAL device is located during enumeration, you should use it for your application—though if your program is written to take advantage of hardware transformation and lighting, the TnLHAL is even better.

The TnLHAL ("Transform 'n' Lighting HAL") device implements all the transformation, lighting, and rasterization modules in hardware and tends to be the fastest device type. Unlike the HAL device, this device performs hardware-accelerated transformation and lighting operations. Thus, it offloads these tasks from the CPU, speeding up an application considerably. You can tell whether a device provides hardware-accelerated transformation and lighting by checking for the D3DDEVCAPS_HWTRANSFORMANDLIGHT device capability.

The RGB device is provided for systems that don't have any hardware capable of 3D acceleration. The RGB device emulates the 3D operations in software. This means that it runs significantly slower than the HAL device, but it does utilize any special instructions provided by the system's CPU. This rasterizer will use CPUs supporting the MMX instruction set (on some Intel processors) or the AMD 3DNow! (on some AMD processors) to speed rendering. The MMX instruction set is used to accelerate rasterization and the 3DNow! instruction set accelerates transformation and lighting operations. But even with these special instruction sets, the RGB device is still slower than the HAL or TnLHAL.

The final device type is the reference rasterizer device. This renderer supports all Direct3D features, but the implementation is optimized for accuracy rather than for speed. Because of this, the reference rasterizer is quite slow and should be used only for testing Direct3D features your card doesn't support.

Direct3D doesn't enumerate the reference rasterizer by default. To enumerate it, you first need to use RegEdit to set the *EnumReference* value in the HKEY_LOCAL_MACHINE\SOFTWARE\Microsoft\Direct3D\Drivers registry key to a nonzero DWORD value.

Direct3DVertexBuffer Object

This object is a memory buffer that contains vertices that are rendered with the vertex buffer rendering methods provided in the *IDirect3DDevice7* interface. A vertex buffer is created, and an interface for it retrieved, using the *IDirect3D7::CreateVertexBuffer* method. Vertices and vertex buffers are explained in detail in the next chapter.

Creating an Immediate Mode Application

Setting up your program to use Direct3D involves the following steps, several of which were covered in Chapter 3. I'll go over a few additional aspects of the first five steps and then describe the final process of creating the Direct3D device and the depth buffer.

1. Initializing the application

2. Determining the version of DirectX that's available (if you choose not to assume that DirectX 7 is available as we do in our code for this book)

3. Enumerating the available Direct3D devices

4. Selecting the Direct3D device

5. Getting an *IDirectDraw7* interface with *DirectDrawCreateEx*

6. Getting an *IDirect3D7* interface by using the *QueryInterface* method of the *IDirectDraw7* interface, then creating a Direct3D device

7. Enumerating the depth-buffer format and creating a depth buffer to use for rendering your 3D world

In this chapter, you'll find all the code necessary to perform these steps and create a valid Direct3D device, thus enabling you to render your 3D world.

We now need to modify the *CD3DFramework7::CreateEnvironment* routine from Chapter 3 to create the Direct3D, Direct3DDevice, and depth buffer objects. Here's the revised version of this routine:

```
//------------------------------------------------------------------
// Name: CreateEnvironment
// Desc: Creates the internal objects for the framework
//------------------------------------------------------------------
HRESULT CD3DFramework7::CreateEnvironment( GUID* pDriverGUID,
                                           GUID* pDeviceGUID,
                                           DDSURFACEDESC2* pMode,
                                           DWORD dwFlags )
{
    HRESULT hr;

    // Select the default memory type, depending on whether the
    // device is a hardware device or a software device.
    if( IsEqualIID( *pDeviceGUID, IID_IDirect3DHALDevice ) )
        m_dwDeviceMemType = DDSCAPS_VIDEOMEMORY;
    else if( IsEqualIID( *pDeviceGUID, IID_IDirect3DTnLHalDevice ) )
```

```
        m_dwDeviceMemType = DDSCAPS_VIDEOMEMORY;
    else
        m_dwDeviceMemType = DDSCAPS_SYSTEMMEMORY;

    // Create the DirectDraw object.
    hr = CreateDirectDraw( pDriverGUID, dwFlags );
    if( FAILED( hr ) )
        return hr;

    // Create the front and back buffers, and attach a clipper.
    if( dwFlags & D3DFW_FULLSCREEN )
        hr = CreateFullscreenBuffers( pMode, dwFlags );
    else
        hr = CreateWindowedBuffers( pMode, dwFlags );
    if( FAILED( hr ) )
        return hr;

    // Create the Direct3D object and the Direct3DDevice object.
    hr = CreateDirect3D( pDeviceGUID, dwFlags );
    if( FAILED( hr ) )
        return hr;

    // Create and attach the z-buffer.
    if( dwFlags & D3DFW_ZBUFFER )
        hr = CreateZBuffer( pDeviceGUID, dwFlags );
    if( FAILED( hr ) )
        return hr;

    return S_OK;
}
```

We'll go over the added calls to this routine later in the chapter.

Depending on the device type you create (HAL, RGB, and so on), you should have your software select the memory type used for your main surfaces, textures, and vertex buffers that works most effectively with your code design. In addition to standard video memory, DirectDraw provides support for the Accelerated Graphics Port (AGP) architecture that allows creating surfaces in nonlocal video memory. There are two AGP architecture implementations: the *execute model* and the *DMA model*. With the execute model, display devices support the same features for both nonlocal (AGP) and local (standard) video memory surfaces. With the DMA model, DirectDraw uses nonlocal video memory for any texture surfaces you create if there is no local video memory remaining (unless you ask for local video memory). For other surface types, surfaces will be created only in local video memory unless your program requests that nonlocal video memory be used.

To determine whether the device driver supports texturing from nonlocal video memory surfaces, you can check to see whether the D3DDEVCAPS_ TEXTURENONLOCALVIDMEM flag is set. You can acquire this flag from the 3D device capabilities list, which you can acquire by using the *IDirect3DDevice7:: GetCaps* method.

Step 1: Initializing the Application

The first step in creating the Direct3D portion of your program is to initialize all the variables you'll be using. The main objective of this step is to clear out all the objects and structures so that you can create the objects you need and then fill in the structures with the settings you want to use for your 3D world, such as shading parameters and clippers. The *CD3DFramework7* constructor shown below initializes all its member variables, defining items such as the z-buffer, the back buffers, and the device.

```
//-------------------------------------------------------------------
// Name: CD3DFramework7
// Desc: The constructor, which clears static variables
//-------------------------------------------------------------------
CD3DFramework7::CD3DFramework7()
{
    m_hWnd                = NULL;
    m_bIsFullscreen       = FALSE;
    m_bIsStereo           = FALSE;
    m_dwRenderWidth       = 0L;
    m_dwRenderHeight      = 0L;
    m_pddsFrontBuffer     = NULL;
    m_pddsBackBuffer      = NULL;
    m_pddsBackBufferLeft  = NULL;
    m_pddsZBuffer         = NULL;
    m_pd3dDevice          = NULL;
    m_pDD                 = NULL;
    m_pD3D                = NULL;
    m_dwDeviceMemType     = NULL;
}
```

Step 2: Determining the DirectX Version

Version checking is the process of determining which version of DirectX is installed on the target system. The amount of version checking you need to do depends greatly on how you're going to use Direct3D. If you're just a hobbyist developing for your own system, you already know that you have the latest and greatest version of DirectX installed, so you don't have to check. If you're writing a completely new

DirectX 7 application, you'll probably ship your product with the latest DirectX run-time library, which your setup program will install if the target system is running Microsoft Windows 95 or Windows 98. If it's running Microsoft Windows NT 4 or earlier, you can have your software just refuse to install or run. Windows 2000 ships with full DirectX 7 support, so if the target system is running Windows 2000, your software can use the newest DirectX capabilities available. Most companies shipping 3D games and other software rely on your having the newest version of DirectX installed—since they install it from their game CD during the game install.

However, if you choose to support previous versions of DirectX (for whatever reason), you need to perform more elaborate version checking. You might also want to avoid the standard error messages that pop up when you link to ddraw.lib rather than using *LoadLibrary* and *GetProcAddress*. If you don't want the user to receive the standard system error message, just use *QueryInterface* for the interfaces you need, handle failures with an error message, and then exit. Your best option is to create a Windows 95 or Windows 98 setup program that updates the target system to the latest version of DirectX during setup. Keep in mind, however, that on Windows NT and Windows 2000, only administrators are allowed to update critical portions of the operating system (such as DirectX), so your setup programs can't upgrade the DirectX version.

If you choose to use version checking so that your software runs on the greatest number of platforms, you can check for the availability of various DirectX interfaces. By working your way up from interfaces supported by DirectX 2 to interfaces supported only by DirectX 7, you can determine the most current version of DirectX available. By finding out exactly which version of DirectX is available, you can have your application take advantage of all the features a target platform supports. If the target platform has a version of DirectX that isn't as new as you hoped for, you can have your software gracefully degrade the effects it supports. For example, if you wanted DirectX 7 but only DirectX 3 was available, you could drop the use of multitexturing since it isn't supported in DirectX 3. In this way, your application can run properly, albeit with a slightly lesser quality of the visuals. However, as mentioned above, your best bet is to install the newest version of DirectX on the target platform so that your software performs to its potential.

Step 3: Enumerating the Available Direct3D Devices

To create a device you can use later for rendering, you first need to enumerate the Direct3D devices. As described in Chapter 3, this means enumerating DirectDraw devices, then enumerating all Direct3D devices attached to each DirectDraw device. To do this, you can use the *D3DEnum_EnumerateDevices* routine described in Chapter 3.

Step 4: Selecting the Direct3D Device

The next step in setting up your program to use Direct3D involves selecting the Direct3D device that best fits the needs of your application and then creating the device. The code to handle the selection and creation of the device must determine if you want to run in windowed or full-screen mode. This process was shown in Chapter 3 in the *DeviceEnumCallback* routine.

Step 5: Getting an *IDirectDraw7* Interface

After initializing your variables and determining the DirectX version, the next step is to set up a DirectDraw object. Chapter 3 describes in detail how to acquire the new *IDirectDraw7* interface by using the *CD3DFramework7::CreateDirectDraw* member function.

Step 6: Obtaining an *IDirect3D7* Interface from *IDirectDraw7* and Creating the Direct3D Device

To create a Direct3D object, you use the *QueryInterface* method of the DirectDraw object to determine whether it supports the *IID_IDirect3D7* interface, which was introduced in DirectX 7. If the DirectDraw object supports that interface, *QueryInterface* retrieves a pointer to the interface and calls *AddRef* to add this reference.

The following code in d3dframe.cpp shows how to create the Direct3D object and the Direct3DDevice object. (We'll cover the final segment of the routine, creating a viewport, in Chapter 5.)

```
//-----------------------------------------------------------------
// Name: CreateDirect3D
// Desc: Creates the Direct3D interface
//-----------------------------------------------------------------
HRESULT CD3DFramework7::CreateDirect3D( GUID* pDeviceGUID )
{
    // Query DirectDraw for access to Direct3D.
    if( FAILED( m_pDD->QueryInterface( IID_IDirect3D7,
                                       (VOID**)&m_pD3D ) ) )
    {
        DEBUG_MSG( _T("Couldn't get the Direct3D interface") );
        return D3DFWERR_NODIRECT3D;
    }

    // Create the device.
    if( FAILED( m_pD3D->CreateDevice( *pDeviceGUID, m_pddsBackBuffer,
                                      &m_pd3dDevice) ) )
    {
```

```
        DEBUG_MSG( _T("Couldn't create the D3DDevice") );
        return D3DFWERR_NO3DDEVICE;
    }

    // Set the viewport for the newly created device.
    D3DVIEWPORT7 vp = { 0, 0, m_dwRenderWidth, m_dwRenderHeight,
                        0.0f, 1.0f };

    if( FAILED( m_pd3dDevice->SetViewport( &vp ) ) )
    {
        DEBUG_MSG(
            _T("Error: Couldn't set current viewport to device") );
        return D3DFWERR_NOVIEWPORT;
    }

    return S_OK;
}
```

Once this routine returns successfully, you'll have a valid Direct3D object and a valid Direct3D device object to use for your application.

Creating Direct3D Devices

Earlier in this chapter, you saw the types of Direct3D devices available. With DirectX 7, the *IDirect3DDevice7* interface, retrieved with a call to the *IDirect3D7:: CreateDevice* method, includes methods for supporting materials, lights, and viewports rather than requiring the separate Direct3DLight, Direct3DMaterial, and Direct3DViewport objects previous releases of DirectX required.

As we discussed, the device you create must match the capabilities available on the target platform. Direct3D provides rendering capabilities by using 3D hardware on the target computer or through emulating the 3D capabilities in software, so it provides support for both hardware access and software emulation.

You should design your software to use any hardware capabilities available rather than software emulation because the hardware runs much faster. Also keep in mind that software devices don't necessarily support the same features as hardware devices. Because of this, you should query for device capabilities to find out which are supported in hardware and then use software emulation only for those systems without hardware accelerators.

The HAL and TnLHAL devices are hardware-accelerated, so you should use them whenever possible. Direct3D applications access the 3D hardware through Direct3D methods via the HAL. If the target system has a Direct3D-capable 3D hardware accelerator, you should use it for any Direct3D features the hardware implements. If no hardware acceleration is available, the RGB device (which will use MMX if it's available) is the next best choice. The RGB device is a software rasterizer, so it will be slower than a hardware-accelerated device. However, the RGB device uses any CPU extensions that are available, such as MMX, 3DNow!, and Katmai, to run as quickly as possible.

The calls to acquire the various device types are as follows:

```
CreateDevice(IID_IDirect3DTnLHalDevice, lpDirectDrawSurface,
            lplpDirect3DDevice);
CreateDevice(IID_IDirect3DHALDevice, lpDirectDrawSurface,
            lplpDirect3DDevice);
CreateDevice(IID_IDirect3DRGBDevice, lpDirectDrawSurface,
            lplpDirect3DDevice);
CreateDevice(IID_IDirect3DRefDevice, lpDirectDrawSurface,
            lplpDirect3DDevice);
```

The *IDirect3DDevice7* interface's member function, *IDirect3DDevice7::Get-Caps*, obtains all the capabilities of the Direct3D device. This method stores the data that describes those capabilities in a D3DDEVICEDESC7 structure.

The D3DDEVICEDESC7 structure is defined as follows:

```
typedef struct _D3DDeviceDesc7 {
    DWORD        dwDevCaps;                  // Capabilities of device
    D3DPRIMCAPS  dpcLineCaps;
    D3DPRIMCAPS  dpcTriCaps;
    DWORD        dwDeviceRenderBitDepth;  // One of DDBB_8, 16, etc.
    DWORD        dwDeviceZBufferBitDepth; // One of DDBD_16, 32, etc.
    DWORD        dwMinTextureWidth, dwMinTextureHeight;
    DWORD        dwMaxTextureWidth, dwMaxTextureHeight;
    DWORD        dwMaxTextureRepeat;
    DWORD        dwMaxTextureAspectRatio;
    DWORD        dwMaxAnisotropy;
    D3DVALUE     dvGuardBandLeft;
    D3DVALUE     dvGuardBandTop;
    D3DVALUE     dvGuardBandRight;
    D3DVALUE     dvGuardBandBottom;
    D3DVALUE     dvExtentsAdjust;
    DWORD        dwStencilCaps;
    DWORD        dwFVFCaps;
    DWORD        dwTextureOpCaps;
    WORD         wMaxTextureBlendStages;
    WORD         wMaxSimultaneousTextures;
    DWORD        dwMaxActiveLights;
    D3DVALUE     dvMaxVertexW;
    GUID         deviceGUID;
    WORD         wMaxUserClipPlanes;
```

```
    WORD        wMaxVertexBlendMatrices;
    DWORD       dwVertexProcessingCaps;
    DWORD       dwReserved1;
    DWORD       dwReserved2;
    DWORD       dwReserved3;
    DWORD       dwReserved4;
} D3DDEVICEDESC7, *LPD3DDEVICEDESC7;
```

The members of this structure are defined as follows:

- ◾ *dwDevCaps*   Includes flags identifying the device's capabilities.

- ◾ *dpcLineCaps* **and** *dpcTriCaps*   D3DPRIMCAPS structures that define the device's support for line-drawing and triangle primitives.

- ◾ *dwDeviceRenderBitDepth*   The device's rendering bit depth. This member can be one or more of the DirectDraw bit-depth constants: DDBD_8, DDBD_16, DDBD_24, or DDBD_32.

- ◾ *dwDeviceZBufferBitDepth*   Indicates the device's depth-buffer bit depth. This member can be one of the DirectDraw bit-depth constants: DDBD_8, DDBD_16, DDBD_24, or DDBD_32.

- ◾ *dwMinTextureWidth, dwMinTextureHeight*   Indicates the minimum texture width and height for this device.

- ◾ *dwMaxTextureWidth, dwMaxTextureHeight*   Indicates the maximum texture width and height for this device.

- ◾ *dwMaxTextureRepeat*   Includes the full range of the integer (nonfractional) bits of the postnormalized texture indices. If the D3DDEVCAPS_TEXREPEATNOTSCALEDBYSIZE bit is set, the device defers scaling by the texture size until after the texture address mode is applied. If it isn't set, the device scales the texture indices by the texture size (largest level of detail) prior to interpolation.

- ◾ *dwMaxTextureAspectRatio*   Indicates the maximum texture aspect ratio that the hardware supports; this value will typically be a power of 2.

- ◾ *dwMaxAnisotropy*   Indicates the maximum valid value for the D3DRENDERSTATE_ANISOTROPY render state.

- ◾ *dvGuardBandLeft, dvGuardBandTop, dvGuardBandRight,* **and** *dvGuardBandBottom*   Define the screen-space coordinates of the guard-band clipping region. Coordinates inside this rectangle but outside the viewport rectangle are automatically clipped.

- **dvExtentsAdjust**   Indicates the number of pixels required to adjust the extents rectangle outward to accommodate antialiasing kernels.

- **dwStencilCaps**   Includes flags that specify which stencil-buffer operations are supported.

- **dwFVFCaps**   Indicates the flexible vertex format capabilities.

- **dwTextureOpCaps**   Includes the combination of flags that describe the texture operations this device supports.

- **wMaxTextureBlendStages**   Indicates the maximum number of texture-blending stages this device supports.

- **wMaxSimultaneousTextures**   Indicates the maximum number of textures that can be simultaneously bound to this device's texture-blending stages.

- **dwMaxActiveLights**   Indicates the maximum number of lights that can be active simultaneously.

- **dvMaxVertexW**   Indicates the maximum w-based depth value that the device supports.

- **deviceGUID**   Indicates the globally unique identifier (GUID) that identifies this device.

- **wMaxUserClipPlanes**   Indicates the maximum number of user-defined clipping planes this device supports. This member can range from 0 to D3DMAXUSERCLIPPLANES. User-defined clipping planes are manipulated by using the *IDirect3DDevice7:: GetClipPlane* and *IDirect3DDevice7:: SetClipPlane* methods.

- **wMaxVertexBlendMatrices**   Indicates the maximum number of matrices that this device can apply when performing multimatrix vertex blending.

- **dwVertexProcessingCaps**   Indicates the device's vertex processing.

- **dwReserved1** through **dwReserved4**   Reserved for future use.

As you can see, many capabilities are available. You'll have to decide which of these to check for based on the requirements of your application. You should use as many as possible, however, to produce the most realistic 3D environment you can. As an example, the RoadRage code we're developing in this book uses fog and alpha blending to provide as realistic a rendered and animated 3D world as possible.

You also need to provide the user with a way to select one of the other available devices (or modes) so that he or she can change from the initially selected ones (for example, RGB vs. HAL; full-screen mode vs. windowed mode; a lower resolution mode, such as 800 × 600 vs. 640 × 480; and so on).

The following code will handle user selection of the Change Device/Mode item from the File menu. It produces a dialog box that presents the available devices and modes, allows the user to select which device and mode to switch to, and then makes the switch. Here's the code we need to add to the *CD3DApplication::MsgProc* member function, contained in the d3dapp.cpp file, to handle user selection of this menu item:

```
case IDM_CHANGEDEVICE:
    // Display the device-selection dialog box.
    if (m_bActive && m_bReady)
    {
        Pause(TRUE);
        if (SUCCEEDED( D3DEnum_UserChangeDevice(&m_pDeviceInfo)))
        {
            if( FAILED( hr = Change3DEnvironment() ) )
                return 0;
        }
        Pause(FALSE);
    }
    return 0;
```

Figure 4-1 shows the drop-down menu the code produces for selecting a new device or mode.

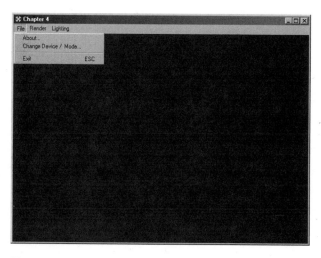

Figure 4-1
Selecting a new device or mode

The dialog box this menu selection produces when the user selects it is shown in Figure 4-2. The user can select the desired device (for example, the primary device or any of the secondary devices) and the mode.

Figure 4-2
The Change Device dialog box

The new case statement added to the *CD3DApplication::MsgProc* member function for this chapter calls *D3DEnum_UserChangeDevice* to produce a dialog box that presents all the available devices and modes on the host system and allows the user to select a new device or mode. As you saw above, each device is displayed in a list box at the top of the dialog box and each mode is displayed in a list box at the bottom of the dialog box. The *D3DEnum_UserChangeDevice* routine follows:

```
//-----------------------------------------------------------------
// Name: D3DEnum_UserChangeDevice
// Desc: Pops up a dialog box that allows the user to select a new
//       device
//-----------------------------------------------------------------
HRESULT D3DEnum_UserChangeDevice( D3DEnum_DeviceInfo** ppDevice )
{
    if( IDOK == DialogBoxParam( (HINSTANCE)GetModuleHandle(NULL),
                                MAKEINTRESOURCE(IDD_CHANGEDEVICE),
                                GetForegroundWindow(),
                                ChangeDeviceProc, (LPARAM)ppDevice ) )
        return S_OK;

    return E_FAIL;
}
```

This routine calls the Windows *DialogBoxParam* function and creates a modal dialog box from a dialog box template resource you specify. It takes a callback function in the *lpDialogFunc* parameter. The modal dialog box won't return control until this callback function terminates the modal dialog box by calling the *EndDialog* function. The *ChangeDeviceProc* callback specified in the call to DialogBoxParam handles all Windows messages for the device-selection dialog box:

```
//-------------------------------------------------------------------
// Name: ChangeDeviceProc
// Desc: Windows message-handling function for the device-selection
//       dialog box
//-------------------------------------------------------------------
static BOOL CALLBACK ChangeDeviceProc( HWND hDlg, UINT uiMsg,
    WPARAM wParam, LPARAM lParam )
{
    static D3DEnum_DeviceInfo** ppDeviceArg;
    static D3DEnum_DeviceInfo* pCurrentDevice;
    static DWORD dwCurrentMode;
    static BOOL  bCurrentWindowed;
    static BOOL  bCurrentStereo;

    // Get access to the enumerated device list.
    D3DEnum_DeviceInfo* pDeviceList;
    DWORD               dwNumDevices;
    D3DEnum_GetDevices( &pDeviceList, &dwNumDevices );

    // Handle the initialization message.
    if( WM_INITDIALOG == uiMsg )
    {
        // Get the application's current device, passed in as an
        // lParam argument.
        ppDeviceArg = (D3DEnum_DeviceInfo**)lParam;
        if( NULL == ppDeviceArg )
            return FALSE;

        // Set up temporary storage pointers for the dialog box.
        pCurrentDevice = (*ppDeviceArg);
        dwCurrentMode    = pCurrentDevice->dwCurrentMode;
        bCurrentWindowed = pCurrentDevice->bWindowed;
        bCurrentStereo   = pCurrentDevice->bStereo;

        UpdateDialogControls( hDlg, pCurrentDevice, dwCurrentMode,
                              bCurrentWindowed, bCurrentStereo );

        return TRUE;
    }
    else if( WM_COMMAND == uiMsg )
    {
        HWND hwndDevice   = GetDlgItem( hDlg, IDC_DEVICE_COMBO );
        HWND hwndMode     = GetDlgItem( hDlg, IDC_MODE_COMBO );
        HWND hwndWindowed = GetDlgItem( hDlg, IDC_WINDOWED_CHECKBOX );
```

(continued)

```
HWND hwndStereo   = GetDlgItem( hDlg, IDC_STEREO_CHECKBOX );

// Get current user interface state.
DWORD dwDevice   = ComboBox_GetCurSel( hwndDevice );
DWORD dwModeItem = ComboBox_GetCurSel( hwndMode );
DWORD dwMode =
        ComboBox_GetItemData( hwndMode, dwModeItem );
BOOL  bWindowed =
        hwndWindowed ? Button_GetCheck( hwndWindowed ) : 0;
BOOL  bStereo =
        hwndStereo   ? Button_GetCheck( hwndStereo )   : 0;

D3DEnum_DeviceInfo* pDevice = &pDeviceList[dwDevice];

if( IDOK == LOWORD(wParam) )
{
    // Handle the case in which the user clicks OK. Check to
    // see whether the user changed any options.
    if( pDevice    != pCurrentDevice   ||
        dwMode     != dwCurrentMode     ||
        bWindowed  != bCurrentWindowed ||
        bStereo    != bCurrentStereo )
    {
        // Return the newly selected device and its new
        // properties.
        (*ppDeviceArg)              = pDevice;
        pDevice->bWindowed          = bWindowed;
        pDevice->bStereo            = bStereo;
        pDevice->dwCurrentMode      = dwMode;
        pDevice->ddsdFullscreenMode =
            pDevice->pddsdModes[dwMode];

        EndDialog( hDlg, IDOK );
    }
    else
        EndDialog( hDlg, IDCANCEL );

    return TRUE;
}
else if( IDCANCEL == LOWORD(wParam) )
{
    // Handle the case in which the user clicks Cancel.
    EndDialog( hDlg, IDCANCEL );
    return TRUE;
}
```

```
        else if( CBN_SELENDOK == HIWORD(wParam) )
        {
            if( LOWORD(wParam) == IDC_DEVICE_COMBO )
            {
                // Handle the case in which the user chooses the
                // device combo.
                dwMode    = pDeviceList[dwDevice].dwCurrentMode;
                bWindowed = pDeviceList[dwDevice].bWindowed;
                bStereo   = pDeviceList[dwDevice].bStereo;
            }
        }

        // Keep the user interface current.
        UpdateDialogControls( hDlg, &pDeviceList[dwDevice], dwMode,
                              bWindowed, bStereo );
        return TRUE;
    }
```

When the dialog box is created, the *ChangeDeviceProc* callback calls the *GetDlgItem* function to get the handle of the various list box controls. Once it has the handles for the various controls, it calls the *D3DEnum_GetDevices* routine to build a list of devices and modes. Each device is added to the device list box by looping through the *g_d3dDevices* global array of devices created during enumeration. All the modes for each device are then added to the modes list box.

If the device can render to a window, it adds a windowed mode. After this, it loops through each full-screen mode (the number of which is stored in the *pDevice->dwNumModes* global variable). Each mode, stored in the *pDevice->pddsdModes* array, which is an array of DDSURFACEDESC2 structures that each contains a description of a mode, is added to the mode list box. Finally, the selected item in the list box is set to the current mode.

```
//----------------------------------------------------------------
// Name: UpdateDialogControls
// Desc: Builds the list of devices and modes for the combo boxes in
//       the device-selection dialog box
//----------------------------------------------------------------
static VOID UpdateDialogControls( HWND hDlg,
    D3DEnum_DeviceInfo* pCurrentDevice,
                                  DWORD dwCurrentMode, BOOL bWindowed,
                                  BOOL bStereo )
{
    // Get access to the enumerated device list.
    D3DEnum_DeviceInfo* pDeviceList;
```

(continued)

```
DWORD              dwNumDevices;
D3DEnum_GetDevices( &pDeviceList, &dwNumDevices );

// Get access to the UI controls.
HWND hwndDevice        = GetDlgItem( hDlg, IDC_DEVICE_COMBO );
HWND hwndMode          = GetDlgItem( hDlg, IDC_MODE_COMBO );
HWND hwndWindowed      =
    GetDlgItem( hDlg, IDC_WINDOWED_CHECKBOX );
HWND hwndStereo        = GetDlgItem( hDlg, IDC_STEREO_CHECKBOX );
HWND hwndFullscreenText = GetDlgItem( hDlg, IDC_FULLSCREEN_TEXT );

// Reset the content in each combo box.
ComboBox_ResetContent( hwndDevice );
ComboBox_ResetContent( hwndMode );

// Don't let non-GDI devices be windowed.
if( FALSE == pCurrentDevice->bDesktopCompatible )
    bWindowed = FALSE;

// Add a list of devices to the device combo box.
for( DWORD device = 0; device < dwNumDevices; device++ )
{
    D3DEnum_DeviceInfo* pDevice = &pDeviceList[device];

    // Add device name to the combo box.
    DWORD dwItem = ComboBox_AddString( hwndDevice,
                                       pDevice->strDesc );

    // Set the remaining UI states for the current device.
    if( pDevice == pCurrentDevice )
    {
        // Set the combo box selection on the current device.
        ComboBox_SetCurSel( hwndDevice, dwItem );

        // Enable/set the full-screen checkbox, as appropriate.
        if( hwndWindowed )
        {
            EnableWindow( hwndWindowed,
                          pDevice->bDesktopCompatible );
            Button_SetCheck( hwndWindowed, bWindowed );
        }

        // Enable/set the stereo check box, as appropriate.
        if( hwndStereo )
        {
            EnableWindow( hwndStereo,
                          pDevice->bStereoCompatible && !bWindowed );
```

```
            Button_SetCheck( hwndStereo, bStereo );
        }

        // Enable/set the full-screen modes combo box, as
        // appropriate.
        EnableWindow( hwndMode, !bWindowed );
        EnableWindow( hwndFullscreenText, !bWindowed );

        // Build the list of full-screen modes.
        for( DWORD mode = 0; mode < pDevice->dwNumModes; mode++ )
        {
            DDSURFACEDESC2* pddsdMode =
                            &pDevice->pddsdModes[mode];

            // Skip nonstereo modes, if the device is in stereo
            // mode.
            if( 0 == ( pddsdMode->ddsCaps.dwCaps2 &
                       DDSCAPS2_STEREOSURFACELEFT ) )
                if( bStereo )
                    continue;

            TCHAR strMode[80];
            wsprintf( strMode, _T("%ld x %ld x %ld"),
                    pddsdMode->dwWidth, pddsdMode->dwHeight,
                    pddsdMode->ddpfPixelFormat.dwRGBBitCount );

            // Add the mode description to the combo box.
            DWORD dwItem =
                ComboBox_AddString( hwndMode, strMode );

            // Set the item data to identify this mode.
            ComboBox_SetItemData( hwndMode, dwItem, mode );

            // Set the combo box selection on the current mode.
            if( mode == dwCurrentMode )
                ComboBox_SetCurSel( hwndMode, dwItem );

            // Not all modes support stereo, so select a default
            // mode in case none was chosen yet.
            if( bStereo &&
                ( CB_ERR == ComboBox_GetCurSel( hwndMode )))
                ComboBox_SetCurSel( hwndMode, dwItem );
        }
    }
}
}
```

Step 7: Creating a Depth Buffer

A depth buffer is a DirectDraw surface that stores depth information that Direct3D uses. When a Direct3D application renders a 3D scene to a target surface, the memory in an attached depth-buffer surface is used to determine how the pixels of rasterized polygons end up occluding others. Direct3D uses an off-screen DirectDraw surface as the target that the final color values are written to. The depth-buffer surface attached to the render-target surface stores the depth information indicating how far away every visible pixel in the scene is. The depth buffer is often what is called a *z-buffer*. A related type of depth buffer is called a *w-buffer*, which can be more accurate in some cases. Some Direct3D devices support a structure called a *stencil buffer*, which can be used to generate some interesting effects such as shadows. (Stencil buffers are covered in Chapter 12.) Stencil buffers are usually interleaved with the depth buffer. For example, a 32-bit depth buffer might consist of a 24-bit z-buffer and an 8-bit stencil buffer.

Before rendering a 3D scene, you usually have Direct3D set all depth values in the depth buffer to the greatest value for the scene. The render target's color can be set to a constant color at this time as well. Then, as each polygon in the scene is rasterized (converted to pixels), the z-value or w-value at each pixel is computed. Then the depth value (the *z* coordinate in the z-buffer case and the *w* coordinate in the w-buffer case) at the current point is tested to determine whether it is smaller than the value already in the depth buffer at that location. If it is smaller (nearer to the viewer than any other polygon), this new value is stored in the depth buffer and the color from the polygon is stored in the current point on the rendering surface. In the case that the depth value of the polygon at that point is larger (farther from the viewer than another polygon), nothing is written and the next polygon in the list is tested.

Almost every 3D accelerator supports z-buffering, but not all 3D accelerators support w-buffering. The advantage of w-buffering is that the *z* values generated for z-buffers aren't always evenly distributed across the z-buffer range (usually 0.0 through 1.0 inclusive). The ratio between the far and near clipping planes affects how the *z* values are distributed. Using a far-plane distance to near-plane distance ratio of 100, 90 percent of the depth-buffer range is spent on the first 10 percent of the scene depth range. At higher ratios, a much higher percentage (97 to 98 percent) can be spent in the first 2 percent of the depth range.

If you use a w-buffer instead of a z-buffer, the depth values tend to be more evenly distributed between the near and far clipping planes. The benefit is that this lets programs support large maximum ranges while achieving accurate depth close to the eye point. A limitation is that it can sometimes produce hidden surface artifacts for near objects. You'll need to decide which approach you like based on your application's design.

A few 3D accelerators have special hardware that can resolve which surfaces are visible without a depth buffer. These hardware devices set a caps bit named D3DPRASTERCAPS_ZBUFFERLESSHSR ("HSR" stands for "hidden surface removal"). When you detect a device with this bit set, you shouldn't create a depth buffer so that more memory is available on the accelerator for textures or other objects.

To create and attach a depth buffer, you need to perform the tasks listed in the following code:

```
//-----------------------------------------------------------------
// Name: CreateZBuffer
// Desc: Internal function called by Create to make and attach a
//       depth buffer to the renderer
//-----------------------------------------------------------------
HRESULT CD3DFramework7::CreateZBuffer ( GUID* pDeviceGUID )
{
    HRESULT hr;

    // Check whether the device supports z-bufferless hidden surface
    // removal. If so, a z-buffer isn't necessary.
    D3DDEVICEDESC7 ddDesc;
    m_pd3dDevice->GetCaps( &ddDesc );
    if( ddDesc.dpcTriCaps.dwRasterCaps &
            D3DPRASTERCAPS_ZBUFFERLESSHSR )
        return S_OK;

    // Get z-buffer dimensions from the render target.
    DDSURFACEDESC2 ddsd;
    ddsd.dwSize = sizeof(ddsd);
    m_pddsBackBuffer->GetSurfaceDesc( &ddsd );

    // Set up the surface description for the z-buffer.
    ddsd.dwFlags = DDSD_WIDTH | DDSD_HEIGHT |
                    DDSD_CAPS  | DDSD_PIXELFORMAT;
    ddsd.ddsCaps.dwCaps = DDSCAPS_ZBUFFER | m_dwDeviceMemType;
    // Tag the pixel format as uninitialized.
    ddsd.ddpfPixelFormat.dwSize = 0;
    // Get an appropriate pixel format from enumeration of the
    // formats. On the first pass, look for a z-buffer depth equal
```

(continued)

```
            // to the frame buffer depth (unfortunately, some cards
            // require this).
            m_pD3D->EnumZBufferFormats( *pDeviceGUID,
                                        EnumZBufferFormatsCallback,
                                        (VOID*)&ddsd.ddpfPixelFormat );
            if( 0 == ddsd.ddpfPixelFormat.dwSize )
            {
                // Try again, just accepting any 16-bit z-buffer.
                ddsd.ddpfPixelFormat.dwRGBBitCount = 16;
                m_pD3D->EnumZBufferFormats( *pDeviceGUID,
                                            EnumZBufferFormatsCallback,
                                            (VOID*)&ddsd.ddpfPixelFormat );

                if( 0 == ddsd.ddpfPixelFormat.dwSize )
                {
                    DEBUG_MSG( _T(
                            "Device doesn't support requested z-buffer format") );
                    return D3DFWERR_NOZBUFFER;
                }
            }

            // Create and attach a z-buffer.
            if( FAILED( hr = m_pDD->CreateSurface( &ddsd,
                                                   &m_pddsZBuffer,
                                                   NULL )))
            {
                DEBUG_MSG( _T("Error: Couldn't create a ZBuffer surface") );
                if( hr != DDERR_OUTOFVIDEOMEMORY )
                    return D3DFWERR_NOZBUFFER;
                DEBUG_MSG( _T("Error: Out of video memory") );
                return DDERR_OUTOFVIDEOMEMORY;
            }

            if( FAILED( m_pddsBackBuffer->
                        AddAttachedSurface( m_pddsZBuffer ) ) )
            {
                DEBUG_MSG(
                    _T("Error: Couldn't attach z-buffer to render surface") );
                return D3DFWERR_NOZBUFFER;
            }

            // For stereoscopic viewing, attach z-buffer to left surface
            // as well.
            if( m_bIsStereo )
            {
                if( FAILED( m_pddsBackBufferLeft->
                            AddAttachedSurface( m_pddsZBuffer )))
                {
```

```
            DEBUG_MSG(_T(
              "Error: Couldn't attach z-buffer to left render surface"
              ) );
            return D3DFWERR_NOZBUFFER;
        }
    }

    // Finally, this call rebuilds internal structures.
    if( FAILED( m_pd3dDevice->
                SetRenderTarget( m_pddsBackBuffer, 0L ) ) )
    {
        DEBUG_MSG(_T(
          "Error: SetRenderTarget() failed after attaching z-buffer!"
          ) );
        return D3DFWERR_NOZBUFFER;
    }

    return S_OK;
}
```

In the first segment of this routine, we check the capabilities (the D3DP-RASTERCAPS_ZBUFFERLESSHSR member of the *dwRasterCaps* member) to see whether this device supports z-bufferless hidden surface removal. If it does, the function exits without creating a depth buffer. If not, the function sets up the surface description for the z-buffer by setting the *ddsd.ddsCaps.dwCaps* member to DDSCAPS_ZBUFFER | *m_dwDeviceMemType* to indicate that it's setting up a z-buffer.

Before you can create a depth buffer, you need to verify which depth-buffer formats (if any) the rendering device supports. To enumerate the depth-buffer formats that the device supports, call *IDirect3D7::EnumZBuffersFormats* and specify the *EnumZBufferFormatsCallback* routine.

When the system calls the callback function, it will pass the function a DDPIXELFORMAT structure that describes the pixel format of the depth buffer. The *dwFlags* member will be set to DDPF_ZBUFFER for any pixel formats that include depth-buffer bits. If this is the case, the *dwZBufferBitDepth* member will hold an integer specifying the number of bits in the pixel format reserved for depth information, and the *dwZBitMask* member will mask the relevant bits.

The *IDirect3D7::EnumZBufferFormats* method is defined as follows:

```
HRESULT EnumZBufferFormats(
    REFCLSID riidDevice,
    LPD3DENUMPIXELFORMATSCALLBACK lpEnumCallback,
    LPVOID lpContext
);
```

Parameter	Description
riidDevice	Reference to a GUID for the device whose depth-buffer formats will be enumerated
lpEnumCallback	Address of a *D3DEnumPixelFormatsCallback* callback function that will be called for each supported depth-buffer format
lpContext	Application-defined data passed to the callback function

If the attempt to get a particular pixel format fails (that is, isn't found during enumeration), you'll need to look for a z-buffer depth equal to the frame-buffer depth since some 3D cards require this.

After an attempt to get a pixel format succeeds, check the *m_bIsStereo* flag. If you're creating stereo flipping surfaces (meaning that you're creating a stereo video application for a virtual reality, such as a head-mounted display, or other application purpose), you need to call the *AddAttachedSurface* method to attach the depth buffer to this additional back buffer. The *IDirectDrawSurface7::AddAttachedSurface* method is defined as follows:

```
HRESULT AddAttachedSurface(
    LPDIRECTDRAWSURFACE7 lpDDSAttachedSurface
);
```

This method has one parameter, *lpDDSAttachedSurface*, which is the address of an *IDirectDrawSuface7* interface for the surface to be attached.

The *IDirectDrawSurface7::AddAttachedSurface* method increments the reference count of the surface being attached. You can explicitly unattach the surface and decrement its reference count by using the *IDirectDrawSurface7::Delete-AttachedSurface* method. Unlike complex surfaces that you create with a single call to *IDirectDraw7::CreateSurface*, surfaces attached with this method are not automatically released. It is your responsibility to release these surfaces.

Several interactions and rules define the surface attachment of z-buffers and back buffers:

- Attachment isn't bidirectional.

- A surface can't be attached to itself.

- Emulated surfaces (in system memory) can't be attached to nonemulated surfaces.

- A flipping surface can't be attached to another flipping surface of the same type.

- Two surfaces of different types can be attached. For example, you can attach a flipping z-buffer to a regular flipping surface.

- If a nonflipping surface is attached to another nonflipping surface of the same type, the two surfaces will become a flipping chain.

- If a nonflipping surface is attached to a flipping surface, it becomes part of the existing flipping chain. Additional surfaces can be added to this chain, and each call of the *IDirectDrawSurface7::Flip* method will advance one step through the surfaces.

The callback function you create for the z-buffer enumeration process needs to specify the capabilities you want for z-buffering. In the code for this chapter, just check the RGB bits per pixel (4, 8, 16, 24, or 32) to make sure it matches the z-buffer bits per pixel. This is because some cards require us to match a 16-bit z-buffer with a 16-bit RGB buffer, and so on. If it does, we return, indicating that the format is OK. As with any enumeration, it's up to you to request the capabilities you absolutely need for your application but to skip those that aren't important.

The *EnumZBufferFormatsCallback* routine is defined as follows:

```
//------------------------------------------------------------------
// Name: EnumZBufferFormatsCallback
// Desc: Returns the first matching enumerated z-buffer format
//------------------------------------------------------------------
static HRESULT WINAPI EnumZBufferFormatsCallback(
                        DDPIXELFORMAT* pddpf,
                        VOID* pContext )
{
    DDPIXELFORMAT* pddpfOut = (DDPIXELFORMAT*)pContext;

    if( pddpfOut->dwRGBBitCount == pddpf->dwRGBBitCount )
    {
        (*pddpfOut) = (*pddpf);
        return D3DENUMRET_CANCEL;
    }

    return D3DENUMRET_OK;
}
```

The Code So Far

At this point, you can compile the code for this chapter. When you run the executable, you'll notice that the window displayed (shown in Figure 4-3) looks much like the one you saw in Chapter 3. However, the window now supports Direct3D and is ready to display and animate your 3D world. Also, you can select the menu option Change Device/Mode menu item and choose a new device or mode to switch to.

If you select a full-screen window from the pop-up window, when you deselect the Use Desktop Window check box and click OK, the window will switch to a full-screen view. The window displays only the frame rate, no graphic content (frames per second) at this point. To go back to the windowed mode, you can press F2 and click in the Use Desktop Window check box.

Figure 4-3
The screen from this chapter's code

Conclusion

In this chapter, we covered all the commands (and the code to use them) you need to create the framework of a Direct3D Immediate Mode application. You can reuse this code for any applications you develop in the future, so be sure to take the time to understand it thoroughly.

Combining the code from Chapters 2 and 3 and this chapter, we now have an application that runs in the Windows environment, determines what DirectX features are supported in both hardware and software, supports multiple buffers for rendering (front buffer, back buffer, and z-buffer plus flipping chains), and selects the best 3D device available on the target system. If the system has more than one 3D accelerator, you now know how to make sure you select the best one (or more than one of you want to run in multimon mode). You can also now easily switch between any available devices and display modes.

In Chapter 5, we'll turn to the topic of Direct3D vertices and how they are transformed and lit.

CHAPTER FIVE

Direct3D Vertices and the Transformation and Lighting Pipeline

The task of rendering a 3D object is divided into two stages. The first stage is called *transformation and lighting* (and is often abbreviated as "T&L"). In this stage, each *vertex* of the object is transformed from an abstract, floating-point coordinate space into pixel-based screen space, taking into account the properties of the virtual camera used to render the scene. In addition, the effect of various types of lights can be applied to the vertices. (A few other important tasks, such as clipping and viewport scaling, take place in the first stage too.) In the second stage, called *rasterization,* primitives are used to organize these transformed and lit vertices into points, lines, and triangles. The rasterizer draws the resulting shapes into the DirectDraw surface known as the render target while applying texture maps and interpolating various properties such as color between connected vertices. Rasterization is also where the depth buffer is used to determine which of the resulting pixels will be visible to the user and which are obscured by the pixels of other primitives. Figure 5-1 shows how these stages work together to implement the task of rendering a 3D object.

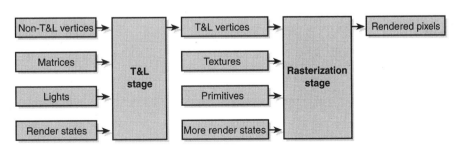

Figure 5-1
The two stages of rendering a 3D object

Direct3D can perform both the T&L stage and the rasterization stage. You can configure Direct3D to perform the steps separately or together in a single function call, depending on the needs of your program. If you want, you can provide your own transformation and lighting, and pass processed vertices directly to the Direct3D rasterizer, bypassing Direct3D's T&L stage. This chapter discusses Direct3D vertices and the process of transforming and lighting them. Chapter 6 will talk about rasterizing primitives onto the render target, using the transformed and lit vertices.

Overview of the T&L Pipeline

The process of transformation and lighting is often thought of as a pipeline (though perhaps a factory assembly line would be a better metaphor), in which untransformed and unlit vertices enter one end, several sequential operations are performed on the vertices inside, and then the transformed and lit vertices exit from the other end. Your application sets up the T&L pipeline by specifying several matrices, the viewport, and any lights you want to use. Then the application feeds vertices into the pipeline, which transforms the vertices, lights them, clips them, projects them into screen space, and scales them as specified by the viewport. Vertices exiting the pipeline are considered to be "processed" and are ready to be handed to the rasterizer. The T&L pipeline is depicted in Figure 5-2.

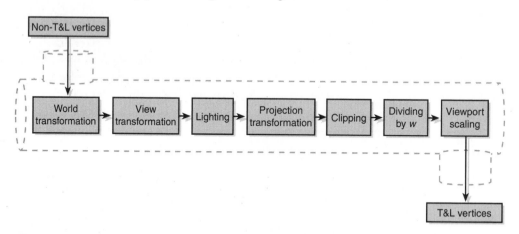

Figure 5-2
The T&L pipeline

It is possible to configure the T&L pipeline to skip some or all of the steps shown here. Programmers who have implemented their own transformation and lighting algorithms can disable parts of the pipeline and send vertices that are already transformed and lit to Direct3D. In most cases, however, it's best to use Direct3D's full T&L pipeline. This code has been optimized to make use of all the latest CPU extensions, and on some 3D graphics cards, T&L can be performed extremely quickly by dedicated hardware. For this discussion, let's assume that the programmer wants Direct3D to perform the full T&L process, and let's watch what happens to a vertex as it passes through the various stages of the pipeline.

World Transformation

During the T&L process, all the coordinates of the various objects to be rendered need to be converted into a common coordinate system, known as *world space*. But it is usually convenient for your program to express the coordinates of each object in its own, local coordinate system, known as *model space* (or *local space*). The matrix defining the transformation between model space and world space is called the *world transformation matrix*. Using model space makes life easier in several ways. For example, it's easier and faster to move an object by simply redefining the transformation from model space to world space than it would be to manually change all the coordinates of the object in world space. Model space also allows *instancing*, in which you can draw an object, such as a sphere, using one model-to-world transformation, and then draw it again somewhere else using a different model-to-world transformation. The model space also allows more natural local transformations. For example, rotating a sphere around its center is easiest when the origin is at the center of the sphere, regardless of where in world space the sphere is positioned.

The first stage of the T&L pipeline uses the world transformation matrix that you specify to transform the location coordinates in the object's vertices from local space into world space. The world transformation matrix can use any combination of rotations (rotating the object about the *x*-axis, *y*-axis, or *z*-axis), translations (moving the object along the *x*-axis, *y*-axis, or *z*-axis), and scaling (enlarging or shrinking the object). Figure 5-3 shows the relationship between the world coordinate system and a model's local coordinate system.

The most important aspect of the world coordinate system is that it provides a coordinate space that all the 3D objects share instead of requiring a unique coordinate system for each 3D object. Once the vertices are specified in world coordinates, Direct3D doesn't have to remember any local coordinates or deal with any model-to-world transformations. The conversion from the local coordinate system to the world coordinate system is analogous to converting various objects expressed in pounds, kilograms, and tons into grams, providing a common denominator for all the world's objects. If you don't need to use a separate model space and want to specify an object's vertices directly in world coordinates, you can just make the world transformation matrix an identity matrix. This indicates that the object's model space is equivalent to the common world space.

World coordinates

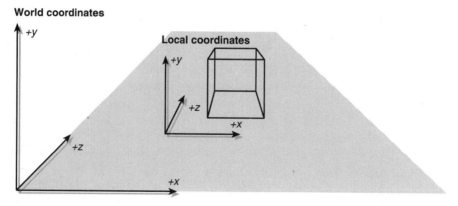

Figure 5-3
World transformation (world and local coordinate systems)

View Transformation

World space is still fairly abstract in the sense that the location of the origin and the axes of the space are completely up to the programmer and have no significance to Direct3D. The second stage of the T&L pipeline transforms the vertices from world space into *camera space*, in which the virtual camera is at the origin and is pointing directly down the positive z-axis. Lights (which are specified in world space) are also transformed into camera space at this stage. Figure 5-4 illustrates this concept.

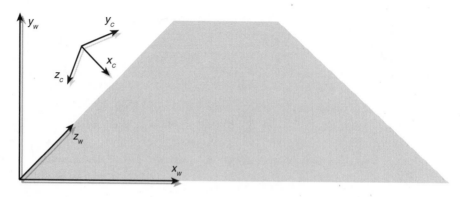

Figure 5-4
View transformation

Lighting

At this point, the effect of any current lights is calculated and applied to the vertices. The lighting code looks at the position of each vertex, its *normal vector* (the vector pointing away from the polygon containing the vertex), its color, and the current material properties. It calculates the effect of each light on the vertex based on all these factors and on the properties of the light, and stores the resulting color of the vertex back into the vertex structure. From this point forward, Direct3D doesn't need to deal with lights or materials.

Projection Transformation and the Viewing Frustum

The next stage of the pipeline scales the objects in the scene based on their distance from the viewpoint specified. This scaling, called *projection transformation,* produces the appearance of depth in the rendered scene by making objects in the distance appear smaller than those closer to the viewpoint. After the projection transformation is applied, the vertices are considered to be in *projection space.*

To understand how the projection transformation works, it is helpful to think about the *viewing frustum.* A *frustum* is the geometric term for a pyramid with its pointed tip removed. In computer graphics, the viewing frustum is formed by conceptually placing a pyramid such that its pointed tip is at the camera position, with the camera pointing down the middle of the pyramid, projecting the pyramid's four "walls" through the four sides of the screen and chopping off the front and back of the pyramid at the near and far *clipping planes* (explained below). The resulting viewing frustum represents the volume of the camera space that will be visible in the rendered scene. Although you can use many types of projections, which affect how the 3D models are projected from the camera space onto the screen, this book describes the most common type: *perspective projection,* which means that objects farther from the camera are made smaller than those close to the camera. Another type of transformation, which doesn't scale the size of the objects in the scene, is *orthogonal projection.* Although orthogonal projection is useful for some applications, you'll probably want to use the standard approach of scaling objects based on distance for most first-person-perspective games.

To perform perspective projection, the projection transformation converts the viewing frustum into a *cuboid,* a cubelike shape in which the dimensions are not all equal. Because the near end of a viewing frustum is smaller than the far end, closer objects appear larger than farther ones, generating the perspective effect in the scene.

Figure 5-5 illustrates the viewing frustum's components.

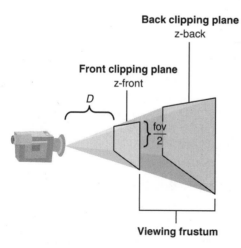

Figure 5-5
The viewing frustum

In Figure 5-5, you also see the front and back clipping planes represented. The clipping planes are used together to define what is visible to the viewer when the scene is rendered. The front clipping plane defines the closest distance an object can be to be included in the rendered scene, and the back clipping plane defines the farthest distance included. Any objects outside the frustum are not rendered. The near and far clipping planes are necessary because they're used to set the minimum and maximum values in the z-buffer. If there were no far plane, the renderer wouldn't know what value to map to the maximum z value. Keep in mind that the range you set for the far plane will affect the speed and visual quality of the scene. If you set the plane too close, you'll end up with *popping*, which is the perception that objects are jumping into view suddenly rather than transitioning in gradually from far out when they are small and thus less noticeable. If you set the plane too far away, you're making clipping ineffective because more objects will be rendered, causing the rendering to take longer.

The viewing frustum is described by the *field of view* (fov), which is the angle formed by the planes coming out of the camera and by the distances from the viewpoint to the front and back clipping planes. These distances are defined as the z coordinates of the front and back planes. The D variable is the distance from the camera to the front clipping plane (the origin of the space defined by the viewing transformation).

Figure 5-6 illustrates how the projection transformation converts the viewing frustum into a new coordinate space. Because we're using a perspective projection, the frustum becomes a cuboid. After projection is complete, the limits of the x dimension are −1 for the left plane and 1 for the right plane, the limits of the y dimension are −1 for the bottom plane and 1 for the top plane, and the limits of the z dimension are 0 for the front plane and 1 for the back plane.

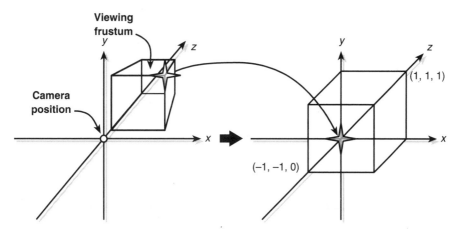

Figure 5-6
Perspective projection

Clipping

At this point, *clipping* takes place. Clipping is the process of ensuring that objects that are completely outside of the viewing frustum don't get rendered, and those objects that intersect the viewing frustum are drawn in such a way that no pixels are drawn outside the rectangle specified by the viewport. Clipping is the only part of the T&L pipeline that needs information about the primitives that connect the vertices. For example, if one vertex of a triangle is outside the view frustum, the clipping code needs to determine the two points at which the edges of the triangle intersect the frustum, and it needs to break the triangle into two triangles because the outline of the clipped triangle now has four sides. So if primitive information is available to the T&L pipeline (as with a *DrawPrimitive* call), full clipping takes place. If the T&L pipeline is just transforming and lighting a vertex buffer (which has no associated primitive information), as with a *ProcessVertices* call, the pipeline just determines and records which vertices are outside each plane of the viewing frustum. This information is used in a later DrawPrimitive call to clip the primitives using that vertex buffer.

Dividing by *w*, or Nonhomogenization

At this point, Direct3D needs to convert the vertices from being *homogeneous* to *nonhomogeneous*. When you specify Direct3D vertices, you provide x, y, and z coordinates for each one. But in order to perform transformation and lighting, an additional coordinate, called *w*, is added and given an initial value of 1.0. As the vertex is passed through various matrices in the T&L pipeline, the w coordinate changes its value. A vertex with a w value other than 1.0 is called homogeneous. Once transformation is finished, the vertex is restored to nonhomogeneous form by dividing the x, y, and z coordinates by w. The reciprocal of the w coordinate is stored as well. This process is also known as "dividing by w." This conversion is necessary because the rasterizer expects to receive vertices in terms of their nonhomogeneous x, y, and z locations as well as the reciprocal-of-homogeneous-w (RHW).

Viewport Scaling

The final step of the T&L pipeline is to adjust the vertices to fit the viewport. The viewport lets you specify how to map the rendered image onto the render target surface. You can specify both a translation and a scaling operation. Generally, you want to fill the entire render target, so you specify no translation, and scale the vertex coordinates so that an x coordinate of −1 maps to the left edge, an x of 1 maps to the right edge, a y of −1 maps to the bottom edge, and a y of 1 maps to the top. You can also specify a scaling of the z coordinates if you want to render into a particular depth range. To use the full range, you set the viewport to use a minimum z of 0.0 and a maximum z of 1.0.

Vertices

All primitives that DirectX can render are made from vertices. In geometry, a *vertex* is a point in space that defines a corner of a polygon. A Direct3D vertex holds the coordinates of its position and can also store information such as a normal vector, texture coordinates, and color information. Vertices get transformed by Direct3D from a user-specified format to a format that is ready to be rasterized.

DirectX 6 introduced the flexible vertex format that lets us define vertices in several new ways. Before this, only the following three predefined types of vertices were available:

- **D3DVERTEX (untransformed, unlit vertices)**   If you choose not to light or transform your vertices before passing them to Direct3D, use this vertex type. You need to declare the lighting parameters and transformation matrices, but Direct3D computes the lighting and transformation for you.

- **D3DLVERTEX (untransformed, lit vertices)**   If you choose to light but not transform your vertices before passing them to Direct3D, you should use this vertex type. Also use these vertices if you want to compute your own custom lighting effects.

- **D3DTLVERTEX (transformed, lit vertices)**   If you choose to light and transform your vertices before passing them to Direct3D, you should use this vertex type. The T&L pipeline will skip transforming and lighting the vertices, but it will clip them if necessary. You can tell Direct3D that you intend to do your own clipping by using the D3DDP_DONOTCLIP flag when you call a rendering method. You should use the D3DDP_DONOTCLIP option with this type of vertex because if Direct3D is told to clip the transformed and lit vertices, it will have to back-transform them to projection space for clipping and then transform them back to screen space. This additional transformation causes additional overhead that you should attempt to avoid so that your application will run efficiently.

Flexible Vertex Formats

Although the original types are still very useful, the flexible vertex formats are even better. In the flexible vertex format, only the necessary vertex components are used, saving a fair amount of memory bandwidth and rendering time. Vertices are defined with a combination of flexible vertex format flags. Each rendering method available through the *IDirect3DDevice7* interface takes a combination of these flags to describe the format of the vertices being passed to Direct3D. These flags indicate which vertex components (position, normal, colors, and the number of texture coordinates) you want to use—and thus are currently in memory—and which portions of the rendering pipeline you want applied to them.

When using the flexible vertex format, you must format all the vertices in the following order (although you'll never use all of these at once):

1. Position (untransformed or transformed x, y, z)—(float) x coordinate, y coordinate, and z coordinate

2. RHW (only transformed vertices)—(float) rhw (the reciprocal-of-homogeneous-w)

3. Blending weight values—1–5 floats

4. Vertex normal (only untransformed vertices)—(float) normal x, normal y, normal z

5. Diffuse color—(DWORD) diffuse RGBA

6. Specular color—(DWORD) specular RGBA

7. Texture coordinate sets 1–8—(float) u coordinate, v coordinate

To request the untransformed and unlit vertex type, use the D3DFVF_XYZ and D3DFVF_NORMAL flags together in the vertex description passed to the rendering methods. This vertex type requests that Direct3D perform all transformation and lighting operations using its internal algorithms, unless you pass the D3DDP_DONOTLIGHT flag to the rendering methods, which asks Direct3D to disable the lighting engine for the primitives being rendered.

If you use just the D3DFVF_XYZ flag, the vertices are considered by Direct3D to be untransformed but already lit. Direct3D doesn't perform any lighting calculations on untransformed and lit vertices, but it still transforms them using the previously set world, view, and projection matrices.

The D3DFVF_XYZRHW flag indicates that the vertices are already transformed and lit. Direct3D doesn't transform vertices with the world, view, or projection matrix, and it doesn't do any lighting calculations because this flag indicates that these operations have already been performed.

With DirectX 7, you can specify texture coordinates in different formats. This capability allows textures to be addressed using from one to three texture coordinates. (You'd use three if you were using 2D-projected texture coordinates.) The D3DFVF_TEXCOORDSIZEn series of macros create bit patterns that define the texture coordinate formats that our vertex format will use.

Left-Handed and Right-Handed Coordinate Systems

Direct3D uses a left-handed coordinate system. In both left-handed and right-handed coordinate systems (the two most popular coordinate systems in 3D programming), the positive x-axis points to the right and the positive y-axis points up.

The z-axis, however, points in a different direction in each system. You can remember the direction in which the positive z-axis points by turning your palm up and pointing the fingers of your hand in the positive *x* direction and curling them in the positive *y* direction. The direction your thumb points, which in the left-handed coordinate system is away from you, is the direction the positive z-axis points for the coordinate system. Figure 5-7 illustrates this concept.

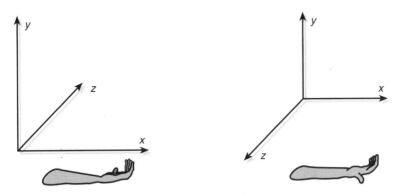

Figure 5-7
The left-handed and right-handed coordinate systems

To port an application from a right-handed to a left-handed coordinate system, change the 3D data as follows:

1. Flip the order of the vertices of each triangle in an object so that they are transversed clockwise from the front. For example, if the vertices are defined as V_0, V_1, and V_2 in the original triangle, you should switch them and pass them as V_0, V_2, and V_1.

2. Set up a view matrix to scale the world space by –1 in the z direction by just flipping the sign of the third row in the matrix (the _31, _32, _33, and _34 members of the view matrix's D3DMATRIX structure).

Strided Vertex Format

Direct3D provides a vertex type called the *strided vertex format* that can be used to represent *untransformed* vertices. Unlike a regular vertex, which consists of a structure that contains all the components of a vertex, a strided vertex contains pointers to those components. This gives you the freedom to organize the vertex components in different ways. Without strided vertices, all the information for one vertex is provided, then all the information for the second vertex, and so on. With strided vertices, you can remove some or all of this interleaving of information. As an example, you could have the position information for all the vertices in a contiguous array, followed by all the normal information, followed by all the texture coordinates.

You're not restricted to any specific interleaving scheme, so any approach that sets the data pointers and their strides correctly is acceptable. Strided vertices are a fairly advanced feature that you can use to ultra-optimize your program (for example, increasing the CPU cache performance). You'll probably find that you don't need to use them.

The D3DDRAWPRIMITIVESTRIDEDDATA structure used with the *IDirect3DDevice7::DrawPrimitiveStrided* and *IDirect3DDevice7::DrawIndexed-PrimitiveStrided* methods is defined as follows:

```
typedef struct D3DDRAWPRIMITIVESTRIDEDDATA  {
    D3DDP_PTRSTRIDE position;
    D3DDP_PTRSTRIDE normal;
    D3DDP_PTRSTRIDE diffuse;
    D3DDP_PTRSTRIDE specular;
    D3DDP_PTRSTRIDE textureCoords[D3DDP_MAXTEXCOORD];
} D3DDRAWPRIMITIVESTRIDEDDATA , *LPD3DDRAWPRIMITIVESTRIDEDDATA;
```

This structure contains the following members:

- *position* and *normal* Hold D3DDP_PTRSTRIDE structures that point to an array of position and normal vectors for a collection of vertices. Each of these vectors is a three-element array of float values.

- *diffuse* and *specular* Hold D3DDP_PTRSTRIDE structures that point to an array with diffuse and specular color information for a collection of vertices. Each element of the array is a 32-bit RGBA value, with 8 bits allocated for each color component (R, G, B, and A).

- *textureCoords* Holds an eight-element array of D3DDP_PTRSTRIDE structures. Each element in the array is, in turn, an array of texture coordinates for the collection of vertices. You can find which array of texture coordinates you need to use for a given texture stage by calling the *IDirect3DDevice3::SetTextureStageState* method with the D3DTSS_TEXCOORDINDEX value.

The D3DDRAWPRIMITIVESTRIDEDDATA structure holds 12 D3DDP_PTRSTRIDE structures, one for each position, normal, diffuse color, and specular color member, plus four structures for the texture coordinates member. The D3DDP_PTRSTRIDE structure is defined as shown here:

```
typedef struct _D3DDP_PTRSTRIDE {
    LPVOID lpvData;
    DWORD  dwStride;
} D3DDP_PTRSTRIDE;
```

This structure contains the following members:

- *lpvData*   The address of an array of data.

- *dwStride*   The memory stride between elements in the array.

Each of the D3DDP_PTRSTRIDE structures in the D3DDRAWPRIM-ITIVESTRIDEDDATA structure holds a pointer to an array of data and to the stride (the distance between elements in the array) of that array. You can set the *dwStride* member of the D3DDP_PTRSTRIDE structure to the memory stride (in bytes) from one entry in the array to the next. You can use the 12 structures you define to arrange the vertex components however you want. For example, suppose you want to use separate arrays for each vertex component, such as a set of arrays holding the position (float), normal (float), diffuse (RGBA value), specular (RGBA value), and texture (float) information. In this case, an untransformed position or a vertex normal has a stride of three *float* variables: (x, y, z) for position and (n_x, n_y, n_z) for vertex normal. Furthermore, diffuse and specular color have a stride of one DWORD (RGBA), and a texture coordinate has a stride of two *float* values (u, v).

Vertex Buffers

It is possible to have your program allocate memory for an array of vertices and pass a pointer to that array to a Direct3D primitive-drawing function. The preferred approach, however, is to let Direct3D manage the memory that holds the vertex array in an object called a *vertex buffer*. Using vertex buffers has several advantages over managing the vertex memory yourself. Vertex buffers can be placed in video memory rather than system memory if that will improve performance (as it will when transformation and lighting takes place in hardware). Vertex buffers also let the programmer separate the T&L stage from the rasterization stage, by calling *IDirect3DVertexBuffer7::ProcessVertices* to transform and light the vertices but not rasterize them yet. This is useful when doing multipass rendering, in which the same object is rendered multiple times with different textures or other properties. Without vertex buffers, your program couldn't specify that vertices be transformed and lit once but rasterized multiple times.

Here's the function declaration for this method:

```
HRESULT IDirect3DVertexBuffer7::ProcessVertices(
    DWORD dwVertexOp,
    DWORD dwDestIndex,
    DWORD dwCount,
    LPDIRECT3DVERTEXBUFFER7 lpSrcBuffer,
    DWORD dwSrcIndex,
    LPDIRECT3DDEVICE7 lpD3DDevice,
    DWORD dwFlags
);
```

Parameter	Description
dwVertexOp	Can hold a combination of the following flags to describe how the method will process the vertices as they are transferred from the source buffer: **D3DVOP_CLIP** Used with vertex buffers containing clipping information; vertices are transformed and clipped if they are outside the viewing frustum. **D3DVOP_EXTENTS** Updates the extents of the screen rectangle when the vertices are rendered after they are transformed. The extents returned by *IDirect3DDevice7::GetClipStatus* won't have been updated with the new vertex information when they are rendered. **D3DVOP_LIGHT** Indicates that you want to light the vertices. **D3DVOP_TRANSFORM** Requests transformation of the vertices using the world, view, and projection matrices. This flag always needs to be set.
dwDestIndex	The index into this destination vertex buffer where the vertices are placed after processing.
dwCount	The number of vertices in the source buffer to process.
lpSrcBuffer	The address of the *IDirect3DVertexBuffer7* interface for the source vertex buffer.
dwSrcIndex	The index of the first vertex in the source vertex buffer to be processed.
lpD3DDevice	The address of the *IDirect3DDevice7* interface for the device that will be used to transform the vertices.
dwFlags	Processing options. Set this parameter to 0 for default processing. Set it to D3DPV_DONOTCOPYDATA to prevent the system from copying vertex data not affected by the current vertex operation into the destination buffer.

Setting Up the T&L Pipeline Matrices

This section discusses the details of building the three transformation matrices—world, view, and projection—that must be specified for the T&L pipeline.

The World Matrix

Recall that the world matrix transforms coordinates from model space (in which vertices are defined relative to the model's local origin) to world space (in which vertices are defined relative to an origin that is common to every object in the scene). If the term *world matrix* seems ambiguous to you, think of this matrix as a "local-to-world matrix." Because you'll probably render several objects in a scene, each with its own local coordinate space, you'll change the world matrix several times in the process of rendering a single frame. (The relationship between the world coordinate system and the model's local coordinate system was shown in Figure 5-3.)

You create the world matrix as you do all transformations: using a combination of transformation matrices to produce a final matrix that performs all the transformations each separate matrix produces. In the code below, I show how to create an example world matrix and then modify it with additional matrices to translate a model into world space. The code then rotates the model to place it in its final orientation.

If a model is at the world origin and its local coordinate axes are oriented the same as world space, the world matrix is just the identity matrix. Usually the world matrix is a combination of a translation into world space and potentially one or more rotations to turn the model to its proper position.

The variables for defining the matrix are shown below. The D3DMATRIX type used for the matrices is declared in Direct3D as a two-dimensional array containing a 4 × 4 matrix.

```
HRESULT hr;
D3DMATRIX   matWorld, // World matrix being constructed
            matTemp,  // Temporary matrix for rotations
            matRot;   // Final rotation matrix (applied to
                      // matWorld)
    // Using the left-to-right order of matrix concatenation,
    // apply the translation to the object's world position
    // before applying the rotations.
    D3DUtil_SetTranslateMatrix(matWorld, m_vPos);
```

(continued)

```
D3DUtil_SetIdentityMatrix(matRot);
//
// Now apply the orientation variables to the
// world matrix.
//
if(m_fPitch || m_fYaw || m_fRoll)
{
    // Produce and combine the rotation matrices.
    D3DUtil_SetRotateXMatrix(matTemp, m_fPitch);  // Pitch
    D3DMath_MatrixMultiply(matRot,matRot,matTemp);
    D3DUtil_SetRotateYMatrix(matTemp, m_fYaw);    // Yaw
    D3DMath_MatrixMultiply(matRot,matRot,matTemp);
    D3DUtil_SetRotateZMatrix(matTemp, m_fRoll);   // Roll
    D3DMath_MatrixMultiply(matRot,matRot,matTemp);
    // Apply the rotation matrices to complete the
    // world matrix.
    D3DMath_MatrixMultiply(matWorld, matRot, matWorld);
}

hr = lpDev->SetTransform(D3DTRANSFORMSTATE_WORLD, &matWorld);
```

This code block calls the *D3DUtil_SetTranslateMatrix* routine, passing in the viewpoint. The routine then calls the *D3DUtil_SetIdentityMatrix* routine to initialize the matrix with the identity matrix. This identity matrix is organized as an all-zero matrix with 1s along the diagonal, as shown here:

$$\begin{bmatrix} 1 & 0 & 0 & 0 \\ 0 & 1 & 0 & 0 \\ 0 & 0 & 1 & 0 \\ 0 & 0 & 0 & 1 \end{bmatrix}$$

The identity matrix represents a "no-op" transformation; that is, a point transformed through an identity matrix has the same coordinates coming out as going in.

```
inline VOID D3DUtil_SetIdentityMatrix( D3DMATRIX& m )
{
    m._12 = m._13 = m._14 = m._21 = m._23 = m._24 = 0.0f;
    m._31 = m._32 = m._34 = m._41 = m._42 = m._43 = 0.0f;
    m._11 = m._22 = m._33 = m._44 = 1.0f;
}
```

You should also use routines to enable your program to perform rotations, translations, and scaling in the x, y, and z axes. A translation transformation translates the point (x, y, z) to a new point (x', y', z') using the following formula:

$$[x'\,y'\,z'\,1]=[x\,y\,z\,1]\begin{bmatrix} 1 & 0 & 0 & 0 \\ 0 & 1 & 0 & 0 \\ 0 & 0 & 1 & 0 \\ T_x & T_y & T_z & 1 \end{bmatrix}$$

D3DUtil_SetTranslateMatrix, which takes the amount to translate along the *x*, *y*, and *z* axes (*tx*, *ty*, *tz*), and creates a translation matrix, is defined as follows:

```
inline VOID D3DUtil_SetTranslateMatrix( D3DMATRIX& m, FLOAT tx,
                                        FLOAT ty, FLOAT tz )
{ D3DUtil_SetIdentityMatrix( m );
  m._41 = tx; m._42 = ty; m._43 = tz; }

inline VOID D3DUtil_SetTranslateMatrix( D3DMATRIX& m, D3DVECTOR& v )
{ D3DUtil_SetTranslateMatrix( m, v.x, v.y, v.z ); }
```

Once the translation matrix is filled, you could multiply it with the current world matrix to translate it. The following call does this for you:

```
D3DMath_MatrixMultiply (WorldMatrix, TranslateMatrix, WorldMatrix);
```

The *D3DMath_MatrixMultiply* routine multiplies two matrices together and places the result into a third matrix. This call will multiply the world matrix by the translation matrix to move the point along all three axes the distance specified in the *x*, *y*, and *z* directions and place the result back into the world matrix. When you're working with matrices, you need to remember that matrix concatenation/ multiplication isn't commutative. Because of this, you need to make sure your parameters are in the right order when calling *D3DMath_MatrixMultiply* and when building up matrices from transformations in general.

The *D3DMath_MatrixMultiply* routine is defined as follows:

```
VOID D3DMath_MatrixMultiply( D3DMATRIX& q, D3DMATRIX& a,
                             D3DMATRIX& b )
{
    FLOAT* pA = (FLOAT*)&a;
    FLOAT* pB = (FLOAT*)&b;
    FLOAT  pM[16];

    ZeroMemory( pM, sizeof(D3DMATRIX) );

    for( WORD i=0; i<4; i++ )
        for( WORD j=0; j<4; j++ )
            for( WORD k=0; k<4; k++ )
```

(continued)

119

```
                    pM[4*i+j]  +=   pA[4*i+k]  *  pB[4*k+j];

        memcpy( &q, pM, sizeof(D3DMATRIX) );
    }
```

One additional useful helper function for multiplying a vertex by a matrix, *D3DMath_VertexMatrixMultiply*, follows.

```
//-------------------------------------------------------------------
// Name: D3DMath_VertexMatrixMultiply
// Desc: Multiplies a vertex by a matrix
//-------------------------------------------------------------------
HRESULT D3DMath_VertexMatrixMultiply( D3DVERTEX& vDest,
                                      D3DVERTEX& vSrc, D3DMATRIX& mat)
{
    HRESULT    hr;
    D3DVECTOR* pSrcVec  = (D3DVECTOR*)&vSrc.x;
    D3DVECTOR* pDestVec = (D3DVECTOR*)&vDest.x;

    if( SUCCEEDED( hr = D3DMath_VectorMatrixMultiply( *pDestVec,
                                                      *pSrcVec,
                                                      mat ) ) )
    {
        pSrcVec  = (D3DVECTOR*)&vSrc.nx;
        pDestVec = (D3DVECTOR*)&vDest.nx;
        hr = D3DMath_VectorMatrixMultiply( *pDestVec, *pSrcVec, mat );
    }
    return hr;
}
```

Once you've set up the matrix to translate the desired distances, you need to add the rotations you want. In the code for this book, we just need to rotate about the *y*-axis to orient ourselves properly to our 3D world if we're just walking straight or driving on a flat surface. If you need to orient your objects differently (which often happens if the 3D tool you use to create 3D objects uses a different orientation than the ones used here), you rotate about the *x* and *z* axes. Because you'll want to handle all three axes sooner or later, I show the matrices and list the routines for performing rotations about the *x*, *y*, and *z* axes.

The matrix to perform a rotation about the *x*-axis, where θ equals the amount you want to rotate about this axis, follows:

$$[x'\ y'\ z'\ 1] = [x\ y\ z\ 1] \begin{bmatrix} 1 & 0 & 0 & 0 \\ 0 & \cos\theta & \sin\theta & 0 \\ 0 & -\sin\theta & \cos\theta & 0 \\ 0 & 0 & 0 & 1 \end{bmatrix}$$

The matrix to perform a rotation about the *y*-axis, where θ equals the amount you want to rotate about this axis, looks like this:

$$[x'\ y'\ z'\ 1]=[x\ y\ z\ 1]\begin{bmatrix} \cos\theta & 0 & -\sin\theta & 0 \\ 0 & 1 & 0 & 0 \\ \sin\theta & & \cos\theta & 0 \\ 0 & 0 & 0 & 1 \end{bmatrix}$$

To perform a rotation about the *z*-axis, where θ equals the amount you want to rotate about this axis, use this matrix:

$$[x'\ y'\ z'\ 1]=[x\ y\ z\ 1]\begin{bmatrix} \cos\theta & \sin\theta & 0 & 0 \\ -\sin\theta & \cos\theta & 0 & 0 \\ 0 & 0 & 1 & 0 \\ 0 & 0 & 0 & 1 \end{bmatrix}$$

Once you've defined the world transformation matrix, you need to call the *IDirect3DDevice7::SetTransform* method to set it, specifying the D3DTRANSFORMSTATE_WORLD flag in the first parameter.

This method uses the D3DTRANSFORMSTATETYPE enumerated type to describe the transformation state for the D3DOP_STATETRANSFORM opcode in the D3DOPCODE enumerated type, which is organized as follows:

```
typedef enum _D3DTRANSFORMSTATETYPE {
    D3DTRANSFORMSTATE_WORLD        = 1,
    D3DTRANSFORMSTATE_VIEW         = 2,
    D3DTRANSFORMSTATE_PROJECTION   = 3,
    D3DTRANSFORMSTATE_FORCE_DWORD  = 0x7fffffff,
} D3DTRANSFORMSTATETYPE;
```

These members are defined as follows:

- **D3DTRANSFORMSTATE_WORLD, D3DTRANSFORMSTATE_VIEW, and D3DTRANSFORMSTATE_PROJECTION**   Used to define the matrices for world, view, and projection transformations. The default value for each member is NULL, indicating the identity matrices.

- **D3DTRANSFORMSTATE_FORCE_DWORD**   Used to force this enumerated type to 32 bits.

The View Matrix

The view transformation transforms the vertices from world space into camera space. The camera, which represents the viewer, is positioned at the origin looking in the positive z direction (because of the left-handed coordinate system Direct3D uses) in camera space. The view matrix is used to translate and rotate the objects in the 3D world around the camera's position and orientation. (Again, the camera's position is the origin.)

You can create a view matrix in a number of ways. The approach I often use is to directly create the composite (a single matrix derived from multiple transformation matrices) view matrix. By taking the camera's world space position and a position in the scene to look at, you can have vectors computed to define the orientation of the camera space coordinate axes. The camera's position is subtracted from the position of the viewer, and the resulting vector is used as the camera's direction vector (n). The cross product of this vector and the y-axis of the world space is computed and normalized to produce a "right" vector (u).

The cross product of the vectors (u and n) is then computed to obtain an *up* vector (v). The three vectors—up, right, and view—define the orientation of the coordinate axes for the camera space in terms of the world space. You compute the x, y, and z translation factors by taking the negative of the dot product between the camera position and the u, v, and n vectors.

You then place these values into the following matrix, where c is the camera's world space position, to generate the view matrix. This matrix translates and rotates the vertices from world space to camera space:

$$\begin{bmatrix} v_x & u_x & n_x & 0 \\ v_y & u_y & n_y & 0 \\ v_z & u_z & n_z & 0 \\ -(v \cdot c) & -(u \cdot c) & -(n \cdot c) & 1 \end{bmatrix}$$

Although the above computation might seem complicated, the code to perform these tasks is fairly straightforward. Best of all, you can reuse the code for all your applications.

This math is all done for you by the following function from the Direct3D Framework:

```
HRESULT D3DUtil_SetViewMatrix( D3DMATRIX& mat, D3DVECTOR& vFrom,
    D3DVECTOR& vAt, D3DVECTOR& vUp );
```

The Projection Matrix

The final matrix you need to create is the projection matrix, which is used to control how the viewer sees the contents of the 3D world. The projection matrix works like a lens on a camera. To produce this matrix, you usually create a scale and perspective projection.

The code below sets up a projection matrix, taking the front and back clipping planes and the field of view in radians. The *IDirect3DDevice7::SetTransform* method is then called to set the projection transformation, just as for the world and view transformations, except this time D3DTRANSFORMSTATE_PROJECTION is specified in the first parameter.

Here are the calls and the routine to set up the matrix and use this method:

```
D3DUtil_SetProjectionMatrix( matProj, 1.57f, 1.0f, 1.0f, 100.0f );
    m_pd3dDevice->SetTransform( D3DTRANSFORMSTATE_PROJECTION,
                              &matProj );
    ⋮
//------------------------------------------------------------
// Name: D3DUtil_SetProjectionMatrix
// Desc: Sets the passed-in 4 x 4 matrix to a perspective projection
//       matrix built from the field of view (fov, in y), aspect
//       ratio, near plane (D), and far plane (F). The projection
//       matrix is normalized for element [3][4] to be 1.0. This is
//       performed so that w-based range fog will work correctly.
//------------------------------------------------------------
HRESULT D3DUtil_SetProjectionMatrix( D3DMATRIX& mat, FLOAT fFOV,
                              FLOAT fAspect, FLOAT fNearPlane,
                              FLOAT fFarPlane )
{
    if( fabs(fFarPlane-fNearPlane) < 0.01f )
        return E_INVALIDARG;
```

(continued)

```
    if( fabs(sin(fFOV/2)) < 0.01f )
        return E_INVALIDARG;

    FLOAT w = fAspect * ( cosf(fFOV/2)/sinf(fFOV/2) );
    FLOAT h =    1.0f  * ( cosf(fFOV/2)/sinf(fFOV/2) );
    FLOAT Q = fFarPlane / ( fFarPlane - fNearPlane );

    ZeroMemory( &mat, sizeof(D3DMATRIX) );
    mat._11 = w;
    mat._22 = h;
    mat._33 = Q;
    mat._34 = 1.0f;
    mat._43 = -Q*fNearPlane;

    return S_OK;
}
```

The Viewport

As you saw earlier in this chapter, the last stage of the T&L pipeline is to transform the vertices from projection space into screen space based on the viewport. In screen space, the *x* and *y* coordinates of the vertices correspond to pixels, and the *z* coordinate is the value that will be stored in the z-buffer. Before sending any vertices through the T&L pipeline, you need to pass Direct3D a structure that specifies the viewport parameters.

Creating the Viewport

With DirectX 7, the viewport rectangle is defined using the D3DVIEWPORT7 structure. This structure, shown earlier, is used by the viewport manipulation methods of the *IDirect3DDevice7* interface: *IDirect3DDevice7::SetViewport* and *IDirect3DDevice7::GetViewport*.

The D3DVIEWPORT7 structure, specified as the only parameter of the *IDirect3DDevice7::SetViewport* method, describes the viewport parameters and is defined as follows:

```
typedef struct _D3DVIEWPORT7 {
    DWORD       dwX;
    DWORD       dwY;
    DWORD       dwWidth;
    DWORD       dwHeight;
    D3DVALUE    dvMinZ;
    D3DVALUE    dvMaxZ;
} D3DVIEWPORT7, *LPD3DVIEWPORT7;
```

Parameter	Description
dwX and *dwY*	The pixel coordinates of the top-left corner of the viewport on the render-target surface. Set these members to 0 unless you want to render to a subset of the surface.
dwWidth and *dwHeight*	The dimensions, in pixels, of the viewport on the render-target surface. Set these members to the dimensions of the render-target surface unless you're rendering only to a subset of the surface.
dvMinZ and *dvMaxZ*	These members define the maximum and minimum nonhomogeneous z coordinates that result from the perspective divide and are projected onto the $w = 1$ plane.

The *dwX*, *dwY*, *dwWidth*, and *dwHeight* members (defined as screen coordinates that are relative to the upper-left corner of the render-target surface) of the D3DVIEWPORT7 structure define the area of the render-target surface into which the scene will be rendered. This is known as the *viewport rectangle* or the *destination rectangle*.

Setting Up the Viewport

The following code sets up the viewport by setting various members of the D3DVIEWPORT7 structure:

```
//
// Set up the viewport for a reasonable viewing area.
//
D3DVIEWPORT7 viewData;
memset(&viewData, 0, sizeof(D3DVIEWPORT7));
viewData.dwSize = sizeof(D3DVIEWPORT7);
viewData.dwX = viewData.dwY = 0;
viewData.dwWidth = w;
viewData.dwHeight = h;
viewData.dvMinZ = 0.0f;
viewData.dvMaxZ = 1.0f;
```

Once you've set the D3DVIEWPORT7 structure's members, you can pass the structure to Direct3D by using the *IDirect3DDevice7::SetViewport* method, which has the following function declaration:

```
HRESULT IDirect3DDevice7::SetViewport(
    LPD3DVIEWPORT7 lpViewport
);
```

IDirect3DDevice7::SetViewport has one parameter, *lpViewport*, which holds the address of a D3DVIEWPORT7 structure containing the new viewport.

Clearing the Viewport

Once the viewport is prepared, you can clear it to reset the contents of the viewport rectangle on the render-target surface and the rectangles in the depth and stencil buffer surfaces if it was specified. *IDirect3DDevice7* provides the *IDirect3DDevice7::Clear* method to clear the viewport. Because our focus is on real-time 3D games and simulations, we usually need to update the entire viewport rectangle—after all, every portion of the scene is changing. However, this method can accept one or more rectangles describing the area or areas on the surfaces being cleared if you need to clear only portions of the viewport, which is the case when you're using a portion of the display to represent a HUD or a game-scoring frame around the viewport.

Here's the declaration for this method:

```
HRESULT IDirect3DDevice7::Clear(
    DWORD dwCount,
    LPD3DRECT lpRects,
    DWORD dwFlags,
    DWORD dwColor,
    D3DVALUE dvZ,
    DWORD dwStencil
);
```

Parameter	Description
dwCount	The number of rectangles in the array *lpRects*.
lpRects	An array of D3DRECT structures defining the rectangles to be cleared. Each rectangle contains screen coordinates that correspond to points on the render-target surface.
dwFlags	Holds the flags defining how the surface will be cleared. At least one of the following flags (or a combination of them) must be used: **D3DCLEAR_TARGET** Clears the rendering target to the color in the *dwColor* parameter. **D3DCLEAR_ZBUFFER** Clears the depth buffer to the value in the *dvZ* parameter. **D3DCLEAR_STENCIL** Clears the stencil buffer to the value in the *dwStencil* parameter.

(continued)

Parameter	Description
dwColor	A 32-bit RGBA color value the render-target surface will be cleared to.
dvZ	The new *z* value that this method stores in the depth buffer. This parameter can range from 0.0 (closest) through 1.0 (farthest).
dwStencil	The value to store in each stencil-buffer entry, with a valid range from 0 through $2^n - 1$ inclusive, where *n* is the bit depth of the stencil buffer.

You can specify the D3DCLEAR_TARGET flag so that the viewport is cleared using an RGBA color specified in the *dwColor* parameter. You can use the D3DCLEAR_ZBUFFER flag to clear the depth buffer to a depth specified in *dvZ*. This value can range between 0.0 (the closest distance) through 1.0 (the farthest distance). Finally, you can use the D3DCLEAR_STENCIL flag to reset the stencil bits to the value specified in the *dwStencil* parameter. This value can range in value from 0 through $2^n - 1$, where *n* is the stencil buffer's bit depth.

Lighting

Unlike interfaces in earlier versions of DirectX, the *IDirect3DDevice7* interface doesn't use COM objects to represent each light. Methods such as *IDirect-3DDevice7::SetLight* now use the D3DLIGHT7 structure to describe a set of lighting properties rather than the lighting semantics that previous versions of the device interface used.

In Direct3D, the light model approximates real-world lighting by calculating the mathematical interaction of a surface's color and the color of light reflecting off that surface. The result of this computation is used as the color to apply to the surface when rendered to the screen. In real life, light bounces (reflects) off thousands of surfaces before it reaches the eye. With each reflection, some of the light is absorbed by the surface it bounces off, some is scattered randomly, and the rest hits the next surface or the eye. This real-life effect of light bouncing until it is seen or it attenuates to 0 is what raytracing algorithms attempt to simulate. Although raytracers create very realistic scenes that approximate what we see in nature, no real-time program can perform these computations (yet). Direct3D uses a simpler approach to provide real-time lighting for performance reasons. In Direct3D, light is defined as the red, green, and blue components that combine to create a specific light color. If you enable lighting in your application, as Direct3D rasterizes a scene in its final stage of rendering, it computes the color of each vertex as a combination of the following:

■ The current material color and the texels in an associated texture map

■ The diffuse and specular components associated with the vertex

■ The color and intensity of the light generated by any light objects in the scene

■ The scene's ambient light level

The diffuse reflectance of a material is the most important component in determining the color of a vertex. Because diffuse light is directional, the angle of incidence for diffuse lights controls the intensity of the reflected light. The diffuse reflection is greatest when the light hits a vertex parallel to the vertex normal. As this angle is increased, the diffuse reflectance decreases. The specular reflection creates highlights on an object's surface, making the object appear shiny.

If you use Direct3D lighting and materials and pass unlit vertices to it, Direct3D performs lighting computations for you. Remember that materials are used to describe how light reflects off surfaces. A polygon's material possesses properties that affect how the polygon reflects the light it receives. A reflectance trait that defines how the material reflects ambient light, as well as other traits that define the material's specular and diffuse reflectance, can be set by our software.

In Direct3D, two light types, *direct light* and *ambient light,* are used to describe how light will be reflected. Although you can write your own lighting computations, Direct3D has built-in algorithms that do an excellent job and save you a great deal of time. If you do choose to turn off lighting for vertices that include normals, you would set the D3DRENDERSTATE_LIGHTING render state to FALSE.

You need to consider one important thing when you're using Direct3D's lighting: in Direct3D, lighting is computed only per vertex, not per pixel. Thus, if you shine a spotlight on the middle of a large triangle, it's not going to look pretty.

(In fact, this characteristic makes spotlights almost useless unless you happen to have dense vertex distribution.) Many programmers bypass this problem via light mapping, by which the lighting is calculated, often in advance, independently of vertex positions. It is then stored in a sort of monochrome low-resolution texture map that is applied on top of the object's regular texture. Light mapping is a lot more work but it can create much more sophisticated lighting effects because lighting isn't limited to being per vertex.

Ambient Light

Ambient light is light that has no determinable direction or source because it's been scattered so many times. This light produces low-intensity illumination everywhere in a scene. It contains only color and intensity and doesn't add to specular reflection. It is also independent of any light-generating objects that you've placed in your scene.

In previous versions of DirectX, we specified light states and render states. In DirectX 7, all states are render states. You set the ambient light level with a call to the *IDirect3DDevice7::SetRenderState* method, specifying D3DRENDER-STATE_AMBIENT as the *dwRenderStateType* parameter and the desired RGBA color as the *dwRenderState* parameter, as follows:

```
// lpD3DDevice is a valid pointer to an IDirect3DDevice7 interface.
//
// Set the ambient light.
D3DCOLOR d3dclrAmbientLightColor = D3DRGBA(1.0f,1.0f,1.0f,1.0f);
lpD3DDevice->SetRenderState(D3DRENDERSTATE_AMBIENT,
                            d3dclrAmbientLightColor);
```

Each RGBA color component value used to define an ambient light can range from 0 through 255. The D3DRGBA macro creates an RGBA D3DCOLOR value from the red, green, blue, and alpha components you specify. This macro is defined as follows:

```
#define D3DRGBA (r, g, b, a) \
    ((((long)((a) * 255)) << 24) |
    (((long)((r) * 255)) << 16) |
    (((long)((g) * 255)) << 8) |
    (long)((b) * 255))
```

Direct Light

Whereas ambient light adds simple, general lighting to a scene, direct light simulates light coming from a particular location or direction. This light interacts with a surface's material and changes the surface's color. Direct3D uses its direction when computing Gouraud and other shading. To simplify computation, when a direct light is reflected, it doesn't affect the ambient light level of the scene.

To create a direct light, just define a variable of type D3DLIGHT7 and fill its members. The following code illustrates how to create a point light and fill the diffuse, ambient, and specular RGB values to a value of 1.0. By setting the *dvPosition.x*, *dvPosition.y*, and *dvPosition.z* values, you position the light in the scene.

```
//
// m_pd3dDevice is a valid pointer to an IDirect3DDevice7
// interface.
//
D3DLIGHT7 d3dLight;
HRESULT   hr;
//
// Initialize the structure.
//
ZeroMemory(&d3dLight, sizeof(D3DLIGHT7));
//
// Set up for a white point light.
//
d3dLight.dltType = D3DLIGHT_POINT;
d3dLight.dcvDiffuse.r = 1.0f;
d3dLight.dcvDiffuse.g = 1.0f;
d3dLight.dcvDiffuse.b = 1.0f;
d3dLight.dcvAmbient.r = 1.0f;
d3dLight.dcvAmbient.g = 1.0f;
d3dLight.dcvAmbient.b = 1.0f;
d3dLight.dcvSpecular.r = 1.0f;
d3dLight.dcvSpecular.g = 1.0f;
d3dLight.dcvSpecular.b = 1.0f;


// Position the point light high in the scene and behind the
// viewer. These coordinates are in world space, so the
// viewer can be anywhere in world space too.
// For the purposes of this example, assume the viewer
// is at the origin of world space.
d3dLight.dvPosition.x = 0.0f;
```

```
d3dLight.dvPosition.y = 1000.0f;
d3dLight.dvPosition.z = -100.0f;

// Don't attenuate.
d3dLight.dvAttenuation0 = 1.0f;
d3dLight.dvRange = D3DLIGHT_RANGE_MAX;

// Set the property information for the first light.
hr = m_pd3dDevice->SetLight(0, d3dLight);
if (FAILED(hr))
{
    // Code to handle the error goes here.
}
```

Color for Lights and Materials

In Direct3D, color is described using four components: red (R), green (G), blue (B), and alpha (A). The D3DCOLORVALUE structure holds the values for each component describing a particular color. Each of its members holds a floating-point value that usually ranges between 0.0 through 1.0 inclusive.

When defining a color for a light, the color values represent the amount of each light component the light emits. Lights use only the three RGB components, and not the A component. A value of 0.0 for an RGB component is equivalent to *off,* and a value of 1.0 indicates a value of *fully on.* Combining these values produces a final color for a light. An RGB triplet value of (1.0, 1.0, 1.0) defines a bright white light, (0.0, 0.0, 0.0) defines a light that emits no light, (0.0, 0.0, 1.0) defines a bright blue light, and (1.0, 0.0, 1.0) defines a bright purple light. Other combinations produce other colors of light.

Beyond the typical 0.0 through 1.0 range of values, Direct3D also allows you to specify negative values for the light's color components, so you can create *dark lights,* which are used to remove light from a scene. Additionally, you can set values greater than 1.0 to define a very bright light.

When describing a color for a material, the color component values define the amount of each light component that is reflected by a surface that uses the material. For example, a material with RGB values of (1.0, 1.0, 1.0) reflects all the light that hits it, and a material with RGB values of (0.0, 0.0, 0.0) reflects no light. So if you shine a red light on an object with a blue material, the object won't be affected by the light.

Types of Lights

Direct3D provides three types of direct lights: directional lights, point lights, and spotlights.

The D3DLIGHTTYPE enumerated type is used to define the light type. This enumerated type is used with the D3DLIGHT7 structure.

```
typedef enum _D3DLIGHTTYPE {
    D3DLIGHT_POINT        = 1,
    D3DLIGHT_SPOT         = 2,
    D3DLIGHT_DIRECTIONAL  = 3,
    D3DLIGHT_FORCE_DWORD  = 0x7fffffff,
} D3DLIGHTTYPE;
```

- **D3DLIGHT_POINT** Light is a point source. The light has a position in space and radiates light in all directions.

- **D3DLIGHT_SPOT** Light is a spotlight source. This light is something like a point light except that the illumination is limited to a cone. This light type has a direction and several other parameters that determine the shape of the cone it produces. For information about these parameters, see the D3DLIGHT7 structure.

- **D3DLIGHT_DIRECTIONAL** Light is a directional source. Using this light type is equivalent to using a point light source at an infinite distance.

- **D3DLIGHT_FORCE_DWORD** Forces this enumerated type to be 32 bits.

Directional Lights

Directional lights represent lights that are at an effectively infinite distance (for example, the sun) and thus have only color and direction, not position. These lights give off parallel light so that all the light they produce moves through a scene in the same direction. These lights are not affected by attenuation or range. Because of this, Direct3D uses only the color and direction you define for computing vertex colors. These lights are the least computationally intensive lights available in Direct3D, so using them strategically can help accelerate your applications.

Point Lights

Point lights are lights that give off light in all directions equally from a particular point, as shown in Figure 5-8.

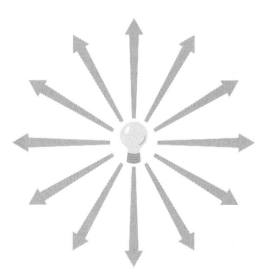

Figure 5-8
Point light

The point light's position in world space and the coordinates of a vertex being lit are used to compute a vector defining the light's direction and the distance the light has traveled. These are also used, along with the vertex normal, to compute how the light affects the illumination of a surface. An example of a point light is a standard light bulb. These light types are affected by attenuation and range, and they illuminate any 3D object meshes they affect.

Spotlights

Spotlights are used to simulate real-world lights that have both a point of origin and a direction, such as a desk lamp or a car's headlights. In Direct3D, spotlights produce a light as illustrated in Figure 5-9.

The light that a spotlight emits is composed of a bright inner cone and a larger outer cone, with the light intensity diminishing between the two. Spotlights are affected by falloff (light attenuation that occurs between a spotlight's inner and outer cones), attenuation, and range, which, together with the distance light travels to each vertex, are used in the computation of lighting effects for objects in a scene.

Spotlights are the most computationally expensive of the Direct3D Immediate Mode lights, so you should use these only when you find the realistic lighting that spotlights produce important enough to your application to be worth the computational cost.

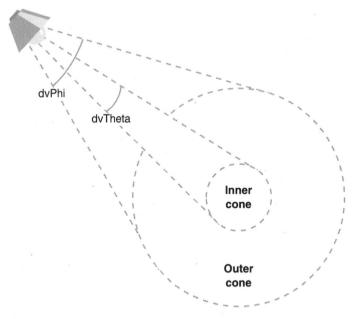

Figure 5-9
Spotlight

Light Properties

You use light properties to define a light's type and color and, for some lights, also the position, direction, attenuation, range, and spotlight effects. These properties control how the light illuminates the contents of a scene. The D3DLIGHT7 structure is used to describe the light properties for all the available light types.

Here's the D3DLIGHT7 structure you use for defining the light type:

```
typedef struct _D3DLIGHT7 {
    D3DLIGHTTYPE    dltType;
    D3DCOLORVALUE   dcvDiffuse;
    D3DCOLORVALUE   dcvSpecular;
    D3DCOLORVALUE   dcvAmbient;
    D3DVECTOR       dvPosition;
    D3DVECTOR       dvDirection;
    D3DVALUE        dvRange;
    D3DVALUE        dvFalloff;
    D3DVALUE        dvAttenuation0;
    D3DVALUE        dvAttenuation1;
    D3DVALUE        dvAttenuation2;
    D3DVALUE        dvTheta;
    D3DVALUE        dvPhi;
} D3DLIGHT7, *LPD3DLIGHT7;
```

Parameter	Description
dltType	Type of the light source. This value is one of the members of the D3DLIGHTTYPE enumerated type.
dcvDiffuse	Diffuse color emitted by the light. This member is a D3DCOLORVALUE structure.
dcvSpecular	Specular color emitted by the light. This member is a D3DCOLORVALUE structure.
dcvAmbient	Ambient color emitted by the light. This member is a D3DCOLORVALUE structure.
dvPosition	Position of the light in world space. This member has no meaning for directional lights.
dvDirection	Direction the light is pointing in world space. This member has meaning only for directional and spot-lights. This vector doesn't need to be normalized, but it should have a nonzero length.
dvRange	Distance beyond which the light has no effect. The maximum allowable value for this member is D3D-LIGHT_RANGE_MAX, which is defined as the square root of FLT_MAX. This member doesn't affect directional lights.
dvFalloff	Decrease in illumination between a spotlight's inner cone (the angle specified by the *dvTheta* member) and the outer edge of the outer cone (the angle specified by the *dvPhi* member). The effect of falloff on the lighting is subtle. Furthermore, a small performance penalty is incurred by shaping the falloff curve. For these reasons, most developers set this value to 1.0.
dvAttenuation0, *dvAttenuation1*, and *dvAttenuation2*	Values specifying how the light intensity changes over distance. (Attenuation doesn't affect directional lights.) These members represent a light's constant, linear, and quadratic attenuation factors. Valid values for these members range from 0.0 to infinity, inclusive.
dvTheta	Angle, in radians, of a spotlight's inner cone—that is, the fully illuminated spotlight cone. This value must be between 0 and the value specified by the *dvPhi* member.
dvPhi	Angle, in radians, defining the outer edge of the spotlight's outer cone. The spotlight doesn't light points outside this cone. This value must be between 0 and pi.

Light Attenuation

Attenuation is how a light's intensity decreases as it reaches the maximum distance you define with the range property. Three of the D3DLIGHT7 structure members—*dvAttenuation0*, *dvAttenuation1*, and *dvAttenuation2*—define the light attenuation effects. These members usually range from 0.0 through 1.0 and are used to define the constant, linear, and quadratic attenuation for a light. If you set the *dvAttenuation1* member to 1.0 and the *dvAttenuation0* and *dvAttenuation2* members to 0.0, the light intensity will attenuate evenly over distance from maximum intensity at the source to zero intensity at the maximum range.

Light Color

You set the color of a light by using the color property in the *dcvDiffuse, dcvSpecular,* and *dcvAmbient* members of the D3DLIGHT7 structure. These members specify RGBA color defining the diffuse, specular, and ambient colors for the object. The *dcvDiffuse* variable defines the diffuse color emitted by the light, the *dcvSpecular* variable the specular color, and the *dcvAmbient* variable the ambient color.

As mentioned earlier, the RGB values typically range from 0.0 through 1.0 (the alpha value is unused), but you can specify numbers below 0.0 for dark lights or greater than 1.0 for very bright lights.

Light Direction

You use this property to define the direction that light emitted by the object travels. Only directional lights and spotlights use it. The direction is defined using a D3DVECTOR structure in the *dvDirection* member of the light's D3DLIGHT7 structure. The direction vector is the distance from an origin. As an example, an overhead light could be defined using a directional light with a direction of <0,–1,0>.

Light Position

You define the light position by using a D3DVECTOR structure in the *dvPosition* member of the D3DLIGHT7 structure. The coordinates are defined in world space. Remember that directional lights don't use the position property because the light hits all objects at the same angle.

Light Range

You use the light range property to define the distance (in world space) at which the meshes are no longer affected by the light an object emits. The *dvRange* member defines the light's maximum range in world space. You typically set this range to the maximum possible value, D3DLIGHT_RANGE_MAX. Directional lights don't use the range property.

Light Type

You use the light type property to define the Direct3D light object type. You set the light type with a value from the D3DLIGHTTYPE enumeration in the *dltType* member of the light's D3DLIGHT7 structure. This light can be any of the three types described earlier: directional lights, point lights, and spotlights.

Spotlight Properties

Only spotlights use the final three properties in the D3DLIGHT7 structure: *dvFalloff*, *dvTheta*, and *dvPhi*. You use these members to define the size of a spotlight's inner and outer cones and to indicate how light decreases between them. (Refer to Figure 5-9 to see how spotlights emit light.)

The *dvFalloff* member defines how the light intensity decreases between the outer edge of the inner cone and the inner edge of the outer cone. Setting *dvFalloff* to 1.0 causes the falloff to transition evenly between the two cones. The *dvTheta* value describes the radian angle of the spotlight's inner cone. The *dvPhi* value describes the angle for the outer cone.

Setting the Light's Properties

To set the preceding properties for a direct light you've created, you use the *IDirect3DDevice7::SetLight* method. Here's the function declaration for this method:

```
HRESULT IDirect3DDevice7::SetLight(
    DWORD dwLightIndex,
    LPD3DLIGHT7 lpLight
);
```

The *IDirect3DDevice7::SetLight* method has a parameter, *lpLight*, which is the address of a D3DLIGHT7 structure used to set the current light data. You set the light's properties by filling a D3DLIGHT7 structure and then calling the *IDirect3DDevice7::SetLight* method with the address of a filled D3DLIGHT7 structure. The *dwLightIndex* parameter defines the index that specifies which light in the scene you're working with.

The following code segment shows how to set up properties for a white point light that doesn't attenuate over distance. It then uses the *IDirect3DDevice7::SetLight* method to enable these new properties.

```
//  g_lpd3dDev variable is a valid pointer to an IDirect3DDevice7
//  interface.
D3DLIGHT7 d3dLight;
HRESULT   hr;     // Initialize the structure.
ZeroMemory(&d3dLight, sizeof(D3DLIGHT7));
```

(continued)

137

```
// Set up for a white point light.
d3dLight.dltType = D3DLIGHT_POINT;
d3dLight.dcvDiffuse.r = 1.0f;
d3dLight.dcvDiffuse.g = 1.0f;
d3dLight.dcvDiffuse.b = 1.0f;
d3dLight.dcvAmbient.r = 1.0f;
d3dLight.dcvAmbient.g = 1.0f;
d3dLight.dcvAmbient.b = 1.0f;
d3dLight.dcvSpecular.r = 1.0f;
d3dLight.dcvSpecular.g = 1.0f;
d3dLight.dcvSpecular.b = 1.0f;

// Set the light high and behind the viewer (who is at
// (0.0,0.0,0.0) - world space origin.
// These coordinates are in world space, so
// the viewer could be anywhere in world space.
d3dLight.dvPosition.x = 0.0f;
d3dLight.dvPosition.y = 1000.0f;
d3dLight.dvPosition.z = -100.0f;
// Don't have the light attenuate.
d3dLight.dvAttenuation0 = 1.0f;
d3dLight.dvRange = D3DLIGHT_RANGE_MAX;

// Set the property information for the first light--index  0.
hr = g_lpd3dDev->SetLight(0, d3dLight);
if (FAILED(hr))
{
    // Code to handle the error goes here.
}
```

Retrieving Light Properties

Once a light has been created, you can acquire the set of lighting properties the device uses for it by using its *IDirect3DDevice7::GetLight* method. You can then use and modify the light as needed. Here's the function declaration for this method:

```
HRESULT IDirect3DDevice7::GetLight(
    DWORD dwLightIndex,
    LPD3DLIGHT7 lpLight
);
```

Parameter	Description
dwLightIndex	Zero-based index of the lighting property set to be retrieved
lpLight	The address of a D3DLIGHT7 structure that will be filled with the retrieved lighting-parameter set

This method takes the index of the light you want information about and the address of a D3DLIGHT7 structure. Here's an example of getting the first light we defined:

```
//
// g_lpd3dDev variable is a valid pointer to an IDirect3DDevice7
// interface.
//
HRESULT hr;
D3DLIGHT7 light;

// Get the property information for the first light.
hr = g_lpd3dDev->GetLight(0, &light);
if (FAILED(hr))
{
    // Handle your error here.
}
```

Enabling and Disabling the Lighting Engine

Direct3D defaults to performing lighting calculations on all vertices, even those that don't contain a vertex normal. (Note that this behavior differs from that of earlier versions of Direct3D, which lit only vertices that contained vertex normals.) You can enable lighting by setting the D3DRENDERSTATE_LIGHTING render state to TRUE or disable it by setting D3DRENDERSTATE_LIGHTING to FALSE.

Enabling and Disabling a Light

Once the lights have been created and placed in the scene, you can enable or disable each set of lighting parameters within a device by using the *IDirect3DDevice7:: LightEnable* method, which is defined as follows:

```
HRESULT LightEnable(
    DWORD dwLightIndex,
    BOOL bEnable
);
```

Parameter	Description
dwLightIndex	Zero-based index of the set of lighting parameters that are the target of this method.
bEnable	Value indicating whether the set of lighting parameters is being enabled or disabled. Set this parameter to TRUE to enable lighting with the parameters at the specified index or FALSE to disable it.

The Code So Far

You're now at the point where you can write an application that creates every object necessary to generate a window capable of rendering and presenting a Direct3D scene (even though we haven't yet covered the actual 3D content). Figure 5-10 shows a screen shot of the output of the code for this chapter. This code generates two lights—one red and one green. Each light moves around the scene and cycles between the point light, directional light, and spotlight types. By watching this code in action, you'll be able to see firsthand how the various lights can be used to illuminate a scene and how different each effect is.

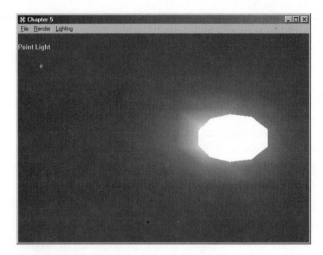

Figure 5-10
The scene with rendered colored lights.

Conclusion

In this chapter, we covered the T&L pipeline, vertices, T&L matrices, the viewport, and lighting. This is a great deal of information to digest, but I hope you now feel that you have enough background information to be comfortable creating and using these objects. You'll use these objects in every 3D project you create, so make sure you look carefully through the code for this chapter.

CHAPTER SIX

Rendering 3D Primitives

Now that you've learned how to set up a 3D environment with Microsoft Direct3D Immediate Mode, you can add the last key piece of the puzzle: creating a 3D object and rendering it. In Chapter 5, you saw all the vertex types available in Direct3D. You also saw how you can allocate the memory for vertices yourself or use vertex buffers to manage this memory for you. In this chapter, you'll use these vertices to create what's known as a *3D primitive*.

A 3D primitive is an object composed of a group of vertices. The most basic primitive you can create is a *point list,* which is nothing more than a collection of single-pixel points. You can also create and render a *line list*, which is a collection of 1-pixel-thick lines. Usually, however, you create 3D primitives that are *triangles*. Direct3D uses triangles (rather than another kind of polygon) to describe the faces of 3D objects because triangles are always coplanar and convex (which means that they are easy to render quickly). Direct3D lets you combine triangles to create more complex polygons and meshes. By using large numbers of triangles, you can approximate curved surfaces such as spheres.

The *BeginScene* and *EndScene* Methods

Before getting into the details of rendering primitives, you should know about *BeginScene* and *EndScene*. In Direct3D, you indicate that you want to begin rendering a scene by using the *IDirect3DDevice7::BeginScene* method. This method tells DirectX to verify the rendering data and make sure the rendering surfaces are set up correctly.

After using this method to begin the scene, you can begin using the Direct3D methods to render the primitives constituting the objects in your scene. If you call these methods before calling *BeginScene*, Direct3D will return

D3DERR_SCENE_NOT_IN_SCENE. Once your rendering is complete, you need to call *IDirect3DDevice7::EndScene* to clear the internal flag that indicates the scene is in progress, flushes the cached data, and makes sure the rendering surfaces are OK.

You need to wrap all your rendering method calls with the *BeginScene/ EndScene* pair. If *BeginScene* fails, the scene won't begin and any calls to *EndScene* will fail (since you didn't start the scene in the first place). If a surface isn't restored before a call to *BeginScene*, it will return DDERR_SURFACELOST. If a surface is lost during rendering, *EndScene* will return this error value also and calls to the scene methods will return errors also. Note that after *BeginScene* succeeds, if an error is returned during scene rendering, you need to call *EndScene* to clean up your rendering process.

One important point to remember is that you must always end rendering one scene before beginning another. If you attempt to nest *BeginScene/EndScene* pairs, the D3DERR_SCENE_IN_SCENE error will be returned. You'll also get this error if you call *EndScene* without calling *BeginScene*.

Indexed and Nonindexed Primitives

Immediate Mode offers two ways of grouping the vertices that define a primitive: using *nonindexed primitives* and using *indexed primitives*. To create a nonindexed primitive, you fill an array with an *ordered* list of vertices. By ordered, I mean that the order of the vertices in the array indicates how to build the triangles. The first triangle consists of the first three vertices in the array, the second triangle consists of the next three vertices, and so on. This means that vertices can't be shared by multiple triangles. If you have two triangles that are connected, you'll have to specify the same vertices multiple times. To create an indexed primitive, you fill an array with an *unordered* list of vertices and create a second array with an ordered list of indices into the unordered array. With indexed primitives, the order of vertices in the array isn't important. Instead, the order of the indices in the index array indicates how to build the triangles. The first triangle consists of the vertices referenced by the first three indices in the index array, the second triangle consists of the vertices referenced by the next three indices, and so forth. This means that vertices can be shared by multiple triangles, simply by having multiple entries in the index array refer to the same vertex. Triangle strips and fans, discussed later in this chapter, share vertices also, so you should choose between indexed and nonindexed primitives based on a 3D object's structure.

Most 3D models share a number of vertices. Therefore, you can save memory, bandwidth, and CPU time by sharing these vertices among multiple triangles (or lines). When 3D models share vertices, indexed vertices are quite useful. However, be aware that some vertices that look like candidates for sharing actually aren't. A cube is a classic example of this. It's tempting to use only 8 vertices and share them among the 12 triangles needed to form a cube. But if you do this, you'll have problems with the vertices' normal vectors. The face of each triangle has a vector, called a *face normal,* that is perpendicular to the face's plane. The face normal points away from the front side of the triangle's face, which in Direct3D is the only visible side. Because normals are defined per vertex rather than per face, two triangles with different normals won't be able to share a vertex. Well, they *could,* but the shared vertex would have only one normal, so the lighting effect probably wouldn't be what you want. In the case of the cube, it's actually better to use 24 vertices, which is still better than the 36 vertices that you'd need for the 12 triangles if you didn't use indexing. Figure 6-1 illustrates how these normals are organized.

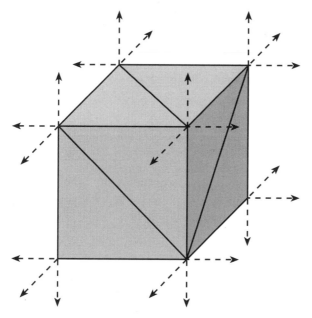

Figure 6-1
Vertex normals of a cube's surface

The DrawPrimitive Methods

You might be starting to get the impression that there are a lot of different cases to deal with when rendering primitives. You've seen that vertices can be stored in three ways: user arrays, strided vertices, and vertex buffers. And you've seen that Direct3D can render three kinds of primitives: points, lines, and triangles. Lines can be specified in two ways: line lists and line strips. Triangles can be specified in three ways: lists, strips, and fans. Finally, primitives can be indexed or nonindexed. That adds up to a lot of different ways to render primitives! The six DrawPrimitive methods of the *IDirect3DDevice7* interface can handle all these cases. Table 6-1 shows that a different method exists for each combination of vertex type and indexing type.

Table 6-1   Methods for Rendering Primitives

Type of Primitive	Normal User Vertices	Strided User Vertices	Vertex Buffer
Nonindexed	*DrawPrimitive*	*DrawPrimitiveStrided*	*DrawPrimitiveVB*
Indexed	*DrawIndexedPrimitive*	*DrawIndexedPrimitiveStrided*	*DrawIndexedPrimitiveVB*

Let's take a closer look at each of these methods.

DrawPrimitive

The *IDirect3DDevice7::DrawPrimitive* method renders the array of vertices you provide as a sequence of geometric primitives of whichever type you specify. Here's the function declaration for this method:

```
HRESULT IDirect3DDevice7::DrawPrimitive(
    D3DPRIMITIVETYPE dptPrimitiveType,
    DWORD dwVertexTypeDesc,
    LPVOID lpvVertices,
    DWORD dwVertexCount,
    DWORD dwFlags
);
```

Parameter	Description
dptPrimitiveType	The type of primitive that this command will render. This primitive type must be one of the members of the D3DPRIMITIVETYPE enumerated type.
dwVertexTypeDesc	Holds a combination of the flexible vertex format flags that defines the vertex format this set of primitives will use.
lpvVertices	A pointer to the array of vertices to use in the primitive sequence.
dwVertexCount	Holds the number of vertices to draw in the array. The maximum value you can specify here is D3DMAXNUM-VERTICES (65,535).
dwFlags	Set this parameter to 0 to render the primitive without waiting, or set it to D3DDP_WAIT to cause the method to wait until the polygons have been rendered before it returns. By default, the method returns as soon as it sends the polygons to the video card. Use the D3DDP_WAIT flag for debugging. Applications shouldn't use the D3DDP_WAIT flag to wait for a scene to be up-to-date before rendering.

DrawPrimitiveStrided

The *IDirect3DDevice7::DrawPrimitiveStrided* method is used to render an array of strided vertices as a sequence of geometric primitives. You need to verify that the vertices you want rendered use the format you specify. Because Direct3D doesn't check whether the vertex size and stride match the specified flexible vertex format, you need to make sure they do or a memory fault error will probably occur.

Here's the function declaration for this method:

```
HRESULT DrawPrimitiveStrided(
    D3DPRIMITIVETYPE dptPrimitiveType,
    DWORD    dwVertexTypeDesc,
    LPD3DDRAWPRIMITIVESTRIDEDDATA lpVertexArray,
    DWORD    dwVertexCount,
    DWORD    dwFlags
);
```

Parameter	Description
dptPrimitiveType	Type of primitive to be rendered by this command. This parameter must be one of the members of the D3DPRIMITIVETYPE enumerated type.
dwVertexTypeDesc	A combination of flexible vertex format flags that describes the vertex format.
lpVertexArray	Address of a D3DDRAWPRIMITIVESTRIDEDDATA structure that contains pointers and memory strides for the vertex components for this primitive, in the format specified by the flags in *dwVertexTypeDesc*.
dwVertexCount	Number of vertices in the array at *lpVertexArray*. The maximum number of vertices allowed is D3DMAXNUM-VERTICES (0xFFFF).
dwFlags	Set to 0 to render the primitive without waiting, or use the D3DDP_WAIT flag, which causes the method to wait until the polygons have been rendered before it returns, instead of returning as soon as the polygons have been sent to the card. (On scene-capture cards, the method returns as soon as the card responds.) This flag is typically used for debugging. Applications should not attempt to use this flag to ensure that a scene is up-to-date before continuing.

DrawPrimitiveVB

The *IDirect3DDevice7::DrawPrimitiveVB* method is used to render an array of vertices in a vertex buffer as a sequence of geometric primitives. Here's the function declaration for this method:

```
HRESULT DrawPrimitiveVB(
    D3DPRIMITIVETYPE        d3dptPrimitiveType,
    LPDIRECT3DVERTEXBUFFER7 lpd3dVertexBuffer,
    DWORD dwStartVertex,
    DWORD dwNumVertices,
    DWORD dwFlags
);
```

Parameter	Description
dptPrimitiveType	Type of primitive to be rendered by this command. This parameter must be one of the members of the D3DPRIMITIVETYPE enumerated type.
lpd3dVertexBuffer	Address of the *IDirect3DVertexBuffer7* interface for the vertex buffer that contains the array of vertices. Vertices can be transformed or untransformed, optimized or unoptimized.
dwStartVertex	Index value of the first vertex in the primitive. The highest possible starting index is D3DMAXNUMVERTICES (0xFFFF). In debug builds, specifying a starting index value that exceeds this limit causes the method to fail and return DDERR_INVALIDPARAMS.
dwNumVertices	Number of vertices to be rendered. The maximum number of vertices allowed is D3DMAXNUMVERTICES (0xFFFF).
dwFlags	Set to 0 to render the primitive without waiting, or use the D3DDP_WAIT flag, which causes the method to wait until the polygons have been rendered before it returns, instead of returning as soon as the polygons have been sent to the card. (On scene-capture cards, the method returns as soon as the card responds.)
	This flag is typically used for debugging. Applications should not attempt to use this flag to ensure that a scene is up-to-date before continuing.

DrawIndexedPrimitive

The *IDirect3DDevice7::DrawIndexedPrimitive* method is designed to render the geometric primitive you specify based on indexing into an array of vertices rather than on using an array of vertices directly. Here's the function declaration for this method:

```
HRESULT IDirect3DDevice7::DrawIndexedPrimitive(
    D3DPRIMITIVETYPE d3dptPrimitiveType,
    DWORD dwVertexTypeDesc,
    LPVOID lpvVertices,
    DWORD dwVertexCount,
    LPWORD lpwIndices,
```

(continued)

```
    DWORD dwIndexCount,
    DWORD dwFlags
);
```

Parameter	Description
d3dptPrimitiveType	The type of primitive that this command will render. (This primitive type must be one of the members of the D3DPRIMITIVETYPE enumerated type.) The D3DPT_POINTLIST member of D3DPRIMITIVE-TYPE isn't indexed, so you can't use it.
dwVertexTypeDesc	Holds a combination of the flexible vertex format flags that defines the vertex format this set of primitives will use.
lpvVertices	A pointer to an array of vertices you want to use in the primitive sequence.
dwVertexCount	Holds the total number of vertices in the array the *lpvVertices* parameter points to.
lpwIndices	A pointer to a list of WORDs used to index the vertex list when creating the geometry to render.
dwIndexCount	Used to define the number of indices provided for creating the geometry. The maximum value you can use here is D3DMAXNUMVERTICES (65,535).
dwFlags	Set this parameter to 0 to render the primitive without waiting, or set it to D3DDP_WAIT to cause the method to wait until the polygons have been rendered before it returns. By default, the method returns as soon as it sends the polygons to the video card. Use the D3DDP_WAIT flag for debugging. Applications shouldn't use the D3DDP_WAIT flag to wait for a scene to be up-to-date before rendering.

DrawIndexedPrimitiveStrided

The *IDirect3DDevice7::DrawIndexedPrimitiveStrided* method allows you to render a geometric primitive, based on indexing into an array of strided vertices. Here's the function declaration for this method:

```
HRESULT DrawIndexedPrimitiveStrided(
    D3DPRIMITIVETYPE d3dptPrimitiveType,
    DWORD    dwVertexTypeDesc,
    LPD3DDRAWPRIMITIVESTRIDEDDATA lpVertexArray,
    DWORD    dwVertexCount,
```

```
    LPWORD  lpwIndices,
    DWORD   dwIndexCount,
    DWORD   dwFlags
);
```

Parameter	Description
d3dptPrimitiveType	Type of primitive to be rendered by this command. This parameter must be one of the members of the D3DPRIMITIVETYPE enumerated type. The D3DPT_POINTLIST member of D3DPRIMITIVETYPE is not indexed.
dwVertexTypeDesc	A combination of flexible vertex format flags that describes the vertex format for this primitive.
lpVertexArray	Address of a **D3DDRAWPRIMITIVESTRIDEDDATA** structure that contains pointers and memory strides for the vertex components of this primitive, in the format specified by the flags in *dwVertexTypeDesc*.
dwVertexCount	Defines the number of vertices in the list. This parameter is used differently from the *dwVertexCount* parameter in the *IDirect3DDevice7::DrawPrimitive* method. In that method, the *dwVertexCount* parameter gives the number of vertices to draw, but here it gives the total number of vertices in the array pointed to by the *lpVertexArray* parameter. When you call *IDirect-3DDevice7::DrawIndexedPrimitiveStrided*, you specify the number of vertices to draw in the *dwIndexCount* parameter.
lpwIndices	Pointer to a list of WORDs that are to be used to index into the specified vertex list when creating the geometry to render.
dwIndexCount	Specifies the number of indices provided for creating the geometry. The maximum number of indices allowed is D3DMAXNUMVERTICES (0xFFFF).
dwFlags	Set to 0 to render the primitive without waiting, or use the D3DDP_WAIT flag, which causes the method to wait until the polygons have been rendered before it returns, instead of returning as soon as the polygons have been sent to the card. (On scene-capture cards, the method returns as soon as the card responds.) This flag is typically used for debugging. Applications should not attempt to use this flag to ensure that a scene is up-to-date before continuing.

DrawIndexedPrimitiveVB

The *IDirect3DDevice7::DrawIndexedPrimitiveVB* method is used to render a geometric primitive using indexing into an array of vertices within a vertex buffer. Here's the function declaration for this method:

```
HRESULT DrawIndexedPrimitiveVB(
    D3DPRIMITIVETYPE         d3dptPrimitiveType,
    LPDIRECT3DVERTEXBUFFER7  lpd3dVertexBuffer,
    DWORD   dwStartVertex,
    DWORD   dwNumVertices,
    LPWORD  lpwIndices,
    DWORD   dwIndexCount,
    DWORD   dwFlags
);
```

Parameter	Description
d3dptPrimitiveType	The type of primitive to be rendered by this command. This parameter must be one of the members of the D3DPRIMITIVETYPE enumerated type. The D3DPT_POINTLIST member of D3DPRIMITIVETYPE is not indexed.
lpd3dVertexBuffer	The address of the *IDirect3DVertexBuffer7* interface for the vertex buffer that contains the array of vertices. Vertices can be transformed or untransformed, optimized or unoptimized.
dwStartVertex	Index of the first vertex in the vertex buffer to be rendered.
dwNumVertices	Total number of vertices in the vertex buffer to be rendered.
lpwIndices	The address of an array of WORDs that is used to index into the vertices in the vertex buffer. The values in the array must index vertices within the range [0, *dwNumVertices* − 1].
dwIndexCount	The number of indices in the array at *lpwIndices*. The maximum number of indices allowed is D3DMAXNUMVERTICES (0xFFFF).

(continued)

Parameter	Description
dwFlags	Set to 0 to render the primitive without waiting, or use the D3DDP_WAIT flag, which causes the method to wait until the polygons have been rendered before it returns, instead of returning as soon as the polygons have been sent to the card. (On scene-capture cards, the method returns as soon as the card responds.)
	This flag is typically used for debugging. Applications should not attempt to use this flag to ensure that a scene is up-to-date before continuing.

Primitive Types

The D3DPRIMITIVETYPE enumerated type used by the DrawPrimitive methods lists all the primitives that these methods support. Here's the definition for this type:

```
typedef enum _D3DPRIMITIVETYPE {
    D3DPT_POINTLIST      = 1,
    D3DPT_LINELIST       = 2,
    D3DPT_LINESTRIP      = 3,
    D3DPT_TRIANGLELIST   = 4,
    D3DPT_TRIANGLESTRIP  = 5,
    D3DPT_TRIANGLEFAN    = 6
    D3DPT_FORCE_DWORD    = 0x7fffffff,
} D3DPRIMITIVETYPE;
```

These are the members of the D3DPRIMITIVETYPE enumerated type:

- **D3DPT_POINTLIST**   Causes the DrawPrimitive methods to render the vertices as a collection of isolated points.

- **D3DPT_LINELIST**   Causes the DrawPrimitive methods to render the vertices as a list of isolated straight-line segments. You must specify an even number of vertices that is greater than or equal to 2.

- **D3DPT_LINESTRIP**   Causes the DrawPrimitive methods to render the vertices as a single polyline. You must specify at least two vertices.

■ **D3DPT_TRIANGLELIST** Causes the DrawPrimitive methods to render the vertices as a sequence of isolated triangles. Each group of three vertices defines a separate triangle. You must specify at least three vertices and ensure that the number of vertices is divisible by 3. The winding-order render state defines how backface culling (backface removal) is performed. (We'll discuss backface culling and the winding-order render state later in the chapter.)

■ **D3DPT_TRIANGLESTRIP** Causes the DrawPrimitive methods to render the vertices as a triangle strip. You must provide at least three vertices. The DrawPrimitive method will take the vertices of even-numbered triangles out of order, to ensure that the triangles are drawn in a clockwise orientation. (For more information, see the section "Culling State" later in the chapter.)

■ **D3DPT_TRIANGLEFAN** Causes the DrawPrimitive methods to render the vertices as a triangle fan. You must define at least three vertices.

■ **D3DPT_FORCE_DWORD** Forces this enumerated type into a 32-bit type.

The following sections cover each of these primitive types, which you can use to create the 3D content for your applications.

Point Lists

You can use the first primitive type, the point list, to define a collection of vertices that are rendered as isolated points. You can use a point list in a 3D scene to represent objects such as dotted lines.

To create a point list, you need to fill an array of vertices. The code that follows shows an example of how to perform this task. Although I show a simple six-element list, you could use a point list to create a star field if you wanted; of course, your list would need many more points. I tend to create star fields using a texture-wrapped sphere surrounding the 3D world because it allows me to create a number of effects using texture animation.

```
const DWORD TOTAL_VERTICES = 6;
D3DVERTEX lpVertices[TOTAL_VERTICES];
⋮
D3DVECTOR v1(-1, 4, 0);
D3DVECTOR v2( 2,-1, 0);
D3DVECTOR v3( 1, 3, 0);
D3DVECTOR v4(-3,-2, 0);
D3DVECTOR v5( 3, 2, 0);
D3DVECTOR v6( 2, 1, 0);
D3DVECTOR vNormal(0, 0, -1);
```

```
lpVertices[0] = D3DVERTEX(v1, vNormal, 0, 0);
lpVertices[1] = D3DVERTEX(v2, vNormal, 0, 0);
lpVertices[2] = D3DVERTEX(v3, vNormal, 0, 0);
lpVertices[3] = D3DVERTEX(v4, vNormal, 0, 0);
lpVertices[4] = D3DVERTEX(v5, vNormal, 0, 0);
lpVertices[5] = D3DVERTEX(v6, vNormal, 0, 0);
```

Once you've defined the point list, you can render it by using the *IDirect-3DDevice7::DrawPrimitive* method discussed earlier. The code for rendering the point list follows. As you also learned earlier in the chapter, any call you make to *IDirect3DDevice7::DrawPrimitive* must occur between calls to *IDirect3D-Device7::BeginScene* and *IDirect3DDevice7::EndScene*.

```
if (FAILED(lpDirect3DDevice7->BeginScene()))
{
    // Handle any error here.
}
⋮
if (FAILED(lpDirect3DDevice7->DrawPrimitive(D3DPT_POINTLIST,
    D3DFVF_VERTEX, lpVertices, TOTAL_VERTICES, 0)))
{
    // Handle any error here.
}
⋮
if (FAILED(lpDirect3DDevice7->EndScene()))
{
    // Handle any error here.
}
```

You can apply materials and textures to a point list, but one tiny pixel on the screen probably won't represent a texture or a material very well. Also, be aware that these points are always 1 pixel in diameter regardless of their distance from the camera. To produce bigger points, you need to use small triangles to represent them. When the rendering is complete, you'll see a scene similar to that shown in Figure 6-2.

Figure 6-2
A rendered point list

Line Lists

You can use the second primitive type, the line list, to define a group of straight-line segments. You can use this type to define groups of simple single-line objects.

To create a line list, simply fill an array of vertices as shown in the next code snippet. Always remember that the amount of vertices defined in a line list must be an even number that is greater than or equal to 2. This example shows the code needed to define three lines:

```
const DWORD TOTAL_VERTICES = 6;
D3DVERTEX lpVertices[TOTAL_VERTICES];
⋮
D3DVECTOR v1(-10, 10, 0);
D3DVECTOR v2( -8, -5, 0);
D3DVECTOR v3( -4,  3, 0);
D3DVECTOR v4(  1, -6, 0);
D3DVECTOR v5(  2, -1, 0);
D3DVECTOR v6( 12,  9, 0);
D3DVECTOR vNormal(0, 0, -1);

lpVertices[0] = D3DVERTEX(v1, vNormal, 0, 0);
lpVertices[1] = D3DVERTEX(v2, vNormal, 0, 0);
lpVertices[2] = D3DVERTEX(v3, vNormal, 0, 0);
lpVertices[3] = D3DVERTEX(v4, vNormal, 0, 0);
lpVertices[4] = D3DVERTEX(v5, vNormal, 0, 0);
lpVertices[5] = D3DVERTEX(v6, vNormal, 0, 0);
```

Once you've defined the line list, you can render it by using the *IDirect-3DDevice7::DrawPrimitive* method as you did with the point list. The code for rendering the line list follows. When the rendering is complete, you'll see a scene similar to that shown in Figure 6-3.

```
if (FAILED(lpDirect3DDevice7->BeginScene()))
{
    // Handle any error here.
}
⋮
if (FAILED(lpDirect3DDevice7->DrawPrimitive(D3DPT_LINELIST,
    D3DFVF_VERTEX, lpVertices, TOTAL_VERTICES, 0)))
{
    // Handle any error here.
}
⋮
if (FAILED(lpDirect3DDevice7->EndScene()))
{
    // Handle any error here.
}
```

Figure 6-3
A rendered line list

As with point lists, you can apply materials and textures to line lists. And like points, which always remain 1 pixel in size, lines are always 1 pixel wide. If you need to render wider lines or if you want the width to vary according to a line's distance from the camera, you should instead use pairs of thin triangles to represent the lines.

Line Strips

You can use the third primitive type, the line strip, to describe a series of connected line segments. You can use line strips to create polygons that are open—in other words, polygons whose last vertex isn't connected to the first vertex with a line segment.

You can create a line strip by filling an array of vertices the same way you did for point and line lists. This next code segment presents an example of how to fill this list:

```
const DWORD TOTAL_VERTICES = 5;
D3DVERTEX lpVertices[TOTAL_VERTICES];
⋮
D3DVECTOR v1(-8, -8, 0);
D3DVECTOR v2(-3, -9, 0);
D3DVECTOR v3(-1,  0, 0);
D3DVECTOR v4( 9, -2, 0);
D3DVECTOR v5( 7, -6, 0);
D3DVECTOR vNormal(0, 0, -1);

lpVertices[0] = D3DVERTEX(v1, vNormal, 0, 0);
lpVertices[1] = D3DVERTEX(v2, vNormal, 0, 0);
lpVertices[2] = D3DVERTEX(v3, vNormal, 0, 0);
lpVertices[3] = D3DVERTEX(v4, vNormal, 0, 0);
lpVertices[4] = D3DVERTEX(v5, vNormal, 0, 0);
```

Once you've defined the line strip, you can render it by using the *IDirect-3DDevice7::DrawPrimitive* method as you did for the point and line lists. The code to render the line strip follows, and Figure 6-4 shows the line strip produced by this code.

```
if (FAILED(lpDirect3DDevice7->BeginScene()))
{
    // Handle any error here.
}
⋮
if (FAILED(lpDirect3DDevice7->DrawPrimitive(D3DPT_LINESTRIP,
    D3DFVF_VERTEX, lpVertices, TOTAL_VERTICES, 0)))
{
    // Handle any error here.
}
⋮
if (FAILED(lpDirect3DDevice7->EndScene()))
{
    // Handle any error here.
}
```

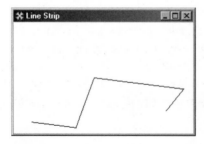

Figure 6-4
A rendered line strip

Triangle Lists

You can use the fourth primitive type, the triangle list, to create lists of isolated triangles. Always remember that the number of vertices defined in a triangle list must be divisible by 3. You can use these lists to create objects that are made up of unconnected pieces. A code example that defines a list of two triangles follows:

```
const DWORD TOTAL_VERTICES = 6;
D3DVERTEX lpVertices[TOTAL_VERTICES];
⋮
D3DVECTOR v1(-10, -5, 0);
```

```
D3DVECTOR v2( -5,  5, 0);
D3DVECTOR v3(  0, -5, 0);
D3DVECTOR v4(  1, -5, 0);
D3DVECTOR v5(  6,  5, 0);
D3DVECTOR v6( 11, -5, 0);
D3DVECTOR vNormal(0, 0, -1);

lpVertices[0] = D3DVERTEX(v1, vNormal, 0, 0);
lpVertices[1] = D3DVERTEX(v2, vNormal, 0, 0);
lpVertices[2] = D3DVERTEX(v3, vNormal, 0, 0);
lpVertices[3] = D3DVERTEX(v4, vNormal, 0, 0);
lpVertices[4] = D3DVERTEX(v5, vNormal, 0, 0);
lpVertices[5] = D3DVERTEX(v6, vNormal, 0, 0);
```

As with the other primitive types, you can render the triangle list by using the *IDirect3DDevice7::DrawPrimitive* method. The following code shows an example of how to render a triangle list. Figure 6-5 shows the result.

```
if (FAILED(lpDirect3DDevice7->BeginScene()))
{
    // Handle any error here.
}
⋮
if (FAILED(lpDirect3DDevice7->DrawPrimitive(D3DPT_TRIANGLELIST,
    D3DFVF_VERTEX, lpVertices, TOTAL_VERTICES, 0)))
{
    // Handle error here.
}
⋮
if (FAILED(lpDirect3DDevice7->EndScene()))
{
    // Handle any error here.
}
```

Figure 6-5
A rendered triangle list

Triangle Strips

You can use the fifth primitive type, the triangle strip, to create a series of connected triangles. When you use connected triangles, the code will have to specify shared vertices only once. For example, you need only six vertices to define the triangle strip illustrated in Figure 6-6, which is composed of four triangles.

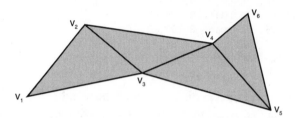

Figure 6-6
A triangle strip

As Figure 6-6 shows, the first three triangles share v_3, two of the triangles share v_4, and so on. By default, Direct3D culls triangles that are specified in counterclockwise order. Therefore, when rendering triangle strips, Direct3D reads the vertices out of order for every even triangle in the strip. To render the triangle strip in Figure 6-6, Direct3D reads vertices from the vertex list as follows: v_1, v_2, and v_3 for the first triangle; v_2, v_4, and v_3 for the second triangle; v_3, v_4, and v_5 for the third triangle; v_4, v_6, and v_5 for the fourth triangle; and so on. That way, the front side of the strip is always shown when it faces the camera, and the back side of the strip is always culled.

Triangle strips make efficient use of memory and processing time, so it's a good idea to use them whenever possible. The following code segment produces the triangle strip illustrated in Figure 6-6 by filling an array of vertices, just as you did with the other primitive types:

```
const DWORD TOTAL_VERTICES=6;
D3DVERTEX lpVertices[TOTAL_VERTICES];
    :
D3DVECTOR v1(-10, -5, 0);
D3DVECTOR v2( -5,  7, 0);
D3DVECTOR v3(  0, -1, 0);
D3DVECTOR v4(  6,  4, 0);
D3DVECTOR v5( 11, -7, 0);
D3DVECTOR v6(  9,  9, 0);
D3DVECTOR vNormal(0, 0, -1);
```

```
lpVertices[0] = D3DVERTEX(v1, vNormal, 0, 0);
lpVertices[1] = D3DVERTEX(v2, vNormal, 0, 0);
lpVertices[2] = D3DVERTEX(v3, vNormal, 0, 0);
lpVertices[3] = D3DVERTEX(v4, vNormal, 0, 0);
lpVertices[4] = D3DVERTEX(v5, vNormal, 0, 0);
lpVertices[5] = D3DVERTEX(v6, vNormal, 0, 0);
```

This next code snippet shows how to render a triangle strip by using the *IDirect3DDevice7::DrawPrimitive* method, just as you've done with all the other primitive types. Figure 6-7 illustrates the rendered strip.

```
if (FAILED(lpDirect3DDevice7->BeginScene()))
{
    // Handle any error here.
}
⋮
if (FAILED(lpDirect3DDevice7->DrawPrimitive(D3DPT_TRIANGLESTRIP,
    D3DFVF_VERTEX, lpVertices, TOTAL_VERTICES, 0)))
{
    // Handle error here.
}
⋮
if (FAILED(lpDirect3DDevice7->EndScene()))
{
    // Handle any error here.
}
```

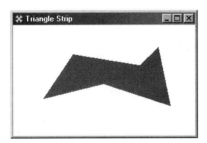

Figure 6-7
The rendered triangle strip

Triangle Fans

The sixth primitive type, the triangle fan, is a lot like a triangle strip. The difference is that all the triangles share one vertex, as Figure 6-8 shows.

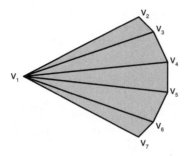

Figure 6-8
A triangle fan

Here's an example of the code needed to fill an array that defines a triangle fan:

```
const DWORD TOTAL_VERTICES = 6;
D3DVERTEX lpVertices[TOTAL_VERTICES];
⋮
D3DVECTOR v1( -3,  0,  0);
D3DVECTOR v2(  1,  4,  0);
D3DVECTOR v3(1.5,  3,  0);
D3DVECTOR v4(  2,  1,  0);
D3DVECTOR v5(  2, -1,  0);
D3DVECTOR v6(1.5, -3,  0);
D3DVECTOR v7(  1, -4,  0);
D3DVECTOR vNormal(0, 0, -1);

lpVertices[0] = D3DVERTEX(v1, vNormal, 0, 0);
lpVertices[1] = D3DVERTEX(v2, vNormal, 0, 0);
lpVertices[2] = D3DVERTEX(v3, vNormal, 0, 0);
lpVertices[3] = D3DVERTEX(v4, vNormal, 0, 0);
lpVertices[4] = D3DVERTEX(v5, vNormal, 0, 0);
lpVertices[5] = D3DVERTEX(v6, vNormal, 0, 0);
lpVertices[6] = D3DVERTEX(v7, vNormal, 0, 0);
```

The code can then render the triangle fan by using the *IDirect3DDevice3:: DrawPrimitive* method you've been using, specifying D3DPT_TRIANGLEFAN as the first parameter. Figure 6-9 shows the rendered triangle fan.

```
if (FAILED(lpDirect3DDevice7->BeginScene()))
{
    // Handle any error here.
}
⋮
if (FAILED(lpDirect3DDevice3->DrawPrimitive(D3DPT_TRIANGLEFAN,
    D3DFVF_VERTEX, lpVertices, TOTAL_VERTICES, 0)))
{
    // Handle any error here.
```

```
}
⋮
if (FAILED(lpDirect3DDevice7->EndScene()))
{
    // Handle any error here.
}
```

Figure 6-9
A rendered triangle fan

Setting Render States

A Direct3D device has dozens of settings that you can change to affect how primitives are rendered. These settings are called *render states*. You can use the *IDirect3D-Device7::SetRenderState* method to change a render state. This method takes as parameters a member of the D3DRENDERSTATETYPE enumerated type and a new value for the specified render state. The meaning of the second parameter is dependent on the value specified for *dwRenderStateType*.

Here's the function declaration for this method:

```
HRESULT IDirect3DDevice7::SetRenderState(
    D3DRENDERSTATETYPE dwRenderStateType,
    DWORD dwRenderState
);
```

Parameter	Description
dwRenderStateType	The device state variable that this function changes. This parameter can be any member of the D3DRENDER-STATETYPE enumerated type.
dwRenderState	The new value for the Direct3DDevice render state. This parameter is dependent on the *dwRenderStateType* parameter.

All the Direct3D render states have default values, so you don't have to set every single render state before you start rendering primitives. The render states that you choose to change will depend on the needs of your program. In some cases, you will set a render state once upon creation of the Direct3D device. In other cases, you will change the render state when the user changes a program setting or when rendering a particular object. As an example, the following code segment uses *SetRenderState* to set the render state for the cull, shade, and fill modes, and the ambient light level of a simple scene.

```
HRESULT CMyD3DApplication::Render()
{
    // Clear the viewport.
    lpDev7->Clear( 0, NULL, D3DCLEAR_TARGET|D3DCLEAR_ZBUFFER,
                   0x000000ff, 1.0f, 0L );

    DWORD dwCullMode  = m_bCull ? D3DCULL_CCW : D3DCULL_NONE;
    DWORD dwShadeMode = m_bFlat ? D3DSHADE_FLAT : D3DSHADE_GOURAUD;
    DWORD dwFillMode  = m_bWire ? D3DFILL_WIREFRAME : D3DFILL_SOLID;
    lpDev7->SetRenderState( D3DRENDERSTATE_CULLMODE,  dwCullMode );
    lpDev7->SetRenderState( D3DRENDERSTATE_SHADEMODE, dwShadeMode );
    lpDev7->SetRenderState( D3DRENDERSTATE_FILLMODE,  dwFillMode );
    lpDev7->SetRenderState( D3DRENDERSTATE_AMBIENT,
                            RGBA_MAKE(128,128,128,128) );

    // Begin the scene.
    if( SUCCEEDED( m_pd3dDevice->BeginScene() ) )
    {
        if( m_pFileObject )
            m_pFileObject->Render( m_pd3dDevice );

        // End the scene.
        m_pd3dDevice->EndScene();
    }

    return S_OK;
}
```

When rendering primitives, keep in mind that 3D acceleration hardware can quickly process a series of primitives that are all the same type, but it can be slowed down by changing the type of rendering more than is necessary. Switching to a different texture map can slow down rendering, as can changing the render state. To maximize performance, try to render all primitives that share a texture (and ideally, the same render states) at once, then change texture (and render state if necessary), then render more primitives, and so on.

The following sections describe the render states that you'll most likely want to use. In subsequent chapters, we'll be covering several of these states in detail, but for now, I'll provide a quick overview of the available states so that you can begin to see how these commands work together.

Alpha Blending States

Alpha blending (which allows the rendering of semitransparent objects) can be activated through the setting of a few render states. You can use the D3DRENDER-STATE_ALPHABLENDENABLE render state to enable alpha transparency blending on devices that support it. The D3DRENDERSTATE_SRCBLEND and D3DRENDERSTATE_DESTBLEND render states define the type of alpha blending that is performed. An example is shown here:

```
//
// Enable alpha blending.
//
lpDev7->SetRenderState(D3DRENDERSTATE_ALPHABLENDENABLE,
                       TRUE);
//
// Set the source blend state.
//
lpDev7->SetRenderState(D3DRENDERSTATE_SRCBLEND,
                       D3DBLEND_SRCCOLOR);
//
// Set the destination blend state.
//
lpDev7->SetRenderState(D3DRENDERSTATE_DESTBLEND,
                       D3DBLEND_INVSRCCOLOR);
```

After setting these states, you can render primitives that contain alpha in their vertex color, material, or texture map. Where the alpha value is 1.0, the object will be opaque. Where the alpha value is 0.0, the object will be transparent. Values between 0.0 and 1.0 will cause the object to be semitransparent.

Alpha Testing State

Alpha testing controls whether pixels are written to the render-target surface—that is, it verifies whether the pixels are accepted or rejected. The D3DRENDERSTATE_ALPHAREF render state lets you use alpha testing to determine whether a color about to be rendered for a pixel is more opaque than the one already at that pixel by using the D3DPCMPCAPS_GREATEREQUAL render state. If the color about to be rendered is more opaque, the pixel is written. If the color isn't more opaque, that pixel is skipped. This approach saves the time required to blend the colors.

The following command sets the current Direct3D device so that it tests each pixel according to an alpha test function:

```
//
// Set the alpha testing state.
//
if (pd3dDeviceDesc.dpcTriCaps.dwAlphaCmpCaps &
    D3DPCMPCAPS_GREATEREQUAL)
{
    lpDev7->SetRenderState( D3DRENDERSTATE_ALPHAREF,
                            (DWORD)0x00000001);
    lpDev7->SetRenderState( D3DRENDERSTATE_ALPHATESTENABLE,
                            TRUE );
    lpDev7->SetRenderState( D3DRENDERSTATE_ALPHAFUNC,
                            D3DCMP_GREATEREQUAL);
}
```

You can set the alpha test function with the D3DRENDERSTATE_ALPHAFUNC enumerated value. You can set a reference alpha value for all pixels to be compared against by using the D3DRENDERSTATE_ALPHAREF render state.

The code to perform alpha testing and determine whether the available device supports alpha testing appears in detail in Chapter 10.

Ambient Lighting State

As mentioned in Chapter 5, ambient light is the light that surrounds the object and emanates from all directions. This lighting is used as the background lighting for the RoadRage application. You control the color of the ambient lighting by using the *IDirect3DDevice7::SetRenderState* method and passing it the enumerated value D3DLIGHTSTATE_AMBIENT as the first parameter. The second parameter is a color in RGBA format. The following code sets the ambient light color:

```
//
// Set the ambient light.
//
D3DCOLOR d3dclrAmbientLightColor = D3DRGBA(1.0f,1.0f,1.0f,1.0f);
lpDev7->SetRenderState(D3DRENDERSTATE_AMBIENT,
                       d3dclrAmbientLightColor);
```

Antialiasing State

Antialiasing makes lines and edges look as smooth as possible on the screen. Direct3D provides a render state for full-scene antialiasing if the Direct3D device supports it but defaults to not performing antialiasing (D3DRENDERSTATE_ ANTIALIAS set to D3DANTIALIAS_NONE, a member of D3DANTIALIAS-MODE, which disables full-screen antialiasing). The following command enables sort-independent antialiasing, which means that antialiasing isn't to depend on the order in which the polygons are rendered:

```
//
// Set up antialiasing.
//
lpDev7->SetRenderState(D3DRENDERSTATE_ANTIALIAS,
    D3DANTIALIAS_SORTINDEPENDENT);
```

Clipping State

Primitives being rendered partially outside the viewport can be clipped. You can disable clipping (it is enabled by default) by setting the D3DRENDERSTATE_ CLIPPING render state to FALSE, as follows:

```
//
// Set the clipping state.
//
lpDev7->SetRenderState(D3DRENDERSTATE_CLIPPING, FALSE);
```

The primitive clipping render state is different than those used for vertices in a vertex buffer.

Color Keying State

You can set a color key to treat the key color as transparent. Once set, whenever a texture is applied to one of the primitives, all the texels that match the key color won't be rendered on the primitive (making the primitive effectively transparent at that point). You can set the color key by using the *IDirectDrawSurface7:: SetColorKey* method for the surface that will be using the color key and then toggle it on and off with a call, as follows:

```
//
// Turn on color keying.
//
lpDev7->SetRenderState(D3DRENDERSTATE_COLORKEYENABLE, FALSE);
```

Setting the second parameter to TRUE enables color keying; setting it to FALSE disables color keying.

Culling State

When you set up a triangle that you want to see both sides of, you usually should make sure that you create *two* triangles instead of one—one that represents the front of the triangle and one that represents the back. You need to do this because Direct3D culls any primitives that are facing away from the camera during rendering. By rendering both the front and back triangles, the triangle is visible from both sides because you've rendered two triangles instead of just one.

Direct3D defaults to culling backfaces with counterclockwise vertices. In other words, Direct3D assumes that you specify the vertices in counterclockwise order when facing the triangle from the side that you want to be visible. You can change the *culling mode* of a Direct3D device by calling *SetRenderState* with render-state type D3DRENDERSTATE_CULLMODE and a constant from the D3DCULL enumerated type. Although you'll rarely need to change the culling mode, you might need to do so in either of these two cases:

- You need to import 3D content that specifies triangles in the counterclockwise direction.

- You're attempting to find out why you can't see an object, so you use D3DCULL_NONE to keep Direct3D from culling any objects.

This next code segment shows how to set the culling mode to cull backfaces with clockwise vertices:

```
//
// Set the culling mode.
//
lpD3DDevice7->SetRenderState(D3DRENDERSTATE_CULLMODE, D3DCULL_CW);
```

You can use the D3DCULL enumerated type just mentioned to define the supported cull modes that specify how backfaces are culled when rendering 3D objects. Here's the definition for this type:

```
typedef enum _D3DCULL {
    D3DCULL_NONE = 1,
    D3DCULL_CW   = 2,
    D3DCULL_CCW  = 3,
    D3DCULL_FORCE_DWORD  = 0x7fffffff,
} D3DCULL;
```

These members have the following uses:

- **D3DCULL_NONE**   Backfaces aren't culled.

- **D3DCULL_CW**   Backfaces with clockwise vertices are culled.

■ **D3DCULL_CCW**   Backfaces with counterclockwise vertices are culled.

■ **D3DCULL_FORCE_DWORD**   Forces this enumerated type to be 32 bits.

Depth-Buffering State

Depth buffering removes hidden lines and surfaces. By default, Direct3D doesn't perform depth buffering. You can set the depth-buffering state by using the D3DRENDERSTATE_ZENABLE render state and passing it one of the members of the D3DZBUFFERTYPE enumerated type. The following code sets the depth-buffer state to enable z-buffering:

```
//
// Enable z-buffering.
//
lpDev7->SetRenderState(D3DRENDERSTATE_ZENABLE, D3DZB_TRUE);
```

Fill State

By default, Direct3D fills in the contents of the triangles that you specify. But it can also be configured to draw just the "wireframe" outline of the triangle or render just a single pixel at each vertex of the triangle. You can select the method for filling primitives by using D3DRENDERSTATE_FILLMODE and specifying a value from the D3DFILLMODE enumerated type. This enumerated type holds the constants that define the possible fill modes and is defined as follows:

```
typedef enum _D3DFILLMODE {
    D3DFILL_POINT     = 1,
    D3DFILL_WIREFRAME = 2,
    D3DFILL_SOLID     = 3
    D3DFILL_FORCE_DWORD  = 0x7fffffff,
} D3DFILLMODE;
```

These members cause Direct3D to fill primitives as follows:

■ **D3DFILL_POINT**   Causes Direct3D to draw a 1-pixel point at each specified vertex.

■ **D3DFILL_WIREFRAME**   Causes Direct3D to draw lines between specified vertices. This mode doesn't work for clipped primitives when you're using the DrawPrimitive methods.

■ **D3DFILL_SOLID**   Causes Direct3D to fill the interiors of the specified triangles.

■ **D3DFILL_FORCE_DWORD**   Forces this enumerated type to be 32 bits.

167

Fog State

You can use fog effects to simulate fog or to decrease the clarity of a scene with distance. The latter technique causes objects to become hazy as they become more distant from the viewer, as happens in real life. To enable fog, you can use the following code:

```
//
// Turn on fog.
//
FLOAT fFogStart =  1.0f;
FLOAT fFogEnd   = 50.0f;
lpDev7->SetRenderState( D3DRENDERSTATE_FOGENABLE,    TRUE );
lpDev7->SetRenderState( D3DRENDERSTATE_FOGCOLOR,     WATER_COLOR );
lpDev7->SetRenderState( D3DRENDERSTATE_FOGTABLEMODE, D3DFOG_NONE );
lpDev7->SetRenderState( D3DRENDERSTATE_FOGVERTEXMODE, D3DFOG_LINEAR);
lpDev7->SetRenderState( D3DRENDERSTATE_FOGSTART,
                        *((DWORD *)(&fFogStart)));
lpDev7->SetRenderState( D3DRENDERSTATE_FOGEND,
                        *((DWORD *)(&fFogEnd)) );
```

Chapter 9 includes more detail about the fog types supplied by Direct3D. In that chapter you'll also find out how to add support for the various fog types.

Lighting State

You can enable or disable lighting calculations. (They are enabled by default.) Vertices containing a vertex normal are the only ones that will be properly lit. Any others will use a dot product of 0 in all lighting computations, so they will end up receiving no lighting.

```
//
// Turn off lighting.
//
lpDev7->SetRenderState(D3DRENDERSTATE_LIGHTING, FALSE);
```

Outline State

Direct3D devices default to using a solid outline for primitives. You can easily change the outline pattern by using the **D3DLINEPATTERN** structure, as this code segment shows:

```
//
// Set the outline pattern.
//
```

```
// Line pattern of 1100110011001100 (0xCCCC) produces a dashed line.
DWORD linePattern= 0xCCCC;
lpD3DDevice7->SetRenderState(D3DRENDERSTATE_LINEPATTERN,
                             linePattern);
```

Per-Vertex Color States

The flexible vertex format allows vertices to contain both vertex color and vertex normal information (though the D3DVERTEX, D3DLVERTEX, and D3DTL-VERTEX vertex types can't contain both color and normal information). The color and normal are used for lighting computation. If you choose to disable using vertex color lighting information, you make the following call:

```
lpDev7->SetRenderState(D3DRENDERSTATE_COLORVERTEX, FALSE);
```

You can set the source from which the system gets the color information for a vertex (when per-vertex color is enabled) with the following render states:

- D3DRENDERSTATE_DIFFUSEMATERIALSOURCE
- D3DRENDERSTATE_SPECULARMATERIALSOURCE
- D3DRENDERSTATE_AMBIENTMATERIALSOURCE
- D3DRENDERSTATE_EMISSIVEMATERIALSOURCE

These render states control the color sources for the diffuse, specular, ambient, and emissive color component sources. By setting these states to members of the D3DMATERIALCOLORSOURCE enumerated type, constants are set to request the use of the current material, diffuse color, or specular color as the source for the specified color component.

Shading State

Although Direct3D defaults to Gouraud shading, you can use flat shading. You can set the shading state to flat-shading mode as follows:

```
//
// Set the shading state.
//
lpDev7->SetRenderState(D3DRENDERSTATE_SHADEMODE,  D3DSHADE_FLAT);
```

Stencil Buffering States

You can use the stencil buffer to decide whether a pixel is written to the rendering target surface. You can enable stenciling by using the following call:

```
//
// Set the stencil buffer state.
//
lpDev7->SetRenderState(D3DRENDERSTATE_STENCILENABLE, TRUE);
```

Once this state is set, you can set the comparison function that performs the stencil test as follows, passing a member of the **D3DCMPFUNC** enumerated type as the second value:

```
//
// Set the stencil test comparison test to less than or equal.
//
lpDev7->SetRenderState(D3DRENDERSTATE_STENCILFUNC,
                       D3DCMP_LESSEQUAL);
```

You also need to set the stencil reference value, which is the stencil buffer that the stencil function uses for its test, as follows:

```
//
// Set the stencil reference value.
//
lpDev7->SetRenderState(D3DRENDERSTATE_STENCILREF, newRef);
```

Before performing the stencil test for a pixel, Direct3D does a bitwise AND of the stencil reference value and a stencil mask value and compares the result against the contents of the stencil buffer using the stencil comparison function. You can set the stencil mask with the following command:

```
//
// Set the stencil mask.
//
lpDev7->SetRenderState(D3DRENDERSTATE_STENCILMASK,
                       newStencilMask);
```

You can define what occurs when the stencil test fails with this command:

```
//
// Define what happens when the stencil test fails.
//
lpDev7->SetRenderState(D3DRENDERSTATE_STENCILFAIL,
                       D3DSTENCILOP_REPLACE);
```

The second argument is a value from the **D3DSTENCILOP** enumerated type.

You can define what occurs when the stencil test passes but the depth-buffer test fails with this command:

```
//
// Define what happens when the stencil test
// passes but the depth-buffer text fails.
//
lpDev7->SetRenderState(D3DRENDERSTATE_STENCILZFAIL,
                       D3DSTENCILOP_REPLACE);
```

The second argument is passed as a value from the D3DSTENCILOP enumerated type.

Finally, you can define what occurs when both the stencil test and the depth-buffer test pass with this command:

```
//
// Define what happens when both the stencil and depth-buffer
// tests pass.
//
lpDev7->SetRenderState(D3DRENDERSTATE_STENCILPASS,
                       D3DSTENCILOP_REPLACE);
```

The second argument is passed as a value from the D3DSTENCILOP enumerated type.

Texture Perspective State

You can apply perspective correction to textures to make them fit properly onto primitives that diminish in size as they get farther away from the viewer. You must enable perspective correction to use w-based fog and w-buffers.

The default value is TRUE, which enables perspective-correct texture mapping. Also, many of today's adaptors will apply perspective correction automatically.

The D3DRENDERSTATE_TEXTUREPERSPECTIVE render state is used to do this as follows:

```
// Enable texture perspective.
lpD3DDevice7->SetRenderState(D3DRENDERSTATE_TEXTUREPERSPECTIVE,
                             TRUE);
```

Texture Wrapping State

The D3DRENDERSTATE_WRAP0 through D3DRENDERSTATE_WRAP7 render states are used to enable and disable *u*-wrapping and *v*-wrapping for various textures in the device's multitexture cascade.

The states allow you to enable wrapping in first, second, third, and fourth directions of the texture. You can set these render states to a combination of the D3DWRAPCOORD_0, D3DWRAPCOORD_1, D3DWRAPCOORD_2, and

D3DWRAPCOORD_3 flags. If you specify a value of 0, wrapping will be disabled completely, but texture wrapping is disabled in all directions for all texture stages by default anyway.

The following code segment illustrates the calls to set the texture-wrapping state:

```
//
// Set wrap flags for both coordinates in first set of texcoords:
//
m_pd3dDevice->SetRenderState( D3DRENDERSTATE_WRAP0,
D3DWRAPCOORD_0|D3DWRAPCOORD_1 );
```

Vertex Color Lighting State

The flexible vertex format allows vertices to contain both vertex color and vertex normal information. Direct3D defaults to using this information when it calculates lighting.

```
//
// Disable vertex lighting.
//
lpDev7->SetRenderState(D3DRENDERSTATE_COLORVERTEX, FALSE);
```

If you want your application to disable the use of vertex color lighting information, call the *IDirect3DDevice7::SetRenderState* method and pass D3DRENDER-STATE_COLORVERTEX as the first parameter and set the second parameter to FALSE. This setting causes the output alpha value to be equal to the alpha component of diffuse material, clamped to a range from 0 through 255. If you set the second parameter to TRUE and specify a diffuse vertex color, the output alpha value will be equal to the diffuse alpha value for the vertex.

z-Biasing State

With *z*-biasing, Direct3D allows you to display one surface in front of another even if the surfaces have the same depth values. You can use this technique to produce effects such as shadows. By providing a *z*-bias to a shadow, you can make the shadow display properly (appear *on* the wall) even though the shadow is at the same depth as the wall. The *dwRenderState* parameter, set to 12 in the following code segment, can be set to a value from 0 through 16:

```
//
// Use z-biasing.
//
lpDev7->SetRenderState(D3DRENDERSTATE_ZBIAS, 12);
```

Setting a high *z*-bias makes it more likely that your polygons will be visible when they're displayed with other polygons that are coplanar.

Interpolants: Gouraud Shading and Specular Lighting

In Direct3D, the Gouraud shading technique, like all shading techniques, defines how lighting is interpolated between vertices. Lighting techniques, such as *specular lighting,* are used to incorporate the vector that runs from the object to the viewer's eye into the lighting computation. Therefore, unless you use flat shading, Direct3D interpolates the characteristics of a triangle's vertices across the triangle when it renders a face. The triangle interpolants are *color, specular, fog,* and *alpha.* Although it seems that texture coordinates would also be interpolants, they aren't affected by the shading model. (Chapter 8 covers texture coordinates in more detail.)

The current shade mode (the mode being used for the primitives being rendered) modifies the triangle interpolants. If you're using flat shading, Direct3D performs no interpolation; the renderer applies the color of the first vertex in the triangle to the entire face. If instead you use Gouraud shading, Direct3D applies linear interpolation using all three of the triangles' vertices. The final shading mode, Phong shading, which isn't yet implemented by the hardware on today's market, computes the color and lighting for every pixel. Direct3D is ready to use this feature when the appropriate hardware emerges.

Be aware that the color and specular interpolants are treated differently, depending on which color model you're using. If you're using the RGB color model, Direct3D uses the red, green, and blue color components in the interpolation. If you're using the monochromatic (ramp) model (which is obsolete in DirectX 7), Direct3D uses only the blue component of the vertex color. The alpha component of a color (the component that controls the color's transparency) is used as a separate interpolant since device drivers implement transparency in two different ways: through texture blending and through stippling.

To determine which forms of interpolation the current driver supports, check the *dwShadeCaps* member of the D3DPRIMCAPS structure. Direct3D assumes that if a primitive type is supported, at least the D3DSHADE_FLAT mode (as specified in the D3DSHADEMODE enumerated type) is available.

This *dwShadeCaps* member can have one or more of the following flags:

- **D3DPSHADECAPS_ALPHAFLATBLEND and D3DPSHADE-CAPS_ALPHAFLATSTIPPLED**   Indicate that the device can support an alpha component for flat-blended and flat-stippled transparency, respectively (the D3DSHADE_FLAT state as specified in the D3DSHADEMODE enumerated type). Applications provide the alpha color component for a primitive as part of the color for the first vertex of the primitive.

- **D3DPSHADECAPS_ALPHAGOURAUDBLEND and D3DP-SHADECAPS_ALPHAGOURAUDSTIPPLED** Indicate that the device can support an alpha component for Gouraud-blended and Gouraud-stippled transparency, respectively (the D3DSHADE_GOURAUD state as defined in the D3DSHADEMODE enumerated type). Applications provide the alpha color component for a primitive at the vertices and the device interpolates the alpha component across a face along with the other color components.

- **D3DPSHADECAPS_COLORFLATMONO and D3DPSHADE-CAPS_COLORFLATRGB** Indicate that the device can support colored flat shading in the D3DCOLOR_MONO and D3DCOLOR_RGB color modes, respectively. In these modes, the application provides the color component for a primitive as part of the color for the first vertex of the primitive. If you use a monochromatic lighting mode, the driver interpolates only the blue component of the color. If you use RGB lighting modes, the red, green, and blue components are interpolated.

- **D3DPSHADECAPS_COLORGOURAUDMONO and D3DP-SHADECAPS_COLORGOURAUDRGB** Indicate that the device can support colored Gouraud shading in the D3DCOLOR_MONO and D3DCOLOR_RGB color modes, respectively. In these modes, the application provides the color component for a primitive at the vertices and the driver interpolates the color component across a face. In monochromatic lighting modes, the driver interpolates only the blue component of the color. If you're using RGB lighting modes, the red, green, and blue components are interpolated.

- **D3DPSHADECAPS_FOGFLAT and D3DPSHADECAPS_FOGGOURAUD** Indicate that the device can support fog in the flat and Gouraud shading models, respectively.

- **D3DPSHADECAPS_SPECULARFLATMONO and D3DP-SHADECAPS_SPECULARFLATRGB** Indicate that the device can support specular highlights in flat shading in the D3DCOLOR_MONO and D3DCOLOR_RGB color models, respectively.

- **D3DPSHADECAPS_SPECULARGOURAUDMONO and D3DPSHADECAPS_SPECULARGOURAUDRGB** Indicate that the device can support specular highlights in Gouraud shading in the D3DCOLOR_MONO and D3DCOLOR_RGB color models, respectively.

Creating a 3D Application

Now that you've learned the basics of 3D primitives and the render states you can use to affect how the primitives are rendered, let's look at a program that actually renders something interesting! The RoadRage code for this chapter is a lot bigger than in previous chapters, but the steps that it is taking should make sense to you. Aside from all the initialization and Windows code that we've talked about in previous chapters, here's how RoadRage works.

Loading the Models

For simple programs, you can specify the 3D models in the code itself. But for a significant 3D program, you'll probably want to load 3D model information from external files. In RoadRage, the function *CMyD3DApplication::LoadRR_Resources* loads all the media that the program will use. *LoadRR_Resources* and *CMyD3D-Application::InitRRVariables*, which sets up some application state, are called by *WinMain* before calling *CMyD3DApplication::Run* to start the main message loop. You could also load the media in the *CMyD3DApplication::OneTimeSceneInit* function.

Initializing the Device

Every time the Direct3D device is created or changed, you'll want to initialize some settings. RoadRage does this in the *CMyD3DApplication::InitDeviceObjects* function shown here:

```
//------------------------------------------------------------------
// Name: InitDeviceObjects
// Desc: Initializes scene objects
//------------------------------------------------------------------
HRESULT CMyD3DApplication::InitDeviceObjects()
{
    // Create and set up the object material.
    D3DMATERIAL7 mtrl;
    D3DUtil_InitMaterial( mtrl, 1.0f, 1.0f, 1.0f, 0.0f );
    mtrl.power = 40.0f;
    m_pd3dDevice->SetMaterial( &mtrl );
    m_pd3dDevice->SetRenderState( D3DRENDERSTATE_AMBIENT,
                                  0x00505050 );

    // Set the transform matrices.
    D3DUtil_SetIdentityMatrix( matWorld );
    D3DUtil_SetProjectionMatrix( matProj, 1.57f,
                                 1.0f, 1.0f, 100.0f );
```

(continued)

```
m_pd3dDevice->SetTransform( D3DTRANSFORMSTATE_WORLD,
                            &matWorld );
m_pd3dDevice->SetTransform( D3DTRANSFORMSTATE_PROJECTION,
                            &matProj );

// Turn on lighting. Light will be set during the FrameMove()
// call.
m_pd3dDevice->SetRenderState( D3DRENDERSTATE_LIGHTING,
                              bEnableLighting );

// Set miscellaneous render states.
m_pd3dDevice->SetRenderState(D3DRENDERSTATE_DITHERENABLE, TRUE);
m_pd3dDevice->SetRenderState(D3DRENDERSTATE_CULLMODE,
                             D3DCULL_NONE);
m_pd3dDevice->SetRenderState(D3DRENDERSTATE_ZENABLE, D3DZB_TRUE);
m_pd3dDevice->SetRenderState(D3DRENDERSTATE_FILLMODE,
                             D3DFILL_SOLID);
m_pd3dDevice->SetRenderState(D3DRENDERSTATE_SHADEMODE,
                             D3DSHADE_GOURAUD);

return S_OK;
}
```

You can see that it sets the material on the device to be a normal white material. Then it sets the ambient light level. Then it sets up the world and projection matrices. (The view matrix will be set later.) Finally, it sets some render states to affect how the graphics will be rendered.

Handling Per-Frame Activity

Before rendering each frame, the program needs to react to user input, update object positions, and so on. In RoadRage, this is all handled in the *CMyD3D-Application::FrameMove* function. We haven't added input support to RoadRage, so the function doesn't do much yet. But you can see that at the end of the function, it adjusts the view matrix based on the user's position and orientation.

Rendering the Frame

After updating the world state, it's time to render the scene. This task is done by *CMyD3DApplication::Render*. RoadRage uses a culling system that renders a subset of the world depending on the camera's position and orientation. Management of that culling system takes up a lot of the code in this function, but the core tasks in *Render* are pretty simple:

1. Call *IDirect3DDevice7::Clear* to clear the back buffer and the depth buffer.

2. Decide which objects to render.

3. Call *IDirect3DDevice7::BeginScene* to indicate that rendering is about to begin.

4. Use the DrawPrimitive functions to render all the 3D objects.

5. Call *EndScene* to indicate that all primitives for the frame have been submitted.

The Code So Far

That's all there is to creating a DrawPrimitive-based application! Try compiling the code for this chapter (in the Chap6 subproject for the RoadRage project on the companion CD). When you execute it, you'll see a screen similar to the one shown in Figure 6-10.

Figure 6-10
The rendered scene

The view you see is of a street with buildings, street lights, sidewalks, and so on along it. The scene uses Direct3D lights to cast lighting on the street from each of the street lights. It also uses a low-level ambient light.

As you can see, there are no textures applied to the scene yet, so everything appears white. In Chapter 8, we'll be adding textures, including an animated texture for the cloudy sky in the background, but for now, you can see that we're rendering all the polygons we load from our 3D world database (stored in the level1.map file). This map file was created using the Road Rage Editor contained in the RR_EDITOR subproject. This program allows you to graphically create a complex 3D world using a graphic editor for placing the 3D objects into your world. Using this program, you can create new 3D worlds whenever you want to. You can easily add new 3D objects into your world using the editor. Details on this project can be found in the Using the Companion CD section in the front of this book.

Conclusion

In this chapter, you learned what types of primitives are available in Direct3D and how to use them to create 3D objects. You also learned about render states and discovered how to use them when rendering primitives. You then saw how to apply Gouraud and specular interpolants when rendering primitives to make them look more realistic. Finally, you looked at all the code required to create a running application, which specified and rendered a complex 3D scene.

Chapter 7 covers all the DirectInput capabilities needed to enable keyboard and joystick input. (In DirectInput terminology, a joystick device can be a traditional joystick, a steering wheel, or any number of other controlling devices.) Although this book focuses on Direct3D, when developing a complete 3D application, it's almost always critical to provide some form of control and input capability. In addition to covering all the code needed to implement and enable keyboard and joystick input, you'll learn how to implement force feedback—an intriguing capability provided on many new devices that lets your application mimic real-world forces.

By covering how to use input devices in Direct3D applications before discussing how to add additional 3D content, I'll show you how to set up your program to allow for manual control of motion through the scene as you add content to it. You'll be able to render and move through your 3D world easily to verify that it looks as you expect it to.

CHAPTER SEVEN

Keyboard and Joystick Input

As you know, the focus of this book is Microsoft Direct3D Immediate Mode. However, it's impossible to create a quality Direct3D application without using a few other Microsoft DirectX components. The additional three DirectX components this book covers are DirectDraw (described in Chapter 3), DirectInput (covered in this chapter), and DirectPlay (Chapter 15). We went over DirectDraw early in the book because it's an integral component of Direct3D and it isn't possible to explain Immediate Mode without covering at least the basics of DirectDraw. We'll continue to discuss aspects of DirectDraw because it is so integral to Direct3D.

DirectInput, on the other hand, isn't a requirement for creating a Direct3D-based application. If you create a Direct3D-based application that doesn't require any user input (such as a stand-alone demonstration program), you can get away with using only two DirectX components: DirectDraw and Direct3D. Furthermore, if speed and efficiency aren't issues, you can use the Microsoft Windows messages and APIs to acquire user input rather than using DirectInput.

However, for most useful 3D applications—such as games or simulations—you can't create a program without using an efficient form of input. DirectInput provides support for using input devices such as keyboards, mouse devices, joysticks and other game controllers, and force-feedback devices. The most important reason many developers use DirectInput is that it provides faster, more flexible access to input data by communicating directly with the hardware drivers rather than relying on Windows messaging. This way, DirectInput avoids the delays Windows can normally impose on software.

You access DirectInput via the DirectInput object, which supports the *IDirectInput7* COM interface, and a *DirectInputDevice2* object associated with each individual control or switches such as keys, buttons, axes, or even an individual force-input device that provides data. Each input device has *object instances,* which are feedback effects.

NOTE To use DirectInput in your programs, you need to remember to include dinput.lib when you build your project so that the DirectInput library is included in your build.

Creating a DirectInput Object

Integrating DirectInput support into your applications is reasonably simple. You need to create just two main objects. The first is the LPDIRECTINPUT7 variable, *g_pDI* in the code below, which is the interface to the DirectInput object. You use this interface to handle all the DirectInput aspects of your game.

The second object is the LPDIRECTINPUTDEVICE2 object, *g_pdid-Device2* in the code below, which is a pointer to an *IDirectInputDevice2* interface. *IDirectInputDevice2* inherits all the methods of *IDirectInputDevice* and adds methods for polling devices and using force feedback.

In the following code, the variable *g_guidJoystick* holds the globally unique identifier (GUID) for the joystick. Finally, the *g_bUseMouse* and *g_bUseJoystick* variables specify whether the mouse or the joystick is currently being used as the input device. If neither the mouse nor the joystick is available, the keyboard becomes the default input device.

```
#include <dinput.h>
extern LPDIRECTINPUTDEVICE2 g_Keyboard_pdidDevice2;
extern LPDIRECTINPUT7        g_Keyboard_pDI;

LPDIRECTINPUT7        g_pDI;              // The DInput object
LPDIRECTINPUT7        g_Keyboard_pDI;     // The DInput object
LPDIRECTINPUTDEVICE2 g_pdidDevice2;       // The DIDevice2 interface
LPDIRECTINPUTDEVICE2 g_Keyboard_pdidDevice2;   // The DIDevice2
                                               // interface
GUID                 g_guidJoystick;      // The GUID for the joystick

BOOL g_bUseKeyboard = TRUE;
BOOL g_bUseMouse    = FALSE;
BOOL g_bUseJoystick = FALSE;
BOOL bMouseLookOn   = TRUE;
BOOL bMouseLookup_is_mouse_forward = TRUE;
```

Once the variables are defined, you need to add the code to create the DirectInput7 object. In the *WinMain* routine, you can create the DirectInput7 object by using the *CreateDInput* routine. You then create the keyboard input device by using *CreateInputDevice* because you should always support at least keyboard input for any game you create. You won't need to perform an enumeration process for the keyboard because all computers are required to have one. (Computers won't even boot without a keyboard device in place.)

When the user exits the game, you'll need to call the *DestroyInputDevice* and *DestroyDInput* routines to destroy the DirectInput device and the DirectInput interface to make sure that you clean up the objects you generated to support the DirectInput activities.

The calls necessary to add the creation and destruction of these objects during game startup and end (in this case, they are added to the *WinMain* routine) are shown here:

```
//---------------------------------------------------------------
// WinMain
// Desc: Application entry point
//---------------------------------------------------------------
int PASCAL WinMain( HINSTANCE hInst, HINSTANCE, LPSTR, int nCmdShow )
{
    ⋮
    //
    // Create the DInput object.
    //
    if( FAILED(d3dApp.CreateDInput( d3dApp.Get_hWnd() ) ) ) )
    {
        return FALSE;
    }

    if( FAILED( hr = CoInitialize( NULL ) ) )
        return FALSE;

    // Create a keyboard device.
    if( FAILED(d3dApp.CreateInputDevice( d3dApp.Get_hWnd(),
                                g_Keyboard_pDI,
                                g_Keyboard_pdidDevice2,
                                GUID_SysKeyboard,
                                &c_dfDIKeyboard,
                                DISCL_NONEXCLUSIVE |
                                DISCL_FOREGROUND )))
    {
        return FALSE;
    }
    ⋮
    d3dApp.InitRRvariables();
    d3dApp.LoadRR_Resources();
    d3dApp.Run();

    PrintMessage(NULL, "Quitting", NULL, LOGFILE_ONLY);

    d3dApp.DestroyInputDevice();
```

(continued)

```
        d3dApp.DestroyDInput();

        d3dApp.FreeDirectSound();

        CoUninitialize();
        return TRUE;
}
```

You create the actual DirectInput object by calling the *DirectInputCreateEx* function. This function creates an instance of a DirectInput object that supplies the newest set of DirectInput interfaces. You pass the value DIRECTINPUT_VERSION as defined in dinput.h. This value, when passed in, will request the use of the newest DirectInput version. You must set the third parameter to *IID_IDirectInput7* or an error will be returned.

If the call is successful, this function returns a pointer to an *IDirectInput7* COM interface. The *CreateDInput* routine you'll see in a moment acquires all the DirectInput devices available on the target system. In this routine, you acquire a DirectX 7 DirectInput interface by using the *DirectInputCreateEx* routine.

Here's the function declaration for *DirectInputCreateEx*:

```
HRESULT WINAPI DirectInputCreateEx (
    HINSTANCE hInst,
    DWORD dwVersion,
    REFIID riidltf,
    LPVOID * ppvOut,
    LPUNKNOWN punkOuter
);
```

Parameter	Description
hInst	Instance handle of the application or DLL creating the DirectInput object.
dwVersion	Version number, which must be DIRECTINPUT_VERSION, of the dinput.h header file used; determines which version of DirectInput your code was designed for.
riidltf	GUID of the desired DirectInput interface. Acceptable values are *IID_IDirectInput*, *IID_IDirectInput2*, and *IID_IDirectInput7*.
ppvOut	Address of a pointer to be initialized with a DirectInput interface pointer.
punkOuter	Address of the controlling object's *IUnknown* interface. If the interface isn't aggregated, pass NULL for this parameter. Most callers pass NULL for this parameter.

```
//-------------------------------------------------------------------
// Name: CreateDInput
// Desc: Initializes the DirectInput objects
//-------------------------------------------------------------------
HRESULT CMyD3DApplication::CreateDInput( HWND hWnd )
{
    // Create the main DirectInput object.

    PrintMessage(NULL, "CD3DApplication::CreateDInput()", NULL,
                LOGFILE_ONLY);

    if( FAILED( DirectInputCreateEx( (HINSTANCE)GetWindowLong(
                hWnd, GWL_HINSTANCE ), DIRECTINPUT_VERSION,
                IID_IDirectInput7, (LPVOID*) &g_pDI, NULL) ) )
    {
        DisplayError( "DirectInputCreate() failed." );
            return E_FAIL;
    }

    // Check to see whether a joystick is present. If one is, the
    // enumeration callback will save the joystick's GUID, so we can
    // create it later.
    ZeroMemory( &g_guidJoystick, sizeof(GUID) );

    g_pDI->EnumDevices( DIDEVTYPE_JOYSTICK, EnumJoysticksCallback,
                    &g_guidJoystick, DIEDFL_ATTACHEDONLY );

    // Keyboard
    if( FAILED( DirectInputCreateEx( (HINSTANCE)GetWindowLong( hWnd,
                GWL_HINSTANCE ), DIRECTINPUT_VERSION,
                IID_IDirectInput7, (LPVOID*) &g_Keyboard_pDI,
                NULL) ) )
    {
        DisplayError( "DirectInputCreate() failed." );
        return E_FAIL;
    }

    return S_OK;
}
```

After creating the DirectInput object, the *CreateDInput* routine enumerates the joystick devices on the target system since, other than the keyboard, you can't be sure which devices exist. To do this, the routine calls the *IDirectInput7:: EnumDevices* method with the first parameter set to DIDEVTYPE_JOYSTICK to locate all the joystick devices connected to the machine. (You can set it to DIDEV-TYPE_KEYBOARD if you want to locate attached keyboards or to NULL if you want to locate all available input devices.) In DirectInput terminology, a *joystick* can be any of a wide range of devices, including standard joysticks, steering wheels, game pads, and force-feedback devices.

Here's the function declaration for this method:

```
BOOL IDirectInput::EnumDevices(
    DWORD dwDevType,
    LPDIENUMCALLBACK lpCallback,
    LPVOID pvRef,
    DWORD dwFlags
);
```

Parameter	Description
dwDevType	Device type filter. If you set this parameter to 0, the function enumerates all device types. If you want to enumerate a specific device type, pass a device type constant, such as DIDEVTYPE_MOUSE or DIDEVTYPE_KEYBOARD.
lpCallback	Address of a callback function that will be called with a description of each DirectInput device.
pvRef	Application-defined 32-bit value that is passed to the enumeration callback each time it's called.
dwFlags	Indicates the scope of the enumeration. The values can be any of the following flags: **DIEDFL_ALLDEVICES** The default value in which all installed devices will be enumerated **DIEDFL_ATTACHEDONLY** Enumerate only attached and installed devices **DIEDFL_FORCEFEEDBACK** Enumerate only devices that support force feedback **DIEDFL_INCLUDEALIASES** Include devices that are aliases for other devices **DIEDFL_INCLUDEPHANTOMS** Include phantom (placeholder) devices

You'll notice that I used the DIEDFL_ATTACHEDONLY value as the last value to the call to indicate that I care about only the devices that are attached to and installed in the system. In most cases, this is what you'll want to do too.

The enumeration routine you pass to the *EnumDevices* call is the *EnumJoysticksCallback* routine. This routine is called once for each enumerated joystick.

For each of these enumerated devices, you create a device interface so that you can use it in your application.

```
//---------------------------------------------------------------
// Name: EnumJoysticksCallback
// Desc: Called once for each enumerated joystick. If we find one,
//       create a device interface on it so that we can play with it.
//---------------------------------------------------------------
BOOL CALLBACK EnumJoysticksCallback( LPCDIDEVICEINSTANCE pInst,
                                     VOID* pvContext )
{
    memcpy( pvContext, &pInst->guidInstance, sizeof(GUID) );

    return DIENUM_STOP;
}
```

In addition to the code you added to the *WinMain* routine, you also need to add code to the *WndProc* routine to handle acquiring and unacquiring the DirectInput device you want to use for the application. In DirectInput, when you *acquire* a device, you give the application access to it. While the device is acquired, DirectInput will allow your application to use its data. When a device is not acquired, you can change its characteristics, but you can't acquire its data.

By setting the cooperative level (we'll cover this in a moment), a device can be unacquired automatically when your application moves into the background. As an example, the mouse will be unacquired automatically when the user clicks on a menu because Windows will take over the device at this point. You also need to unacquire a device manually if you want to change its properties (unless you're changing the gain of a force-feedback device while it's in an acquired state). If you didn't unacquire it and something like a hardware interrupt were to be performed, accessing a data buffer just as you were changing the buffer size could completely corrupt the data.

One other issue you should remember is that Windows doesn't have access to the mouse when your application is using it in exclusive mode, so you need to release the mouse if you want Windows to use it.

The additions to the *MsgProc* routine below handle selecting the input device.

```
LRESULT CMyD3DApplication::MsgProc( HWND hWnd, UINT uMsg, WPARAM wParam,
                                    LPARAM lParam )
{
    switch( msg )
    {
    ⋮
```

(continued)

```
        case WM_COMMAND:
            switch( LOWORD(wParam) )
            {

                case IDM_SELECTINPUTDEVICE:
                    DialogBox( (HINSTANCE)GetWindowLong( hWnd,
                        GWL_HINSTANCE ),
                        MAKEINTRESOURCE(IDD_SELECTINPUTDEVICE),
                        hWnd,(DLGPROC)InputDeviceSelectProc );
                    break;

                ⋮
                default:
                    return CD3DApplication::MsgProc( hWnd, uMsg,
                                                wParam, lParam );
            }
            break;
        ⋮
        default:
            return CD3DApplication::MsgProc( hWnd, uMsg, wParam,
                                        lParam );
    }

    return DefWindowProc( hWnd, msg, wParam, lParam );
}
```

Getting the Keyboard, the Mouse, or the Joystick

Once the input devices have been enumerated, you need to allow the user to select the input device he or she wants to use. The *InputDeviceSelectProc* callback routine below illustrates one way you can allow users to select the input device they want to use. This routine lets the user make a selection from the *Select Input Device* drop-down menu: joystick, keyboard, or keyboard with mouse.

The *DirectInputDevice2* object represents input devices. Keep in mind that, as I mentioned earlier, Microsoft refers to many different input devices—including game pads and steering wheels—as joysticks. Therefore, my code also uses this terminology. I refer to all devices besides the keyboard and mouse as *joysticks*. Two GUIDs—*GUID_SysKeyboard* and *GUID_SysMouse*—are predefined for the keyboard and mouse. When creating *DirectInputDevice2* objects for any devices other than the system mouse or keyboard, you must use the device's instance GUID, which you obtained via your call to the *IDirectInput7::EnumDevices* method.

After the user has determined which device he or she wants to create, the *CreateInputDevice* routine is called for the keyboard, the mouse, or the joystick.

```
//--------------------------------------------------------------------
// Name: InputDeviceSelectProc
// Desc: Dialog procedure for selecting an input device
//--------------------------------------------------------------------
BOOL CALLBACK InputDeviceSelectProc( HWND hWnd, UINT msg,
                                     WPARAM wParam, LPARAM lParam )
{
    HWND hwndKeyboardButton = GetDlgItem( hWnd, IDC_KEYBOARD );
    HWND hwndMouseButton    = GetDlgItem( hWnd, IDC_MOUSE );
    HWND hwndJoystickButton = GetDlgItem( hWnd, IDC_JOYSTICK );

    if( WM_INITDIALOG == msg )
    {
        SendMessage( hwndKeyboardButton, BM_SETCHECK,
                     g_bUseKeyboard, 0L );
        SendMessage( hwndMouseButton,    BM_SETCHECK,
                     g_bUseMouse,    0L );
        SendMessage( hwndJoystickButton, BM_SETCHECK,
                     g_bUseJoystick, 0L );

        EnableWindow( hwndJoystickButton,
                      (g_guidJoystick != GUID_NULL) );

        return TRUE;
    }

    if( WM_COMMAND == msg && IDOK == LOWORD(wParam) )
    {
        // Destroy the old device.
        pCMyApp->DestroyInputDevice();

        // Check the dialog controls to see which type of device
        // to create.
        g_bUseKeyboard = SendMessage(hwndKeyboardButton,
                                     BM_GETCHECK,0, 0L);
        g_bUseMouse    = SendMessage(hwndMouseButton,
                                     BM_GETCHECK,0, 0L);
        g_bUseJoystick = SendMessage(hwndJoystickButton,
                                     BM_GETCHECK,0, 0L);

        if( g_bUseKeyboard )
        {
            pCMyApp->CreateInputDevice( GetParent(hWnd),
                                        g_Keyboard_pDI,
                                        g_Keyboard_pdidDevice2,
                                        GUID_SysKeyboard,
```

(continued)

187

```
                                        &c_dfDIKeyboard,
                                        DISCL_NONEXCLUSIVE |
                                        DISCL_FOREGROUND );
        g_Keyboard_pdidDevice2->Acquire();
    }

    if( g_bUseMouse )
    {
        pCMyApp->CreateInputDevice( GetParent(hWnd), g_pDI,
                                    g_pdidDevice2,
                                    GUID_SysMouse,
                                    &c_dfDIMouse,
                                    DISCL_EXCLUSIVE |
                                    DISCL_FOREGROUND );
        g_pdidDevice2->Acquire();

        pCMyApp->CreateInputDevice( GetParent(hWnd),
                                    g_Keyboard_pDI,
                                    g_Keyboard_pdidDevice2,
                                    GUID_SysKeyboard,
                                    &c_dfDIKeyboard,
                                    DISCL_NONEXCLUSIVE |
                                    DISCL_FOREGROUND );
        g_Keyboard_pdidDevice2->Acquire();
    }

    if( g_bUseJoystick )
    {
        pCMyApp->CreateInputDevice( GetParent(hWnd), g_pDI,
                                    g_pdidDevice2,
                                    g_guidJoystick,
                                    &c_dfDIJoystick,
                                    DISCL_EXCLUSIVE |
                                    DISCL_FOREGROUND );
        g_pdidDevice2->Acquire();


        // Set the range of the joystick axes tp [-1000,+1000].
        DIPROPRANGE diprg;
        diprg.diph.dwSize      = sizeof(DIPROPRANGE);
        diprg.diph.dwHeaderSize = sizeof(DIPROPHEADER);
        diprg.diph.dwHow       = DIPH_BYOFFSET;
        diprg.lMin             = -10;
        diprg.lMax             = +10;

        diprg.diph.dwObj = DIJOFS_X;     // Set the x-axis range.
```

```
            g_pdidDevice2->SetProperty( DIPROP_RANGE, &diprg.diph );

            diprg.diph.dwObj = DIJOFS_Y;    // Set the y-axis range.
            g_pdidDevice2->SetProperty( DIPROP_RANGE, &diprg.diph );

            // Set the dead zone for the joystick axes (because many
            // joysticks aren't perfectly calibrated to be 0 when
            // centered).
            DIPROPDWORD dipdw;
            dipdw.diph.dwSize      = sizeof(DIPROPDWORD);
            dipdw.diph.dwHeaderSize = sizeof(DIPROPHEADER);
            dipdw.diph.dwHow       = DIPH_DEVICE;
            dipdw.dwData           = 1000; // Here, 1000 = 10%

            dipdw.diph.dwObj = DIJOFS_X; // Set the x-axis dead zone.
            g_pdidDevice2->SetProperty( DIPROP_DEADZONE,
                                        &dipdw.diph );

            dipdw.diph.dwObj = DIJOFS_Y; // Set the y-axis dead zone.
            g_pdidDevice2->SetProperty( DIPROP_RANGE, &dipdw.diph );
        }

        EndDialog( hWnd, IDOK );
        return TRUE;
    }

    if( WM_COMMAND == msg && IDCANCEL == LOWORD(wParam) )
    {
        EndDialog( hWnd, IDCANCEL );
        return TRUE;
    }

    return FALSE;
}
```

If the user requests the use of a keyboard, this routine just calls the *Create-InputDevice* routine with the global variable *c_dfDIKeyboard* and with *GUID_SysKeyboard*, which is the system keyboard's GUID.

If the user requests the use of a mouse, this routine calls the *CreateInputDevice* routine with the global variable *c_dfDIMouse* and with *GUID_SysMouse*, which is the system mouse's GUID.

If the user requests the use of a joystick, this routine calls the *CreateInputDevice* routine with the global variable *c_dfDIJoystick* and the *g_guidJoystick* global variable specifying the joystick to use.

The code calls the *IDirectInputDevice2::SetProperty* method to set the device's properties (such as the size or the value specified in *dwValue*). In DirectInput, properties define a device's data buffer size, the range and granularity of the values received from an axis, the saturation values of an axis (discussed below), the dead zone, and whether axis data is absolute or relative.

In the routine above, you called the method four times: first to set the *x*-axis range, second to set the *y*-axis range, third to set the *x*-axis dead zone, and fourth to set the *y*-axis dead zone.

NOTE The saturation property of an axis allows you to define tolerance zones at the extremes of a range. Normally, a force-feedback joystick that doesn't support saturation reports axis values to an application depending on the exact position of the stick. A device that supports saturation reports axis values in the same way but allows for tolerance zones near the minimum and maximum of the axis's range. Such a device reports an axis value in the tolerance zones as a minimum or a maximum axis value, regardless of the actual value. For example, if an application defines positive and negative saturation value of 7 on an axis with a range 0 through 10, the device will report the maximum axis value (10) as a user moves the stick past the position that would normally cause the device to report the value 7.

Before you get or set a property, you need to set up a property structure, which consists of a DIPROPHEADER structure followed by one or more data elements. The DIPROHEADER structure defines the size of the property and indicates how the data will be interpreted. These are the predefined property structures:

- **DIPROPDWORD** Consists of a DIPROPHEADER structure and a DWORD data member for properties that require a single value, such as a buffer size.

- **DIPROPRANGE** Used for range properties that require maximum and minimum values.

- **DIPROPGUIDANDPATH** Allows applications to perform operations that are not supported by DirectInput.

- **DIPROPSTRING** Allows applications to set Unicode string properties.

In addition, before you call the *IDirectInputDevice2::SetProperty* method, you must initialize the DIPROPHEADER structure by setting its members, which define the size of the property structure, the size of the DIPROPHEADER structure, a value that identifies the object whose property you want to set, and code indicating how the object identifier should be interpreted. Once you've done so, you can get or set properties for a whole device (as opposed to a device object) by setting the *dwObj* DIRPOPHEADER member to 0 and the *dwHow* member to the value DIPH_DEVICE. To get or set individual properties for a device object (such as a particular axis) fill the *dwObj* and *dwHow* with values to identify the object.

The *CreateInputDevice* routine, shown below, calls the *IDirectInput7:: CreateDeviceEx* method to create the desired DirectInput device. This method is defined as follows:

```
HRESULT CreateDeviceEx(
    REFGUID rguid,
    REFIID riid,
    LPVOID *pvOut,
    LPUNKNOWN pUnkOuter
);
```

Parameter	Description
rguid	Reference to (C++) or address of (C) the instance GUID for the desired input device. The GUID is retrieved through the *IDirectInput::EnumDevices* method, or it can be one of the following predefined GUIDs: **GUID_SysKeyboard** The default system keyboard **GUID_SysMouse** The default system mouse For the preceding GUID values to be valid, the application must define INITGUID before all other preprocessor directives at the beginning of the source file, or link to dxguid.lib.
riid	GUID for the desired interface. Currently accepted values are *IID_IDirectInputDevice*, *IID_IDirectInputDevice2*, and *IID_IDirectInputDevice7*.
pvOut	Address of a variable to receive the interface pointer if successful.
pUnkOuter	Address of the controlling object's *IUnknown* interface for COM aggregation, or NULL if the interface is not aggregated. Most callers will pass NULL.

The routine itself follows.

```
//-------------------------------------------------------------
// Name: CreateInputDevice
// Desc: Creates a DirectInput device
```

(continued)

```
//-----------------------------------------------------------------
HRESULT CMyD3DApplication::CreateInputDevice( HWND hWnd,
                    LPDIRECTINPUT7          pDI,
                    LPDIRECTINPUTDEVICE2 pDIdDevice,
                    GUID guidDevice,
                            const DIDATAFORMAT* pdidDataFormat,
DWORD dwFlags )
{

    PrintMessage(NULL, "CD3DApplication::CreateInputDevice()",NULL,
                LOGFILE_ONLY);

    // Obtain an interface to the input device.
    if( FAILED( pDI->CreateDeviceEx( guidDevice,
                                     IID_IDirectInputDevice2,
                                     (VOID**)&pDIdDevice, NULL ) ) )
    {
        PrintMessage(NULL, "CD3DApplication::CreateInputDevice() - "
                    "CreateDeviceEx FAILED", NULL, LOGFILE_ONLY);
        DisplayError( "CreateDeviceEx() failed" );
        return E_FAIL;
    }
    else
        PrintMessage(NULL, "CD3DApplication::CreateInputDevice() - "
                    "CreateDeviceEx ok", NULL, LOGFILE_ONLY);

    // Set the device data format. A data format specifies which
    // controls on a device you're interested in and indicates how
    // they should be reported.
    if( FAILED( pDIdDevice->SetDataFormat( pdidDataFormat ) ) )
    {
        DisplayError( "SetDataFormat() failed" );
        return E_FAIL;
    }

    // Set the cooperative level to let DirectInput know how this
    // device should interact with the system and with other
    // DirectInput applications.
    if( FAILED( pDIdDevice->SetCooperativeLevel( hWnd, dwFlags ) ) )
    {
        DisplayError( "SetCooperativeLevel() failed" );
        return E_FAIL;
    }

    if(guidDevice == GUID_SysKeyboard)
        g_Keyboard_pdidDevice2 = pDIdDevice;
```

```
    else
        g_pdidDevice2 = pDIdDevice;

    return S_OK;
}
```

Once the device has been created, call the *IDirectInputDevice2::SetDataFormat* method. Here's the declaration for this method:

```
BOOL IDirectInputDevice::SetDataFormat(
    LPCDIDATAFORMAT lpdf
);
```

IDirectInputDevice2::SetDataFormat has one parameter: *lpdf*. This parameter accepts the address of a structure that defines the data format that *DirectInputDevice2* should return. You can define your own DIDATAFORMAT structure, or you can use one of the predefined global constants: *c_dfDIKeyboard*, *c_dfDIMouse*, *c_dfDI-Mouse2*, *c_dfDIJoystick*, or *c_dfDIJoystick2*. These predefined constants suffice to allow your application to use most off-the-shelf devices; generally, you won't need to define a custom DIDATAFORMAT structure.

Before your application acquires and uses an input or output device, you must call the *SetDataFormat* method to tell DirectInput what device objects your application will use and how the data will be arranged.

The next step you need to perform before you can access the DirectInput device (in this case, the keyboard) is to use the method *IDirectInputDevice:: SetCooperativeLevel* to set the device's behavior. This method sets the device's exclusivity, which determines how the input from the device is shared with other applications. Call the *SetCooperativeLevel* method with the handle of the window you want to associate with the device. For your first device—the keyboard—you must use the DISCL_NONEXCLUSIVE flag in the *dwFlags* parameter because DirectInput doesn't support exclusive access to keyboard devices. If it did, the user wouldn't even be able to use the Ctrl+Alt+Esc sequence to restart a computer with a DirectInput application running. If you're running in windowed mode, you also need to use the keyboard for any other existing Windows processes. The code following this discussion is used to set the device's cooperative level.

The next routine you'll need to define to properly clean up after your application, *DestroyInputDevice*, is the last routine you call when you're finished with the DirectInput device. This routine calls the *IDirectInputDevice2::Unacquire* and *IDirectInputDevice2::Release* methods to clean up the objects you created for handling the input devices.

```
//------------------------------------------------------------------
// Name: DestroyInputDevice
// Desc: Releases the DirectInput device
//------------------------------------------------------------------
VOID CMyD3DApplication::DestroyInputDevice()
{
    // Unacquire and release the device's interfaces.
    if( g_pdidDevice2 )
    {
        g_pdidDevice2->Unacquire();
        g_pdidDevice2->Release();
        g_pdidDevice2 = NULL;
    }

    // Keyboard

    if( g_Keyboard_pdidDevice2 )
    {
        g_Keyboard_pdidDevice2->Unacquire();
        g_Keyboard_pdidDevice2->Release();
        g_Keyboard_pdidDevice2 = NULL;
    }
}
```

With the devices enumerated, and once the user has selected an input device, you need to call a routine to handle the user input. The routine to handle the user input, *CMyD3DApplication::UpdateControls*, is shown here.

```
VOID CMyD3DApplication::UpdateControls()
{
    int i;
    int look_up = 0;
    int look_down = 0;

    // Get the relative time, in seconds.
    FLOAT fTime = ( timeGetTime() - GetBaseTime() ) * 0.001f;

    g_fCurrentTime = timeGetTime() * 0.001f;

    if( (g_Keyboard_pdidDevice2) || (g_pdidDevice2) )
    {
        HRESULT       hr;
        BYTE          diks[256]; // DInput keyboard state buffer
        DIMOUSESTATE  dims;      // DInput mouse state structure
        DIJOYSTATE    dijs;      //. DInput joystick state structure

        // Read the current keyboard state.
```

```
if( g_bUseKeyboard )
{
    g_Keyboard_pdidDevice2->Acquire();
    hr = g_Keyboard_pdidDevice2->GetDeviceState(sizeof(diks),
                                                &diks );
}

// Read the current mouse and keyboard state.
if( g_bUseMouse )
{
    g_Keyboard_pdidDevice2->Acquire();
    hr=g_Keyboard_pdidDevice2->GetDeviceState(sizeof(diks),
                                              &diks );

    g_pdidDevice2->Acquire();
    hr = g_pdidDevice2->GetDeviceState(sizeof(DIMOUSESTATE),
                                        &dims);
}

// Read the current joystick state.
if( g_bUseJoystick )
{
    // Poll the device before reading the current state.
    // Polling is required for some devices (joysticks) but
    // has no effect for others (keyboard and mouse). Note:
    // Polling uses a DIDevice2 interface for the device.

    g_pdidDevice2->Poll();

    g_pdidDevice2->Acquire();
    hr = g_pdidDevice2->GetDeviceState( sizeof(DIJOYSTATE),
                                        &dijs );

}

// Check whether the input stream has been interrupted. If
// it has been interrupted, reacquire the input device and
// try again.
if( hr == DIERR_INPUTLOST )
{
    PrintMessage(NULL, "DIERR_INPUTLOST", NULL,
                 LOGFILE_ONLY);

    hr = g_pdidDevice2->Acquire();
    if( FAILED(hr) )
    {
```

(continued)

195

```
            PrintMessage(NULL, "Acquire input device FAILED",
        NULL, LOGFILE_ONLY);
            return; // S_OK;
        }
    }

    // Read keyboard input only.
    if( g_bUseKeyboard )
    {
        Controls.bLeft       = diks[DIK_LEFT]        && 0x80;
        Controls.bRight      = diks[DIK_RIGHT]       && 0x80;
        Controls.bForward    = diks[DIK_UP]          && 0x80;
        Controls.bBackward   = diks[DIK_DOWN]        && 0x80;
        Controls.bUp         = diks[DIK_NUMPADPLUS]  && 0x80;
        Controls.bDown       = diks[DIK_NUMPADMINUS] && 0x80;
        Controls.bHeadUp     = diks[DIK_PGUP]        && 0x80;
        Controls.bHeadDown   = diks[DIK_PGDN]        && 0x80;
        Controls.bStepLeft   = diks[DIK_COMMA]       && 0x80;
        Controls.bStepRight  = diks[DIK_PERIOD]      && 0x80;
        Controls.bFire       = diks[DIK_RCONTROL]    && 0x80;
        Controls.bScores     = diks[DIK_S]           && 0x80;
        Controls.bPrevWeap   = diks[DIK_INSERT]      && 0x80;
        Controls.bNextWeap   = diks[DIK_DELETE]      && 0x80;
        Controls.bTravelMode = diks[DIK_SPACE]       && 0x80;
    }

    // Read mouse and keyboard input.
    if( g_bUseMouse )
    {
        // On really fast computers, the mouse appears to be
        // still most of the time and moves in jumps. To combat
        // this, we'll keep 0.1 second of persistence for any
        // up/down values we read.
        static FLOAT fUpTime = 0.0f;
        static FLOAT fDnTime = 0.0f;
        if( dims.lY < 0 ) fDnTime = 0.0f, fUpTime =
g_fCurrentTime+0.1f;
        if( dims.lY > 0 ) fUpTime = 0.0f, fDnTime =
g_fCurrentTime+0.1f;

            if(bMouseLookOn == TRUE )
            {
                if(bMouseLookup_is_mouse_forward == TRUE)
                {
                    look_up   = fDnTime-g_fCurrentTime > 0.0f;
                    look_down = fUpTime-g_fCurrentTime > 0.0f;
                }
```

```
        else
        {
            look_down = fDnTime-g_fCurrentTime > 0.0f;
            look_up   = fUpTime-g_fCurrentTime > 0.0f;
        }
    }

    Controls.bLeft       = dims.lX<0;
    Controls.bRight      = dims.lX>0;
    Controls.bForward    = diks[DIK_UP]       && 0x80;
    Controls.bBackward   = diks[DIK_DOWN]     && 0x80;
    Controls.bUp         = diks[DIK_ADD]      && 0x80;
    Controls.bDown       = diks[DIK_SUBTRACT] && 0x80;
    Controls.bHeadUp     = look_up;
    Controls.bHeadDown   = look_down;
    Controls.bStepLeft   = diks[DIK_COMMA]    && 0x80;
    Controls.bStepRight  = diks[DIK_PERIOD]   && 0x80;
    Controls.bFire       = dims.rgbButtons[0] && 0x80;
    Controls.bScores     = diks[DIK_S]        && 0x80;
    Controls.bPrevWeap   = diks[DIK_INSERT]   && 0x80;
    Controls.bNextWeap   = diks[DIK_DELETE]   && 0x80;
    Controls.bTravelMode = diks[DIK_SPACE]    && 0x80;
}

// Read joystick input.
if( g_bUseJoystick )
{
    Controls.bLeft       = dijs.lX<0;
    Controls.bRight      = dijs.lX>0;
    Controls.bForward    = dijs.lY<0;
    Controls.bBackward   = dijs.lY>0;
    Controls.bUp         = diks[DIK_ADD]      && 0x80;
    Controls.bDown       = diks[DIK_SUBTRACT] && 0x80;
    Controls.bHeadUp     = look_up;
    Controls.bHeadDown   = look_down;
    Controls.bStepLeft   = diks[DIK_COMMA]    && 0x80;
    Controls.bStepRight  = diks[DIK_PERIOD]   && 0x80;
    Controls.bFire       = dijs.rgbButtons[0] && 0x80;
    Controls.bScores     = diks[DIK_S]        && 0x80;
    Controls.bPrevWeap   = diks[DIK_INSERT]   && 0x80;
    Controls.bNextWeap   = diks[DIK_DELETE]   && 0x80;
    Controls.bTravelMode = diks[DIK_SPACE]    && 0x80;
}

for(i = 0; i < 256; i++)
{
```

(continued)

```
        if( (diks[i] && 0x80) == FALSE)
            DelayKey2[i] = FALSE;
    }

    if(RRAppActive == TRUE)
    {
        MovePlayer(&Controls);
    }

    }

}
```

This routine verifies that you have created a keyboard, mouse, or joystick DirectInput device. If you have a joystick, it calls the *IDirectInputDevice2::Poll* method. This method has no effect on keyboards or mouse devices, but for joysticks and other similar devices, it will update the device state, generate input events (if the buffer data is enabled), or set notification events (if notification is enabled).

The *IDirectInputDevice7::Acquire* method is then used to get access to the input device. Before acquiring a device, however, you must set a data format with the *IDirectInputDevice7::SetDataFormat* method covered earlier in the chapter.

You can define your own DIDATAFORMAT structure or use one of the following predefined global constants:

- *c_dfDIKeyboard*
- *c_dfDIMouse*
- *c_dfDIMouse2*
- *c_dfDIJoystick*
- c_*dfDIJoystick2*

As mentioned earlier, you should rarely need to create your own DIDATA-FORMAT structure. The five predefined global variables listed here will handle almost any device you'll need to deal with.

Once the format is set and the device is acquired, you can use the *IDirect-InputDevice2::GetDeviceState* method to get the immediate data on the attached input device. This method fills a DIDATAFORMAT structure, which is defined as follows:

```
typedef struct DIDATAFORMAT {
    DWORD dwSize;
    DWORD dwObjSize;
    DWORD dwFlags;
```

```
    DWORD dwDataSize;
    DWORD dwNumObjs;
    LPDIOBJECTDATAFORMAT rgodf;
} DIDATAFORMAT, *LPDIDATAFORMAT;

typedef const DIDATAFORMAT *LPCDIDATAFORMAT;
```

This structure has the following members.

dwSize   Size of this structure, in bytes.

dwObjSize   Size of the DIOBJECTDATAFORMAT structure, in bytes.

dwFlags   Flags describing other attributes of the data format. This value can be one of the following flags:

■ **DIDF_ABSAXIS**   The axes are in absolute mode. Setting this flag in the data format is equivalent to manually setting the axis mode property by using the *IDirectInputDevice7::SetProperty* method. This flag can't be combined with the DIDF_RELAXIS flag.

■ **DIDF_RELAXIS**   The axes are in relative mode. Setting this flag in the data format is equivalent to manually setting the axis mode property by using the *IDirectInputDevice7::SetProperty* method. This flag can't be combined with the DIDF_ABSAXIS flag.

dwDataSize   Size of a data packet returned by the device, in bytes. This value must be a multiple of 4 and must exceed the largest offset value for an object's data within the data packet.

dwNumObjs   Number of objects in the *rgodf* array.

rgodf   Address to an array of DIOBJECTDATAFORMAT structures. Each structure describes how one object's data should be reported in the device data. Typical errors include placing two pieces of information in the same location and placing one piece of information in more than one location.

The DIDATAFORMAT structure is filled with information about the device.

The declaration for the *IDirectInputDevice2::GetDeviceState* method follows:

```
HRESULT GetDeviceState(
    DWORD cbData,
    LPVOID lpvData,
);
```

The *lpvData* parameter is used to indicate the address of a structure for the function to fill with information about the device's state. The *cbData* member is used to specify the size, in bytes, of the buffer in the *lpvData* parameter.

At this point, you'll have all the information you need about the type of device you've found, and you'll be able to read the various states of the devices' axes, buttons, and so on. In the *CMyD3DApplication::UpdateControls* routine, the *diks* variable holds the keyboard information, the *dijs* variable holds the joystick information, and the *dims* variable holds the mouse information.

As an example, the line

```
Controls.bFire        = diks[DIK_LCONTROL]    && 0x80;
```

assigns TRUE or FALSE (1 or 0) to the *Controls.bFire* member. If the left CONTROL key is pressed, the member is set to TRUE. If the left CONTROL key is not pressed, the member is set to FALSE. The remainder of the *CMyD3DApplication::UpdateControls* routine sets the members of the Controls structure to the settings received from the keyboard, mouse and keyboard, or joystick devices, depending on what devices are currently selected from the IDD_SELECTINPUT-DEVICE pop-up window.

You now have all the code you need to implement support for any type of input device.

Force Feedback

Force feedback can add a great deal of realism to your 3D game or simulation. In fact, I recommend including it in every 3D application you create. DirectX has supported force feedback since version 5, with the *DirectInputEffect* interface. Using DirectInput, you can control force-feedback devices. You can use these devices to produce effects such as resistance or vibration when a character or vehicle collides with another prop or when the user presses a button.

In DirectInput, an *effect* is an instance of movement or resistance over a period of time. A number of standard categories of effects, called *forces,* are available for use in your applications. Here are some examples:

- **Constant force**   A steady force exerted in a single direction
- **Ramp force**   A force that increases or decreases in magnitude
- **Periodic effect**   A force that pulsates according to a defined wave pattern, such as a sine wave or a square wave
- **SawtoothUp/SawtoothDown force**   A waveform that rises or drops after reaching a maximum positive or negative force

DirectInput defines the following force types: *GUID_ConstantForce, GUID_CustomForce, GUID_Damper, GUID_Friction, GUID_Inertia, GUID_RampForce, GUID_SawtoothDown, GUID_SawtoothUp, GUID_Sine, GUID_Spring, GUID_Square,* and *GUID_Triangle.*

To create a force-feedback–capable device, you need to define an *IDirectInputDevice2* interface along with an *IDirectInputEffect* interface. You need the following variables:

```
//-----------------------------------------------------------------
// Global variables for the DirectMusic sample
//-----------------------------------------------------------------
LPDIRECTINPUT7          g_pDI        = NULL;
LPDIRECTINPUTDEVICE2    g_pJoystick  = NULL;
LPDIRECTINPUTEFFECT     g_pEffect    = NULL;
HINSTANCE               g_hInst      = NULL;
BOOL                    g_bActive    = TRUE;
int                     g_nXForce;
int                     g_nYForce;
```

To handle a force-feedback device, you need to add a number of new features to your code. The first (labeled STEP 1) is to modify the call to the *IDirectInput7:: EnumDevices* method in the *CMyD3DApplication::CreateDInput* routine. In this call, you set the first parameter to DIDEVTYPE_JOYSTICK to restrict the enumeration to just joystick-type devices, as we did for regular joystick enumeration. You also now need to pass the DIEDFL_FORCEFEEDBACK flag to restrict the enumeration further to devices attached to the system that actually support force feedback.

Next you need to disable the autocentering spring of the joystick so that it will be able to properly generate a force (labeled STEP 2). Finally, in STEP 3, you place the call to the routine that creates the force you want to play.

```
// Because we'll be playing force-feedback effects, disable the
// autocentering spring.
    HRESULT hr;
    ⋮
    // Create a DInput object.
    hr = DirectInputCreateEx( g_hInst, DIRECTINPUT_VERSION,
                              IID_IDirectInput7,
                              (VOID**)&g_pDI, NULL );
    if( FAILED(hr) )
        return hr;
    // STEP 1
    // Look for a usable force-feedback joystick.
    hr = g_pDI->EnumDevices( DIDEVTYPE_JOYSTICK,
```

(continued)

```
                                  EnumFFJoysticksCallback,
                                  NULL, DIEDFL_ATTACHEDONLY |
                                  DIEDFL_FORCEFEEDBACK );
    if( FAILED(hr) )
        return hr;

    if( NULL == g_pJoystick )
    {
        MessageBox( NULL, "Force-feedback joystick not found",
                    "DirectInput Sample", MB_ICONERROR | MB_OK );
        return E_FAIL;
    }

    // Set the data format to "simple joystick" - a predefined data
    // format. A data format specifies which controls on a device we
    // are interested in, and how they should be reported.
    //
    // This setting tells DirectInput that at some point in the
    // application (though not in this sample) it will be passed a
    // DIJOYSTATE structure to IDirectInputDevice2::GetDeviceState.
    // Setting the data format is important so that the DIJOFS_*
    // values work properly.
    hr = g_pJoystick->SetDataFormat( &c_dfDIJoystick );
    if( FAILED(hr) )
        return hr;

    // Set the cooperative level to let DInput know how this device
    // should interact with the system and with other DInput
    // applications. Exclusive access is required to perform force
    // feedback.
    hr = g_pJoystick->SetCooperativeLevel( hDlg,
                                           DISCL_EXCLUSIVE |
                                           DISCL_FOREGROUND );
    if( FAILED(hr) )
        return hr;

    // Because we'll be playing force-feedback effects, disable
    // the autocentering spring.
    DIPROPDWORD dipdw;
    dipdw.diph.dwSize       = sizeof(DIPROPDWORD);
    dipdw.diph.dwHeaderSize = sizeof(DIPROPHEADER);
    dipdw.diph.dwObj        = 0;
    dipdw.diph.dwHow        = DIPH_DEVICE;
    dipdw.dwData            = FALSE;
    //
    // STEP 2
    //
```

```
hr = g_pJoystick->SetProperty( DIPROP_AUTOCENTER, &dipdw.diph );
if( FAILED(hr) )
    return hr;
//
// STEP 3
//
// Call the routine to create the force-feedback effect here.
//
return S_OK;
```

Creating a Force

Magnitude, a force's strength, is measured in units ranging from 0 (no force) to 10,000 (the maximum force for the device). In DirectInput, magnitudes are linear, which means that a force of 5000 is twice as great as one of 2500. A negative value for magnitude will cause a device to exert force in the opposite direction of a positive value. The *direction* of a force refers to the direction it is exerted from. If you create a force on an axis, it will push along that axis from the positive direction toward the negative.

Each DirectInput effect has a *duration* that is measured in microseconds. If you define a periodic effect, you must specify its period (the duration of one cycle) in microseconds. The *phase* of this periodic effect describes the point along the wave at which playback begins. The magnitude of this periodic effect is the force at the peak of the wave.

You can change a force using a wrapper, known in DirectInput as an *envelope.* This envelope constrains the force in a set of ranges over time. It can define *attack* values and *fade* values, which you can use to modify the beginning and ending magnitude of the effect. These attack and fade values have durations that define the time it takes the magnitude to reach or recede from the *sustain value,* which is the magnitude in the middle portion of the effect.

Creating DirectInput Forces

To add force feedback to your code, you'll need to create the force-feedback effects and the routines to play them back either through a code control or a user hardware event (such as the user pressing a button).

By specifying periodic forces exerted in both the x-axis and the y-axis of a device, you can control joystick devices that have two axes (x and y) and devices with only one axis (x), such as a force-feedback steering wheel. If your code can drive (cause a device to exert a force on) both axes, it can handle any input device; the code can drive one axis for a steering wheel or both axes for a traditional joystick.

This code block shows how to describe two DirectInput effects, *m_pPeriodicX* and *m_pPeriodicY*, which are used to create forces for a force-feedback device:

```
void UpdatePeriodicType(int);
    LPDIRECTINPUTEFFECT m_pPeriodicX;
    LPDIRECTINPUTEFFECT m_pPeriodicY;
    BOOL CreateEffect(void);
    BOOL UpdatePeriodic(DWORD, DWORD);
```

You can use the *UpdatePeriodicType* routine to create DirectInput effects. This routine takes one argument specifying a force type (square, triangle, and so on). The local variables you define include the GUID variable used to request a force type and *diEffect*, and a DirectInput effect structure used to define a new effect (such as a periodic effect). The first segment of the routine, which appears below, declares these variables.

```
void UpdatePeriodicType(int type)
{

    HRESULT hRes;
    GUID tmpguid;
    DIEFFECT diEffect;
    DIPERIODIC diPer;
    DWORD rgdwAxes[2];
    LONG rglDirection[2];
```

The DirectInput DIEFFECT structure you use is defined as:

```
typedef struct DIEFFECT {
    DWORD dwSize;
    DWORD dwFlags;
    DWORD dwDuration;
    DWORD dwSamplePeriod;
    DWORD dwGain;
    DWORD dwTriggerButton;
    DWORD dwTriggerRepeatInterval;
    DWORD cAxes;
    LPDWORD rgdwAxes;
    LPLONG rglDirection;
    LPDIENVELOPE lpEnvelope;
    DWORD cbTypeSpecificParams;
    LPVOID lpvTypeSpecificParams;
    DWORD  dwStartDelay;
} DIEFFECT, *LPDIEFFECT;

typedef const DIEFFECT *LPCDIEFFECT;
```

The DIEFFECT structure has the following members.

dwSize   Specifies the size, in bytes, of the structure. This member must be initialized before the structure is used.

dwFlags   Flags associated with the effect. This value can be a combination of one or more of the following values:

- **DIEFF_CARTESIAN**   The values of *rglDirection* are to be interpreted as Cartesian coordinates.

- **DIEFF_OBJECTIDS**   The values of *dwTriggerButton* and *rgdwAxes* are object identifiers as obtained by *IDirectInputDevice7::EnumObjects*.

- **DIEFF_OBJECTOFFSETS**   The values of *dwTriggerButton* and *rgdwAxes* are data format offsets, relative to the data format selected by *IDirectInputDevice7::SetDataFormat*.

- **DIEFF_POLAR**   The values of *rglDirection* are to be interpreted as polar coordinates.

- **DIEFF_SPHERICAL**   The values of *rglDirection* are to be interpreted as spherical coordinates.

dwDuration   The total duration of the effect, in microseconds. If this value is INFINITE, the effect has infinite duration. If an envelope has been applied to the effect, the attack is applied, followed by an infinite sustain.

dwSamplePeriod   The period at which the device should play back the effect, in microseconds. A value of 0 indicates that the default playback sample rate should be used. If the device isn't capable of playing back the effect at the specified rate, it chooses the supported rate that is closest to the requested value. Setting a custom *dwSamplePeriod* can be used for special effects. For example, playing a sine wave at an artificially large sample period results in a rougher texture.

dwGain   The gain to be applied to the effect, in the range from 0 through 10,000. The gain is a scaling factor applied to all magnitudes of the effect and its envelope.

dwTriggerButton   The identifier or offset of the button to be used to trigger playback of the effect. The flags DIEFF_OBJECTIDS and DIEFF_OBJECTOFFSETS determine the semantics of the value. If this member is set to DIEB_NOTRIGGER, no trigger button is associated with the effect.

dwTriggerRepeatInterval The interval, in microseconds, between the end of one playback and the start of the next when the effect is triggered by a button press and the button is held down. Setting this value to INFINITE suppresses repetition. Support for trigger repeat for an effect is indicated by the presence of the DIEP_TRIGGERREPEATINTERVAL flag in the *dwStaticParams* member of the DIEFFECTINFO structure.

cAxes The number of axes involved in the effect. This member must be filled in by the caller if changing or setting the axis list or the direction list. Once it's been set, the number of axes for an effect can't be changed.

rgdwAxes Pointer to a DWORD array (of *cAxes* elements) containing identifiers or offsets identifying the axes to which the effect is to be applied. The flags DIEFF_OBJECTIDS and DIEFF_OBJECTOFFSETS determine the semantics of the values in the array. Once it's been set, the list of axes associated with an effect can't be changed. No more than 32 axes can be associated with a single effect.

rglDirection Pointer to a LONG array (of *cAxes* elements) containing either Cartesian coordinates or polar coordinates. The flags DIEFF_CARTESIAN, DIEFF_POLAR, and DIEFF_SPHERICAL determine the semantics of the values in the array.

If Cartesian, each value in *rglDirection* is associated with the corresponding axis in *rgdwAxes*. If polar, the angle is measured in hundredths of degrees from the $(0, -1)$ direction, rotated in the direction of $(1, 0)$. This usually means that north is away from the user and east is to the user's right. The last element isn't used. If spherical, the first angle is measured in hundredths of a degree from the $(1, 0)$ direction, rotated in the direction of $(0, 1)$. The second angle (if the number of axes is three or more) is measured in hundredths of a degree toward $(0, 0, 1)$. The third angle (if the number of axes is four or more) is measured in hundredths of a degree toward $(0, 0, 0, 1)$, and so on. The last element isn't used.

> **NOTE** The *rglDirection* array must contain *cAxes* entries, even if polar or spherical coordinates are given. In these cases, the last element in the *rglDirection* array is reserved for future use and must be 0.

lpEnvelope Optional pointer to a DIENVELOPE structure that describes the envelope to be used by this effect. Not all effect types use envelopes. If no envelope is to be applied, the member should be set to NULL.

cbTypeSpecificParams Number of bytes of additional type-specific parameters for the corresponding effect type.

lpvTypeSpecificParams   Pointer to type-specific parameters, or NULL if there are no type-specific parameters. If the effect is of type DIEFT_CONDITION, this member contains a pointer to an array of DICONDITION structures that define the parameters for the condition. A single structure can be used, in which case the condition is applied in the direction specified in the *rglDirection* array. Otherwise, there must be one structure for each axis, in the same order as the axes in the *rgdwAxes* array. If a structure is supplied for each axis, the effect should not be rotated; you should use the following values in the *rglDirection* array:

- DIEFF_SPHERICAL: 0, 0, ...

- DIEFF_POLAR: 9000, 0, ...

- DIEFF_CARTESIAN: 1, 0, ...

If the effect is of type DIEFT_CUSTOMFORCE, this member contains a pointer to a DICUSTOMFORCE structure that defines the parameters for the custom force.

If the effect is of type DIEFT_PERIODIC, this member contains a pointer to a DIPERIODIC structure that defines the parameters for the effect. If the effect is of type DIEFT_CONSTANTFORCE, this member contains a pointer to a DICONSTANTFORCE structure that defines the parameters for the constant force. If the effect is of type DIEFT_RAMPFORCE, this member contains a pointer to a DIRAMPFORCE structure that defines the parameters for the ramp force.

dwStartDelay   Time (in microseconds) that the device should wait after an *IDirect-InputEffect::Start* call before playing the effect. If this value is 0, effect playback begins immediately. This member isn't present in versions prior to DirectX 7.

After specifying the variables, you can fill in the periodic force structure, defined as follows:

```
typedef struct DIPERIODIC {
    DWORD dwMagnitude;
    LONG  lOffset;
    DWORD dwPhase;
    DWORD dwPeriod;
} DIPERIODIC, *LPDIPERIODIC;

typedef const DIPERIODIC *LPCDIPERIODIC;
```

The values you need to be concerned with follow.

dwMagnitude   As you just learned, the magnitude of an effect ranges from 0 to 10,000. If no envelope is applied, this value will describe the amplitude of the effect.

If you choose to apply an envelope to an effect (as shown in Figure 7-1), *dwMagnitude* defines the effect's sustain value.

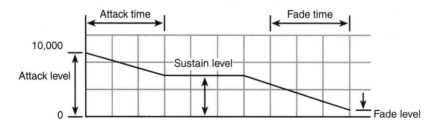

Figure 7-1
DirectInput envelope

lOffset This value specifies the amount the waveform is shifted up or down from the base level.

dwPhase As mentioned earlier, this is the point along the wave at which playback begins.

dwPeriod This value marks the duration of one cycle, in microseconds.
    This is the code for setting up a periodic force:

```
// Initialize DIEFFECT and DIENVELOPE structures.
   ZeroMemory(&diEffect, sizeof(DIEFFECT));
   //
   // Prepare the DIPERIODIC structure.
   //
   // This is the type-specific data for this force.
   diPer.dwMagnitude = 5000;
   diPer.lOffset     = 0;
   diPer.dwPhase     = 0;
   diPer.dwPeriod    = 100000; //10Hz
```

    Once you've defined these parameters, you can fill the *DirectInput Effect* structure used to create a force-feedback effect. The *dwSize* field of this structure describes its size in bytes. The *dwSamplePeriod* field defines the period in the number of microseconds in which the device will play back the effect. By specifying the value 0, you're requesting that the system use the default playback sample rate. The *dwTriggerButton* member indicates the trigger button you want to use. In the code segment that follows, the DIEB_NOTRIGGER value indicates that no trigger button will be associated with this effect. The final variable that this code segment sets, the *dwTriggerRepeatInterval* member of the structure, defines the interval (in microseconds) between the end of one playback and the beginning of the next when the effect is triggered by a button press and the user holds down the button.

```
// Prepare the DIEFFECT structure.
    //
    // Fill in the force-specific values.
    // These fields are the same for all effects you'll be creating.
    diEffect.dwSize                     = sizeof(DIEFFECT);
    // Use the default sample period.
    diEffect.dwSamplePeriod             = 0;
    diEffect.dwTriggerButton            = DIEB_NOTRIGGER;
    diEffect.dwTriggerRepeatInterval    = 0;
```

The *rgdwAxes* field specifies the axes you'll use. Both axes are used for a joystick, and one—the *x*-axis—is used for a steering wheel. The direction of an effect refers to the direction that it originates from. For example, if an effect has a direction along the negative *y*-axis (defined in the *rglDirection* field of the DIEFFECT structure), the effect will push the joystick toward the user along the positive *y*-axis. The *dwGain* field defines a gain between 0 and 10,000 that will be applied to the effect. This gain is a scaling factor that's applied to all magnitudes of the effect and its envelope. The last field, the *dwFlags* field, is set to a combination of the DIEFF_CARTESIAN and DIEFF_OBJECTOFFSETS flags. The DIEFF_CARTESIAN flag requests that values in the *rglDirection* field be interpreted as Cartesian coordinates. The DIEFF_OBJECTOFFSETS flag indicates that the values of the *dwTriggerButton* and *rgdwAxes* fields be used as data format offsets that are relative to the data format requested by a call to *IDirectInput:: SetDataFormat*.

```
// Which axes and directions to use?
    rgdwAxes[0]                 = DIJOFS_X;
    rgdwAxes[1]                 = DIJOFS_Y;
    diEffect.rgdwAxes           = rgdwAxes;
    rglDirection[0]             = 0;
    rglDirection[1]             = 1;
    diEffect.rglDirection       = rglDirection;
    diEffect.dwGain             = 10000;
    diEffect.dwFlags            = DIEFF_OBJECTOFFSETS |
                                  DIEFF_CARTESIAN;
```

The last values you must set in the effect's structure are *dwDuration*, *cAxes*, *lpEnvelope*, *cbTypeSpecificParams*, and *lpvTypeSpecificParams*. The *dwDuration* field describes the duration of an effect in microseconds. If you set it to a value of

INFINITE, the effect will occur infinitely. The *cAxes* field defines the number of axes in the effect. For a force-feedback steering wheel, you'd use only the *x*-axis. The *lpEnvelope* field defines the effect's envelope. By specifying NULL, you won't need an envelope for the effect you're creating. The *cbTypeSpecificParams* field defines the number of bytes used for the effect. The *lpvTypeSpecificParams* field defines a pointer to the type-specific parameters, contained in the DIPERIODIC structure specified earlier.

```
diEffect.dwDuration                 = INFINITE;
    diEffect.cAxes                  = 2;
    diEffect.lpEnvelope             = NULL;
    diEffect.cbTypeSpecificParams   = sizeof(DIPERIODIC);
    diEffect.lpvTypeSpecificParams  = &diPer;
```

In the next segment of code, you'll set the GUID for the effect type, selecting from the types we discussed earlier:

```
switch(type)
    {
        case 0:
            tmpguid = GUID_Sine;
            break;

        case 1:
            tmpguid = GUID_Square;
            break;

        case 2:
            tmpguid = GUID_Triangle;
            break;

        case 3:
            tmpguid = GUID_SawtoothUp;
            break;

        case 4:
            tmpguid = GUID_SawtoothDown;
            break;

        default:
            tmpguid = GUID_Sine;
    }

if (m_pPeriodicY)
    m_pPeriodicY->Release();
if (m_pPeriodicX)
    m_pPeriodicX->Release();
```

Now that you've defined your forces in the *x* and *y* directions, you have only one more step to perform. Call the *IDirectInputDevice2::CreateEffect* method to create and initialize two effects that are identified by the GUID selected in the previous case statement:

```
//
    // Call CreateEffect.
    //
    hRes = g_pJoystick->CreateEffect(tmpguid, &diEffect,
                                    &m_pPeriodicY, NULL);
    if(FAILED(hRes))
    {
        OutputDebugString("CreateEffect(VibrationY) failed\n");
    }

    rgdwAxes[0]                     = DIJOFS_X;
    rgdwAxes[1]                     = DIJOFS_Y;
    rglDirection[0]                 = 1;
    rglDirection[1]                 = 0;
    //
    // Call CreateEffect.
    //
    hRes = g_pJoystick->CreateEffect(tmpguid, &diEffect,
                                    &m_pPeriodicX, NULL);
    if(FAILED(hRes))
    {
        OutputDebugString("CreateEffect(VibrationX) failed\n");
    }
}
```

The *SetAcquire* routine determines whether the application is active; if the application is active, this routine calls the *IDirectInputDevice2::Acquire* method to gain access to the device. Once you have access to the device, you can call the *IDirectInputEffect::Start* method.

The *IDirectInputEffect::Start* method is used to start playing an effect. If the effect happens to already be playing, it will be started again from the beginning. DirectInput devices need to have the effects we want played downloaded to them initially. So if the effect hasn't yet been downloaded to the device, or if it's been modified since it was last downloaded, it is downloaded first. This method is defined as follows:

```
HRESULT Start(
    DWORD dwIterations,
    DWORD dwFlags,
);
```

The *IDirectInputEffect::Start* method has the following parameters.

dwIterations   Number of times to play the effect in sequence. The envelope is rearticulated with each iteration. To play the effect exactly once, pass 1. To play the effect repeatedly until explicitly stopped, pass INFINITE. To play the effect until explicitly stopped without rearticulating the envelope, modify the effect parameters with the *IDirectInputEffect::SetParameters* method and change the *dwDuration* member to INFINITE.

dwFlags   Flags that describe how the effect should be played by the device. The value can be 0 or one or more of the following values:

- **DIES_SOLO**   All other effects on the device should be stopped before the specified effect is played. If this flag is omitted, the effect is mixed with existing effects already started on the device.

- **DIES_NODOWNLOAD**   Do not automatically download the effect.

The *SetAcquire* function is defined as follows.

```
//------------------------------------------------------------------
// Name: SetAcquire
// Desc: Acquire or unacquire the mouse, depending on whether the
// application is active. The input device must be acquired before
// GetDeviceState is called.
//------------------------------------------------------------------
HRESULT SetAcquire( HWND hDlg )
{
    if( NULL == g_pJoystick )
        return S_FALSE;

    if( g_bActive )
    {
        // Acquire the input device.
        g_pJoystick->Acquire();

        if( g_pEffect )
            g_pEffect->Start( 1, 0 ); // Start the effect.
    }
    else
    {
        // Unacquire the input device.
        g_pJoystick->Unacquire();
    }
```

```
    return S_OK;
}
```

If you want to play forces to both the *x* and *y* axes rather than on just one axis, you would perform the following:

```
BOOL PlayVibration()
{
    HRESULT hRes;

    if(m_bYAxisOn)
        hRes = m_pPeriodicY->Start(1,0);

    if (FAILED(hRes))
        return FALSE;

    if(m_bXAxisOn)
        hRes = m_pPeriodicX->Start(1,0);

    if (FAILED(hRes))
        return FALSE;

    return TRUE;
    UpdatePeriodic(1);
}
```

The last routine you'll need to define is one to modify the effect you create so that you can vary the force-feedback effect that is produced. Doing this is basically the same as producing a new effect. You just set the parameters of the effect to the new settings you want and call the *IDirectInputEffect::SetParameters* method to set the effect to the new values.

```
//------------------------------------------------------------------
// Name: SetJoyForcesXY
// Desc: Apply the X and Y forces to the effect we prepared.
//------------------------------------------------------------------
HRESULT SetJoyForcesXY()
{
    // Modifying an effect is basically the same as creating a new
    // one except that you need to specify only the parameters you're
    // modifying.
    LONG rglDirection[2] = { g_nXForce, g_nYForce };

    DICONSTANTFORCE cf;
    cf.lMagnitude =
        (DWORD)sqrt( (double)g_nXForce * (double)g_nXForce +
                     (double)g_nYForce * (double)g_nYForce );
```

(continued)

213

```
        DIEFFECT eff;
        eff.dwSize                 = sizeof(DIEFFECT);
        eff.dwFlags                = DIEFF_CARTESIAN |
                                     DIEFF_OBJECTOFFSETS;
        eff.cAxes                  = 2;
        eff.rglDirection           = rglDirection;
        eff.lpEnvelope             = 0;
        eff.cbTypeSpecificParams   = sizeof(DICONSTANTFORCE);
        eff.lpvTypeSpecificParams = &cf;

        // Now set the new parameters and start the effect immediately.
        return g_pEffect->SetParameters( &eff, DIEP_DIRECTION |
                                         DIEP_TYPESPECIFICPARAMS |
                                         DIEP_START );
    }
```

Conclusion

This chapter covered all the critical aspects of DirectInput that you need to understand to add device input support to your program. It's not possible to detail every aspect of DirectInput in a single chapter. However, with an understanding of the commands and code covered in this chapter, you should be able to implement keyboard, mouse, and joystick support for any program you write. If you want additional information on working with DirectInput, I recommend you pick up a copy of *Inside DirectX* (Microsoft Press, 1998).

Having completed this chapter, you should now find the concepts of input device handling and force feedback less daunting. Conceptually, force feedback isn't difficult to use in DirectX. You just need to remember to set all the parameters defining the various forces required to generate the real-world force that you want to simulate. You might want to take some time now to add support for other joystick features that weren't addressed in this chapter's code.

In Chapter 8, you'll learn about the many texturing capabilities Direct3D provides. Texturing makes 3D worlds appear realistic to the user and is a must for any 3D simulation that intends to draw the user into the virtual world. Direct3D offers many features for texturing, and once you understand how to use them, you'll be able to create beautiful, engaging 3D worlds.

CHAPTER EIGHT

Texturing

To make a rendered scene look more realistic, Microsoft Direct3D provides the capability of applying textures to 3D primitives. You can apply textures to a 3D world to simulate wall coverings and materials such as tapestries and bricks. Direct3D provides an advanced set of texturing methods that you can use to create vivid, real-time games and simulations. Once rendered, your 3D scenes will successfully mimic the images and environments you see in the real world.

Think of a texture as a bitmap of pixel colors that you apply to the surface of a 3D object. In the real world, *texture* refers to an object's color, pattern, and tactile characteristics. In Direct3D, however, *texture* is simply the color pattern of the object; it doesn't change the geometric form of the object at all. This color pattern makes the object *appear* textured or bumpy. (We'll go over bump maps, which produce the appearance of raised textures on an object's surfaces, later in this chapter.) Direct3D textures don't actually create a geometric texture on the object's surface. That would be a computationally intensive endeavor, to say the least.

Although textures are only bitmaps, you can apply them to 3D primitives to make them look like real-world objects. In this chapter's code, you'll see how to use textures to render blacktop roads—complete with the painted line down the middle—sidewalks, and brick walls. You'll also see how to apply textures to cars and signs to give them the appearance of having windows, posters, and so on.

This chapter will also cover how to apply advanced texturing approaches, including mipmapping and texture blending. Mipmapping allows you to create textures with multiple levels of detail so that, as the user moves closer to an object in the virtual world, more complex textures gradually replace the simpler ones. Mipmapping enables you to produce realistic, highly detailed objects without excessive computational overhead. Texture blending allows you to apply multiple texture maps to the same surface. You can use this technique to simulate subtle lighting or material effects.

Texture Coordinates

A Direct3D texture is nothing more than a bitmap—a two-dimensional array of color values. Each entry in the array is an individual color value called a *texel*. Each texel has a unique address in the texture that is basically the column and row position, defined as *u* (column) and *v* (row). This address is called a *texture coordinate* and is represented in the texture's own coordinate space. A position in texture space is specified in relation to the texture's origin $(0, 0)$.

When you apply a texture to a 3D primitive, Direct3D needs to map the texel addresses into object coordinates and then translate those addresses into screen coordinates (pixel locations). Direct3D maps texels from texture space directly into pixels in screen space. Direct3D also determines the texel or texels needed to color each pixel in screen space. The texture color of the point on the polygon that maps to the 2D pixel location is determined in a process known as *texture filtering,* which is described in detail later in this chapter. You can access each texel in a texture by specifying its texel coordinates. However, Direct3D needs a uniform address range for all the texels in a texture so that it can map them onto a primitive. To do this, Direct 3D uses a normalized addressing scheme in which texture addresses consist of texel coordinates that map to the address range 0.0 to 1.0. The texture addresses are defined using (u, v) values, which are analogous to (x, y) coordinates in screen space. Be aware that mapping from texture space to screen space means that texels from differently sized textures can have identical texture addresses but can be mapped to different screen coordinates. In short, by using normalized coordinates for textures, Direct3D allows you to deal with texture coordinates without worrying about the dimensions of the texture map you're using.

Assigning Texture Coordinates

You can assign texture coordinates to the vertices (see the D3DVERTEX structure) that define the primitives in your 3D world. This way, you can control which part of the texture is mapped onto the primitive. Also, when multitexturing (texture blending), you can use flexible vertex formats to specify a (u, v) pair for each *texture stage*. (You'll learn more about texture stages later in this chapter.) For example, if you have a rectangular primitive that represents a wall segment and that has the same aspect ratio (the ratio of width to height) as a texture, you can assign the texture coordinates $(0.0, 0.0)$, $(1.0, 0.0)$, $(1.0, 1.0)$, and $(0.0, 1.0)$ to the primitive's vertices, causing Direct3D to stretch the texture over the entire rectangle.

If you instead choose to apply the texture to a rectangle that's half as wide, you have to decide how to apply it. The first option is to apply the entire texture to the rectangle, which requires you to change the texture's aspect ratio (squash the texture) so that it fits the narrower wall. When you scale the texture, the texture-filtering method you choose will impact the quality of the rendered image.

The second option is to apply the left or right half of the texture to the wall. If you choose to apply the left side of the texture, assign the texture coordinates (0.0, 0.0), (0.5, 0.0), (0.5, 1.0), and (0.0, 1.0) to the vertices. If you've designed textures with edges that blend well together, this approach might be problematic for some applications because it effectively cuts the texture in half, preventing the edges from matching colorwise.

The third option is to change the texture-addressing mode to allow techniques such as wrapping, clamping, and mirroring (which you'll learn about later in the chapter).

Creating Texture Surfaces

In Microsoft DirectX 7, textures are actually DirectDraw surfaces. To create a new surface for a texture and copy a bitmap as a texture into it, you could use the following *CreateTextureFromBitmap* routine. This routine also turns on texture management (described later) for hardware Direct3D devices.

```
//-----------------------------------------------------------------
// Name: CreateTextureFromBitmap
// Desc: Uses a bitmap to create a texture for the specified device.
//       This code gets the attributes of the texture from the
//       bitmap, creates the texture, and then copies the bitmap into
//       the texture.
//-----------------------------------------------------------------
static LPDIRECTDRAWSURFACE7 CreateTextureFromBitmap(
                                LPDIRECT3DDEVICE7 pd3dDevice,
                                HBITMAP hbm )
{
    LPDIRECTDRAWSURFACE7 pddsTexture;
    HRESULT hr;

    // Get the device caps so that you can check whether the device
    // has any constraints when using textures.
    D3DDEVICEDESC7 ddDesc;
    if( FAILED( pd3dDevice->GetCaps( &ddDesc ) ) )
        return NULL;

    // Get the bitmap structure (to extract width, height, and bpp).
    BITMAP bm;
    GetObject( hbm, sizeof(BITMAP), &bm );
```

(continued)

```
DWORD dwWidth  = (DWORD)bm.bmWidth;
DWORD dwHeight = (DWORD)bm.bmHeight;

// Set up the new surface description for the texture. Because
// we're using the texture management attribute, Direct3D does
// a lot of the dirty work for us.
DDSURFACEDESC2 ddsd;
ZeroMemory( &ddsd, sizeof(DDSURFACEDESC2) );
ddsd.dwSize           = sizeof(DDSURFACEDESC2);
ddsd.dwFlags          = DDSD_CAPS | DDSD_HEIGHT |
                        DDSD_WIDTH | DDSD_PIXELFORMAT;
ddsd.ddsCaps.dwCaps   = DDSCAPS_TEXTURE;
ddsd.dwWidth          = dwWidth;
ddsd.dwHeight         = dwHeight;

// Turn on texture management for hardware devices.
if( ddDesc.deviceGUID == IID_IDirect3DHALDevice )
    ddsd.ddsCaps.dwCaps2 = DDSCAPS2_TEXTUREMANAGE;
else if( ddDesc.deviceGUID == IID_IDirect3DTnLHalDevice )
    ddsd.ddsCaps.dwCaps2 = DDSCAPS2_TEXTUREMANAGE;
else
    ddsd.ddsCaps.dwCaps |= DDSCAPS_SYSTEMMEMORY;

// Adjust width and height if the driver requires you to.
if( ddDesc.dpcTriCaps.dwTextureCaps & D3DPTEXTURECAPS_POW2 )
{
    for( ddsd.dwWidth=1;  dwWidth>ddsd.dwWidth;
         ddsd.dwWidth<<=1 );
    for( ddsd.dwHeight=1; dwHeight>ddsd.dwHeight;
         ddsd.dwHeight<<=1 );
}
if( ddDesc.dpcTriCaps.dwTextureCaps & D3DPTEXTURECAPS_SQUAREONLY )
{
    if( ddsd.dwWidth > ddsd.dwHeight )
        ddsd.dwHeight = ddsd.dwWidth;
    else
        ddsd.dwWidth  = ddsd.dwHeight;
}

// Enumerate the texture formats, and find the closest device-
// supported texture pixel format. The TextureSearchCallback
// function here is simply looking for a 16-bit texture. Real
// applications might be interested in other formats, such as
// for alpha textures, bump maps, and so on.
pd3dDevice->EnumTextureFormats( TextureSearchCallback,
                                &ddsd.ddpfPixelFormat );
if( 0L == ddsd.ddpfPixelFormat.dwRGBBitCount )
```

```
        return NULL;

// Get the device's render target so that we can use the render
// target to get a pointer to a DDraw object. We need the
// DirectDraw interface for creating surfaces.
LPDIRECTDRAWSURFACE7 pddsRender;
LPDIRECTDRAW7        pDD;
pd3dDevice->GetRenderTarget( &pddsRender );
pddsRender->GetDDInterface( (VOID**)&pDD );
pddsRender->Release();

// Create a new surface for the texture.
if( FAILED( hr = pDD->CreateSurface( &ddsd, &pddsTexture,
                                     NULL ) ) )
{
    pDD->Release();
    return NULL;
}

// Done with DDraw.
pDD->Release();

// Now copy the bitmap to the texture surface. To do this, we're
// creating a device context (DC) for the bitmap and a DC for
// the surface so that we can use the BitBlt() call to copy the
// actual bits.

// Get a DC for the bitmap.
HDC hdcBitmap = CreateCompatibleDC( NULL );
if( NULL == hdcBitmap )
{
    pddsTexture->Release();
    return NULL;
}
SelectObject( hdcBitmap, hbm );

// Get a DC for the surface.
HDC hdcTexture;
if( SUCCEEDED( pddsTexture->GetDC( &hdcTexture ) ) )
{
    // Copy the bitmap image to the surface.
    BitBlt( hdcTexture, 0, 0, bm.bmWidth, bm.bmHeight, hdcBitmap,
            0, 0, SRCCOPY );
    pddsTexture->ReleaseDC( hdcTexture );
}
```

(continued)

```
        DeleteDC( hdcBitmap );

        // Return the newly created texture.
        return pddsTexture;
}
```

Palettized Textures

Although a simple texture surface like the one in the previous code will work for many texturing needs, you'll often want to use more advanced approaches so that your applications use less memory or to enhance the application's visual effects. The first of these approaches involves using *palettized textures,* which are texture surfaces that use an attached palette. Palettized textures represent the simplest form of *texture compression* (which is described later in this chapter). Palettized textures are DirectDrawSurface7 objects that you create by specifying the DDSCAPS_ TEXTURE flag and using one of the DDPF_PALETTEINDEXEDn pixel formats (in which n is 1, 2, 4, or 8). Palettized textures allow you to save a large amount of memory (much more than using RGBA colors for every pixel allows) and are thus useful for many applications.

To create a palettized texture, you must specify the DirectDraw and Direct3D capabilities you need. Specify these capabilities in the DDSURFACEDESC2 structure used to create the surface. You specify dimensions for the surface when you create it, along with the DDSCAPS_TEXTURE flag and one of the DDPF_ PALETTEINDEXEDn pixel-format flags. After creating this surface, you'll create and initialize a DirectDrawPalette object by using the *IDirectDraw7::Create-Palette* method.

The last step in creating a palettized texture is to attach the palette to a surface by using the *IDirectDrawSurface7::SetPalette* method. If you forget to attach the palette, an access violation will occur during rendering.

Each pixel in a palettized surface (a surface with a palette attached to it) is an index to a table of values held within the attached DirectDrawPalette object. You should use the *IDirect3DDevice7::EnumTextureFormats* method to identify the texture formats that the current driver supports.

The following code shows how to create a texture that uses a palette:

```
//------------------------------------------------------------
// Name: CopyBitmapToSurface
// Desc: Copies the image of a bitmap into a surface
//------------------------------------------------------------
HRESULT TextureContainer::CopyBitmapToSurface()
{
        // Get a DDraw object to create a temporary surface.
```

```
LPDIRECTDRAW7 pDD;
m_pddsSurface->GetDDInterface( (VOID**)&pDD );

// Get the bitmap structure (to extract width, height, and bpp).
BITMAP bm;
GetObject( m_hbmBitmap, sizeof(BITMAP), &bm );

// Set up the new surface description.
DDSURFACEDESC2 ddsd;
ddsd.dwSize = sizeof(ddsd);
m_pddsSurface->GetSurfaceDesc( &ddsd );
ddsd.dwFlags            = DDSD_CAPS | DDSD_HEIGHT | DDSD_WIDTH |
                          DDSD_PIXELFORMAT | DDSD_TEXTURESTAGE;
ddsd.ddsCaps.dwCaps     = DDSCAPS_TEXTURE | DDSCAPS_SYSTEMMEMORY;
ddsd.ddsCaps.dwCaps2    = 0L;
ddsd.dwWidth            = bm.bmWidth;
ddsd.dwHeight           = bm.bmHeight;

// Create a new surface for the texture.
LPDIRECTDRAWSURFACE7 pddsTempSurface;
HRESULT hr;
if( FAILED( hr = pDD->CreateSurface( &ddsd, &pddsTempSurface,
                                     NULL ) ) )
{
    pDD->Release();
    return hr;
}

// Get a DC for the bitmap.
HDC hdcBitmap = CreateCompatibleDC( NULL );
if( NULL == hdcBitmap )
{
    pddsTempSurface->Release();
    pDD->Release();
    return hr;
}
SelectObject( hdcBitmap, m_hbmBitmap );

// Handle palettized textures. You'll need to attach a palette.
if( ddsd.ddpfPixelFormat.dwRGBBitCount == 8 )
{
    LPDIRECTDRAWPALETTE  pPalette;
    DWORD dwPaletteFlags = DDPCAPS_8BIT|DDPCAPS_ALLOW256;
    DWORD pe[256];
    WORD  wNumColors     = GetDIBColorTable( hdcBitmap, 0, 256,
                                             (RGBQUAD*)pe );
```

(continued)

```
              // Create the color table.
              for( WORD i=0; i<wNumColors; i++ )
              {
                  pe[i] = RGB(GetBValue(pe[i]),
                              GetGValue(pe[i]),
                              GetRValue(pe[i]));

                  // Handle textures with transparent pixels.
                  if( m_dwFlags & (D3DTEXTR_TRANSPARENTWHITE |
                                   D3DTEXTR_TRANSPARENTBLACK) )
                  {
                      // Set alpha for opaque pixels.
                      if( m_dwFlags & D3DTEXTR_TRANSPARENTBLACK )
                      {
                          if( pe[i] != 0x00000000 )
                              pe[i] |= 0xff000000;
                      }
                      else if( m_dwFlags & D3DTEXTR_TRANSPARENTWHITE )
                      {
                          if( pe[i] != 0x00ffffff )
                              pe[i] |= 0xff000000;
                      }
                  }
              }
              // Add the DDPCAPS_ALPHA flag for textures with transparent
              // pixels.
              if( m_dwFlags & (D3DTEXTR_TRANSPARENTWHITE |
                               D3DTEXTR_TRANSPARENTBLACK))
                  dwPaletteFlags |= DDPCAPS_ALPHA;

              // Create and attach a palette.
              pDD->CreatePalette(dwPaletteFlags,(PALETTEENTRY*)pe,
                                 &pPalette, NULL);
              pddsTempSurface->SetPalette( pPalette );
              m_pddsSurface->SetPalette( pPalette );
              SAFE_RELEASE( pPalette );
          }

          // Copy the bitmap image to the surface.
          HDC hdcSurface;
          if( SUCCEEDED( pddsTempSurface->GetDC( &hdcSurface ) ) )
          {
              BitBlt( hdcSurface, 0, 0, bm.bmWidth, bm.bmHeight, hdcBitmap,
                      0, 0, SRCCOPY );
              pddsTempSurface->ReleaseDC( hdcSurface );
          }
```

```
DeleteDC( hdcBitmap );

// Copy the temporary surface to the real texture surface.
m_pddsSurface->Blt( NULL, pddsTempSurface, NULL,
                    DDBLT_WAIT, NULL );

// Done with the temporary surface.
pddsTempSurface->Release();

// For textures with real alpha (not palettized), set
// transparent bits.
if( ddsd.ddpfPixelFormat.dwRGBAlphaBitMask )
{
    if(m_dwFlags & (D3DTEXTR_TRANSPARENTWHITE |
                    D3DTEXTR_TRANSPARENTBLACK) )
    {
        // Lock the texture surface.
        DDSURFACEDESC2 ddsd;
        ddsd.dwSize = sizeof(ddsd);
        while( m_pddsSurface->Lock( NULL, &ddsd, 0, NULL ) ==
                DDERR_WASSTILLDRAWING );

        DWORD dwAlphaMask =
            ddsd.ddpfPixelFormat.dwRGBAlphaBitMask;
        DWORD dwRGBMask   = ( ddsd.ddpfPixelFormat.dwRBitMask |
                              ddsd.ddpfPixelFormat.dwGBitMask |
                              ddsd.ddpfPixelFormat.dwBBitMask );
        DWORD dwColorkey = 0x00000000; // Color key on black
        if( m_dwFlags & D3DTEXTR_TRANSPARENTWHITE )
            dwColorkey = dwRGBMask;     // Color key on white

        // Add an opaque alpha value to each non-color-keyed pixel.
        for( DWORD y=0; y<ddsd.dwHeight; y++ )
        {
            WORD*  p16 =
                (WORD*)((BYTE*)ddsd.lpSurface + y*ddsd.lPitch);
            DWORD* p32 =
                (DWORD*)((BYTE*)ddsd.lpSurface + y*ddsd.lPitch);

            for( DWORD x=0; x<ddsd.dwWidth; x++ )
            {
                if( ddsd.ddpfPixelFormat.dwRGBBitCount == 16 )
```

(continued)

```
                                {
                                    if( ( *p16 &= dwRGBMask ) != dwColorkey )
                                        *p16 |= dwAlphaMask;
                                    p16++;
                                }
                                if( ddsd.ddpfPixelFormat.dwRGBBitCount == 32 )
                                {
                                    if( ( *p32 &= dwRGBMask ) != dwColorkey )
                                        *p32 |= dwAlphaMask;
                                    p32++;
                                }
                        }
                    }
                }
                m_pddsSurface->Unlock( NULL );
            }
        }

        pDD->Release();

        return S_OK;
    }
```

Texture Management

Texture management is the process of determining which textures are needed for rendering, and making sure that those textures are loaded in video memory so that Direct3D can apply them to objects. Three primary tasks are required for performing texture management:

■ Tracking the available texture memory

■ Determining which textures are needed for rendering the current frame

■ Deciding which of the existing texture surfaces you can reload with another texture image and which surfaces you should replace with new texture surfaces

Before the release of DirectX 6, you had to implement your own texture management scheme, which entailed spending extra time on software development that you probably would've preferred to spend on content development. Current versions of Direct3D can perform texture management for you, guaranteeing that textures are automatically loaded for optimal performance. The texture surfaces that Direct3D manages are known as *managed textures.* You can still do your own texture management if you prefer, but Direct3D's texture management does everything you need for most purposes.

The *CreateTextureFromBitmap* function shown in the "Creating Texture Surfaces" section of this chapter illustrates how to turn on texture management when a hardware Direct3D device is being used. You should not turn on texture management when using a software Direct3D device. If the GUID of the current Direct3D device is IID_IDirect3DHALDevice or IID_IDirect3DTnLHalDevice, the DDSCAPS2_TEXTUREMANAGE flag is set to make the new texture use Direct3D's texture management.

Three other flags pertain to texture management and help the system understand what the application will do with its textures: DDSCAPS2_HINTDYNAMIC, DDSCAPS2_HINTSTATIC, and DDSCAPS2_OPAQUE. You can use these flags only for texture surfaces, which are defined with the DDSCAPS_TEXTURE flag set in the *dwCaps* member. These flags are optional, but they can improve performance. You can't set more than one of these flags on a texture.

Here are the definitions of these flags:

- **DDSCAPS2_HINTDYNAMIC** Tells the driver that the texture surface will often be locked. This is frequently the case for procedural textures (computer-generated textures), dynamic light maps (dynamic computer-generated textures that simulate lighting conditions), and similar objects.

- **DDSCAPS2_HINTSTATIC** Tells the driver that a texture surface can be reordered or retiled on load. This operation is fairly fast and symmetrical because an application can lock these bits. (Remember, the application will take a performance hit when this operation occurs.) Reordering or retiling a texture doesn't affect its size.

- **DDSCAPS2_OPAQUE** Tells the driver that this texture surface won't be locked again. The driver can therefore optimize this surface by retiling and compressing it when it needs to. You can't lock this surface. You also can't used it in blit operations. If you try to either lock or blit a surface with this capability, the call will fail.

Direct3D's texture-management scheme automatically loads textures into video memory as needed. Be aware that Direct3D can store managed textures in local or nonlocal video memory. Direct3D doesn't indicate where the texture is cached because it determines when an application is trying to use more textures than will fit in video memory. If an application exceeds video-memory capacity with its textures, Direct3D will remove, or *evict*, older textures from video memory to free up space for new ones.

If an application needs to reuse a texture that Direct 3D has evicted, Direct3D will reload the original texture surface from system memory into the video memory cache. Each time a texture requires reloading, it will slow your application slightly.

However, the lag time is minimal and, of course, unavoidable when implementing this efficient approach of texture handling.

You can dynamically modify the system memory's original copy of a texture by blitting to or locking the texture surface. Once a blit is completed or the surface is unlocked—in other words, once Direct3D finds a *dirty* texture—the texture manager will automatically update the video memory's copy of the texture. This update will cause a performance hit comparable to that of reloading an evicted texture. Typically you'll need to evict all the managed textures from video memory when you move from one game level to another or when you load a new segment of a map (as with the RoadRage application we're building in this book). You can evict all managed textures using the *IDirect3D7::EvictManagedTextures* method, which destroys any cached local and nonlocal textures in video memory and leaves the original copies in system memory alone.

Here's the declaration for the *IDirect3D7::EvictManagedTextures* method:

```
HRESULT IDirect3D7::EvictManagedTextures()
```

This method doesn't have any parameters.

One performance enhancement related to textures that you might want to consider is to reverse the order in which you render polygons from frame to frame. This prevents texture thrashing during the process of evicting textures used in the current frame to reclaim texture memory for subsequent frames. Texture thrashing can occur when the textures you require exceed the available video memory. If your frame requires textures A, B, C, and D but you have only enough video memory for three textures, you should render the polygons that need A first, followed by those that need B, then those that need C, and finally those that need D. For the next frame, you should start with the polygons that need texture D, followed by those that need C, then B, then A. This way, you'll need to evict and reload only one texture (A); this is obviously preferable to having the Least Recently Used algorithm in the texture manager force you to reload every texture!

You might be wondering, "Why not always use Direct3D's texture management?" The answer is the same as the answer to the question, "Why not always use Direct3D's transformation and lighting?" Start with using the facilities that Direct3D provides and when your application is fully fleshed out, profile it to determine whether writing your own algorithms will improve its performance. Most of the time, you'll be quite happy with Direct3D's performance.

Texture Compression

To render the most realistic-looking scenes, it's best to use high-resolution textures with rich color depth. However, such textures can consume a lot of memory. For example, a 256 × 256 texture with 16 bits of color per pixel will use 128 KB of memory. Adding mipmaps to this texture costs an additional 43 KB of memory. A scene with 50 such textures will require more than 8 MB of memory. For added realism, you can use 512×512 textures with 32 bits of color per pixel, but that uses eight times as much memory!

Managing this much data can hurt your application's performance in several ways. First, the texture data must be loaded from disk into the computer. Second, the texture data needs to be transferred to memory that the video card can access (unless the renderer can use textures directly from system RAM or AGP memory). If the video card doesn't have enough memory to hold all the textures you're using, expensive transfers from system to video memory will constantly occur. Finally the rendering hardware needs to access all those textures—often many times per texel—while rasterizing primitives. Texture compression is therefore an essential technique for using high-quality textures without overwhelming the video memory subsystem. Early 3D accelerator cards didn't use compressed textures, but now that DirectX promotes a standard for compressed textures, hardware support is much more prevalent.

DXT Formats

Microsoft introduced DXT-compressed texture surfaces with DirectX 6. DXT is a type of DirectDraw surface that stores its image data in compressed form. Several 3D accelerator cards can render textures directly from DXT surfaces, which affords tremendous memory and bandwidth savings. But even when working with a renderer that doesn't use DXT surfaces directly, you can save disk space by authoring textures in the DXT format.

Five varieties of the DXT format exist: DXT1, DXT2, DXT3, DXT4, and DXT5. The compression ratio for the DXT1 format is 4:1. (A 4×4 block of 16-bit RGB565 texels is compressed to 64 bits: two 16-bit RGB565 values and sixteen 2-bit indices.) This level of compression isn't spectacular (when compared with compression technologies such as JPEG), but it's enough to effectively quadruple a 3D accelerator card's capacity for storing textures.

In return for this modest compression ratio, the compressed texture format has the following advantages compared with more sophisticated compression algorithms such as JPEG:

■ Each 4×4 texel block can be compressed and decompressed independently of the other blocks. Techniques that provide higher compression ratios might also require decompressing larger portions of the texture image.

- Each compressed block is always the same size (for example, in the DXT1 format it's 64 bits), which simplifies the problem of finding the block that contains a particular 4 × 4 region of the texture. The blocks representing the image can be stored in an array, and the offset into this array is easily calculated from the *x* and *y* indices and the block size.

- The decompression algorithm is fast. It simply uses the 2-bit indices in the compressed block to select colors from a four-value lookup table.

Although it's not necessary to know all the details about how DXT compression works, a few concepts are worth noting. The following table describes the five DXT formats:

Setting for DDPIXELFORMAT's *dwFourCC* Member	Description	Alpha Premultiplied?
DXT1	Opaque; 1-bit alpha	Not applicable
DXT2	Explicit alpha	Yes
DXT3	Explicit alpha	No
DXT4	Interpolated alpha	Yes
DXT5	Interpolated alpha	No

As you can see, the primary difference among these variations is the treatment of alpha. DXT1 works for opaque images or images with 1 bit of alpha, which means that it works well for most textures, including those that have traditionally used color-keyed transparency. DXT2 and DXT3 use four levels of alpha that are evenly spaced between full transparency and full opacity. DXT4 and DXT5 can have values indicating full transparency and full opacity, plus four other levels interpolated between two values that the application specifies. As an alternative, DXT4 and DXT5 can instead simply have six alpha levels interpolated between two specified values. DXT2 and DXT4 use premultiplied alpha, in which the RGB values for each pixel have already been scaled down by the alpha value at that pixel, while DXT3 and DXT5 use non-premultiplied alpha, in which the RGB values remain independent of the alpha value. Whether you use premultiplied or non-premultiplied alpha depends on what your hardware supports and how you plan to use the texture.

DXT works by breaking images into 4 × 4 texel chunks and exploiting color coherence within each chunk. For example, in the DXT1 format the compression software converts the 4 × 4 texel data into two 16-bit color values (RGB 5:6:5 format) plus 2 bits per texel. The 2 bits represent an index into a table containing the two 16-bit color values plus two more values. The compressor derives the two additional values from the 16-bit color values through linear interpolation. This compression procedure can cause images with a large number of colors in a small area to suffer some loss in quality. DXT is a fixed-rate compression format, meaning that a compressed, solid white image will take up as much space as a compressed photograph. However, DXT does a remarkable job of efficiently compressing a wide range of images that will likely be useful as texture maps. DXT1 uses 4 bits per texel, while the DXT2 through DXT5 formats use 8 bits per texel. (The DXT2 through DXT5 formats are larger because of their extra alpha information.) Therefore, compressing a 24-bit RGB image to DXT1 format can yield a sixfold compression savings, and compressing a 32-bit RGBA image to any of the DXT2 through DXT5 formats produces a fourfold compression savings. Be aware that you can simply compress a 24-bit pixel to 16-bit RGB565 without using DXT1 at all, which accounts for the difference between the 6:1 ratio for a DXT1 format shown here and the 4:1 ratio listed earlier.

Using DXT Surfaces

In DirectDraw, you create DXT surfaces the same way you create ordinary texture surfaces except that instead of specifying the DDPF_RGB flag, you must specify the DDPF_FOURCC flag and a FOURCC code indicating which DXT format to use. Here's an example of code that creates a 256 × 256 DXT1 texture that uses automatic texture management:

```
DDSURFACEDESC2 ddsd;
LPDIRECTDRAWSURFACE7 pddsCompressed = NULL;
ZeroMemory(&ddsd, sizeof(ddsd));
ddsd.dwSize = sizeof(ddsd);
ddsd.dwFlags = DDSD_CAPS | DDSD_WIDTH |
               DDSD_HEIGHT | DDSD_PIXELFORMAT;
ddsd.ddsCaps.dwCaps = DDSCAPS_TEXTURE;
ddsd.ddsCaps.dwCaps2 = DDSCAPS2_TEXTUREMANAGE;
ddsd.dwWidth = 256;
ddsd.dwHeight = 256;
ddsd.ddpfPixelFormat.dwSize = sizeof(DDPIXELFORMAT);
ddsd.ddpfPixelFormat.dwFlags = DDPF_FOURCC;
ddsd.ddpfPixelFormat.dwFourCC = FOURCC_DXT1;
if (FAILED(hr = pDD->CreateSurface(&ddsd, &pddsCompressed, NULL)))
    return hr;
return S_OK;
```

To move an image from a regular RGB surface into the compressed texture, use DirectDraw's *Blt* function. If the source RGB surface has alpha bits, *Blt* will set alpha information appropriately in the destination DXT surface. If the source RGB surface has a color key attached, *Blt* will set the alpha for each pixel to either opaque or transparent. The reverse operation also works: you can blit from a DXT texture to just about any format of RGB surface to decompress the image. Be aware that compressing an image into a DXT format is much slower than decompressing it. Therefore, applications should avoid compressing textures at run time and use precompressed textures instead.

Another way to fill the compressed texture is to lock the surface and then transfer DXT-compressed data directly into it. This method is the one you should use if you've stored your texture data on file in compressed format. The DirectX SDK illustrates this approach with the DirectX Texture Tool and the Compress sample application. (You'll see the files for these applications if you install DirectX 7 from the CD accompanying this book.) The DirectX Texture Tool lets you load uncompressed images, generate mipmap levels (see the section that follows), compress the resulting surface, and save everything as a DirectDraw surface (DDS) file. The DDS file is a simple format that holds the surface description (which holds the image dimensions, compression format, and other useful parameters), followed by one or more blocks of compressed surface data (one block per mipmap level). Here's the code needed to load a DDS file:

```
HRESULT ReadDDSTexture( CHAR* strTextureName, LPDIRECTDRAW7 pDD,
                        DDSURFACEDESC2* pddsdComp,
                        LPDIRECTDRAWSURFACE7* ppddsCompTop )
{
    HRESULT              hr;
    LPDIRECTDRAWSURFACE7 pddsTop      = NULL;
    LPDIRECTDRAWSURFACE7 pdds         = NULL;
    LPDIRECTDRAWSURFACE7 pddsAttached = NULL;
    DDSURFACEDESC2       ddsd;
    DWORD                dwMagic;

    hr = E_FAIL;
    //
    // Open the compressed texture file.
    //
    FILE* file = fopen( strTextureName, "rb" );
    if( file == NULL )
        return E_FAIL;

    // Read the magic number.
    fread( &dwMagic, sizeof(DWORD), 1, file );
```

```
if( dwMagic != MAKEFOURCC('D','D','S',' ') )
    goto LFail;
//
// Read the surface description.
//
fread( pddsdComp, sizeof(DDSURFACEDESC2), 1, file );
//
// Mask/set surface caps appropriately for the application.
//
pddsdComp->ddsCaps.dwCaps2 |= DDSCAPS2_TEXTUREMANAGE;
//
// Handle the special case in which the hardware doesn't
// support mipmapping.
//
if( !g_bSupportsMipmaps )
{
    pddsdComp->dwMipMapCount = 0;
    pddsdComp->dwFlags &= ~DDSD_MIPMAPCOUNT;
    pddsdComp->ddsCaps.dwCaps &= ~( DDSCAPS_MIPMAP |
                                    DDSCAPS_COMPLEX );
}
//
// Does texture have mipmaps?
//
if( pddsdComp->dwMipMapCount == 0 )
    g_bMipTexture = FALSE;
else
    g_bMipTexture = TRUE;
//
// Clear unwanted flags.
//
pddsdComp->dwFlags &= (~DDSD_PITCH);
pddsdComp->dwFlags &= (~DDSD_LINEARSIZE);
//
// Create a new surface based on the surface description.
//
if( FAILED( hr = pDD->CreateSurface( pddsdComp, ppddsCompTop,
                                     NULL ) ) )
    goto LFail;

pddsTop = *ppddsCompTop;

pdds = pddsTop;
pdds->AddRef();
```

(continued)

231

```
while( TRUE )
{
    ZeroMemory( &ddsd, sizeof(DDSURFACEDESC2) );
    ddsd.dwSize = sizeof(DDSURFACEDESC2);

    if( FAILED( hr = pdds->Lock( NULL, &ddsd, DDLOCK_WAIT,
                                 NULL )))
        goto LFail;

    if( ddsd.dwFlags & DDSD_LINEARSIZE )
    {
        fread( ddsd.lpSurface, ddsd.dwLinearSize, 1, file );
    }
    else
    {
        DWORD yp;
        BYTE* pbDest = (BYTE*)ddsd.lpSurface;
        LONG dataBytesPerRow =
            ddsd.dwWidth * ddsd.ddpfPixelFormat.dwRGBBitCount / 8;
        for( yp = 0; yp < ddsd.dwHeight; yp++ )
        {
            fread( pbDest, dataBytesPerRow, 1, file );
            pbDest += ddsd.lPitch;
        }
    }

    pdds->Unlock( NULL );

    if( !g_bSupportsMipmaps )
    {
        // For mipless hardware, don't copy mipmaps.
        pdds->Release();
        break;
    }

    ddsd.ddsCaps.dwCaps  = DDSCAPS_TEXTURE | DDSCAPS_MIPMAP |
                           DDSCAPS_COMPLEX;
    ddsd.ddsCaps.dwCaps2 = 0;
    ddsd.ddsCaps.dwCaps3 = 0;
    ddsd.ddsCaps.dwCaps4 = 0;

    if( FAILED( hr = pdds->GetAttachedSurface(
                              &ddsd.ddsCaps, &pddsAttached ) ) )
    {
        pdds->Release();
        break;
    }
```

```
        pdds->Release();
        pdds = pddsAttached;
    }

    hr = S_OK;  // Everything worked.

LFail:
    fclose( file );

    return hr;
}
```

One point worth mentioning about accessing DXT surfaces directly is that they always use a linear block of memory—unlike RGB surfaces, in which the pitch (the distance, in bytes, between two memory addresses that represent the beginning of one bitmap row and the beginning of the next bitmap row) isn't necessarily the same as the row width. Therefore, pitch is meaningless for DXT surfaces. The *dwLinearSize* field indicates the total amount of memory used for the compressed image data. The previous code sample can also load DDS files containing uncompressed RGB surfaces. The code uses the DDSD_LINEARSIZE flag to determine whether to load an entire mipmap level in a solid block or one to load it one row at a time, honoring pitch.

If you author textures in DXT-compressed form, when the program runs you'll need to determine whether the renderer directly supports DXT textures. If it does, you can go ahead and pass the DXT textures that you've loaded to the renderer. If not, you need to decompress the texture contents into textures that are in a format supported by the renderer. The Compress sample application on the companion CD shows how to enumerate supported formats. If the renderer doesn't support DXT, Compress chooses an appropriate RGB format and decompresses the texture into it.

Mipmaps

One advanced texturing capability Direct3D provides is mipmapping. A *mipmap* consists of a series of textures, each containing a progressively lower resolution of an image (bitmap) that represents the texture. Each level in the mipmap sequence has a height and width that is half of the height and width of the previous level. You can specify that the textures be either square or rectangular. The mipmap technique is a good way to ensure that textures retain their realism and quality as you move closer or further away from them. Direct3D will automatically pick the appropriate mipmap level to texture from. Mipmaps also provide an effective way of reducing memory traffic for textures so that you don't have to render a single texture for all resolutions. When a texture appears at a distance, Direct3D is required to work with a small texture (the texture might be only 2 × 2 at a distance) rather than mapping the complete, full-size image (which might contain 256 × 256 texels) down to the 2 × 2 screen space the polygon requires.

Mipmapping yields a much more realistic scene than simply using a single texture at any resolution. Although properly filtering the whole 256 × 256 texels into 2 × 2 pixels would look great, it would take too long. To maximize speed, Direct3D samples a small number of texels for each pixel from various places in the texture map. Because the result looks fairly poor when the texture map is much bigger than the rendered primitive, you're better off sticking with mipmapping.

Direct3D picks the mipmap level (or levels) for which the texel-to-pixel ratio is closest to 1. For example, if a polygon is approximately 128 × 128 pixels, Direct3D uses the 128 × 128 mipmap level. In general, as you approach the object, Direct 3D replaces smaller textures with larger ones. Or, if the object's resolution falls between two mipmap levels, Direct3D can combine texels from the two mipmap levels to determine the final colors to render.

Direct 3D stores the mipmap you produce as a chain of attached surfaces. The texture with the highest resolution is stored as the first element—the *head*— of the chain. The texture with the next highest resolution is then attached to the head of the chain. Each successive texture is attached to the previous texture until you reach the lowest resolution image.

Figure 8-1 illustrates a mipmap texture set containing mipmap levels of the following sizes: 256 × 256, 128 × 128, 64 × 64, 32 × 32, 16 × 16, 8 × 8, 4 × 4.

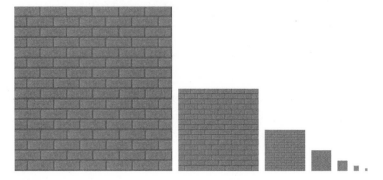

Figure 8-1
Mipmap texture set

The texture shown in Figure 8-1 is one you'd apply to create a brick wall. The first image has the highest resolution in the chain. Each successive image is scaled down to the next power of 2 in both width and height. When you're as far from the wall as possible, Direct3D uses the smallest texture in the mipmap chain (4 × 4 in this set).

The sections that follow describe the steps you need to take to work with a set of mipmaps.

Creating a Mipmap Texture

You can create a surface that represents the levels of a mipmap by using the DDSCAPS_MIPMAP and DDSCAPS_COMPLEX flags in the DDSURFACE-DESC2 structure. You also need to use the DDSCAPS_TEXTURE flag because all mipmaps are textures. The DDSURFACEDESC2 structure is then passed to the *IDirectDraw7::CreateSurface* method. This call will automatically create all the mipmap levels from the original texture.

Direct3D uses dimensions that are powers of 2 (1, 2, 4, 8, and so on) for all mipmap textures but does *not* generally require a texture's width to equal its height (although a few Direct3D devices do require this—check the D3DPTEXTURE-CAPS_SQUAREONLY caps bit). The following code builds a chain of mipmap levels (256 × 256, 128 × 128, 64 × 64, 32 × 32, 16 ×16, 8 × 8, 4 × 4, 2 × 2, and 1 × 1) using the *IDirectDraw7::CreateSurface* method:

```
// Get size information for the top-level bitmap.
BITMAP bm;
GetObject( m_hbmBitmap[0], sizeof(BITMAP), &bm );

// Set up and create the mipmap surface.
DDSURFACEDESC2 ddsd;
ZeroMemory( &ddsd, sizeof(DDSURFACEDESC2) );
ddsd.dwSize          = sizeof(DDSURFACEDESC2);
ddsd.dwFlags         = DDSD_CAPS | DDSD_MIPMAPCOUNT |
                       DDSD_WIDTH | DDSD_HEIGHT |
                       DDSD_PIXELFORMAT;
ddsd.ddsCaps.dwCaps  = DDSCAPS_TEXTURE | DDSCAPS_MIPMAP |
                       DDSCAPS_COMPLEX;
ddsd.dwMipMapCount   = m_dwMipMapCount;
ddsd.dwWidth         = bm.bmWidth;
ddsd.dwHeight        = bm.bmHeight;

// Get the device caps.
D3DDEVICEDESC7 ddDesc;
DWORD          dwDeviceCaps;
```

(continued)

```
if( FAILED( pd3dDevice->GetCaps( &ddDesc ) ) )
    return E_FAIL;
dwDeviceCaps = ddDesc.dpcTriCaps.dwTextureCaps;

// Turn on texture management for hardware devices.
if( IsEqualIID(ddDesc.deviceGUID, IID_IDirect3DHALDevice) ||
    IsEqualIID(ddDesc.deviceGUID, IID_IDirect3DTnLHalDevice) )
    ddsd.ddsCaps.dwCaps2 = DDSCAPS2_TEXTUREMANAGE;
else
    ddsd.ddsCaps.dwCaps |= DDSCAPS_SYSTEMMEMORY;

// Enumerate a good texture format. Search for a 16-bit
// format first.
DDSURFACEDESC2 ddsdSearch;
ddsdSearch. ddpfPixelFormat.dwRGBBitCount = 16;
pd3dDevice->EnumTextureFormats( TextureSearchCallback,
                                &ddsdSearch );

// If a 16-bit format wasn't found, check for a 32-bit format.
if( 16 != ddsdSearch.ddpfPixelFormat.dwRGBBitCount )
{
    ddsdSearch. ddpfPixelFormat.dwRGBBitCount = 32;
    pd3dDevice->EnumTextureFormats( TextureSearchCallback,
                                    &ddsdSearch );
    if( 32 != ddsdSearch.ddpfPixelFormat.dwRGBBitCount )
        return E_FAIL;
}

// If a good texture format is found, use it to create
// the surface.
memcpy( &ddsd.ddpfPixelFormat, &ddsdSearch.ddpfPixelFormat,
        sizeof(DDPIXELFORMAT) );

// Get a DDraw pointer (from the device's render target) for
// creating surfaces. The Release calls just serve to decrement
// the reference count, but the pointers are still valid.
LPDIRECTDRAWSURFACE7 pddsRender;
LPDIRECTDRAW7        pDD  = NULL;
pd3dDevice->GetRenderTarget( &pddsRender );
pddsRender->GetDDInterface( (VOID**)&pDD );
pddsRender->Release();

// Create the mipmap surface.
if( FAILED( pDD->CreateSurface( &ddsd, &m_pddsSurface, NULL ) ) )
```

```
{
    pDD->Release();
    return E_FAIL;
}

// Done with DirectDraw.
pDD->Release();
```

You can set the number of mipmap levels using the *dwMipMapCount* member. If you don't specify a dwMipMapCount value, mipmap levels will be created all the way down to 1x1. The call to *IDirectDraw7::CreateSurface* will create a chain of surfaces, the first of which the method will size according to the width and height the code specifies in the *ddsd.dwWidth* and *ddsd.dwHeight* members. Each of the remaining surfaces in the chain is a power of 2 smaller than the previous surface.

Accessing the Mipmap Levels

After creating the DirectDraw surface, you can traverse the mipmap surface chain by using the *IDirectDrawSurface7::GetAttachedSurface* methods and specifying the *DDSCAPS_MIPMAP* and *DDSCAPS_TEXTURE* flags in the *DDSCAPS2* structure.

The following code segment illustrates how to traverse a mipmap chain from the highest to the lowest resolution.

```
// Loop through each surface in the mipmap, copying the bitmap
// to the temporary surface and then blitting the temporary
// surface to the real one.
LPDIRECTDRAWSURFACE7 pddsDest = m_pddsSurface;

for( WORD wNum=0; wNum < m_dwMipMapCount; wNum++ )
{
    // Copy the bitmap image to the surface.
    BITMAP bm;
    GetObject( m_hbmBitmap[wNum], sizeof(BITMAP), &bm );

    // Create a DC and set up the bitmap.
    HDC hdcBitmap = CreateCompatibleDC( NULL );
    if( NULL == hdcBitmap )
        return E_FAIL;

    SelectObject( hdcBitmap, m_hbmBitmap[wNum] );

    HDC hdcSurface;
```

(continued)

```
if( SUCCEEDED( pddsDest->GetDC( &hdcSurface ) ) )
{
    BitBlt( hdcSurface, 0, 0, bm.bmWidth, bm.bmHeight,
            hdcBitmap, 0, 0, SRCCOPY );
    pddsDest->ReleaseDC( hdcSurface );
}

DeleteDC( hdcBitmap );

// Get the next surface in the chain. Do a Release call to
// avoid increasing the reference counts on the surfaces.
DDSCAPS2 ddsCaps;
ddsCaps.dwCaps  = DDSCAPS_TEXTURE | DDSCAPS_MIPMAP;
ddsCaps.dwCaps2 = 0;
ddsCaps.dwCaps3 = 0;
ddsCaps.dwCaps4 = 0;
if( SUCCEEDED( pddsDest->GetAttachedSurface( &ddsCaps,
                                             &pddsDest ) ) )
    pddsDest->Release();
}
```

Applications need to manually traverse a mipmap chain to load bitmap data into each surface in the chain. This is typically the only reason to traverse the chain.

Direct3D explicitly stores the number of levels in a mipmap chain. When an application obtains the surface description of a mipmap (by calling the *IDirectDrawSurface7::Lock* or *IDirectDrawSurface7::GetSurfaceDesc* method), the *dwMipMapCount* member of the DDSURFACEDESC2 structure contains the number of levels in the mipmap, including the top level. For levels other than the top level in the mipmap, the *dwMipMapCount* member specifies the number of levels from that mipmap to the smallest mipmap in the chain.

Setting the Mipmap LOD Bias

Before we conclude our discussion of mipmaps, let's examine one more helpful texturing technique. Setting the mipmap level of detail (LOD) bias allows you to perform a few special filtering effects. If you set a positive bias on a mipmap texture, the resulting image will be sharper but more aliased. If you set a negative bias, the texture image will look blurred. You can control the LOD bias by setting the D3DRENDERSTATE_MIPMAPLODBIAS state.

Texture Filtering

Whenever a 3D primitive is rendered, it's mapped onto a 2D image. If you apply a texture to the primitive, Direct3D will use the process known as texture filtering to obtain a color value for every pixel in a primitive's on-screen 2D image.

When a texture-mapped polygon is rendered, the texture you're using will usually be *magnified* or *minified* because it's being mapped onto a smaller or larger primitive image. When you magnify a texture (such as when rendering a primitive that takes up 100×100 pixels and has a 16×16 texture), the same texel can end up being mapped to multiple pixels. This magnification of the texture often makes the rendered image look blocky. When you minify a texture (such as when rendering a primitive that takes up 10×10 pixels and has a 256×256 texture), a number of texels will be mapped to a single pixel. This minification can generate an image that looks "sparkly" (especially as the primitive is animated). You can diminish both effects by having Direct3D blend several texel colors to generate a more realistic pixel color.

Direct 3D supplies three settings that change the type of texture filtering: min filtering, mag filtering, and mip filtering. *Min filtering* tells Direct3D how to handle textures that will be minified. *Mag filtering* tells Direct3D how to handle textures that will be magnified. *Mip filtering* tells Direct3D how to use multiple mip levels (if they are present) to improve the image further. These three filtering settings can all be changed independently of each other, allowing for a variety of filtering effects. In a sense, filtering is done in two different ways: *within* a mip level and *between* mip levels. Min filtering and mag filtering tell Direct3D how to filter texels within a particular mip level. Mip filtering tells Direct3D how to filter texels between the two mip levels that best match the primitive's rendered size. When deciding what values to use for these filter settings, you'll basically be trading off image quality vs. rendering time. Often you'll want to leave the choice of filtering quality to the user.

You can set the current texture filtering method by calling the *IDirect3D-Device7::SetTextureStageState* method. Set the first parameter to the stage number (0 to 7) of the texture for which you're selecting a texture filtering method. Set the second parameter to D3DTSS_MAGFILTER, D3DTSS_MINFILTER, or D3DTSS_MIPFILTER to select the method you want to use. Set the third parameter to a member of the D3DTEXTUREMAGFILTER, D3DTEXTUREMINFILTER, or D3DTEXTUREMIPFILTER enumerated types that correspond to the second parameter's value.

Nearest Point Sampling

The fastest, but worst-looking, form of filtering is nearest point sampling, in which Direct3D will directly compute the texel address. This address often won't evaluate to an integer, so Direct3D will copy the color of the texel with the closest integer address. If the texture size is similar to the size of the primitive's on-screen image, using nearest point sampling is a quick way to process textures. However, if the sizes are reasonably different, you'll need to magnify or minify the texture. This will make your image appear blocky or sparkly.

You can use nearest point sampling within a mip level by calling the *IDirect-3DDevice7::SetTextureStageState* method. Set the first parameter to the stage number (0 to 7) of the texture that you want to use for texture filtering. Set the second parameter to D3DTSS_MAGFILTER if you want to set the magnification filter. If you want to set the minification filter, set the second parameter to D3DTSS_MINFILTER. Finally set the third parameter to D3DTFG_POINT for the magnification filter and to D3DTFN_POINT for the minification filter. The following code tells Direct3D to use the nearest point sampling with texture stage 0:

```
m_pd3dDevice->SetTextureStageState(0, D3DTSS_MINFILTER,
                                   D3DTFN_POINT);
m_pd3dDevice->SetTextureStageState(0, D3DTSS_MAGFILTER,
                                   D3DTFG_POINT);
```

Linear Texture Filtering

Linear filtering is another option. The first two steps of performing linear filtering are the same as the first two steps of performing nearest point sampling: computing a texel address and then finding the texel with the integer address closest to the computed address. The third step of performing linear filtering is to compute a weighted average of the four texels surrounding the nearest sample point—above, below, to the left, and to the right. This makes a huge improvement in the smoothness of the resulting rendered primitive, especially if the primitive is animated. However, the filtering sometimes has the side effect of making the resulting pixels look somewhat blurry. Still, it's an improvement in quality over point sampling.

To select linear filtering, call the *IDirect3DDevice7::SetTextureStageState* method. Set the first argument to this method to the stage number (0 to 7) of the texture for which you're choosing a filtering method. Set the second argument to D3DTSS_MAGFILTER if you want to set the magnification filter, or set it to D3DTSS_MINFILTER to set the minification filter. Set the third parameter to D3DTFG_LINEAR for the magnification filter and to D3DTFN_LINEAR for the minification filter.

Linear filtering within a mip level (but not between mip levels) is referred to as *bilinear filtering*, because filtering is done on the nearest texels in the two dimensions of the texture. Here's the code for setting up bilinear filtering for a primitive:

```
m_pd3dDevice->SetTextureStageState(0, D3DTSS_MINFILTER,
                                   D3DTFN_LINEAR);
m_pd3dDevice->SetTextureStageState(0, D3DTSS_MAGFILTER,
                                   D3DTFG_LINEAR);
```

Anisotropic Texture Filtering

Anisotropy is the distortion you see in the texels of a 3D object when its surface isn't parallel with the plane of the screen. The shape of each pixel becomes distorted when a pixel from an anisotropic primitive is mapped into texels. Direct3D measures the anisotropy of a pixel as the elongation of a screen pixel that is inverse-mapped into texture space. Direct3D computes the elongation as the length divided by the width.

Anisotropic filtering samples more texels when a screen pixel is elongated, to reduce the blurriness that standard linear filtering can produce. To enable anisotropic filtering, call the *IDirect3DDevice7::SetTextureStageState* method. Set the first parameter to the stage number (0 to 7) of the texture for which you're choosing a filtering method. Set the second parameter to D3DTSS_MAGFILTER to use the magnification filter or to D3DTSS_MINFILTER to use the minification filter. Set the third parameter to D3DTFG_ANISOTROPIC for the magnification filter and D3DTFN_ANISOTROPIC for the minification filter.

To use anisotropic texture filtering, you also need to set the maximum degree of anisotropy that you want to correct. To do this, call the *IDirect3DDevice7:: SetTextureStageState* method. Set the first argument to the stage of the texture for which you're setting the anisotropy level. Set the second argument to D3DTSS_ MAXANISOTROPY and the third parameter to the degree of anisotropy (any value greater than 1). Here's the code for setting up 4:1 anisotropic filtering:

```
m_pd3dDevice->SetTextureStageState(0, D3DTSS_MINFILTER,
                                   D3DTFN_ANISOTROPIC);
m_pd3dDevice->SetTextureStageState(0, D3DTSS_MAGFILTER,
                                   D3DTFG_ANISOTROPIC);
m_pd3dDevice->SetTextureStageState(0, D3DTSS_MAXANISOTROPY, 4);
```

You can disable anisotropic filtering by setting D3DTSS_MAXANISO-TROPY to 1 or changing to a different filter mode. Before setting the degree of anisotropy, check the D3DPRASTERCAPS_ANISOTROPY flag in the D3DPRIM-CAPS structure to determine the acceptable range of values for the degree of anisotropy. The higher the value you set for D3DPRASTERCAPS_ANISOTROPY, the longer the filtering will take (because more texels are used to determine the final pixel color). As usual, you will have to make the trade-off between rendering speed and image quality.

Mipmap Texture Filtering

As discussed earlier in the chapter, mipmap textures can decrease the time required for rendering a 3D scene and improve its image quality. Because the memory impact is minimal, I recommend using mipmaps in your applications. Usually the primitive being rendered has a pixel density that falls between the density of two mip levels of a texture. The D3DTSS_MIPFILTER setting can be used to tell Direct3D how to use these two mip levels to generate each final image pixel. If you set it to D3DTFP_NONE, the highest mip level will always be used. If you set it to D3DTFP_POINT, Direct3D will only use the mip level that is the closest match for the primitive's pixel density. If you set it to D3DTFP_LINEAR, Direct3D will linearly blend the two mip levels that best match the primitive's pixel density. Remember that mip filtering is combined with the min and mag filtering settings. For example, if you choose linear filtering for the min and mag settings, but point for the mip setting, Direct3D will choose the closest mip level, perform bilinear filtering on that mip level, and use the result as the pixel value. If instead you choose linear filtering for all of the min, mag, and mip settings, Direct3D will do bilinear filtering on each of the two closest mip levels, then linearly combine the results from each mip level into a single pixel value. This technique, which ends up combining eight pixels, is known as *trilinear filtering* because it linearly filters in all three dimensions of the texture: *u*, *v*, and mip level.

Texture Interface Pointers

As we've discussed, the *IDirect3D7* interface allows you to create and apply textures that are exposed through the *IDirectDrawSurface7* interface. You can obtain a pointer to a texture surface interface by creating a DirectDraw Surface object with the *DDSCAPS_TEXTURE* capability set. After creating the surface, you can use the methods of the surface interface to modify its data. You can also use the *IDirect3DDevice7::Load* method to load an image into the texture. You should load textures into video memory using this method rather than using blit operations to achieve the best speed for your application.

The *IDirect3DDevice7::SetTexture* method assigns textures to the set of current textures. This is the declaration for the *SetTexture* method:

```
HRESULT IDirect3DDevice7::SetTexture(
    DWORD dwStage,
    LPDIRECTDRAWSURFACE7 lpTexture
);
```

Parameter	Description
dwStage	Stage identifier that the texture will be set to; devices can currently have up to eight set textures (valid ranges are 0 to 7)
lpTexture	Address of the *IDirectDrawSurface7* interface for the texture you're setting

The *IDirect3DDevice7::SetTexture* method takes a value from 0 through 7 as its first parameter, indicating which texture stage you're assigning, and it takes the texture interface pointer as its second parameter. For mipmapping, you need to specify the surface pointer for the top level of the mipmap. This is the code for setting the main texture stage to a particular texture:

```
// Set the texture.
m_pd3dDevice->SetTexture(0, m_ptexTexture);
```

This code assigns the second texture stage to a particular texture (for operations such as texture blending):

```
//
// Set the second texture.
m_pd3dDevice->SetTexture(1, m_pd3dTexture);
```

Texture Stages

Direct3D supplies advanced texture-blending capabilities that allow you to combine up to eight textures on a primitive at once. The *IDirect3DDevice7* interface provides texture stages as part of Direct3D's multitexturing capability. Each texture stage contains a texture and operations that can be performed on the texture. Together, the textures associated with these stages form the set of current textures.

You set the current textures by using the *IDirect3DDevice7::SetTexture* method as just discussed. Until you change the textures, all the current textures will be blended on any of the rendered primitives in a scene.

Each texture state is defined by its texture stage. You need to set the state of each texture by using the *IDirect3DDevice7::SetTextureStageState* method. The first parameter is passed as the stage number (0 to 7). The second parameter is set to a member of the D3DTEXTURESTAGESTATETYPE enumerated type. The third parameter is passed as the state value for the texture state. Here's the declaration for the *IDirect3DDevice7::SetTextureStageState* method:

```
HRESULT IDirect3DDevice7::SetTextureStageState(
    DWORD dwStage,
    D3DTEXTURESTAGESTATETYPE dwState,
    DWORD dwValue
);
```

Parameter	Description
dwStage	Stage identifier of the texture stage this call will affect; devices can currently have up to eight set textures (valid values are 0 to 7)
dwState	Texture stage to be set; this parameter can be any member of the D3DTEXTURESTAGESTATETYPE enumerated type setting
dwValue	State value to be set; the *dwState* parameter determines the meaning of this value

Here's the definition of the D3DTEXTURESTAGESTATETYPE enumerated type, which defines texture-stage types:

```
typedef enum _D3DTEXTURESTAGESTATETYPE {
    D3DTSS_COLOROP          = 1,
    D3DTSS_COLORARG1        = 2,
    D3DTSS_COLORARG2        = 3,
    D3DTSS_ALPHAOP          = 4,
    D3DTSS_ALPHAARG1        = 5,
    D3DTSS_ALPHAARG2        = 6,
    D3DTSS_BUMPENVMAT00     = 7,
    D3DTSS_BUMPENVMAT01     = 8,
    D3DTSS_BUMPENVMAT10     = 9,
    D3DTSS_BUMPENVMAT11     = 10,
    D3DTSS_TEXCOORDINDEX    = 11,
    D3DTSS_ADDRESS          = 12,
    D3DTSS_ADDRESSU         = 13,
    D3DTSS_ADDRESSV         = 14,
    D3DTSS_BORDERCOLOR      = 15,
    D3DTSS_MAGFILTER        = 16,
    D3DTSS_MINFILTER        = 17,
    D3DTSS_MIPFILTER        = 18,
    D3DTSS_MIPMAPLODBIAS    = 19,
    D3DTSS_MAXMIPLEVEL      = 20,
    D3DTSS_MAXANISOTROPY    = 21,
    D3DTSS_BUMPENVLSCALE    = 22,
    D3DTSS_BUMPENVLOFFSET   = 23,
    D3DTSS_TEXTURETRANSFORMFLAGS = 24,
    D3DTSS_FORCE_DWORD      = 0x7fffffff,
} D3DTEXTURESTAGESTATETYPE;
```

These are the members of the D3DTEXTURESTAGESTATETYPE enumerated type:

- **D3DTSS_COLOROP** The texture-stage state is a color-blending operation identified by one of the members of the D3DTEXTUREOP enumerated type. The default value for the first texture stage, texture stage 0, is D3DTOP_MODULATE. The default for all other stages is D3DTOP_DISABLE.

- **D3DTSS_COLORARG1** The texture-stage state is the first color argument for the stage, which is identified by a texture argument flag. The default argument is D3DTA_TEXTURE.

- **D3DTSS_COLORARG2** The texture-stage state is the second color argument for the stage, identified by a texture argument flag. The default argument is D3DTA_CURRENT.

- **D3DTSS_ALPHAOP** The texture-stage state is an alpha blending operation identified by one of the members of the D3DTEXTUREOP enumerated type. The default value for the first texture stage (stage 0) is D3DTOP_SELECTARG1. The default for all other stages is D3DTOP_DISABLE.

- **D3DTSS_ALPHAARG1** The texture-stage state is the first alpha argument for the stage, identified by a texture argument flag. The default argument is D3DTA_TEXTURE. If you don't set a texture for this stage, the default argument is D3DTA_DIFFUSE.

- **D3DTSS_ALPHAARG2** The texture-stage state is the second alpha argument for the stage, identified by a texture argument flag. The default argument is D3DTA_CURRENT.

- **D3DTSS_BUMPENVMAT00** The texture-stage state is a D3D-VALUE for the [0][0] coefficient in a bump mapping matrix. A bump mapping matrix stores a texture's depth information. (See the section "Bump Mapping" later in the chapter.) The default value is 0.

- **D3DTSS_BUMPENVMAT01** The texture-stage state is a D3D-VALUE for the [0][1] coefficient in a bump mapping matrix. The default value is 0.

- **D3DTSS_BUMPENVMAT10** The texture-stage state is a D3D-VALUE for the [1][0] coefficient in a bump mapping matrix. The default value is 0.

- **D3DTSS_BUMPENVMAT11** The texture-stage state is a D3D-VALUE for the [1][1] coefficient in a bump mapping matrix. The default value is 0.

■ **D3DTSS_TEXCOORDINDEX**   The index of the texture coordinate set to use with this texture stage. The default index is 0. Set this state to the zero-based index of the texture set for each vertex that this texture stage will use. You can specify up to eight sets of texture coordinates for each vertex. If a vertex doesn't include a set of texture coordinates at the specified index, the system defaults to using the (u, v) coordinates $(0, 0)$.

■ **D3DTSS_ADDRESS**   A member of the D3DTEXTUREADDRESS enumerated type. This value selects the texture-addressing mode for both the u and v coordinates. The default is D3DTADDRESS_WRAP.

■ **D3DTSS_ADDRESSU**   A member of the D3DTEXTUREADDRESS enumerated type. This value selects the texture-addressing mode for the u coordinate. The default is D3DTADDRESS_WRAP.

■ **D3DTSS_ADDRESSV**   A member of the D3DTEXTUREADDRESS enumerated type. This value selects the texture-addressing mode for the v coordinate. The default value is D3DTADDRESS_WRAP.

■ **D3DTSS_BORDERCOLOR**   A D3DCOLOR value that describes the color to be used for rasterizing texture coordinates outside the [0.0,1.0] range. The default color is 0x00000000.

■ **D3DTSS_MAGFILTER**   A member of the D3DTEXTUREMAG-FILTER enumerated type that specifies the texture magnification filter to be used when rendering the texture onto primitives. The default value is D3DTFG_POINT.

■ **D3DTSS_MINFILTER**   A member of the D3DTEXTUREMIN-FILTER enumerated type that specifies the texture minification filter to be used when rendering the texture onto primitives. The default value is D3DTFN_POINT.

■ **D3DTSS_MIPFILTER**   A member of the D3DTEXTUREMIP-FILTER enumerated type that indicates the texture magnification filter to be used when rendering the texture onto primitives. The default value is D3DTFP_NONE.

■ **D3DTSS_MIPMAPLODBIAS**   The level of detail bias for mipmaps. You can use this member to make textures appear more chunky or more blurred. The default value is 0.

■ **D3DTSS_MAXMIPLEVEL**   The maximum mipmap level of detail that a program will allow, specified as an index from the top of the mipmap chain. Lower values specify higher levels of detail within the mipmap chain. The default value, which is 0, specifies that all levels can be used. Nonzero values indicate that the application won't display mipmaps that have a higher level of detail than the mipmap at the specified index.

- **D3DTSS_MAXANISOTROPY**   The maximum level of anisotropy. The default value is 1.

- **D3DTSS_BUMPENVLSCALE**   A D3DVALUE scale for bump map luminance. The default value is 0.

- **D3DTSS_BUMPENVLOFFSET**   A D3DVALUE offset for bump map luminance. The default value is 0.

- **D3DTSS_FORCE_DWORD**   A member that forces the D3DTEX-TURESTAGESTATETYPE enumerated type to be 32 bits in size. This value isn't used.

Although most texture properties are set using *SetTextureStageState*, you can set the texture-wrapping state (see the section "Texture Wrapping" near the end of this chapter for more information) for the current textures using the *IDirect-3DDevice7::SetRenderState* method. Pass a value from D3DRENDERSTATE_WRAP0 to D3DRENDERSTATE_WRAP7 for the first parameter, and pass the desired combination of the D3DWRAP_U and D3DWRAP_V flags to enable wrapping in the *u* or *v* directions. This code shows how to set the texture-wrapping state:

```
m_pd3dDevice->SetRenderState(D3DRENDERSTATE_WRAP0, D3DWRAP_U);
```

Texture Blending

You can produce many interesting effects by blending a texture with the underlying primitive's color or another texture on the same primitive. To determine which texture-blending capabilities the target hardware supports, you can check the *dwTextureOpCaps* member of the D3DDEVICEDESC7 structure using the *IDirect3DDevice7::GetCaps* method.

Texture blending allows you to create incredibly realistic scenes by combining multiple textures and adding finishes and light maps to primitives. The three main texture-blending techniques are multipass texture blending, multiple-texture blending, and bump mapping.

Multipass Texture Blending

Multipass texture blending is the process of applying numerous textures to a primitive in several passes. This older process of texture blending is often used for the light and shadow mapping of primitives. All Direct3D device interfaces support this type of blending. Multiple-texture blending, which the next section covers, performs this same process on newer 3D hardware but uses only a single pass. However, if the target system isn't capable of multiple-texture blending, you can use multipass texture blending to produce the same result but at a slower rate.

To enable multipass texture blending, set a texture in texture stage 0 by calling the *IDirect3DDevice7::SetTexture* method. Next select the desired color and alpha blending arguments and operations by using the method *IDirect3DDevice7:: SetTextureStageState*. Next render the objects composing your scene, and set the next texture in texture stage 0. Finally, set the desired color and alpha blending arguments and operations for the second texture, and render the objects again.

Just repeat these steps for all the textures in your scene. For each pass, you must set the current texture. Direct3D blends the texel colors of the current texture with the pixel colors defined in the frame buffer. The following sample code shows how to apply multipass texture blending to a primitive:

```
// Draw the first textures normally. Use the first set of texture
// coordinates.
m_pd3dDevice->SetTextureStageState( 0, D3DTSS_TEXCOORDINDEX, 0 );
m_pd3dDevice->SetTextureStageState( 0, D3DTSS_COLORARG1,
                                    D3DTA_TEXTURE );
m_pd3dDevice->SetTextureStageState( 0, D3DTSS_COLOROP,
                                    D3DTOP_MODULATE );

m_WallData.textureCoords[0].lpvData = &m_avWallVertices[0].tuBase;
m_pd3dDevice->SetTexture( 0, D3DTextr_GetSurface("wall.bmp") );
m_pd3dDevice->DrawPrimitiveStrided( D3DPT_TRIANGLELIST,
                                    D3DFVF_XYZ | D3DFVF_DIFFUSE |
                                    D3DFVF_TEX2,
                                    &m_WallData, 24, NULL );
m_pd3dDevice->SetTexture( 0, D3DTextr_GetSurface("floor.bmp") );
m_pd3dDevice->DrawPrimitiveStrided( D3DPT_TRIANGLELIST,
                                    D3DFVF_XYZ | D3DFVF_DIFFUSE |
                                    D3DFVF_TEX2,
                                    &m_FloorCielData, 12, NULL );

// Draw the light map by using blending, with the second set of
// texture coordinates.
m_pd3dDevice->SetRenderState( D3DRENDERSTATE_ALPHABLENDENABLE,
                              TRUE );
m_pd3dDevice->SetRenderState( D3DRENDERSTATE_SRCBLEND,
                              D3DBLEND_ZERO );
m_pd3dDevice->SetRenderState( D3DRENDERSTATE_DESTBLEND,
                              D3DBLEND_SRCCOLOR );

m_WallData.textureCoords[0].lpvData = &m_avWallVertices[0].tuLightMap;
m_pd3dDevice->SetTexture( 0, D3DTextr_GetSurface("lightmap.bmp") );
m_pd3dDevice->DrawPrimitiveStrided( D3DPT_TRIANGLELIST,
```

```
                              D3DFVF_XYZ | D3DFVF_DIFFUSE |
                              D3DFVF_TEX2,
                              &m_WallData, 36, NULL );
// Restore state.
m_pd3dDevice->SetRenderState( D3DRENDERSTATE_ALPHABLENDENABLE,
                              FALSE );
```

Single-Pass Multiple-Texture Blending

DirectX 6 introduced the ability to apply multiple textures to primitives in a single pass (as opposed to the multipass approach you just learned about). To determine which texture-blending capabilities the target hardware supports, use the *IDirect3DDevice7::GetCaps* method to check the *dwTextureOpCaps* member of the D3DDEVICEDESC7 structure.

The *IDirect3D7* and *IDirect3DDevice7* interfaces allow you to blend up to eight textures on your primitives in a single pass. This texture-blending approach is much faster than the older multipass approach. With single-pass multiple-texture blending, you can combine special effects such as textures, shadows, and diffuse and specular lighting in a single pass. To blend multiple textures, you assign textures to a set of current textures and create the blending stages.

Direct3D provides single-pass multiple-texture blending through the use of texture stages. A texture stage takes two arguments and performs a blending operation on them. You can perform more than 25 operations on the arguments. The arguments for a texture stage can be an associated texture, a color or alpha value iterated during Gouraud shading, an arbitrary color or alpha value, or the result from the previous texture stage.

The results of each stage are carried over to the next one, and the result of the final stage is rasterized on the polygon. This process is called the *texture-blending cascade*. Direct3D provides eight stages (numbered 0 to 7), but some hardware devices provide fewer (or none at all). The stages are blended in increasing order of index. You need to set only the number of stages you want to use. DirectX ignores the remaining (disabled) stages. If an application uses different numbers of stages over time, you can simply disable the first unused stage to prevent Direct3D from applying stages with a higher index.

A blending stage is associated with each texture in the current texture set. The *IDirect3DDevice7::SetTextureStageState* method controls what information from a particular texture stage gets used. You can set color channel operations by using the D3DTSS_COLOROP stage state. The texture-blending arguments use the D3DTSS_COLORARG1, D3DTSS_COLORARG2, D3DTSS_ALPHARG1, and D3DTSS_ALPHARG2 members of the D3DTEXTURESTAGESTATETYPE enumerated type.

An example of single-pass multitexturing follows.

```
D3DTextr_RestoreAllTextures( m_pd3dDevice );
    m_pd3dDevice->SetTexture( 0, D3DTextr_GetSurface("tex1.bmp") );
    m_pd3dDevice->SetTextureStageState( 0, D3DTSS_COLORARG1,
                                        D3DTA_TEXTURE );
    m_pd3dDevice->SetTextureStageState( 0, D3DTSS_COLORARG2,
                                        D3DTA_DIFFUSE );
    m_pd3dDevice->SetTextureStageState( 0, D3DTSS_COLOROP,
                                        D3DTOP_MODULATE );
    m_pd3dDevice->SetTextureStageState( 0, D3DTSS_MINFILTER,
                                        D3DTFN_LINEAR );
    m_pd3dDevice->SetTextureStageState( 0, D3DTSS_MAGFILTER,
                                        D3DTFG_LINEAR );
```

You can also set alpha channel operations (Chapter 10 covers alpha blending) using the D3DTSS_ALPHAOP stage state. The following code segment sets up the base texture in a set of textures to be blended.

```
// Stage 0: The base texture
    m_pd3dDevice->SetTextureStageState(0, D3DTSS_COLOROP,
                                       D3DTOP_MODULATE);
    m_pd3dDevice->SetTextureStageState(0, D3DTSS_COLORARG1,
                                       D3DTA_TEXTURE);
    m_pd3dDevice->SetTextureStageState(0, D3DTSS_COLORARG2,
                                       D3DTA_DIFFUSE);
    m_pd3dDevice->SetTextureStageState(0, D3DTSS_ALPHAOP,
                                       D3DTOP_SELECTARG1);
    m_pd3dDevice->SetTextureStageState(0, D3DTSS_ALPHAARG1,
                                       D3DTA_TEXTURE);
    m_pd3dDevice->SetTextureStageState(0, D3DTSS_TEXCOORDINDEX, 1);
```

To assign textures to the set of current textures, use the *IDirect3DDevice7:: SetTexture* method. This method takes a value from 0 to 7 as the first argument, indicating the texture stage number, and takes the texture interface pointer as the second parameter. You should be aware that software devices don't support assigning the same texture to more than one stage at a time. This code assigns a texture to texture stage 0:

```
m_pd3dDevice->SetTexture( 0,
    D3DTextr_GetSurface("..\\Textures\\Cloud3.bmp") );
m_pd3dDevice->DrawPrimitive( D3DPT_TRIANGLESTRIP, D3DFVF_TLVERTEX,
                             m_pBackground, 4, 0 );
```

Setting Up Texture Stages

The following code shows how to set up a texture stage. The code calls the *IDirect-3DDevice7::SetTextureStageState* method three times. The first call defines the operation that will be performed. The second and third calls set the arguments for the operation the first call specifies.

```
//
// Set texture render states.
// Set texture stage 0 to modulate the texture with the diffuse
// color, and to use point sampling and no mipmapping.
m_pd3dDevice->SetTextureStageState( 0, D3DTSS_COLOROP,
                                    D3DTOP_MODULATE );
m_pd3dDevice->SetTextureStageState( 0,      // The first texture
                        D3DTSS_COLORARG1, // Set the color arg1.
                        D3DTA_TEXTURE );  // Color arg1 value
m_pd3dDevice->SetTextureStageState( 0,      // The first texture
                        D3DTSS_COLORARG2, // Set the color arg2.
                        D3DTA_DIFFUSE);   // Color arg2 value
m_pd3dDevice->SetTextureStageState( 0, D3DTSS_MINFILTER,
                                    D3DTFN_POINT);
m_pd3dDevice->SetTextureStageState( 0, D3DTSS_MAGFILTER,
                                    D3DTFG_POINT);
m_pd3dDevice->SetTextureStageState( 0, D3DTSS_MIPFILTER,
                                    D3DTFP_NONE );
```

The following code example shows how to apply multiple-texture blending to an application:

```
// Set up the texture stages. (You don't need to do this
// every frame.)
m_pd3dDevice->SetTextureStageState( 0, D3DTSS_TEXCOORDINDEX, 0 );
m_pd3dDevice->SetTextureStageState( 0, D3DTSS_COLORARG1,
                                    D3DTA_TEXTURE );
m_pd3dDevice->SetTextureStageState( 0, D3DTSS_COLOROP,
                                    D3DTOP_MODULATE );
m_pd3dDevice->SetTextureStageState( 1, D3DTSS_TEXCOORDINDEX, 1 );
m_pd3dDevice->SetTextureStageState( 1, D3DTSS_COLORARG1,
                                    D3DTA_TEXTURE );
m_pd3dDevice->SetTextureStageState( 1, D3DTSS_COLORARG2,
                                    D3DTA_CURRENT );
m_pd3dDevice->SetTextureStageState( 1, D3DTSS_COLOROP,
                                    D3DTOP_MODULATE );

m_WallData.textureCoords[0].lpvData  =
                  &m_avWallVertices[0].tuBase;
m_WallData.textureCoords[1].lpvData  =
                  &m_avWallVertices[0].tuLightMap;

// Draw the walls in multitexture mode.
m_pd3dDevice->SetTexture( 0, D3DTextr_GetSurface("wall.bmp") );
m_pd3dDevice->SetTexture( 1, D3DTextr_GetSurface("lightmap.bmp") );
m_pd3dDevice->DrawPrimitiveStrided( D3DPT_TRIANGLELIST,
                                    D3DFVF_XYZ | D3DFVF_DIFFUSE |
                                    D3DFVF_TEX2,
```

(continued)

251

```
                                  &m_WallData, 24, NULL );

// Draw the floor in single-texture mode.
m_pd3dDevice->SetTexture( 0, D3DTextr_GetSurface("floor.bmp") );
m_pd3dDevice->SetTexture( 1, NULL );
m_pd3dDevice->DrawPrimitiveStrided( D3DPT_TRIANGLELIST,
                                    D3DFVF_XYZ | D3DFVF_DIFFUSE |
                                    D3DFVF_TEX2,
                                    &m_FloorCielData, 12, NULL );

// Restore state.
m_pd3dDevice->SetTextureStageState( 1, D3DTSS_COLOROP,
                                    D3DTOP_DISABLE );
```

Bump Mapping

Bump mapping is a texture-blending method that creates the appearance of a complex texture on primitives. Although standard texture blending works well for smooth surfaces such as a wood floor, it can't model realistic rough surfaces. Bump mapping provides a texture that contains depth information (tessellation) in the form of values indicating high and low spots on the surface. Bump mapping creates a per-pixel texture coordinate perturbation of specular or diffuse environment maps by taking your specification of the bump map contour using delta values. These are applied to the u and v texture coordinates of an environment map in the next texture stage. These delta values are encoded in the pixel format of the bump map surface.

You can store the contour information in any format you desire (or use approaches such as a procedural bump map). You can apply a bump map to a texture using texture stages. To use bump mapping, set the texture-blending operation of the texture stage that contains the bump map to D3DTOP_BUMP. Using at least three texture-blending stages, you apply the base texture, the bump map, and the environment map in the texture-blending cascade.

A bump map is a DirectDraw surface that uses a pixel format in which each pixel stores the delta values for u and v (D_u and D_v) and sometimes a luminance value (rather than RGB values). You can enumerate the bump map pixel formats by using the *IDirect3DDevice7::EnumTextureFormats* method. The following code is a routine from the Direct3D documentation that determines which devices support bump mapping:

```
BOOL SupportsBumpMapping()
{
    DDPIXELFORMAT ddpfBumpMap;
    D3DDEVICEDESC7 d3dDevDesc;
    ZeroMemory( &d3dDevDesc, sizeof(d3dDevDesc) );
```

```
    // Get the device capabilities.
    m_pd3dDevice->GetCaps( &d3dDevDesc );

    // Does this device support the two bump mapping blend operations?
    DWORD dwBumpOps = d3dDevDesc.dwTextureOpCaps &
                      (D3DTEXOPCAPS_BUMPENVMAP |
                       D3DTEXOPCAPS_BUMPENVMAPLUMINANCE);
    if ( 0 == dwBumpOps)
        return FALSE;

    // Does this device support up to three blending stages?
    if( d3dDevDesc.wMaxTextureBlendStages < 3)
        return FALSE;

    //
    // Check for valid bump map pixel formats.
    //
    // The g_bFoundBumpFormat global variable will be set to TRUE
    // by the callback function if a valid format is found.
    g_bFoundBumpFormat = FALSE;

    m_pd3dDevice->EnumTextureFormats(TextureCallback,
                                     (LPVOID) &ddpfBumpMap);
    if( FALSE == g_bFoundBumpFormat )
        return FALSE;

    // The pixel format now in ddpfBumpMap can be used to create
    // a surface format that's guaranteed to be valid.
    return TRUE;
}
```

The following routine is an example callback function defined to be passed to the *IDirect3DDevice7::EnumTextureFormats* method:

```
HRESULT CALLBACK TextureCallback( DDPIXELFORMAT* pddpf,
                                  VOID* pddpfOut)
{
    // Take the first enumerated DuDv format.
    if( DDPF_BUMPDUDV == pddpf->dwFlags ){
        // Copy the format into the variable at pddpfOut
        // for use when creating the surface later.
        memcpy( pddpfOut, (LPVOID)pddpf, sizeof(DDPIXELFORMAT) );

        // Set the global flag to signal success.
        g_bFoundBumpFormat = TRUE;
        return D3DENUMRET_CANCEL;
    }

    return D3DENUMRET_OK;
}
```

This code verifies that the device supports either the D3DTOP_BUMP-ENVMAP or D3DTOP_BUMPENVMAPLUMINANCE texture-blending operation. It also makes sure that the device supports at least three texture-blending stages and exposes at least one bump mapping pixel format.

Direct3D uses the following formulas and applies them to the D_u and D_v components in each bump map pixel:

$$D_u' = D_u M_{0,0} + D_v M_{1,0}$$
$$D_v' = D_u M_{0,1} + D_v M_{1,1}$$

You can specify the bump map pixel format by using a *DDPIXELFORMAT* structure. The *DDPF_BUMPDUDV* flag in the *dwFlags* member specifies a pixel format for a bump map texture. If this flag is set, the *dwBumpBitCount*, *dwBumpDuBitMask*, *dwBumpDvBitMask*, and *dwBumpLuminanceBitMask* members are used to specify a bit depth for the bump map and the mask values for each pixel component.

The D_u and D_v components of the pixel may range from –1.0 through 1.0, and the luminance component can be from 0 through 255 (if you use it). The D_u and D_v values are taken from the bump map pixel and transformed by a 2×2 matrix to create the output delta values D_u' and D_v'. Direct3D uses these values to modify the texture coordinates that address the environment map in the next texture stage. You set the coefficients of the transformation matrix using the D3DTSS_BUMP-ENVMAT01 through D3DTSS_BUMPENVMAT11 texture stage states. Direct3D also computes the luminance value, which is used to modulate the color of the environment map in the next blending stage, as follows:

$$L' = LS + O$$

where

```
L' = Computed output luminance
L  = Luminance value from the bump map pixel
S  = The scaling factor the luminance value is multiplied by
O  = The offset value
```

The D3DTSS_BUMPENVLSCALE and D3DTSS_BUMPENVLOFFSET texture stage states control the values of the S and O values. This formula will be applied when the texture-blending operation for the stage containing the bump map is set to D3DTOP_BUMPENVMAPLUMINANCE. If you instead use D3DTOP_BUMPENVMAP, Direct3D will use a value of 1.0 for L'.

Once the output delta values D_u' and D_v' are computed, they are added to the texture coordinates in the next texture stage and Direct3D modulates the selected color by the luminance to compute the color to apply to the polygon.

This code shows how to set up a texture stage for bump mapping. The code first sets the color-blending operations and arguments for each stage as well as the base texture map. It then determines whether you have textures turned on, and if you do, it loads the main texture (labeled STEP 1). In STEP 2, it determines whether you've requested bump mapping. If you have, it sets the bump map texture as the second texture. Finally, in STEP 3, if environment mapping is on, you set the specular environment map texture.

```
HRESULT CMyD3DApplication::Render()
{
    m_pd3dDevice->Clear( 0, NULL, D3DCLEAR_TARGET,
                         0x00000000, 1.0f, 0L );

    if( FAILED( m_pd3dDevice->BeginScene() ) )
        return S_OK; // Don't return a "fatal" error.

    m_pd3dDevice->SetRenderState(D3DRENDERSTATE_WRAP0,
                                 D3DWRAP_U | D3DWRAP_V );
    m_pd3dDevice->SetTextureStageState( 0, D3DTSS_COLOROP,
                                 D3DTOP_MODULATE );
    m_pd3dDevice->SetTextureStageState( 0, D3DTSS_COLORARG1,
                                 D3DTA_TEXTURE );
    m_pd3dDevice->SetTextureStageState( 0, D3DTSS_COLORARG2,
                                 D3DTA_DIFFUSE );
    m_pd3dDevice->SetTextureStageState( 0,D3DTSS_ALPHAOP,
                                 D3DTOP_SELECTARG1 );
    m_pd3dDevice->SetTextureStageState( 0, D3DTSS_ALPHAARG1,
                                 D3DTA_TEXTURE );
    m_pd3dDevice->SetTextureStageState( 1, D3DTSS_COLOROP,
                                 D3DTOP_DISABLE );

    // STEP 1
    if( m_bTextureOn )
        m_pd3dDevice->SetTexture( 0,
                         D3DTextr_GetSurface( "earth.bmp" ) );
    else
        m_pd3dDevice->SetTexture( 0,
                         D3DTextr_GetSurface( "block.bmp" ) );

    m_pd3dDevice->SetTextureStageState(0, D3DTSS_TEXCOORDINDEX, 1 );
    m_pd3dDevice->SetTextureStageState(0, D3DTSS_COLOROP,
                                 D3DTOP_SELECTARG1);
    m_pd3dDevice->SetTextureStageState(0, D3DTSS_COLORARG1,
                                 D3DTA_TEXTURE );
    m_pd3dDevice->SetTextureStageState(0, D3DTSS_COLORARG2,
                                 D3DTA_DIFFUSE );
```

(continued)

```
// STEP 2
if( m_bBumpMapOn )
{
    m_pd3dDevice->SetTexture( 1, m_pddsBumpMap );
    m_pd3dDevice->SetTextureStageState( 1,
                                    D3DTSS_TEXCOORDINDEX, 1 );
    m_pd3dDevice->SetTextureStageState( 1, D3DTSS_COLOROP,
                                    D3DTOP_BUMPENVMAPLUMINANCE );
    m_pd3dDevice->SetTextureStageState(1,D3DTSS_COLORARG1,
                                    D3DTA_TEXTURE );
    m_pd3dDevice->SetTextureStageState(1,D3DTSS_COLORARG2,
                                    D3DTA_CURRENT );
    m_pd3dDevice->SetTextureStageState(1,D3DTSS_BUMPENVMAT00,
                                    F2DW(0.5f) );
    m_pd3dDevice->SetTextureStageState(1,D3DTSS_BUMPENVMAT01,
                                    F2DW(0.0f) );
    m_pd3dDevice->SetTextureStageState(1,D3DTSS_BUMPENVMAT10,
                                    F2DW(0.0f) );
    m_pd3dDevice->SetTextureStageState(1,D3DTSS_BUMPENVMAT11,
                                    F2DW(0.5f) );
    m_pd3dDevice->SetTextureStageState(1,D3DTSS_BUMPENVLSCALE,
                                    F2DW(1.0f));
    m_pd3dDevice->SetTextureStageState(1,D3DTSS_BUMPENVLOFFSET,
                                    F2DW(0.0f) );

    // STEP 3
    if( m_bEnvMapOn )
    {
        m_pd3dDevice->SetTexture( 2,
                D3DTextr_GetSurface( "EarthEnvMap.bmp" ) );
        m_pd3dDevice->SetTextureStageState( 2,
                D3DTSS_TEXCOORDINDEX, 0 );
        m_pd3dDevice->SetTextureStageState(2,
                D3DTSS_COLOROP, D3DTOP_ADD );
        m_pd3dDevice->SetTextureStageState(2,
                D3DTSS_COLORARG1, D3DTA_TEXTURE);
        m_pd3dDevice->SetTextureStageState( 2,
                D3DTSS_COLORARG2, D3DTA_CURRENT );
    }
    else
        m_pd3dDevice->SetTextureStageState( 2,
                D3DTSS_COLOROP, D3DTOP_DISABLE );
}
else
{
    if( m_bEnvMapOn )
    {
```

```
        m_pd3dDevice->SetTexture( 1,
                D3DTextr_GetSurface( "EarthEnvMap.bmp" ) );
        m_pd3dDevice->SetTextureStageState(1,
                D3DTSS_TEXCOORDINDEX, 0 );
        m_pd3dDevice->SetTextureStageState(1,
                D3DTSS_COLOROP, D3DTOP_ADD );
        m_pd3dDevice->SetTextureStageState(1,
                D3DTSS_COLORARG1, D3DTA_TEXTURE );
        m_pd3dDevice->SetTextureStageState(1,
                D3DTSS_COLORARG2, D3DTA_CURRENT );
    }
    else
        m_pd3dDevice->SetTextureStageState( 1,
                D3DTSS_COLOROP, D3DTOP_DISABLE );

    m_pd3dDevice->SetTextureStageState(2,
            D3DTSS_COLOROP, D3DTOP_DISABLE );
}

m_pd3dDevice->DrawPrimitive( D3DPT_TRIANGLESTRIP,
                    D3DFVF_XYZ|D3DFVF_NORMAL|D3DFVF_TEX2,
                    m_pSphereVertices, m_dwNumSphereVertices,
                    0x0 );

m_pd3dDevice->EndScene();

return S_OK;
}
```

With the bump mapping parameters configured, you can render your objects and the bump mapping effects will be applied.

Texture-Addressing Modes

Earlier in the chapter, we discussed how to assign texture coordinates to the vertices of primitives. As you learned, the *u* and *v* texture coordinates assigned to a vertex usually range from 0.0 to 1.0. DirectX allows you to use values outside this range to create special texturing effects. You can define how Direct3D handles texture coordinates outside this range by setting the texture-addressing mode, which as you saw earlier in the book allows you to create texturing effects such as tiling, wrapping, and mirroring. Tiling a texture across the surface of a primitive is one of the most common uses of texture-addressing modes. The following sections describe the four texture-addressing modes Direct 3D provides: border color, clamp, mirror, and wrap.

Border Color Texture-Addressing Mode

The *border color* texture-addressing mode is specified by the D3DTADDRESS_ BORDER member of the D3DTEXTUREADDRESS enumerated type. This texture-addressing mode causes Direct3D to use the border color for texture coordinates outside the range 0.0 through 1.0.

To set the border color, call *IDirect3DDevice7::SetTextureStageState* and pass the texture stage identifier as the first argument, the D3DTSS_BORDERCOLOR stage state value as the second argument, and the desired RGBA border color as the third argument. Figure 8-2 illustrates a texture with a border applied.

Figure 8-2
Border color texture-addressing mode

Clamp Texture-Addressing Mode

The *clamp* texture-addressing mode is specified by the D3DTADDRESS_ CLAMP member of the D3DTEXTUREADDRESS enumerated type. This texture-addressing mode causes Direct3D to clamp the texture coordinates to the range

0.0 through 1.0. Direct 3D applies the texture once and then smears the color of the pixels at the edge of the texture in the remaining directions. Even if you set the texture coordinates to (0.0, 0.0), (0.0, 4.0), (4.0, 4.0), and (4.0, 0.0), as in the previous examples, Direct 3D will apply the texture only once. The pixel colors at the top of the columns and the ends of the rows are then extended all the way to the top and right side of the primitive's surface, respectively. This line of code sample shows how to clamp a texture:

```
pd3dDevice->SetTextureStageState( 0, D3DTSS_ADDRESS,
                                  D3DTADDRESS_CLAMP );
```

Figure 8-3 illustrates how this clamped texture will appear once it's applied to a square surface.

Figure 8-3
Clamp texture-addressing mode

Mirror Texture-Addressing Mode

The *mirror* texture-addressing mode is specified using the D3DTADDRESS_ MIRROR member of the D3DTEXTUREADDRESS enumerated type. This texture-addressing mode mirrors a texture at each integer junction. For example, the texture coordinates (0.0, 0.0), (0.0, 4.0), (4.0, 4.0), and (4.0, 0.0) will apply the texture four times in both the *u* and *v* directions. Each row or column that the texture is applied to is a mirror image of the previous row or column. The command used for the mirror texture-addressing mode follows. Figure 8-4 illustrates a texture that's been applied to a square surface using the mirror texture-addressing mode.

```
pd3dDevice->SetTextureStageState( 0, D3DTSS_ADDRESS,
                                  D3DTADDRESS_MIRROR );
```

Figure 8-4
Mirror texture-addressing mode

Wrap Texture-Addressing Mode

The *wrap* texture-addressing mode, the default wrapping mode, is specified using the D3DTADDRESS_WRAP member of the D3DTEXTUREADDRESS enumerated type. This texture-addressing mode causes a texture to repeat at each integer junction. For example, if the texture coordinates (0.0,0.0), (0.0,4.0), (4.0,4.0), and (4.0,0.0) were used, Direct3D would apply the texture to the primitive's surface four times in both the *u* and *v* directions. The command for using this texture-addressing mode follows, and Figure 8-5 shows how a texture looks once it's applied to a square surface using the wrap texture-addressing mode.

```
pd3dDevice->SetTextureStageState( 0, D3DTSS_ADDRESS,
                                  D3DTADDRESS_WRAP );
```

Figure 8-5
Wrap texture-addressing mode

Texture Wrapping

Texture wrapping affects the way Direct3D rasterizes textured polygons and the way it utilizes the texture coordinates specified for each vertex. As polygons are rasterized, Direct3D interpolates between the texture coordinates of each polygon's vertices to determine which texels to use for each pixel in the polygon. Direct3D usually treats a texture as a 2D plane, interpolating new texels by taking the shortest route from point A to point B (where each point represents a u, v position).

By enabling texture wrapping of the u and v coordinates, you change how Direct3D defines the shortest route between texture coordinates in the u and v directions. Texture wrapping always makes the rasterizer take the shortest route between texture coordinate sets, assuming that 0.0 and 1.0 are *coincident* (occupy the same point in space). Enabling texture wrapping in one direction causes DirectX to treat a texture as if it's "wrapped" around a cylinder.

Wrapping in the *u* direction will change how Direct3D interpolates texture coordinates. Figure 8-6 illustrates how the shortest route between points A and B on a "normal" (nonwrapped) texture differs from the shortest route between the same points on a wrapped surface. On a flat, nonwrapped texture, the shortest path between points A and B in the figure is across the texture's middle. On a surface wrapped in the *u* direction, the shortest path between the points in the figure is across the border, where 0.0 and 1.0 coexist. Wrapping a texture in the *v* direction will make it appear as though it's wrapped around a cylinder lying on its side. Finally, when you wrap a surface in both the *u* and *v* directions, the texture is applied (wrapped) as if around a torus.

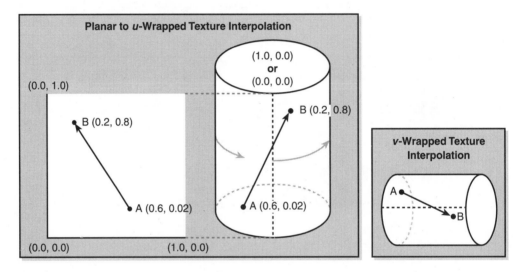

Figure 8-6
Direct3D's perception of the shortest distance between points with and without texture wrapping

Applying a Texture Wrap

When you use the *IDirect3DDevice7* interface, Direct 3D enables texture wrapping individually for texture coordinate sets that are used by vertices rather than for the texture stages themselves. You call the *IDirect3DDevice7::SetRenderState* method to enable texture wrapping. By passing one of the D3DRENDERSTATE_WRAP0 through D3DRENDERSTATE_WRAP7 enumerated values as the first argument, you specify the stage with the wrapping state you want to set. You can set the second argument to one of the D3DWRAPCOORD_0 through D3DWRAPCOORD_3 flags to enable texture wrapping in the *u* or *v* direction. By using these flags together, you can enable wrapping in multiple directions. You can also disable texture wrapping for a set of texture coordinates by setting the value for the render state to 0. Be aware that when you activate texture wrapping, it makes texture coordinates outside the 0.0 to 1.0 range invalid and texture-addressing modes unavailable for use.

The Code So Far

At this point, you should compile this chapter's code and "walk around" the 3D world you've created. Because you now have both keyboard and joystick input supported by DirectInput, you can use the keys or the joystick to maneuver around the 3D environment. Use the up arrow key to move forward, the down arrow key to move backward, the left arrow key to turn left, or the right arrow key to turn right. Different facets of the scene come into focus as you move close enough to them (and disappear as you "step" away) so that the rendering speed remains as high as possible.

Figure 8-7 depicts the 3D world rendered by this chapter's code, illustrating how the textures applied to the primitives you're using for roads, buildings, and gas pumps make this world more realistic. In this figure, the lights actually illuminate the road (because the rendering time required vs. the rendering results make it worth the computation time to use *real* lighting), but you could choose to use light maps and just a simple ambient lighting. The sky texture is animated by adjusting the *u* and *v* coordinates of the sky primitive before rendering each frame.

Figure 8-7
What the code looks like now

Conclusion

This chapter discussed the ways in which you can texture objects in your 3D worlds. Textures are the most important aspect of building 3D worlds because they add realism to 3D models. That said, it's critical that you understand how to use the texturing capabilities and commands.

In Chapter 9, we'll cover how to add fog to a 3D scene. Fog is used for a variety of effects, such as simulating real-world atmospheric conditions and hiding the "popping" of distant objects as they're added to a scene. As you've seen while running the code in this chapter, you don't need to use fog to hide graphics that you plan to add to a scene in the future. However, as you add more animated objects, you might find it useful to take advantage of this feature of Direct3D.

CHAPTER NINE

Fog

You can use fog to achieve a number of effects in Microsoft Direct3D Immediate Mode applications. By adding fog to a scene, you can simulate the real world in a powerful way. Combined with the right sounds and music, fog can help you create worlds that convey a range of atmospheres, from mysterious or creepy to fantastic or other-worldly to pastoral or humorous. Even more important for real-time applications, in which you need to eke out the last possible bit of performance, you can use fog to hide the bizarre and distracting effects of objects popping into existence as they cross into the viewing frustum. To prevent popping, you just set up fog so that users can't see beyond the far clipping plane.

Direct3D implements fog by blending the color of each object in a scene with the fog color you select. The amount of blending that occurs is based on the object's distance from the viewpoint. Direct3D blends the colors of distant objects so that the object's final color approximates the color of the fog. The colors of objects that are near the viewpoint change slightly or not at all. For example, if you use a color such as blue or white as your fog color, your objects will become increasingly obscured the farther away from the viewpoint they are, producing the illusion of fog. If you use black as your fog color, objects will appear to fade into the darkness in a night scene. If the scene has a solid background color (that is, if rendered objects don't cover every screen pixel), you should set the fog color to that background color. If objects are rendered over every screen pixel, however, you can pick any fog color you like. Then, as polygons recede from the camera, they will smoothly fade into the background. In this case, white will give you a realistically fogged scene.

Direct3D supplies two different forms of fog you can use in a scene: vertex fog and pixel fog. (We'll examine these types of fog in detail later in the chapter.) To determine what capabilities the host system has, you can check for the following flags in the *dwShadeCaps* member of the D3DPRIMCAPS structure:

- **D3DSHADECAPS_FOGFLAT**   Indicates that the device supports fog in the flat shading model.

- **D3DSHADECAPS_FOGGOURAUD**   Indicates that the device supports fog in the Gouraud shading model.

- **D3DSHADECAPS_FOGPHONG**   Indicates that the device supports fog in the Phong shading model. This mode isn't supported in DirectX 7.

And you can check for the following flags in the *dwRasterCaps* member of the D3DPRIMCAPS structure:

- **D3DPRASTERCAPS_FOGRANGE**   Indicates that the device supports range-based fog, in which the distance of an object from the viewer rather than the *z* coordinate (the depth of the object) is used to compute a scene's fog effects.

- **D3DPRASTERCAPS_FOGTABLE**   Indicates that the device computes the fog value using a lookup table of fog values indexed to the depth of a pixel.

- **D3DPRASTERCAPS_FOGVERTEX**   Indicates that the device computes the fog effect in its lighting engine. It then fills the alpha component of the D3DCOLOR value specified for the specular member of the D3DTLVERTEX structure with this value. The system then interpolates the fog value when rasterizing.

Before examining how to use the two available types of fog, let's look at how Direct3D computes the fog for a scene.

Fog Formulas

You define how fog affects the color objects in a scene by specifying how Direct3D computes the fog intensity over distance. Fog is a measure of visibility; the lower the value produced by the fog equations, the less visible the object is. You control fog by using the D3DFOGMODE enumerated type, whose members identify the three available fog formulas:

```
typedef enum _D3DFOGMODE {
    D3DFOG_NONE   = 0,
    D3DFOG_EXP    = 1,
    D3DFOG_EXP2   = 2,
    D3DFOG_LINEAR = 3
    D3DFOG_FORCE_DWORD  = 0x7fffffff,
} D3DFOGMODE;
```

These members are defined as follows:

■ **D3DFOG_NONE**   No fog is used.

■ **D3DFOG_LINEAR**   The fog increases linearly between the start and end points, using the following formula:

$$f = \frac{end - d}{end - start}$$

■ **D3DFOG_EXP**   The fog increases exponentially, using the following formula:

$$f = {}^{1}\!/_{e^{d \times density}}$$

■ **D3DFOG_EXP2**   The fog increases exponentially with the square of the distance, using the following formula:

$$f = {}^{1}\!/_{e^{(d \times density)^2}}$$

■ **D3DFOG_FORCE_DWORD**   This member forces this enumerated type to be 32 bits.

Each of the three formulas in the preceding list calculates a fog factor as a function of distance by using the parameters you pass it. How Direct3D computes distance varies depending on the projection matrix you use and on whether you've enabled range-based fog.

You use the first formula for computing linear fog. For linear fog, the *start* value defines the distance at which fog effects begin, *end* defines the distance at which fog effects no longer increase, and *d* specifies the distance from the scene's viewpoint. For all these values, 0.0 corresponds to the near plane and 1.0 corresponds to the far plane. Both pixel fog and vertex fog support linear fog.

The other two formulas Direct3D provides are D3DFOG_EXP and D3D-FOG_EXP2. Only pixel fog supports these exponential fog formulas. In these formulas, e is the base of natural logarithms (~2.71828); *density* is an arbitrary fog density, which can range from 0.0 through 1.0; and d is the distance from the scene's viewpoint.

Figure 9-1 shows a graph of the three fog formulas. Densities of 0.33 and 0.66 are the formula parameters for both exponential formulas.

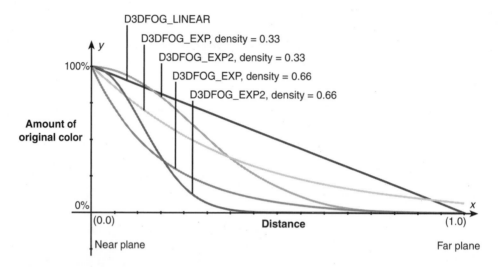

Figure 9-1
Comparison of fog formulas

The fog factors for each of the three fog effects, which are computed using the equations shown in Figure 9-1, are used in the Direct3D blending formula, which is computed as follows:

$$C = f \cdot C_i + (1 - f) \cdot C_f$$

This formula (used for all DirectX devices) scales the color of the current polygon, C_i, by the fog factor, f, and then adds the product to the fog color, C_f, scaled by the inverse of the fog factor. The color value that is computed is a blend of the fog color and the original color, with more of the fog color and less of the original color being blended as the distance increases.

Setting Up Fog

As with most aspects of Direct3D Immediate Mode, you control the fog parameters using device render states. You can set the color used for fog blending by using the D3DRENDERSTATE_FOGCOLOR device render state as shown here:

```
// Set the fog color.
m_pd3dDevice->SetRenderState(D3DRENDERSTATE_FOGCOLOR,
                             RGB_MAKE(0, 0, 80));
```

In the project for this chapter on the companion CD, we add the code to set the fog color to blue using this command to enable proper blending with the scene's background.

You use the D3DRENDERSTATE_FOGTABLEMODE render state to specify the fog mode that will be used when you choose pixel fog. If you choose to use vertex fog, the D3DRENDERSTATE_FOGVERTEXMODE render state specifies the fog mode that will be used.

With vertex fog, fog calculations are applied at each vertex in a polygon and the results are then interpolated across the face of the polygon during rasterization. To enable vertex fog, call the *SetRenderState* method with D3DRENDER-STATE_FOGENABLE as the first parameter and TRUE as the second. Vertex fog supports only the linear fog formula; to specify that formula, call the *SetRenderState* method with D3DRENDERSTATE_FOGVERTEXMODE and the D3DFOG_LINEAR member of the D3DFOGMODE enumerated type. Additionally, you should set the color of the fog based on the color of your rendered 3D world. Here are the necessary calls:

```
m_lpDevice->SetRenderState(D3DRENDERSTATE_FOGENABLE, TRUE);
m_lpDevice->SetRenderState(D3DRENDERSTATE_FOGVERTEXMODE,
                           D3DFOG_LINEAR);
m_lpDevice->SetRenderState(D3DRENDERSTATE_FOGCOLOR, dwColor);
```

The lighting and transformation engines compute vertex fog effects, and the fog is applied during the lighting stage. You also need to set the starting and ending distances (defined in world space) for linear fog by using the D3DRENDER-STATE_FOGSTART and D3DRENDERSTATE_FOGEND lighting states. These two values define the distances at which fog begins and ends in a scene.

The code to set all these states is shown below. This code and the *DoPixelFog* routine we'll cover in the next section are basically the same as the routines of the same name used in many of the Microsoft demo programs contained on this book's companion CD. However, these routines check for any errors and handle them appropriately. Microsoft recommends that you provide any floating-point values required by calls to the *IDirect3DDevice7::SetRenderState* methods without data transitions by casting the address of the floating-point variables as DWORD pointers and then dereferencing them. The calls in this routine illustrate how to use this approach.

```
void DoVertexFog(DWORD dwColor, DWORD dwMode,
                 BOOL fUseRange, FLOAT fDensity)
{
    HRESULT hr;
    float fStart = 0.5f,     // linear fog distances
          fEnd   = 0.8f;

    // Enable fog blending.
    hr = m_lpDevice->SetRenderState(D3DRENDERSTATE_FOGENABLE, TRUE);
    if (FAILED(hr))
        HandleError(hr);

    // Set the fog color.
    hr = m_lpDevice->SetRenderState(D3DRENDERSTATE_FOGCOLOR,
                                    dwColor);
    if (FAILED(hr))
        HandleError(hr);

    // Set the fog parameters.
    if(D3DFOG_LINEAR == dwMode)
    {
        hr = m_lpDevice->SetRenderState(D3DRENDERSTATE_FOGVERTEXMODE,
                                        dwMode);
        if (FAILED(hr)))
            HandleError(hr);
        hr = m_lpDevice->SetRenderState(D3DRENDERSTATE_FOGSTART,
                                        *(DWORD *)(&fStart));
        if (FAILED(hr))
            HandleError(hr);
        hr = m_lpDevice->SetRenderState(D3DRENDERSTATE_FOGEND,
                                        *(DWORD *)(&fEnd));
        if (FAILED(hr))
            HandleError(hr);
    }
    else
    {
        hr = m_lpDevice->SetRenderState(D3DRENDERSTATE_FOGVERTEXMODE,
                                        dwMode);
        if (FAILED(hr))
            HandleError(hr);
```

```
        hr = m_lpDevice->SetRenderState(D3DRENDERSTATE_FOGDENSITY,
                                        *(DWORD *)(&fDensity));
        if (FAILED(hr))
            HandleError(hr);
    }
    //
    // Enable range-based fog if desired (supported only for vertex fog).
    // fUseRange is set to a nonzero value only if the driver exposes
    // the D3DPRASTERCAPS_FOGRANGE capability.
    //
    if(fUseRange)
    {
        hr = m_lpDevice->SetRenderState(D3DRENDERSTATE_RANGEFOGENABLE,
                                        TRUE);
        if (FAILED(hr))
            HandleError(hr);
    }
}
```

Range-Based Fog

Fog can sometimes cause objects to blend with the fog color in odd ways. One situation in which you'd see strange effects is when one of the objects is far enough away to be affected by fog and a second object is close enough not to have been affected yet. This situation is shown in Figure 9-2.

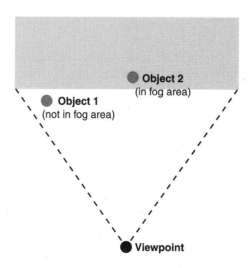

Figure 9-2
An object out of the fog area

271

By rotating the original view shown in Figure 9-2—but without moving the viewpoint—you can change the fog effects even if the objects are stationary. This rotation causes an object that wasn't obscured by fog to become obscured, creating an unrealistic flicker effect as the object becomes brighter or dimmer in relation to the overall scene. Figure 9-3 illustrates what happens to the objects in Figure 9-2 as the view is rotated.

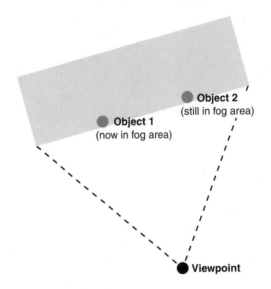

Figure 9-3
Rotating the view so that an object is in the fog area

To address this undesirable effect, and other related problems, Direct3D provides range-based fog. With range-based fog, the distance from the viewpoint to the object's vertices is used to compute the fog. Fog increases as the distance between the viewpoint and each vertex increases, as opposed to the unrealistic-flicker–effect scenario described earlier, in which the depth of the vertex within the scene is used to compute the fog effects. This approach keeps rotational artifacts from occurring. Figure 9-4 shows how range-based fog keeps objects within the fog range. By using the fog's starting and ending ranges in conjunction with the current viewpoint, Direct3D correctly computes fog effects as the view changes.

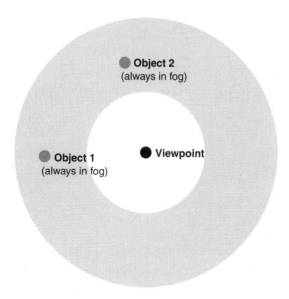

Figure 9-4
Range-based fog

If the device on the target system supports range-based fog, the D3D-PRASTERCAPS_FOGRANGE capability flag will be set in the *dwRasterCaps* member of the D3DPRIMCAPS structure when you call the *IDirect3DDevice7:: GetCaps* method. If it is available on the target system, range-based fog can be enabled by setting the D3DRENDERSTATE_RANGEFOGENABLE render state to TRUE. Here's an example of the call required:

```
m_lpDevice->SetRenderState(D3DRENDERSTATE_RANGEFOGENABLE, TRUE);
```

No one yet manufactures hardware that supports per-pixel range-based fog. Because of this, Direct3D employs range-based fog only when you use vertex fog.

Pixel Fog

Vertex fog is widely supported by 3D hardware, and this type of fog works well in most cases. It causes problems, however, when large polygons are used. If one vertex is extremely close to the camera and another is somewhere in the fog, the fog linearly interpolates between those two vertices, which is probably very different from what the fog equation would generate if applied at each pixel. To provide more accurate fog for such situations, Direct3D supports pixel fog. Pixel fog in Direct3D is calculated on a per-pixel basis in the device. Pixel fog is also known as *table fog* since some devices use a precalculated lookup table to determine the fog factor. The depth of each pixel is used to compute the fog factor that is applied in the blending computations. You can apply pixel fog by using any of the fog formulas defined by members of the D3DFOGMODE enumerated type: D3DFOG_ LINEAR, D3DFOG_EXP, or D3DFOG_EXP2. You implement the pixel fog formula in different ways, depending on the device. If the device doesn't support the complex fog formula you want to use, write your code to request a less complex formula or linear fog if necessary. Also remember that pixel fog doesn't support range-based fog calculations.

Eye-Relative Depth and z-Based Depth Pixel Fog

Eye-relative depth is basically the reciprocal of homogeneous *w* from a device space coordinate set. Most of the available hardware devices use eye-relative depth instead of z-based depth values for pixel fog because eye-relative depth doesn't create the artifacts that uneven distribution of *z* values in the z-buffer causes. The manufacturers of most 3D accelerators use the eye-relative approach because it provides the most realistic effects.

To determine whether a device supports eye-relative fog, check the D3DP-RASTERCAPS_WFOG flag in the *dwRasterCaps* member of D3DPRIMCAPS with a call to the *IDirect3DDevice7::GetCaps* method. Although many hardware devices use the eye-relative approach, software devices (other than the reference rasterizer) always use *z* values to calculate pixel fog effects.

To ensure that Direct3D uses eye-relative depth instead of z-based depth when it's available, make sure that the projection matrix (set with the call to *IDirect3D-Device7::SetTransform* method) you provide produces *z* values in world space that are equivalent to *w* values in device space.

You need to remember that if the projection matrix includes a (3, 4) coefficient that is not 1, you need to scale all coefficients by the inverse of the (3, 4) coefficient to produce a compatible matrix. The following matrix shows a noncompliant projection matrix along with the same matrix scaled properly (compliant) so that eye-relative fog is enabled. (All variables contain nonzero values.) The equations in the matrix show how to scale the noncompliant matrix properly to make it compliant.

Noncompliant

$$\begin{bmatrix} a & 0 & 0 & 0 \\ 0 & b & 0 & 0 \\ 0 & 0 & c & e \\ 0 & 0 & d & 0 \end{bmatrix}$$

Compliant

$$\begin{bmatrix} a/e & 0 & 0 & 0 \\ 0 & b/e & 0 & 0 \\ 0 & 0 & c/e & 1 \\ 0 & 0 & d/e & 0 \end{bmatrix}$$

If you use an affine projection (the coefficients of the fourth column of the projection matrix are [0, 0, 0, 1]), Direct3D uses z-based depth values for the fog. As with vertex fog, if you use the linear fog formula, you need to set the starting and ending distances (defined in world space units) by using the D3DRENDER-STATE_FOGTABLESTART and D3DRENDERSTATE_FOGTABLEEND render states.

To use eye-relative fog, you need to ensure that perspective-correct texture mapping is enabled. You enable it by setting the D3DRENDERSTATE_ TEXTUREPERSPECTIVE render state to TRUE (which is the default value in DirectX 7).

You set the pixel fog parameters by using the device render states. You control the formula you want the system to use by setting D3DRENDERSTATE_ FOGTABLEMODE to the appropriate member from the D3DFOGMODE enumerated type.

Finally, you use the D3DRENDERSTATE_FOGTABLEDENSITY render state to control the fog density, which is applied when you use an exponential fog formula. The fog density is a weighting factor, ranging from 0.0 through 1.0 inclusive, that scales the distance value in the exponent.

You enable pixel fog just as you do vertex fog: by setting the D3DRENDER-STATE_FOGENABLE render state to TRUE. You control the fog color used for fog blending by using the D3DRENDERSTATE_FOGCOLOR render state controls.

Here's an example routine to set up pixel-based fog. As with the routine shown earlier, this routine is similar to the one shown in the Microsoft documentation. In the following "The Code So Far" section, I illustrate code I use for the RoadRage application that allows you to handle these tasks via a drop-down menu. Depending on your final application, using one or the other of these routines, or a combination of both, should allow you to handle any fog code tasks that come up.

```
void DoPixelFog(DWORD dwColor, DWORD dwMode)
{
    HRESULT hr;
    float fStart = 0.5f,      // For linear mode
          fEnd   = 0.8f,
          fDensity = 0.66;    // For exponential modes

    // Enable fog blending.
    hr = m_lpDevice->SetRenderState(D3DRENDERSTATE_FOGENABLE, TRUE);
    if (FAILED(hr))
        HandleError(hr);
    // Set the fog color.
    hr = m_lpDevice->SetRenderState(D3DRENDERSTATE_FOGCOLOR, dwColor);
    if (FAILED(hr))
        HandleError(hr);

    // Set the fog parameters.
    if(D3DFOG_LINEAR == dwMode)
    {
        hr = m_lpDevice->SetRenderState(D3DRENDERSTATE_FOGTABLEMODE,
                                        dwMode);
        if (FAILED(hr))
            HandleError(hr);
        Hr = m_lpDevice->SetRenderState(D3DRENDERSTATE_FOGSTART,
                                        *(DWORD *)(&fStart));
        if (FAILED(hr))
            HandleError(hr);
        hr = m_lpDevice->SetRenderState(D3DRENDERSTATE_FOGEND,
                                        *(DWORD *)(&fEnd));
        if (FAILED(hr))
            HandleError(hr);
    }
    else
    {
        hr = m_lpDevice->SetRenderState(D3DRENDERSTATE_FOGTABLEMODE,
                                        dwMode);
        if (FAILED(hr))
            HandleError(hr);
        hr = m_lpDevice->SetRenderState(D3DRENDERSTATE_FOGDENSITY,
                                        *(DWORD *)(&fDensity));
        if (FAILED(hr))
            HandleError(hr);
    }

}
```

The Code So Far

By varying the lighting, you can simulate day and night in your 3D world, but by adding fog to your application, you can simulate other important atmospheric effects. In addition, as mentioned at the beginning of the chapter, fog hides popping effects.

The code to add fog to our RoadRage application is fairly simple. You first need to add two member variables to your applications class:

```
BOOL m_toggleFog;
BOOL m_tableFog;
```

You then need to add a code segment to set the render states necessary to generate either vertex or pixel fog. In the window's message-handling routine, *CMyD3DApplication::MsgProc* contained in the *RoadRage.cpp* file, you add code to the case statement in which the WM_COMMAND message is handled.

The code to set the appropriate fog states based on the fog type selection follows:

```
//
// Possible modes
// --------------
// Vertex fog (fog type)
//      Linear (fog mode)
//           (Can set to range-based)
//           Start
//           End
//
// Pixel (table) fog (fog type)
//      Fog mode - Linear
//           Start
//           End
//      Fog mode - Exponential
//           Density (0.0 - 1.0)
//
case MENU_FOG_OFF:
    m_pd3dDevice->SetRenderState(D3DRENDERSTATE_FOGENABLE,
                                 FALSE);
    m_toggleFog = FALSE;
    m_tableFog = FALSE;
    break;

case MENU_VERTEXFOG:
    // Set fog render states.
```

(continued)

```
            fStart =  13.0;
            fEnd   = 500.0;
            m_pd3dDevice->SetRenderState(D3DRENDERSTATE_FOGENABLE, TRUE);
            m_pd3dDevice->SetRenderState(D3DRENDERSTATE_FOGCOLOR,
                                         // Highest 8 bits aren't used.
                                         RGB_MAKE(0, 0, 80));

            // Set the fog parameters.
            m_pd3dDevice->SetRenderState(D3DRENDERSTATE_FOGTABLEMODE,
                                         D3DFOG_NONE);
            m_pd3dDevice->SetRenderState(D3DRENDERSTATE_FOGVERTEXMODE,
                                         D3DFOG_LINEAR);
            m_pd3dDevice->SetRenderState(D3DRENDERSTATE_FOGSTART,
                                         *(DWORD *)(&fStart));
            m_pd3dDevice->SetRenderState(D3DRENDERSTATE_FOGEND,
                                         *(DWORD *)(&fEnd));
            m_tableFog = FALSE;
            break;

        case MENU_VERTEXFOG_RANGE:
            // Set fog render states.
            fStart =  13.0;
            fEnd   = 500.0;
            m_pd3dDevice->SetRenderState(D3DRENDERSTATE_FOGENABLE, TRUE);
            m_pd3dDevice->SetRenderState(D3DRENDERSTATE_FOGCOLOR,
                                         // Highest 8 bits aren't used.
                                         RGB_MAKE(0, 0, 80));

            // Set the fog parameters.
            m_pd3dDevice->SetRenderState(D3DRENDERSTATE_FOGTABLEMODE,
                                         D3DFOG_NONE);
            m_pd3dDevice->SetRenderState(D3DRENDERSTATE_FOGVERTEXMODE,
                                         D3DFOG_LINEAR);
            m_pd3dDevice->SetRenderState(D3DRENDERSTATE_FOGSTART,
                                         *(DWORD *)(&fStart));
            m_pd3dDevice->SetRenderState(D3DRENDERSTATE_FOGEND,
                                         *(DWORD *)(&fEnd));

            // Enable range-based fog if desired (supported only for vertex
            // fog). For this example, it is assumed that fUseRange is set
            // to a nonzero value only if the driver exposes the
            // D3DPRASTERCAPS_FOGRANGE capability.
            //
            // Note: This is slightly more performance intensive
            //       than non-range-based fog.
            m_pd3dDevice->SetRenderState(D3DRENDERSTATE_RANGEFOGENABLE,
```

```
                                               TRUE);
        m_tableFog = FALSE;
        break;

    case MENU_TABLEFOGLIN:  // Pixel fog - linear
        m_tableFog = TRUE;
        fStart =  (float)0.8;
        fEnd   =  100.0;

        // Enable fog blending.
        m_pd3dDevice->SetRenderState(D3DRENDERSTATE_FOGENABLE, TRUE);

        // Set the fog color.
        m_pd3dDevice->SetRenderState(D3DRENDERSTATE_FOGCOLOR,
                                     RGB_MAKE(0, 0, 80));

        // Set the fog parameters.
        m_pd3dDevice->SetRenderState(D3DRENDERSTATE_FOGVERTEXMODE,
                                     D3DFOG_NONE );
        m_pd3dDevice->SetRenderState(D3DRENDERSTATE_FOGTABLEMODE,
                                     D3DFOG_LINEAR );
        m_pd3dDevice->SetRenderState(D3DRENDERSTATE_FOGSTART,
                                     *(DWORD *)(&fStart));
        m_pd3dDevice->SetRenderState(D3DRENDERSTATE_FOGEND,
                                     *(DWORD *)(&fEnd));
        break;

    case MENU_TABLEFOGEXP:  // Pixel fog - exponential
        m_tableFog = TRUE;
        fDensity = 0.01f;  // For exponential modes

        // Enable fog blending.
        m_pd3dDevice->SetRenderState(D3DRENDERSTATE_FOGENABLE, TRUE);

        // Set the fog color.
        m_pd3dDevice->SetRenderState(D3DRENDERSTATE_FOGCOLOR,
                                     RGB_MAKE(0, 0, 80));

        // Set the fog parameters.
        m_pd3dDevice->SetRenderState(D3DRENDERSTATE_FOGVERTEXMODE,
                                     D3DFOG_NONE);
        m_pd3dDevice->SetRenderState(D3DRENDERSTATE_FOGTABLEMODE,
                                     D3DFOG_EXP);
        m_pd3dDevice->SetRenderState(D3DRENDERSTATE_FOGDENSITY,
                                     *(DWORD *)(&fDensity));
        break;
```

(continued)

```
case MENU_TABLEFOGEXP2:  // Pixel fog - exponential
    m_tableFog = TRUE;
    fDensity = 0.01f;  // for exponential modes

    // Enable fog blending.
    m_pd3dDevice->SetRenderState(D3DRENDERSTATE_FOGENABLE, TRUE);

    // Set the fog color.
    m_pd3dDevice->SetRenderState(D3DRENDERSTATE_FOGCOLOR,
                                 RGB_MAKE(0, 0, 80));

    // Set the fog parameters.
    m_pd3dDevice->SetRenderState(D3DRENDERSTATE_FOGVERTEXMODE,
                                 D3DFOG_NONE);
    m_pd3dDevice->SetRenderState(D3DRENDERSTATE_FOGTABLEMODE,
                                 D3DFOG_EXP2);
    m_pd3dDevice->SetRenderState(D3DRENDERSTATE_FOGDENSITY,
                                 *(DWORD *)(&fDensity));
    break;
```

With the fog options added to the menu handler, you now need to add the Fog menu option to the *Lighting* drop-down menu. You can add this option when using Microsoft Visual C++ by adding a set of menu items to the lighting menu for each of the fog types to be generated. Figure 9-5 illustrates the lighting menu with the new fog additions (as well as a scene rendered with vertex fog to illustrate the effect).

Figure 9-5
The Lighting menu

With that, you've implemented everything you need to add fog to your programs. Figures 9-6 and 9-7 illustrate the effect you've created by adding fog to your scene. Notice that as you move forward in the scene from the position illustrated in Figure 9-6 to the one in Figure 9-7, the scenery in the distance becomes more visible. Also, you can see how the fog effect adds to the feel of the scene.

Figure 9-6
The effect of fog on distant scenery

Figure 9-7
The effect of fog on objects as the viewpoint moves closer to the objects

Conclusion

In this chapter, you learned how to apply fog to your scenes. Fog adds realism to your applications, hides the effects of popping, and allows you to create imaginative effects to evoke the ambience you want.

At this point, if you haven't already done so, you should compile and run the main application for this chapter. You can enable fog effects by going to the main window (press the Alt key while in full-screen mode) and selecting the desired Fog mode from the Lighting menu. You can switch the fog on and off with the Fog Off menu item to see how it impacts the scene.

The companion CD includes another project, named MFCFog, in the /mssdk/ samples/Multimedia/D3dim/src/MFCFog folder. You should build this project in addition to the overall book project to see another application using fog. MFCFog is a program that simulates a rotating flyover of a terrain with a number of columns sticking out of the ground. The demo lets you select vertex or pixel (table) fog. You can also vary the start and end values using the sliders on the screen. It does a very good job of demonstrating D3D's fog capabilities.

Figure 9-8 presents a screen shot of this demo application.

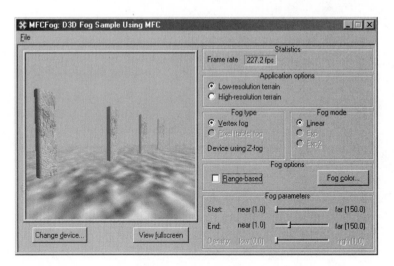

Figure 9-8
MFCFog demo application

In Chapter 10, we'll cover alpha blending. You'll learn how to use it to produce transparency and other special effects in your applications.

CHAPTER TEN

Alpha Blending

As Microsoft Direct3D renders a scene, it can integrate color information from several sources: vertex color, the current material, texture maps, and the color previously written to the render target. Rather than simply choosing the color from only one of these locations, Direct3D can blend several of these colors. A factor called *alpha* can be used to indicate how the blending should be weighted. Alpha values can be stored in vertices, materials, and texture maps. Alpha is usually treated as a measure of opacity; that is, an alpha value of 0 means full transparency, an alpha value of 1 means full opacity, and alpha values between 0 and 1 mean some level of semitransparency. By using alpha blending, you can create interesting and realistic visual effects.

Blending with the Frame Buffer

Whenever Direct3D renders a primitive, it computes the color for each pixel, deriving the color from the primitive's texture, material, and lighting information. You can use alpha blending to combine the primitive's color with the color previously stored in that pixel of the frame buffer (from other primitives or the *clear color,* that is, the color the scene is specified to be cleared to when you use the *IDirect3DDevice7::Clear* method).

Using this form of alpha blending, you can simulate semitransparent objects, combine two images, and add special effects such as force fields, flames, plasma beams, and light mapping. Alpha information can be stored in the polygon's vertex structure or in each texel of a texture map. Direct3D uses the following formula to compute the final color for each pixel in the rendered primitive:

FinalColor = SourcePixelColor · SourceBlendFactor + DestPixelColor · DestBlendFactor

The variables used in this equation are defined as follows:

- **FinalColor**   The pixel color output to the rendering surface
- **SourcePixelColor**   The pixel color computed for the current primitive
- **SourceBlendFactor**   The value used to compute the percentage of the source pixel color that will be applied to create the final color (Valid values are 0.0 through 1.0 inclusive.)
- **DestPixelColor**   The color of the current pixel in the frame buffer
- **DestBlendFactor**   The percentage of the frame buffer's current color that will be used to create the final color (Valid values are 0.0 through 1.0 inclusive.)

Direct3D lets you change the *SourceBlendFactor* and *DestBlendFactor* flags to generate the effect you want. For example, the final pixel will just be the color of the polygon if you set *SourceBlendFactor* to D3DBLEND_ONE (1.0, 1.0, 1.0, 1.0) and *DestBlendFactor* to D3DBLEND_ZERO (0.0, 0.0, 0.0, 0.0). On the other extreme, if you set *SourceBlendFactor* to D3DBLEND_ZERO and *DestBlendFactor* to D3DBLEND_ONE, the polygon will be completely transparent and the final pixel will just be the color that was previously in the frame buffer. If you set up the blend factors to use values between these extremes such that the source factor and end factor add up to 1.0, the polygon will be blended into the frame buffer with varying levels of transparency. For most of the interesting transparency effects (like flames and plasma beams), you need to set *SourceBlendFactor* and *DestBlendFactor* to settings that use the alpha values of the texture or vertices rather than to simple constant values. By varying the alpha values from frame to frame, you can create a shimmering effect. Also, if *FinalColor* has a value over 1.0—for example, if *SourceBlendFactor* and *DestBlendFactor* are both (1.0, 1.0, 1.0, 1.0)—the color values will get saturated at 1.0 because 1.0 is the highest acceptable value.

Recall from earlier chapters that when you set a color, you're actually setting the red, green, blue, and alpha values. Thus you can use the alpha value of the texels in each texture with the *SourceBlendFactor* variable to control the resulting transparency.

Direct3D uses a variety of formulas to combine a source color and a destination color into the final color, based on the blending flags you choose. As an example, let's say the following variables define the source and destination values:

(s_r, s_g, s_b, s_a) is the information in the source pixel.

(d_r, d_g, d_b, d_a) is the information in the destination pixel.

Let's also say that the source blend flag and the destination blend flag are both set to D3DBLEND_SRCALPHA, which generates blend factors represented as (s_a, s_a, s_a, s_a). Given these definitions, this formula will compute the final blended color (f_r, f_g, f_b, f_a):

$$(f_r, f_g, f_b, f_a) = (s_r \cdot s_a + d_r \cdot s_a, s_g \cdot s_a + d_g \cdot s_a, s_b \cdot s_a + d_b \cdot s_a, s_a \cdot s_a + d_a \cdot s_a)$$

Here is a description of each of the possible blend flags. Except where noted, these flags can be applied to either the D3DRENDERSTATE_SRCBLEND state or the D3DRENDERSTATE_DESTBLEND state:

- **D3DBLEND_ZERO**   The blend factor is $(0, 0, 0, 0)$.
- **D3DBLEND_ONE**   The blend factor is $(1, 1, 1, 1)$.
- **D3DBLEND_SRCCOLOR**   The blend factor is (s_r, s_g, s_b, s_a).
- **D3DBLEND_INVSRCCOLOR**   The blend factor is $(1 - s_r, 1 - s_g, 1 - s_b, 1 - s_a)$.
- **D3DBLEND_SRCALPHA**   The blend factor is (s_a, s_a, s_a, s_a).
- **D3DBLEND_INVSRCALPHA**   The blend factor is $(1 - s_a, 1 - s_a, 1 - s_a, 1 - s_a)$.
- **D3DBLEND_DESTALPHA**   The blend factor is (d_a, d_a, d_a, d_a).
- **D3DBLEND_INVDESTALPHA**   The blend factor is $(1 - d_a, 1 - d_a, 1 - d_a, 1 - d_a)$.
- **D3DBLEND_DESTCOLOR**   The blend factor is (d_r, d_g, d_b, d_a).
- **D3DBLEND_INVDESTCOLOR**   The blend factor is $(1 - d_r, 1 - d_g, 1 - d_b, 1 - d_a)$.
- **D3DBLEND_SRCALPHASAT**   The blend factor is $(f, f, f, 1)$, where $f = min(s_a, 1 - d_a)$.

■ **D3DBLEND_BOTHSRCALPHA** This blend factor is obsolete. You can produce the same effect by setting the source and destination blend factors to D3DBLEND_SRCALPHA and D3DBLEND_INVSRCALPHA in separate calls. This blend mode is supported only for the D3DRENDERSTATE_SRCBLEND render state.

■ **D3DBLEND_BOTHINVSRCALPHA** The source blend factor is $(1 - s_a, 1 - s_a, 1 - s_a, 1 - s_a)$, and the destination blend factor is (s_a, s_a, s_a, s_a); the destination blend selection is overridden. This blend mode is supported only for the D3DRENDERSTATE_SRCBLEND render state.

Once you've verified that a target system supports alpha blending, you can pass the D3DRENDERSTATE_ALPHABLENDENABLE enumerated value as the first parameter to *IDirect3DDevice7::SetRenderState* and TRUE as the second parameter to enable alpha transparency blending. Then you can control the blending factors by using the D3DRENDERSTATE_SRCBLEND and D3DRENDERSTATE_DESTBLEND enumerated values, as follows:

```
//
// Set up alpha blending.
//
m_pd3dDevice->SetRenderState( D3DRENDERSTATE_ALPHABLENDENABLE,
                              TRUE );
m_pd3dDevice->SetRenderState( D3DRENDERSTATE_SRCBLEND,
                              D3DBLEND flag );
m_pd3dDevice->SetRenderState( D3DRENDERSTATE_DESTBLEND,
                              D3DBLEND flag );
```

To maximize performance, you should set ALPHABLENDENABLE to FALSE for the primitives you're rendering that don't require alpha blending rather than provide constant alpha values, which produce the same effect—that is, just writing the source pixel into the frame buffer without blending it. Alpha blending requires a fair bit of extra math and memory access, so turning it on and off is worth the effort. You should minimize the need to change render states by grouping the objects that require alpha blending. One way to reduce the number of necessary render state changes is to render all opaque polygons first with alpha blending turned off and then to enable alpha blending and render the alpha polygons second.

Special Effects

Alpha blending lets you create many special effects in your applications, including emissive objects in a foggy atmosphere (such as flames and lasers), lens flare, light maps, and tinted glass. In the following subsections, I'll give you a brief tour of these effects.

Emissive Objects in a Foggy Atmosphere

To simulate emissive objects, such as flames or lasers, in a foggy or dusty atmosphere, you need to set the source and destination blend states to D3DBLEND_ONE. The following code sets up this type of blending:

```
//
// Draw a light as it would appear in a slightly misty room.
//
m_pd3dDevice->SetRenderState(D3DRENDERSTATE_ALPHABLENDENABLE, TRUE);
m_pd3dDevice->SetRenderState(D3DRENDERSTATE_SRCBLEND, D3DBLEND_ONE);
m_pd3dDevice->SetRenderState(D3DRENDERSTATE_DESTBLEND, D3DBLEND_ONE);
m_pd3dDevice->DrawPrimitive(D3DPT_TRIANGLESTRIP, D3DFVF_VERTEX,
                            g_avLightVertices, 4, NULL );
```

Objects such as flames are often generated using *billboarding*. In this process, a 2D object is placed into a 3D scene and rotated so that it always faces the viewer. Although for most objects this effect is fairly unrealistic, for objects such as flames, you can often insert an animated texture into a scene with billboarding and produce a very realistic look.

Lens Flare

Lens flare is used in a variety of applications to simulate the effect of light reflecting off the camera lens. The Flare demo from Microsoft, which this book's companion CD installs in the \mssdk\samples\Multimedia\d3dim\src\Flare directory, illustrates how to generate this lens flare effect. Figure 10-1 shows the resulting animated scene with the lens flare applied.

Figure 10-1
Microsoft's Flare program demonstrating a lens flare effect

Figure 10-2 shows four of the ten textures (Shine0.ppm through Shine9.ppm) used to generate the animated lens flare effect.

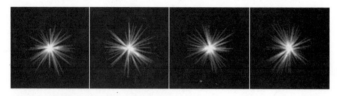

Figure 10-2
Textures for animated lens flare effect

Each image in Figure 10-2 is displayed cyclically, producing the final animated flare effect. Strategic use of this effect can make a scene appear more realistic, by simulating the appearance of light reflection. To create this effect, set both the source and destination blend factors to D3DBLEND_ONE.

Light Maps

As you'll see in Chapter 11 when we cover this topic in detail, light mapping allows you to use one texture as a light map to affect the appearance of the other textures applied to the scene. Using D3DBLEND_ZERO as the source blend state and D3DBLEND_SRCALPHA as the destination blend state, the source primitive is used as a light map to scale the contents of the frame buffer to darken the scene when appropriate.

Keep in mind that several accelerators support alpha blending only with ARGB:4444 , ARGB:1555, or ARGB:8888 format textures. Because of this, you might need to change any code you add alpha blending to so that it uses these texture formats. To guarantee that one of these formats is supported, you need to use the *EnumTextureFormats* method to verify that a format containing 4 (or more) bits of alpha exists:

```
void ChooseTextureFormat(IDirect3DDevice7 *Device, DWORD bpp,
                         DDPIXELFORMAT *pddpf)
{
    FindTextureData FindData;
    ZeroMemory(&FindData, sizeof(FindData));
    FindData.bpp = bpp;
    Device->EnumTextureformats(FindTextureCallback,
                               (LPVOID)&FindData);
    *pddpf = FindData.ddpf;
    ⋮
}
```

Tinted Glass

By using a linear blend of the source color and the destination color, you can create the appearance of tinted glass, in which some of destination object's color appears to flow through the source glass and the rest of it is absorbed by the glass. For glass that is tinted evenly across the surface, it is most efficient to use vertex alpha (and vertex color, too, if the color is uniform). If you want the transparency of the glass to vary nonlinearly across the polygon, use texture alpha instead of vertex alpha.

Alpha Testing

Alpha testing provides the ability to control whether pixels are written to the render-target surface. It is often used to create nonrectangular bitmaps as well as to implement bitmap transparency. Alpha testing allows you to improve your application's performance when nearly transparent objects are being rasterized.

To enable alpha testing, set the D3DRENDERSTATE_ALPHATEST-ENABLE render state to TRUE. With alpha testing, if the color being rasterized at a pixel is more opaque than the color that is already at the pixel, the pixel is written. You determine the state of the color being rasterized at the pixel by using, for example, D3DPCMPCAPS_GREATEREQUAL. If the pixel being rasterized is less opaque than the color already at the pixel, Direct3D skips it completely, saving the time that would have been required to blend the two colors together. In addition, the color buffer, and more important, the z-buffer, aren't updated, avoiding an "invisible" portion of a polygon that obscures a polygon behind it that is rendered afterward. (You can also avoid this problem by rendering the transparent polygons back to front after rendering all the opaque polygons. However, this rendering requires that you sort the polygons in a scene before rendering them.) You can make Direct3D compare the incoming alpha value with a reference alpha value (which you supply) by specifying a comparison function via the D3DRENDER-STATE_ALPHAFUNC render state. When you enable alpha testing, alpha blending will occur only when the test you specify succeeds.

The D3DCMPFUNC enumerated type that defines the possible tests this render state uses is defined as follows:

```
typedef enum _D3DCMPFUNC {
    D3DCMP_NEVER        = 1,
    D3DCMP_LESS         = 2,
    D3DCMP_EQUAL        = 3,
    D3DCMP_LESSEQUAL    = 4,
    D3DCMP_GREATER      = 5,
    D3DCMP_NOTEQUAL     = 6,
    D3DCMP_GREATEREQUAL = 7,
    D3DCMP_ALWAYS       = 8,
    D3DCMP_FORCE_DWORD  = 0x7fffffff,
} D3DCMPFUNC;
```

You supply the reference alpha value for alpha testing via the D3DRENDER-STATE_ALPHAREF render state. In the code below, the call to *SetRenderState* with D3DRENDERSTATE_ALPHAREF sets a value that specifies the reference alpha value that Direct3D tests incoming pixels against when alpha test is enabled. You can specify a reference alpha value between 0x00 and 0xFF; the default value is 0.

The following code checks whether a specific comparison function is supported, and if so, improves rendering performance by causing Direct3D to use that comparison function:

```
LPD3DDEVICEDESC7 lpD3DHWDevDesc;
device->GetCaps(lpD3DHWDevDesc);
//
// lpD3DHWDevDesc is a hardware device D3DDEVICEDESC7 structure
// filled by a call to IDirect3DDevice7::GetCaps.
//
```

```
if (lpD3DHWDevDesc->dpcTriCaps.dwAlphaCmpCaps &
    D3DPCMPCAPS_GREATEREQUAL)
{
    device->SetRenderState(D3DRENDERSTATE_ALPHAREF,
                            (DWORD)0x00000a0);
    device->SetRenderState(D3DRENDERSTATE_ALPHATESTENABLE, TRUE);
    device->SetRenderState(D3DRENDERSTATE_ALPHAFUNC,
                            D3DCMP_GREATEREQUAL);
}
```

If the target system doesn't support the comparison you want to use, just render the primitive as usual. Unfortunately, you won't get the performance gain you hoped for. The *IDirect3DDevice7::GetCaps* method call in the preceding code acquires the capabilities of the current device. By checking the *dwAlphaCmpCaps* member of the D3DPRIMCAPS structure, which is contained in the D3D-DEVICEDESC7 structure associated with the *GetCaps* call, you can determine whether the comparison function you want is available. If this member contains only the D3DPCMPCAPS_ALWAYS or only the D3DPCMPCAPS_NEVER capabilities, the current driver doesn't support alpha testing. Otherwise, *dwAlpha-CmpCaps* contains flags that identify the individual comparisons that the driver supports. If the driver doesn't support the method you want to use, select a comparison function that is available.

If you intend to use alpha in texture maps, you need to make sure that the textures you use are in an ARGB:4444, ARGB:1555, or ARGB:8888 format so that they support alpha channels.

Color-Key Transparency

When you enable *color-key transparency* by setting a *color key,* you tell Direct3D to treat a particular color as transparent. To apply a color key to a texture, you must create the texture by using the DDSD_CKSRCBLT flag. Whenever a texture created with the DDSD_CKSRCBLT flag is applied to a primitive, none of the texels that match the color key are rendered on the primitive.

Like alpha testing, enabling color-key transparency accelerates the rasterization of any invisible pixels because Direct3D performs only a texture read (as opposed to a texture write). Only a read operation is performed because the color-key test result tells Direct3D to skip the write operation for that pixel. Keep in mind, however, that visible pixels incur a slight performance degradation because of the color-key test. Also, unlike alpha blending, in which there are *levels* of transparency, with color-key transparency enabled, the color is always *completely* transparent and thus never rendered.

To set a color key, you use the *IDirectDrawSurface7::SetColorKey* method for the surface you want the color key to be used for. This method is defined as follows:

```
HRESULT SetColorKey(
    DWORD dwFlags,
    LPDDCOLORKEY lpDDColorKey
);
```

Parameter	Description
dwFlags	Determines which color key is requested. The following flags are defined:
	DDCKEY_COLORSPACE The structure contains a color space. Not set if the structure contains a single color key.
	DDCKEY_DESTBLT A color key or color space to be used as a destination color key for blit operations.
	DDCKEY_DESTOVERLAY A color key or color space to be used as a destination color key for overlay operations.
	DDCKEY_SRCBLT A color key or color space to be used as a source color key for blit operations.
	DDCKEY_SRCOVERLAY A color key or color space to be used as a source color key for overlay operations.
lpDDColorKey	Address of the DDCOLORKEY structure that contains the new color-key values for the DirectDrawSurface object. This value can be NULL to remove a previously set color key.

The DDCOLORKEY structure can be used to set the parameters of a source or destination color key. This structure is defined as follows:

```
typedef struct _DDCOLORKEY{
    DWORD dwColorSpaceLowValue;
    DWORD dwColorSpaceHighValue;
} DDCOLORKEY, FAR* LPDDCOLORKEY;
```

The DDCOLORKEY structure has two members:

- **dwColorSpaceLowValue**   Low value of the color range that is to be used as the color key

- **dwColorSpaceHighValue**   High value of the color range that is to be used as the color key

You can toggle color keying on and off by using the *IDirect3DDevice7:: SetRenderState* method and setting the first parameter to D3DRENDERSTATE_ COLORKEYENABLE and the second to TRUE (enabled) or FALSE (disabled).

This code shows how to set up color keying:

```
//
// Enable color keying.
//
m_pd3dDevice->SetRenderState(D3DRENDERSTATE_COLORKEYENABLE, TRUE);
```

Direct3D allows you to use both alpha and color keying together. To combine these two features, you must enable alpha testing to make sure that the textures are rendered properly. To set up the color key, use the *IDirectDrawSurface7:: SetColorKey* method and set the *dwColorSpaceLowValue* and *dwColorSpaceHigh-Value* variables. If you use color keying, be sure to set both color space values to the same color value.

> **NOTE**   Remember that if you want to have *complete* transparency, you can use color keying or one-bit alpha. If you want *levels* of transparency, however, use alpha blending. The Microsoft DirectX team suggests that developers stop using color keying and use one-bit alpha transparency instead because it avoids certain filtering artifacts.

Alpha-Capable Palettized Textures

Direct3D provides the capability to fill texture palettes with alpha information. You can determine whether the current device supports this capability by calling the *IDirectDraw7::GetCaps* method and checking for the DDPCAPS_ALPHA palette capability flag in the *dwPalCaps* member of the associated DDCAPS structure.

Direct3D also allows texturing from alpha-capable palettized textures. To determine whether the target system supports this capability, check for the D3DP-TEXTURECAPS_ALPHAPALETTE flag returned in the two D3DPRIMCAPS structures that are contained in the D3DDEVICEDESC7 structure passed in a call to the *IDirect3DDevice7::GetCaps* method.

Texture Stages Using Alpha

As you saw in Chapter 8, the *IDirect3D7* and *IDirect3DDevice7* interfaces allow you to blend up to eight textures onto primitives in a single pass. The texture stages that use alpha are basically the same as the texture stages described in Chapter 8—except, obviously, that they handle alpha information. For alpha operations, you use the D3DTSS_ALPHAOP stage state (which is similar to the color channel you learned about in Chapter 8), which in turn uses values from the D3DTEXTUREOP enumerated type.

The following texture-blending stages pertain to alpha blending:

- **D3DTSS_ALPHAOP**   A texture alpha-blending operation, identified by one of the members of the D3DTEXTUREOP enumerated type. The default value for the first texture stage (stage 0) is D3DTOP_SELECTARG1. For all other stages, the default is D3DTOP_DISABLE.

- **D3DTSS_ALPHAARG1**   The first alpha argument for the stage, identified by a texture argument flag. The default argument is D3DTA_TEXTURE. If no texture is set for this stage, the default argument is D3DTA_DIFFUSE.

- **D3DTSS_ALPHAARG2**   The second alpha argument for the stage, identified by a texture argument flag. The default argument is D3DTA_CURRENT.

The following code segment illustrates the use of these three states together:

```
m_pd3dDevice->SetTextureStageState( i, D3DTSS_ALPHAOP, op);
m_pd3dDevice->SetTextureStageState( i, D3DTSS_ALPHAARG1, arg1 );
m_pd3dDevice->SetTextureStageState( i, D3DTSS_ALPHAARG2, arg2 );
```

Legacy Blending Modes and Texture Stages

Another aspect of alpha blending you need to know about if you're updating a title created using a prior version of Direct3D is the older D3DRENDERSTATE_ TEXTUREBLEND render state. Earlier versions of Direct3D introduced the texture-blending render state and its texture-blending modes. The Direct3D documentation presents a set of equivalents of the legacy blending modes you can build using texture stages. These modes, defined by the members of the D3DTEXTURE-BLEND enumerated type, are listed below along with an example of how to create the same blend using the texture stage states. I've included this information for those of you who have used these modes or are inheriting legacy code that you need to update to the newest version of DirectX.

D3DTBLEND_ADD

```
// g_lpDev is a valid pointer to an IDirect3DDevice7 interface.
g_lpDev->SetTextureStageState(0, COLOROP, D3DTOP_ADD);
g_lpDev->SetTextureStageState(0, COLORARG1, D3DTA_TEXTURE);
g_lpDev->SetTextureStageState(0, COLORARG2, D3DTA_DIFFUSE);

g_lpDev->SetTextureStageState(0, ALPHAOP, D3DTOP_SELECTARG2);
g_lpDev->SetTextureStageState(0, ALPHAARG2, D3DTA_DIFFUSE);
```

D3DTBLEND_COPY and D3DTBLEND_DECAL

```
// g_lpDev is a valid pointer to an IDirect3DDevice7 interface.
g_lpDev->SetTextureStageState(0, COLOROP, D3DTOP_SELECTARG1);
g_lpDev->SetTextureStageState(0, COLORARG1, D3DTA_TEXTURE);

g_lpDev->SetTextureStageState(0, ALPHAOP, D3DTOP_SELECTARG1);
g_lpDev->SetTextureStageState(0, ALPHAARG2, D3DTA_TEXTURE);
```

D3DTBLEND_DECALALPHA

```
// g_lpDev is a valid pointer to an IDirect3DDevice7 interface.
g_lpDev->SetTextureStageState(0, COLOROP, D3DTOP_BLENDTEXTUREALPHA);
g_lpDev->SetTextureStageState(0, COLORARG1, D3DTA_TEXTURE);
g_lpDev->SetTextureStageState(0, COLORARG2, D3DTA_DIFFUSE);

g_lpDev->SetTextureStageState(0, ALPHAOP, D3DTOP_SELECTARG2);
g_lpDev->SetTextureStageState(0, ALPHAARG2, D3DTA_DIFFUSE);
```

D3DTBLEND_MODULATE

```
// g_lpDev is a valid pointer to an IDirect3DDevice7 interface.
g_lpDev->SetTextureStageState(0, COLOROP, D3DTOP_MODULATE);
g_lpDev->SetTextureStageState(0, COLORARG1, D3DTA_TEXTURE);
g_lpDev->SetTextureStageState(0, COLORARG2, D3DTA_DIFFUSE);

if ( the_texture_has_an_alpha_channel )
{
    g_lpDev->SetTextureStageState(0, ALPHAOP, D3DTOP_SELECTARG1);
    g_lpDev->SetTextureStageState(0, ALPHAARG1, D3DTA_TEXTURE);
}
else
{
    g_lpDev->SetTextureStageState(0, ALPHAOP, D3DTOP_SELECTARG2);
    g_lpDev->SetTextureStageState(0, ALPHAARG2, D3DTA_DIFFUSE);
}
```

D3DTBLEND_MODULATEALPHA

```
// g_lpDev is a valid pointer to an IDirect3DDevice7 interface.
g_lpDev->SetTextureStageState(0, COLOROP, D3DTOP_MODULATE);
g_lpDev->SetTextureStageState(0, COLORARG1, D3DTA_TEXTURE);
g_lpDev->SetTextureStageState(0, COLORARG2, D3DTA_DIFFUSE);

g_lpDev->SetTextureStageState(0, ALPHAOP, D3DTOP_MODULATE);
g_lpDev->SetTextureStageState(0, ALPHAARG1, D3DTA_TEXTURE);
g_lpDev->SetTextureStageState(0, ALPHAARG2, D3DTA_DIFFUSE);
```

Premultiplied vs. Nonpremultiplied Alpha

The last aspect of alpha blending you'll need to consider is how to select whether to use premultiplied or nonpremultiplied alpha in textures. With the premultiplied alpha format, the color components stored in each pixel are already premultiplied by the alpha component. For example, a semitransparent, fully red pixel would be stored as $(0.5, 0.0, 0.0, 0.5)$ in premultiplied format or as $(1.0, 0.0, 0.0, 0.5)$ in nonpremultiplied format.

Premultiplied alpha is starting to gain popularity because it's more useful and more efficient than nonpremultiplied blending in some settings because of the computation time it saves during rendering.

A key point to keep in mind when you're applying a texture with premultiplied alpha is *not* to set up the renderer to use this formula:

$$resultColor = srcColor \cdot srcAlpha + destColor \cdot invSrcAlpha$$

The *srcColor* variable is already multiplied by *srcAlpha*. Instead, you should use the following formula:

resultColor = srcColor · 1 + destColor · invSrcAlpha

To linearly blend a texture stage that uses premultiplied alpha, use the D3D-TOP_BLENDTEXTUREALPHAPM member with the *IDirect3DDevice7::SetTextureStageState* method.

The Code So Far

At this point, you should compile the code for this chapter and select Alpha Transparency from the Textures menu. Now go inside one of the buildings and look out the windows. You can see through the windows because of the alpha values associated with the textures used on the vehicle. The windows are slightly translucent, so if you look closely you'll see that they slightly gray the scene you're looking at outside the window.

To see how the windows look without transparency enabled, select Alpha Transparency from the Textures menu to toggle transparency to an off state. You'll no longer be able to see out the windows.

Figures 10-3 and 10-4 show screen shots of the scene looking out a window of a building along the main street of the RoadRage world.

Figure 10-3
View from RoadRage building with transparency enabled

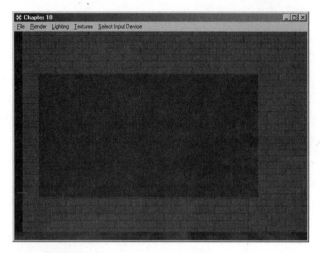

Figure 10-4
View from RoadRage building with transparency turned off

Conclusion

In this chapter, we covered alpha blending and alpha testing as well as some related concepts. Alpha blending allows you to create realistic and interesting special effects. Alpha testing allows you to speed up rendering by avoiding writing pixels that are less opaque than others that occlude them. We also covered several concepts that relate to alpha blending: alpha palettized textures, texture stages using alpha information, and the use of premultiplied vs. nonpremultiplied alpha.

Combining these capabilities, you can create programs that simulate realistic real-world scenes.

In Chapter 11, we'll cover light mapping and environment mapping. These techniques add even more realism to a scene by making the scene appear to be accurately lit and by reflecting the surrounding scenery off other shiny objects in the scene.

CHAPTER ELEVEN

Light Mapping and Environment Mapping

Microsoft Direct3D Immediate Mode offers two capabilities that can greatly enhance the realism of the 3D graphics in your games and simulations: light mapping and environment mapping. In this chapter, you'll learn about the visual effects that these techniques can generate and see how to implement them in your applications.

Light Mapping

Light mapping is the process of applying a texture that contains lighting information (either monochromatic or color) to a primitive that already has a solid color or a base texture. Direct3D needs highly detailed meshes to compute vertex lighting effects because it computes the effects only at the meshes' vertices. Because light mapping doesn't require Direct3D to compute lighting information for every vertex, you don't need to use the highly detailed meshes that vertex lighting requires. So you'll likely see a performance improvement when you render a low-polygon scene with light mapping rather than a high-polygon scene with vertex lighting. And, because you compute light mapping information at authoring time rather than at run time, you'll achieve even higher speeds at run time with this technique.

Light mapping is sometimes referred to as *dark mapping* because it is a technique in which you apply a light-map texture as the second blended texture (on top of the fully lit base texture), darkening a scene rather than lighting it. Light maps can produce dramatic lighting effects in your 3D scenes. By applying a varying light map in an iterative process, you can make these effects range from simple shadows to eerie, undulating degrees of darkness. You generate light maps by sending content through a special renderer—often a raytracer or a radiosity algorithm that simply computes lighting and saves the resulting per-pixel lighting in texture maps. A radiosity program is an image-rendering algorithm that uses the principle of conservation of energy in a closed system to model the diffuse interaction of light from surfaces in a 3D scene (especially room interiors). The algorithm examines the geometric interaction between every pair of discrete polygonal facets (triangles) and sets up a set of simultaneous equations whose solution determines the apparent color of each facet. Because Direct3D doesn't have a per-pixel lighting unit, you either need to write your own renderer or use a free, shareware, or commercial tool. You can then apply the computed light map to a 3D scene.

You can use light maps to add monochromatic or colored light to objects and to add effects such as diffuse lighting and specular highlights. To perform light mapping, you apply two textures to a 3D primitive. One of these textures is a uniformly, fully lit base texture. (A brick wall is an example of this type of texture.) The other texture is the light map. Both textures are blended to produce a scene that appears naturally lit. The light map can contain a bitmap that gives the appearance of complex lighting. You can store this lighting information in the light map's alpha values or color values.

You might be asking yourself, "Won't these light maps take up a lot of memory?" You can reuse "normal" texture maps (bricks, floor, blank walls, and so on) quite a bit, but chances are high that the lighting will differ for each face—meaning you'll have one light map per face, which sounds like a huge drain on the available texture memory. To answer this question about memory, you must consider the following aspects of light mapping:

- A light map can have a much lower resolution than a texture map—for example, a 16×16, bilinear-filtered light map is often sufficient on top of a 256×256 texture map.

- Light maps are often monochromatic, so they can be 4 or 8 bits per pixel rather than 16 or 24. (Plus, light maps often compress well for disk storage.)

- You can analyze the light maps you generate and often discard them in favor of using vertex colors to generate the equivalent effects. For instance, many light maps end up being similar enough to a constant intensity or a linear ramp that you don't need texture maps to create the lighting effect.

- Because light maps typically are small, it's a good idea to combine many of them into a single large texture map to reduce the overhead of changing texture maps while rendering (as discussed Chapter 8).

When combining several light maps into a single texture map, you should be aware of the filtering side effects that can occur between neighboring light maps. Checking the results of the rendered scene is the best way to verify that the light maps stored in the combined textures do what you want.

Figure 11-1, Figure 11-2, and Figure 11-3 illustrate a base texture, a monochromatic light map, and the result of applying both light maps to a surface, respectively.

Figure 11-1
Base texture

Figure 11-2
Monochromatic light map

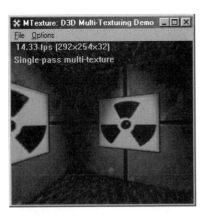

Figure 11-3
Applying the base texture and the light map to a surface

Figure 11-4 and Figure 11-5 show the same scene with a different light map applied. This light map simulates the effect of a flashlight beam hitting the walls in two places. This light map uses a much higher resolution than is necessary. Typically you should use simple textures. As Figure 11-4 illustrates, the higher-resolution light map has only a negligible gain in visual quality—an improvement that's hardly worth its price in memory.

Figure 11-4
Flashlight beam light map

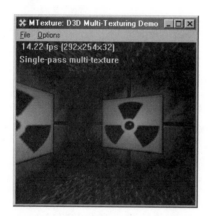

Figure 11-5
Scene with the flashlight beam light map applied

As you can see, effectively applying light maps can greatly enhance a scene's appearance and save rendering time that would be lost if you computed "real" lighting effects.

Light Mapping with Multipass Texture Blending

You can blend the textures used for light mapping in a number of ways. As we discussed in Chapter 8, you can use the older approach of multipass texture blending by applying the D3DRENDERSTATE_SRCBLEND and D3DRENDER-STATE_DESTBLEND enumerated value pair. You can also use the newer

SetTextureStageState method to implement multiple-texture blending. Let's first look at the multipass texture blending technique. Later in the chapter, we'll examine the newer approach, multiple-texture blending.

Monochromatic Light Mapping

You can use monochromatic light mapping to darken a scene based on the source alpha information, which is the lighting information that's stored in the alpha values of the light map textures. With this approach, you can use a source primitive as a light map that darkens the frame by scaling its buffer contents.

When you use multipass texture blending to perform light mapping, you render the base texture onto the primitives in one pass and the light map onto the base texture in another pass—rather than applying the textures in a single pass as you would in multiple-texture blending. To use a monochromatic light map, set the source alpha blend state to D3DBLEND_ZERO and the destination alpha blend state to D3DBLEND_SRCALPHA. This code segment shows you how:

```
device->SetRenderState(D3DRENDERSTATE_ALPHABLENDENABLE, TRUE);
device->SetRenderState(D3DRENDERSTATE_SRCBLEND, D3DBLEND_ZERO);
device->SetRenderState(D3DRENDERSTATE_DESTBLEND, D3DBLEND_SRCALPHA);
```

This code effectively says, "Ignore (multiply by 0) the (nonexistent) color of this light map, and set the final pixel color to be the product of the alpha value of this light map and the color of the underlying texture." In other words, when the alpha value is 1.0, the underlying texture stays at full brightness, and when the alpha value is closer to 0, the underlying texture is further darkened.

Color Light Mapping

You can also use color light mapping, which is similar to the monochromatic light mapping method except that it lets you apply a color light map to a surface. To use color light mapping, set the source alpha blend state to D3DBLEND_ZERO and the destination alpha blend state to D3DBLEND_SRCCOLOR.

The following code illustrates how to color a 3D room by using color light mapping. SEGMENT 1 draws the texture for the room, and SEGMENT 2 draws a light map for the room by blending the light map texture lightmap.bmp with the first textures applied. This code uses multipass rendering.

```
// Draw the first textures normally. Use the first set of
// texture coordinates.
m_pd3dDevice->SetTextureStageState(0, D3DTSS_TEXCOORDINDEX, 0 );
```

(continued)

```
m_pd3dDevice->SetTextureStageState(0, D3DTSS_COLORARG1,
                                   D3DTA_TEXTURE );
m_pd3dDevice->SetTextureStageState(0, D3DTSS_COLOROP,
                                   D3DTOP_MODULATE );
// SEGMENT 1
m_WallData.textureCoords[0].lpvData = &m_avWallVertices[0].tuBase;
m_pd3dDevice->SetTexture( 0, D3DTextr_GetSurface("wall.bmp") );
m_pd3dDevice->DrawPrimitiveStrided( D3DPT_TRIANGLELIST,
                                    D3DFVF_XYZ | D3DFVF_DIFFUSE |
                                    D3DFVF_TEX2,
                                    &m_WallData, 24, NULL );
m_pd3dDevice->SetTexture( 0, D3DTextr_GetSurface("floor.bmp") );
m_pd3dDevice->DrawPrimitiveStrided( D3DPT_TRIANGLELIST,
                                    D3DFVF_XYZ | D3DFVF_DIFFUSE |
                                    D3DFVF_TEX2,
                                    &m_FloorCeilData, 12, NULL );
// SEGMENT 2
// Draw the light map using blending, with the second set of
// texture coordinates.
m_pd3dDevice->SetRenderState( D3DRENDERSTATE_ALPHABLENDENABLE,
                              TRUE );
m_pd3dDevice->SetRenderState( D3DRENDERSTATE_SRCBLEND,
                              D3DBLEND_ZERO );
m_pd3dDevice->SetRenderState( D3DRENDERSTATE_DESTBLEND,
                              D3DBLEND_SRCCOLOR );

m_WallData.textureCoords[0].lpvData = &m_avWallVertices[0].tuLightMap;
m_pd3dDevice->SetTexture( 0, D3DTextr_GetSurface("lightmap.bmp") );
m_pd3dDevice->DrawPrimitiveStrided( D3DPT_TRIANGLELIST,
                                    D3DFVF_XYZ | D3DFVF_DIFFUSE |
                                    D3DFVF_TEX2,
                                    &m_WallData, 36, NULL );
// Restore state.
m_pd3dDevice->SetRenderState( D3DRENDERSTATE_ALPHABLENDENABLE,
                              FALSE );
```

Light Mapping with Texture Stages

Using multiple-texture blending, you can apply one or more light maps to primitives. Although multiple-texture blending effectively produces the same results as multipass texture blending, as stated earlier, this newer feature enables you to render both a light map and a base texture in a single pass. Multiple-texture blending greatly improves the rendering speed, so you should use it whenever the target system hardware supports it.

Multiple-texture blending offers four light-mapping approaches: monochromatic light maps, color light maps, diffuse light maps, and specular light maps. We've already discussed monochromatic and color light maps in this chapter; the sections that follow will explain diffuse and specular light maps.

```
// Set up the texture stages. (You don't need to do this
// every frame.)
m_pd3dDevice->SetTextureStageState( 0, D3DTSS_TEXCOORDINDEX, 0 );
m_pd3dDevice->SetTextureStageState( 0, D3DTSS_COLORARG1,
                                       D3DTA_TEXTURE );
m_pd3dDevice->SetTextureStageState( 0, D3DTSS_COLOROP,
                                       D3DTOP_MODULATE );
m_pd3dDevice->SetTextureStageState( 1, D3DTSS_TEXCOORDINDEX, 1 );
m_pd3dDevice->SetTextureStageState( 1, D3DTSS_COLORARG1,
                                       D3DTA_TEXTURE );
m_pd3dDevice->SetTextureStageState( 1, D3DTSS_COLORARG2,
                                       D3DTA_CURRENT );
m_pd3dDevice->SetTextureStageState( 1, D3DTSS_COLOROP,
                                       D3DTOP_MODULATE );

m_WallData.textureCoords[0].lpvData = &m_avWallVertices[0].tuBase;
m_WallData.textureCoords[1].lpvData = &m_avWallVertices[0].tuLightMap;
// Draw the walls in multi-texture mode.
m_pd3dDevice->SetTexture( 0, D3DTextr_GetSurface("wall.bmp") );
m_pd3dDevice->SetTexture( 1, D3DTextr_GetSurface("lightmap.bmp") );
m_pd3dDevice->DrawPrimitiveStrided( D3DPT_TRIANGLELIST,
                                    D3DFVF_XYZ | D3DFVF_DIFFUSE |
                                    D3DFVF_TEX2,
                                    &m_WallData, 24, NULL );

// Draw the floor in single-texture mode.
m_pd3dDevice->SetTexture( 0, D3DTextr_GetSurface("floor.bmp") );
m_pd3dDevice->SetTexture( 1, NULL );
m_pd3dDevice->DrawPrimitiveStrided( D3DPT_TRIANGLELIST,
                                    D3DFVF_XYZ | D3DFVF_DIFFUSE |
                                    D3DFVF_TEX2,
                                    &m_FloorCielData, 12, NULL );
// Restore state.
m_pd3dDevice->SetTextureStageState( 1, D3DTSS_COLOROP,
                                       D3DTOP_DISABLE );
```

Diffuse Light Mapping

You can generate diffuse light maps to simulate the illumination of matte surfaces by a point light source. When a point source light reflects off a matte surface, it reflects diffuse light. The resultant brightness of this diffuse light is dependent on the distance of the surface from the light source and on the angle between the surface normal and the vector of the light source direction. Because matte surfaces produce a reflection that looks different from the reflection of shiny surfaces, it's useful to generate a matte surface light map.

The following code shows how to simulate diffuse lighting using texture light maps by adding the diffuse light map to the base texture:

```
//
// Set the base texture.
//
dev->SetTexture(0,lpTexureBaseTexture );
//
// Set up the operation and arguments for the base texture.
//
dev->SetTextureStageState(0,D3DTSS_COLOROP, D3DTOP_MODULATE );
dev->SetTextureStageState(0,D3DTSS_COLORARG1, D3DTA_TEXTURE );
dev->SetTextureStageState(0,D3DTSS_COLORARG2, D3DTA_DIFFUSE );
//
// Set the diffuse light map.
//
dev->SetTexture(1,lptexDiffuseLightMap );
//
// Set the blend stage.
//
dev->SetTextureStageState(1, D3DTSS_COLOROP, D3DTOP_ADD );
dev->SetTextureStageState(1, D3DTSS_COLORARG1, D3DTA_TEXTURE );
dev->SetTextureStageState(1, D3DTSS_COLORARG2, D3DTA_CURRENT );
```

Specular Light Mapping

You apply specular light maps to primitives in order to simulate shiny, metallic, or glass surfaces that are illuminated by a point light source. To perform this type of light mapping, you must modulate the specular light map with the primitive's texture and then add the monochromatic or color light map.

Because in the real world specular light varies with a person's point of view, you can generate only an approximation of specular light. You don't recompute the specular light map every time the user moves, and you don't shift the texture coordinates. Therefore, a user paying close attention will realize that the specular reflection is not "moving" as his or her viewpoint changes throughout the scene. However, specular light mapping does produce a fair simulation of this effect at a very low computational cost. The following code segment shows how to create this lighting effect:

```
//
// Set the base texture.
//
```

```
dev->SetTexture(0, lpTexureBaseTexture);
//
// Set up the operation and arguments for the base texture.
//
dev->SetTextureStageState(0, D3DTSS_COLOROP, D3DTOP_MODULATE);
dev->SetTextureStageState(0, D3DTSS_COLORARG1, D3DTA_TEXTURE);
dev->SetTextureStageState(0, D3DTSS_COLORARG2, D3DTA_DIFFUSE);
//
// Set the specular light map.
//
dev->SetTexture(1, lpTexureSpecularLightMap);
//
// Set the specular light map operation and arguments.
//
dev->SetTextureStageState(1, D3DTSS_COLOROP, D3DTOP_MODULATE);
dev->SetTextureStageState(1, D3DTSS_COLORARG1, D3DTA_TEXTURE);
dev->SetTextureStageState(1, D3DTSS_COLORARG2, D3DTA_CURRENT);
//
// Set the color light map.
//
dev->SetTexture(2, lpTexureLightMap);
//
// Set the color light map operation and arguments.
//
dev->SetTextureStageState(2, D3DTSS_COLOROP, D3DTOP_ADD);
dev->SetTextureStageState(2, D3DTSS_COLORARG1, D3DTA_TEXTURE);
dev->SetTextureStageState(2, D3DTSS_COLORARG2, D3DTA_CURRENT);
```

The Microsoft DirectX SDK setup program on the companion CD installs a light map project on your hard drive, in the \mssdk\samples\Multimedia\d3dim\ src\lightmap directory. The project illustrates a light map applied to a simple 3D room. You might want to compile and run this code now while these concepts are fresh in your mind.

Environment Mapping

In the real world, the appearance of many objects is affected not only by the lights around them but also by other objects. Mirrors are an obvious example, and metal and other highly reflective surfaces also fall into this category. One way to generate this effect in Direct3D is with *environment maps*. These are special texture maps that are applied to primitives in such a way as to indicate a reflection of the surrounding scene.

Spherical Environment Maps

With a spherical environment map, a single texture is used to represent the world surrounding an object projected onto a sphere. (Think of the rendered object as being contained in a bubble.) You can also think of each texel as a representation of what you see when looking out from the object in a particular direction. Before the object is rendered, the texture coordinates of the object's vertices need to be adjusted such that the direction in which the vertex normal is pointing maps to the appropriate part of the environment map.

The DirectX SDK has a sample named Sphere Map that demonstrates this technique. It uses the image shown in Figure 11-6 as its sphere map.

Figure 11-6
Sphere map

Before rendering the shiny object (a teapot in the Sphere Map example), the texture coordinates of each vertex get computed as a function of the vertex's normal. Note that the normals first need to be transformed from local space into camera space.

```
//----------------------------------------------------------------
// Name: ApplySphereMapToObject
// Desc: Uses the current orientation of the vertices to calculate
//       the object's sphere-mapped texture coordinates
//----------------------------------------------------------------
HRESULT ApplySphereMapToObject( LPDIRECT3DDEVICE3 pd3dDevice,
                                D3DVERTEX* pvVertices,
                                DWORD dwNumVertices )
{
    // Get the current world-view matrix.
    D3DMATRIX matWorld, matView, matWV;
    pd3dDevice->GetTransform( D3DTRANSFORMSTATE_VIEW,  &matView );
    pd3dDevice->GetTransform( D3DTRANSFORMSTATE_WORLD, &matWorld );
    D3DMath_MatrixMultiply( matWV, matView, matWorld );
```

```
// Extract world-view matrix elements for speed.
FLOAT m11 = matWV._11,   m21 = matWV._21,   m31 = matWV._31;
FLOAT m12 = matWV._12,   m22 = matWV._22,   m32 = matWV._32;
FLOAT m13 = matWV._13,   m23 = matWV._23,   m33 = matWV._33;

// Loop through the vertices, transforming each one and
// calculating the correct texture coordinates.
for( WORD i = 0; i < dwNumVertices; i++ )
{
    FLOAT nx = pvVertices[i].nx;
    FLOAT ny = pvVertices[i].ny;
    FLOAT nz = pvVertices[i].nz;

    // Check the z-component, to skip any vertices that face
    // backward.
    if( nx*m13 + ny*m23 + nz*m33 > 0.0f )
        continue;

    // Assign the sphere map's texture coordinates.
    pvVertices[i].tu =
        0.5f * ( 1.0f + ( nx*m11 + ny*m21 + nz*m31 ) );
    pvVertices[i].tv =
        0.5f * ( 1.0f - ( nx*m12 + ny*m22 + nz*m32 ) );
}

return S_OK;
}
```

Because the sphere map texture is a highly distorted view of the world, Direct3D can't generate it in real time. You'll need to generate this texture before running the program. This means that with spherical environment mapping, the view being reflected is completely static. Whether the user notices this depends on how discernible the reflected scene is.

Cubic Environment Maps

Sphere maps can create a believable reflection effect in many cases, but they aren't perfect. As mentioned earlier, one problem is that they aren't easy to generate in real time. They also have limited resolution, especially near the edges of the map. And if the camera looks in a different direction, the sphere map might not have all the reflection information that is needed. To remedy some of these problems, Direct3D also supports *cube maps*. With cube maps, the reflection is encoded in a conceptual cube around the object rather than a sphere. Whereas a sphere map compresses its conceptual sphere onto a single texture, a cube map is represented as a group of textures—one per face of the cube.

The EnvCube sample in the DirectX SDK illustrates how to use cube maps. This sample loads a cube containing some textures, along with some other objects that animate and will show up in the cube maps. It updates the cube map every frame in the *RenderEnvMap* function by rendering the scene from multiple camera orientations and storing the results in the appropriate faces of the cube map.

```
//-----------------------------------------------------------------
// Name: RenderEnvMap
// Desc: Renders to the device-dependent environment map
//-----------------------------------------------------------------
HRESULT CMyD3DApplication::RenderEnvMap( EnvMapContainer* pEnvMap )
{
    // Check parameters.
    if( NULL==pEnvMap )
        return E_INVALIDARG;

    D3DVIEWPORT7 ViewDataSave;
    D3DMATRIX matWorldSave, matViewSave, matProjSave;
    DWORD dwRSAntiAlias;

    // Save render states of the device.
    m_pd3dDevice->GetViewport( &ViewDataSave );
    m_pd3dDevice->GetTransform( D3DTRANSFORMSTATE_WORLD,
                                &matWorldSave );
    m_pd3dDevice->GetTransform( D3DTRANSFORMSTATE_VIEW,
                                &matViewSave );
    m_pd3dDevice->GetTransform( D3DTRANSFORMSTATE_PROJECTION,
                                &matProjSave );
    m_pd3dDevice->GetRenderState( D3DRENDERSTATE_ANTIALIAS,
                                  &dwRSAntiAlias );

    // Set up a viewport for rendering into the envmap.
    D3DVIEWPORT7 ViewData;
    m_pd3dDevice->GetViewport( &ViewData );
    ViewData.dwWidth  = pEnvMap->dwWidth;
    ViewData.dwHeight = pEnvMap->dwHeight;

    // Because the environment maps are small, antialias when
    // rendering to them.
    m_pd3dDevice->SetRenderState( D3DRENDERSTATE_ANTIALIAS,
                                  D3DANTIALIAS_SORTINDEPENDENT );

    // Render to the six faces of the cube map.
    for( DWORD i=0; i<6; i++ )
    {
```

```
ChangeRenderTarget( pEnvMap->pddsSurface[i] );
m_pd3dDevice->SetViewport( &ViewData );

// Standard view that will be overridden below
D3DVECTOR vEnvEyePt = D3DVECTOR( 0.0f, 0.0f, 0.0f );
D3DVECTOR vLookatPt, vUpVec;

switch( i )
{
    case 0: // pos X
        vLookatPt = D3DVECTOR( 1.0f, 0.0f, 0.0f );
        vUpVec    = D3DVECTOR( 0.0f, 1.0f, 0.0f );
        break;
    case 1: // neg X
        vLookatPt = D3DVECTOR(-1.0f, 0.0f, 0.0f );
        vUpVec    = D3DVECTOR( 0.0f, 1.0f, 0.0f );
        break;
    case 2: // pos Y
        vLookatPt = D3DVECTOR( 0.0f, 1.0f, 0.0f );
        vUpVec    = D3DVECTOR( 0.0f, 0.0f,-1.0f );
        break;
    case 3: // neg Y
        vLookatPt = D3DVECTOR( 0.0f,-1.0f, 0.0f );
        vUpVec    = D3DVECTOR( 0.0f, 0.0f, 1.0f );
        break;
    case 4: // pos Z
        vLookatPt = D3DVECTOR( 0.0f, 0.0f, 1.0f );
        vUpVec    = D3DVECTOR( 0.0f, 1.0f, 0.0f );
        break;
    case 5: // neg Z
        vLookatPt = D3DVECTOR( 0.0f, 0.0f,-1.0f );
        vUpVec    = D3DVECTOR( 0.0f, 1.0f, 0.0f );
        break;
}

D3DMATRIX matWorld, matView, matProj;
D3DUtil_SetIdentityMatrix( matWorld );
D3DUtil_SetViewMatrix( matView, vEnvEyePt, vLookatPt,
                       vUpVec );
D3DUtil_SetProjectionMatrix( matProj, g_PI/2, 1.0f, 0.5f,
                             1000.0f );

// Set the transforms for this view.
m_pd3dDevice->SetTransform( D3DTRANSFORMSTATE_WORLD,
                            &matWorld );
```

(continued)

```
m_pd3dDevice->SetTransform( D3DTRANSFORMSTATE_VIEW,
                            &matView );
m_pd3dDevice->SetTransform( D3DTRANSFORMSTATE_PROJECTION,
                            &matProj );

// Clear the z-buffer.
m_pd3dDevice->Clear( 0, NULL, D3DCLEAR_ZBUFFER, 0x000000ff,
                     1.0f, 0L );

// Begin the scene.
if( SUCCEEDED( m_pd3dDevice->BeginScene() ) )
{
    if( m_pFileObject1 )
        m_pFileObject1->Render( m_pd3dDevice );
    if( m_pFileObject2 )
        m_pFileObject2->Render( m_pd3dDevice );
    if( m_pEnvCubeObject )
        m_pEnvCubeObject->Render( m_pd3dDevice );

    // End the scene.
    m_pd3dDevice->EndScene();
}
}

ChangeRenderTarget( m_pddsRenderTarget );
m_pd3dDevice->SetViewport(&ViewDataSave);
m_pd3dDevice->SetTransform( D3DTRANSFORMSTATE_WORLD,
                            &matWorldSave );
m_pd3dDevice->SetTransform( D3DTRANSFORMSTATE_VIEW,
                            &matViewSave );
m_pd3dDevice->SetTransform( D3DTRANSFORMSTATE_PROJECTION,
                            &matProjSave );
m_pd3dDevice->SetRenderState( D3DRENDERSTATE_ANTIALIAS,
                              dwRSAntiAlias );

return S_OK;
}
```

The shiny object to be rendered, a sphere, is created using special texture coordinates that have three dimensions instead of the usual two. The *ReflectNormals* function reflects the eye's vector off the surface's normal, and the resulting reflection vector is stored in the texture coordinates.

```
//--------------------------------------------------------------------
// Name: ReflectNormals
//--------------------------------------------------------------------
```

```
VOID CMyD3DApplication::ReflectNormals( SPHVERTEX* pVIn, LONG cV )
{
    for( LONG i = 0; i < cV; i++ )
    {
        // Eye vector (doesn't need to be normalized)
        FLOAT fENX = m_vEyePt.x - pVIn->v.x;
        FLOAT fENY = m_vEyePt.y - pVIn->v.y;
        FLOAT fENZ = m_vEyePt.z - pVIn->v.z;

        FLOAT fNDotE = pVIn->v.nx*fENX +
                       pVIn->v.ny*fENY +
                       pVIn->v.nz*fENZ;
        FLOAT fNDotN = pVIn->v.nx*pVIn->v.nx +
                       pVIn->v.ny*pVIn->v.ny +
                       pVIn->v.nz*pVIn->v.nz;
        fNDotE *= 2.0F;
        // Reflected vector
        pVIn->v.tu = pVIn->v.nx*fNDotE - fENX*fNDotN;
        pVIn->v.tv = pVIn->v.ny*fNDotE - fENY*fNDotN;
        pVIn->nz = pVIn->v.nz*fNDotE - fENZ*fNDotN;

        pVIn++;
    }
}
```

When the scene is rendered, the nonshiny objects are rendered normally. Then before the sphere is rendered, the cube-map texture is selected. When the sphere is rendered, the flag D3DFVF_TEXCOORDSIZE3(0) is passed to *DrawPrimitive*, indicating that the texture coordinates have three components. Direct3D does the work of translating the reflection vector into the appropriate texture coordinates on the cube map. The resulting sphere is nice and shiny!

Unlike sphere maps, cube maps require support from the Direct3D device to work. Hardware support for cube maps is growing but is not yet universal. So if the Direct3D device doesn't report the D3DPTEXTURECAPS_CUBEMAP flag, you should use sphere mapping or no environment mapping at all. Keep in mind that in many cases, the accuracy of the environment mapping is lost in the fast-moving action of the game. So take advantage of high-quality environment mapping when you can, but note that even mathematically inaccurate reflections can often fool the eye.

The Code So Far

No new RoadRage code was added in this chapter. Although environment mapping can produce some intriguing effects for a variety of applications, the *EnvCube* demo project Microsoft includes in the DirectX samples does a better job of illustrating this technique than I could do by adding it to an already complex scene such as that generated by the RoadRage project.

Conclusion

This chapter covered light mapping and environment mapping, which are probably the most effective methods for adding realism to a 3D scene. Using these techniques strategically can make your 3D games and simulations truly lifelike.

In Chapter 12, we'll look at another tool you can use for effective texturing: stencil buffers. Stencil buffers allow you to enable or disable drawing to the render-target surface on a pixel-by-pixel basis. This means that your software will mask portions of the rendered image so that they aren't displayed. You'll see that you can use stencil buffers to generate intriguing 3D effects for the scenes you render, such as dissolving, decaling, and outlining.

CHAPTER TWELVE

Stencil Buffers

One aspect of advanced rendering we haven't discussed yet is stenciling, a technique that can be useful for developing commercial applications. If you want your 3D applications to stand apart from the crowd, you'd be wise to combine stenciling with the texturing techniques you learned about in earlier chapters. This chapter will detail how to use stenciling and show you the different types of effects you can generate with it.

Many 3D games and simulations on the market use cinema-quality special effects to add to their dramatic impact. You can use *stencil buffers* to create effects such as composites, decals, dissolves, fades, outlines, silhouettes, swipes, and shadows. Stencil buffers determine whether the pixels in an image are drawn. To perform this function, stencil buffers let you enable or disable drawing to the render-target surface on a pixel-by-pixel basis. This means your software can "mask" portions of the rendered image so that they aren't displayed.

When the stenciling feature is enabled, Microsoft Direct3D performs a *stencil test* for each pixel that it plans to write to the render-target surface. The stencil test uses a stencil reference value, a stencil mask, a comparison function, and a pixel value from the stencil buffer that corresponds to the current pixel in the target surface. Here are the specific steps used in this test:

1. Perform a bitwise AND operation on the stencil reference value with the stencil mask.

2. Perform a bitwise AND operation on the stencil-buffer value for the current pixel with the stencil mask.

3. Compare the results of Step 1 and Step 2 by using the comparison function.

By controlling the comparison function, the stencil mask, the stencil reference value, and the action taken when the stencil test passes or fails, you can control how the stencil buffer works. As long as the test succeeds, the current pixel will be written to the target. The default comparison behavior (the value that the D3DCMPFUNC enumerated type defines for D3DCMP_ALWAYS) is to write the pixel without considering the contents of the stencil buffer. You can change the comparison function to any function you want by setting the value of the D3D-RENDERSTATE_STENCILFUNC render state and passing one of the members of the D3DCMPFUNC enumerated type.

Creating a Stencil Buffer

Before creating a stencil buffer, you need to determine what stenciling capabilities the target system supports. To do this, call the *IDirect3DDevice7::GetCaps* method. The *dwStencilCaps* flags specify the stencil-buffer operations that the device supports. The reported flags are valid for all three stencil-buffer operation render states: D3DRENDERSTATE_STENCILFAIL, D3DRENDERSTATE_STENCILPASS, and D3DRENDERSTATE_STENCILZFAIL. Direct3D defines the following flags for *dwStencilCaps*:

- **D3DSTENCILCAPS_DECR** Indicates that the D3DSTENCILOP_DECR operation is supported
- **D3DSTENCILCAPS_DECRSAT** Indicates that the D3DSTENCIL-OP_DECRSAT operation is supported
- **D3DSTENCILCAPS_INCR** Indicates that the D3DSTENCIL-OP_INCR operation is supported
- **D3DSTENCILCAPS_INCRSAT** Indicates that the D3DSTENCIL-OP_INCRSAT operation is supported
- **D3DSTENCILCAPS_INVERT** Indicates that the D3DSTENCIL-OP_INVERT operation is supported
- **D3DSTENCILCAPS_KEEP** Indicates that the D3DSTENCIL-OP_KEEP operation is supported
- **D3DSTENCILCAPS_REPLACE** Indicates that the D3DSTENCIL-OP_REPLACE operation is supported
- **D3DSTENCILCAPS_ZERO** Indicates that the D3DSTENCIL-OP_ZERO operation is supported

Direct3D embeds the stencil-buffer information with the depth-buffer data. To determine what formats of depth buffers and stencil buffers the target system's hardware supports, call the *IDirect3D7::EnumZBufferFormats* method, which has the following declaration:

```
HRESULT IDirect3D7::EnumZBufferFormats (
    REFCLSID riidDevice,
    LPD3DENUMPIXELFORMATSCALLBACK lpEnumCallback,
    LPVOID lpContext
);
```

Parameter	Description
riidDevice	A reference to a globally unique identifier (GUID) for the device whose depth-buffer formats you want enumerated
lpEnumCallback	The address of a *D3DEnumPixelFormatsCallback* function you want called for each supported depth-buffer format
lpContext	Application-defined data that is passed to the callback function

If the method succeeds, it returns the value D3D_OK. If it fails, the method returns one of these four values:

- DDERR_INVALIDOBJECT

- DDERR_INVALIDPARAMS

- DDERR_NOZBUFFERHW

- DDERR_OUTOFMEMORY

The following code determines what stencil buffer formats are available and what operations are supported and then creates a stencil buffer. As you can see, this code notes whether the stencil buffer supports more than 1 bit—some stenciling techniques must be handled differently if only a 1-bit stencil buffer is available.

```
HRESULT CMyD3DApplication::CreateStencilBuffer()
{
    g_bCanOnlyDoOneBitStencil=FALSE;

    DWORD dwStencilCaps = m_pDeviceInfo->ddDeviceDesc.dwStencilCaps;

    if( (!(dwStencilCaps & D3DSTENCILCAPS_INCR) &&
         !(dwStencilCaps & D3DSTENCILCAPS_INCRSAT)) ||
        (!(dwStencilCaps & D3DSTENCILCAPS_DECR) &&
         !(dwStencilCaps & D3DSTENCILCAPS_DECRSAT)))
    {
```

(continued)

317

```
        // Must do 1-bit stencil buffer.
        g_bCanOnlyDoOneBitStencil=TRUE;
    }
    else
    {
        // Prefer sat ops that cap at 0/max, but can use other
        // ones as long as enough stencil bits.
        g_StencIncOp=(dwStencilCaps & D3DSTENCILCAPS_INCRSAT)?
            D3DSTENCILOP_INCRSAT:D3DSTENCILOP_INCR;
        g_StencDecOp=(dwStencilCaps & D3DSTENCILCAPS_DECRSAT)?
            D3DSTENCILOP_DECRSAT:D3DSTENCILOP_DECR;
    }


    m_pddsRenderTarget->DeleteAttachedSurface( 0,NULL );

    // Get z-buffer dimensions from the render target.
    // Set up the surface description for the z-buffer.
    DDSURFACEDESC2 ddsd;
    D3DUtil_InitSurfaceDesc( ddsd );
    m_pddsRenderTarget->GetSurfaceDesc( &ddsd );
    ddsd.dwFlags          = DDSD_WIDTH | DDSD_HEIGHT | DDSD_CAPS |
                            DDSD_PIXELFORMAT;
    ddsd.ddsCaps.dwCaps   = DDSCAPS_ZBUFFER;
    ddsd.ddsCaps.dwCaps2 = 0;
    ddsd.ddsCaps.dwCaps3 = 0;
    ddsd.ddsCaps.dwCaps4 = 0;
    ddsd.ddpfPixelFormat.dwFlags = DDPF_ZBUFFER | DDPF_STENCILBUFFER;

    if( m_pDeviceInfo->bHardware )
        ddsd.ddsCaps.dwCaps  |= DDSCAPS_VIDEOMEMORY;
    else
        ddsd.ddsCaps.dwCaps  |= DDSCAPS_SYSTEMMEMORY;

    // Get an appropriate pixel format from an enumeration of
    // the formats.
    m_pD3D->EnumZBufferFormats( (*m_pDeviceInfo->pDeviceGUID),
                                EnumZBufferFormatsCallback,
                                (VOID*)&ddsd.ddpfPixelFormat );

    assert(ddsd.ddpfPixelFormat.dwStencilBitDepth!=0);

    g_bCanOnlyDoOneBitStencil=g_bCanOnlyDoOneBitStencil ||
        ((1<<ddsd.ddpfPixelFormat.dwStencilBitDepth)<NUM_SHADOWS);

    g_dwMaxStencilValue=(1<<ddsd.ddpfPixelFormat.dwStencilBitDepth)-1;
```

```
    // Leave g_bUseOneBitStencil set for the window-resize case.
    if( !g_bUseOneBitStencil )
        g_bUseOneBitStencil=g_bCanOnlyDoOneBitStencil;

    SetMenuStates();

    // Create and attach a z-buffer.
    if( FAILED( m_pDD->CreateSurface( &ddsd, &m_pddsDepthBuffer,
                                      NULL ) ) )
        return E_FAIL;

    if( FAILED(m_pddsRenderTarget->AddAttachedSurface(
                                      m_pddsDepthBuffer ) ) )
        return E_FAIL;

    // The SetRenderTarget() call is needed to rebuild internal
    // structures for the newly attached z-buffer.
    return m_pd3dDevice->SetRenderTarget( m_pddsRenderTarget, 0L );
}


//-------------------------------------------------------------------
// Name: EnumZBufferFormatsCallback
// Desc: Enumeration function to report valid pixel formats for
//       z-buffers
//-------------------------------------------------------------------
static
HRESULT WINAPI EnumZBufferFormatsCallback( DDPIXELFORMAT* pddpf,
                                           VOID* pddpfDesired )
{
    if( NULL==pddpf || NULL==pddpfDesired )
        return D3DENUMRET_CANCEL;

    // If the current pixel formats match the desired ones
    // (DDPF_ZBUFFER and possibly DDPF_STENCILBUFFER), copy it and
    // return. This function isn't choosy--it accepts the first valid
    // format that comes along.
    if( pddpf->dwFlags == ((DDPIXELFORMAT*)pddpfDesired)->dwFlags )
    {
        memcpy( pddpfDesired, pddpf, sizeof(DDPIXELFORMAT) );
        return D3DENUMRET_CANCEL;
    }

    return D3DENUMRET_OK;
}
```

Clearing a Stencil Buffer

The *IDirect3DDevice7* interface includes the *Clear* method, which you can use to simultaneously clear the render target's color buffer, depth buffer, and stencil buffer. Here's the declaration for the *IDirect3DDevice7::Clear* method:

```
HRESULT IDirect3DDevice7::Clear(
    DWORD dwCount,
    LPD3DRECT lpRects,
    DWORD dwFlags,
    D3DVALUE dvZ,
    DWORD dwStencil
);
```

Parameter	Description
dwCount	The number of rectangles in the array at *lpRects*.
lpRects	An array of D3DRECT structures defining the rectangles to be cleared. You can set a rectangle to the dimensions of the render-target surface to clear the entire surface. Each of these rectangles uses screen coordinates that correspond to points on the render-target surface. The coordinates are clipped to the bounds of the viewport rectangle.
dwFlags	Flags indicating which surfaces should be cleared. This parameter can be any combination of the following flags, but at least one flag must be used: **D3DCLEAR_TARGET** Clear the render-target surface to the color in the *dwColor* parameter. **D3DCLEAR_STENCIL** Clear the stencil buffer to the value in the *dwStencil* parameter. **D3DCLEAR_ZBUFFER** Clear the depth buffer to the value in the *dvZ* parameter.
dwColor	A 32-bit RGBA color value to which the render-target surface will be cleared.
dvZ	The new *z* value that this method stores in the depth buffer. This parameter can range from 0.0 to 1.0, inclusive. The value of 0.0 represents the nearest distance to the viewer, and 1.0 represents the farthest distance.
dwStencil	The integer value to store in each stencil-buffer entry. This parameter can range from 0 to $2^n - 1$ inclusive, in which *n* is the bit depth of the stencil buffer.

The *IDirect3DDevice7::Clear* method still accepts the older D3DCLEAR_TARGET flag, which clears the render target using an RGBA color you provide in the *dwColor* parameter. This method also still accepts the D3DCLEAR_ZBUFFER flag, which clears the depth buffer to a depth you specify in *dvZ* (in which 0.0 is the closest distance and 1.0 is the farthest). DirectX 6 introduced the D3DCLEAR_STENCIL flag, which you can use to reset the stencil bits to the value you specify in the *dwStencil* parameter. This value can be an integer ranging from 0 to 2^n-1, in which n is the bit depth of the stencil buffer.

Configuring the Stenciling State

You control the various settings for the stencil buffer using the *IDirect3DDevice7:: SetRenderState* method. Here are the stencil-related members of the D3D-RENDERSTATETYPE enumerated type:

```
typedef enum _D3DRENDERSTATETYPE {
    :
    D3DRENDERSTATE_STENCILENABLE    = 52,   // Enable or disable
                                            // stenciling
    D3DRENDERSTATE_STENCILFAIL      = 53,   // Stencil operation
    D3DRENDERSTATE_STENCILZFAIL     = 54,   // Stencil operation
    D3DRENDERSTATE_STENCILPASS      = 55,   // Stencil operation
    D3DRENDERSTATE_STENCILFUNC      = 56,   // Stencil comparison
                                            // function
    D3DRENDERSTATE_STENCILREF       = 57,   // Reference value for
                                            // stencil test
    D3DRENDERSTATE_STENCILMASK      = 58,   // Mask value used in
                                            // stencil test
    D3DRENDERSTATE_STENCILWRITEMASK = 59,   // Stencil-buffer write
                                            // mask
    :
} D3DRENDERSTATETYPE;
```

These are the definitions for the stencil-related render states:

- ◾ **D3DRENDERSTATE_STENCILENABLE**   Use this member to enable or disable stenciling. To enable stenciling, use this member with TRUE; to disable stenciling, use it with FALSE. The default value is FALSE.

- ◾ **D3DRENDERSTATE_STENCILFAIL**   Use this member to indicate the stencil operation to perform if the stencil test fails. The stencil operation can be one of the members of the D3DSTENCILOP enumerated type. The default value is D3DSTENCILOP_KEEP.

- **D3DRENDERSTATE_STENCILZFAIL**   Use this member to indicate the stencil operation to perform if the stencil test passes and the depth test (z-test) fails. The operation can be one of the members of the D3DSTENCILOP enumerated type. The default value is D3D-STENCILOP_KEEP.

- **D3DRENDERSTATE_STENCILPASS**   Use this member to indicate the stencil operation to perform if both the stencil test and the depth test (z-test) pass. The operation can be one of the members of the D3D-STENCILOP enumerated type. The default value is D3DSTENCIL-OP_KEEP.

- **D3DRENDERSTATE_STENCILFUNC**   Use this member to indicate the comparison function for the stencil test. The comparison function can be one of the members of the D3DCMPFUNC enumerated type. The default value is D3DCMP_ALWAYS. This function compares the reference value to a stencil-buffer entry and applies only to the bits in the reference value and stencil-buffer entry that are set in the stencil mask. (The D3DRENDERSTATE_STENCILMASK render state sets the stencil mask.) If the comparison is true, the stencil test passes.

- **D3DRENDERSTATE_STENCILREF**   Use this member to indicate the integer reference value for the stencil test. The default value is 0.

- **D3DRENDERSTATE_STENCILMASK**   Use this member to specify the mask to apply to the reference value and each stencil-buffer entry to determine the significant bits for the stencil test. The default mask is 0xFFFFFFFF.

- **D3DRENDERSTATE_STENCILWRITEMASK**   Use this member to specify the mask to apply to values written into the stencil buffer. The default mask is 0xFFFFFFFF.

The D3DSTENCILOP enumerated type describes the stencil operations for the D3DRENDERSTATE_STENCILFAIL, D3DRENDERSTATE_STENCIL-ZFAIL, and D3DRENDERSTATE_STENCILPASS render states. Here's the definition of D3DSTENCILOP:

```
typedef enum _D3DSTENCILOP {
    D3DSTENCILOP_KEEP         = 1,
    D3DSTENCILOP_ZERO         = 2,
    D3DSTENCILOP_REPLACE      = 3,
    D3DSTENCILOP_INCRSAT      = 4,
    D3DSTENCILOP_DECRSAT      = 5,
    D3DSTENCILOP_INVERT       = 6,
```

```
    D3DSTENCILOP_INCR              = 7,
    D3DSTENCILOP_DECR              = 8,
    D3DSTENCILOP_FORCE_DWORD       = 0x7fffffff
} D3DSTENCILOP;
```

These members serve the following purposes:

- ■ **D3DSTENCILOP_KEEP**   Indicates that you don't want the entry in the stencil buffer updated. This is the default operation.

- ■ **D3DSTENCILOP_ZERO**   Sets the stencil-buffer entry to 0.

- ■ **D3DSTENCILOP_REPLACE**   Replaces the stencil-buffer entry with the reference value.

- ■ **D3DSTENCILOP_INCRSAT**   Increments the stencil-buffer entry, clamping to the maximum value.

- ■ **D3DSTENCILOP_DECRSAT**   Decrements the stencil-buffer entry, clamping to 0.

- ■ **D3DSTENCILOP_INVERT**   Inverts the bits in the stencil-buffer entry.

- ■ **D3DSTENCILOP_INCR**   Increments the stencil-buffer entry, wrapping to 0 if the new value exceeds the maximum value.

- ■ **D3DSTENCILOP_DECR**   Decrements the stencil-buffer entry, wrapping to the maximum value if the new value is less than 0.

- ■ **D3DSTENCILOP_FORCE_DWORD**   Forces this enumeration to be compiled to 32 bits; this value isn't used.

Let's walk through some code that uses the stencil buffer while rendering a scene. This code is from a sample that shows how to draw shadows. For now, don't worry about how all this code generates shadows—the algorithm is described later in the chapter.

The shadow-rendering code starts out by disabling the depth buffer and enabling the stencil buffer:

```
//-------------------------------------------------------------
// Name: RenderShadow
// Desc:
//-------------------------------------------------------------
HRESULT CMyD3DApplication::RenderShadow()
{
    // Turn off depth buffer and turn on stencil buffer.
    m_pd3dDevice->SetRenderState( D3DRENDERSTATE_ZWRITEENABLE,
```

(continued)

```
                                    FALSE );
   m_pd3dDevice->SetRenderState( D3DRENDERSTATE_STENCILENABLE,
                                    TRUE );
```

Next the code sets the comparison function that performs the stencil test by calling the *IDirect3DDevice7::SetRenderState* method and setting the first parameter to D3DRENDERSTATE_STENCILFUNC. The second parameter is set to a member of the D3DCMPFUNC enumerated type. In this code, we want to update the stencil buffer everywhere a primitive is rendered, so we use D3DCMP_ALWAYS:

```
//
// Set up stencil comparison function, reference value, and masks.
// Stencil test passes if ((ref & mask) cmpfn (stencil & mask))
// is true.
//
m_pd3dDevice->SetRenderState( D3DRENDERSTATE_STENCILFUNC,
                              D3DCMP_ALWAYS );
```

In this sample, we don't want the stencil buffer to change if either the stencil buffer test or the depth buffer test fails, so we set the appropriate states to D3D-STENCILOP_KEEP:

```
m_pd3dDevice->SetRenderState( D3DRENDERSTATE_STENCILZFAIL,
                              D3DSTENCILOP_KEEP );
m_pd3dDevice->SetRenderState( D3DRENDERSTATE_STENCILFAIL,
                              D3DSTENCILOP_KEEP );
```

The next settings are different depending on whether a 1-bit or a multibit stencil buffer is present. If the stencil buffer has only 1 bit, the value 1 is stored in the stencil buffer whenever the stencil test passes. Otherwise, an increment operation (either D3DSTENCILOP_INCR or D3DSTENCILOP_INCRSAT) is applied if the stencil test passes.

```
if(g_bUseOneBitStencil)
    {
        pd3dDevice->SetRenderState( D3DRENDERSTATE_STENCILREF,
                                    0x1 );
        pd3dDevice->SetRenderState( D3DRENDERSTATE_STENCILMASK,
                                    0x1 );
        pd3dDevice->SetRenderState( D3DRENDERSTATE_STENCILWRITEMASK,
                                    0x1 );
        pd3dDevice->SetRenderState( D3DRENDERSTATE_STENCILPASS,
                                    D3DSTENCILOP_REPLACE );
    }
    else
    {
        pd3dDevice->SetRenderState( D3DRENDERSTATE_STENCILREF,
                                    0x1 );
```

```
        pd3dDevice->SetRenderState( D3DRENDERSTATE_STENCILMASK,
                                    0xffffffff );
        pd3dDevice->SetRenderState( D3DRENDERSTATE_STENCILWRITEMASK,
                                    0xffffffff );
        pd3dDevice->SetRenderState( D3DRENDERSTATE_STENCILPASS,
                                    g_StencIncOp );
    }
```

At this point, the stencil state is configured and the code is ready to render some primitives.

Creating Effects

Now that you've seen how to create stencil buffers and configure how they work, let's look at some of the effects you can render with them. The following sections describe several ways Microsoft recommends using stencil buffers. Each of these approaches produces impressive results, but a few of them have drawbacks.

Composites

You can use stencil buffers for compositing 2D or 3D images onto a 3D scene. By using a mask in the stencil buffer to occlude a portion of the render-target surface, you can write stored 2D information (such as text or bitmaps). You can also render 3D primitives—or for that matter a complete scene—to the area of the render-target surface that you specify in a stencil mask.

Developers often use this effect to composite several scenes in simulations and games. Many driving games feature a rear view mirror that displays the scene behind the driver. You can composite this second 3D scene with the driver's view forward by using a stencil to block the portion to which you want the mirror image rendered. You can also use composites to create 2D "cockpits" for vehicle simulations by combining a 2D, bitmapped image of the cockpit with the final, rendered 3D scene.

Decals

You can use decals to control which pixels from a primitive image you draw to a render-target surface. When you apply a texture to an object (for example, applying scratch marks to a floor), you need the texture (the scratch marks) to appear immediately on top of the object (the floor). Because the z values of the scratch marks and the floor are equal, the depth buffer might not yield consistent results, meaning that some pixels in the back primitive might be rendered on top of those in the front primitive. This overlap, which is commonly known as *z-fighting* or *flimmering,* can cause the final image to shimmer as you animate from one frame to the next.

You can prevent flimmering by using a stencil to mask the section of the back primitive on which you want the decal to appear. You can then turn off z-buffering and render the image of the front primitive into the masked area of the render-target surface.

Dissolves

You can use dissolves to gradually replace an image by displaying a series of frames that transition from one image to another. In Chapter 8, you saw how to use multiple-texture blending to create this effect by gradually blending two textures together. Stencil buffers allow you to produce similar dissolves, except that a stencil-based dissolve looks more pixelated than a multiple-texture blending one. However, stencil buffers let you use texture-blending capabilities for other effects while performing a dissolve. This capability enables you to efficiently produce more complex effects than you could by using texture blending alone.

A stencil buffer can perform a dissolve by controlling which pixels you draw from two different images to the render-target surface. You can perform a dissolve by defining a base stencil mask for the first frame and altering it incrementally or by defining a series of stencil masks and copying them into the stencil buffer on successive frames.

To start a dissolve, set the stencil function and stencil mask so that most of the pixels from the starting image pass the stencil test and most of the ending image's pixels fail. For each subsequent frame, update the stencil mask to allow fewer pixels in the starting image to pass the test and more pixels in the ending image to pass. By controlling the stencil mask, you can create a variety of dissolve effects.

Although this approach can produce some fantastic effects, it can be a bit slow on some systems. You should test the performance on your target systems to verify that this approach works efficiently for your application.

Fades

You can fade in or out using a form of dissolving. To perform this effect, use any dissolve pattern you want. To fade in, use a stencil buffer to dissolve from a black or white image to a rendered 3D scene. To fade out, start with a rendered 3D scene and dissolve to black or white. As with dissolves, you should check the performance of fades on the target systems to verify that their speed and appearance is acceptable.

Outlines

You can apply a stencil mask to a primitive that's the same shape but slightly smaller than the primitive. The resulting image will contain only the primitive's outline. You can then fill this stencil-masked area of the primitive with a color or set of colors to produce an outline around the image.

Silhouettes

When you set the stencil mask to the same size and shape as the primitive you're rendering, Direct3D produces a final image containing a "black hole" where the primitive should be. By coloring this hole, you can produce a silhouette of the primitive.

Swipes

A swipe makes an image appear as though it's sliding into the scene over another image. You can use stencil masks to disable the writing of pixels from the starting image and enable the writing of pixels from the ending image. To perform a swipe, you can define a series of stencil masks that Direct3D will load into the stencil buffer in a succession of frames, or you can change the starting stencil mask for a series of successive frames. Both methods cause the final image to look as though it's gradually sliding on top of the starting image from right to left, left to right, top to bottom, and so on.

To handle a swipe, remember to read the pixels from the ending image in the reverse order in which you're performing the swipe. For example, if you're performing a swipe from left to right, you need to read pixels from the ending image from right to left. As with dissolves, this effect can render somewhat slowly. Therefore, you should test its performance on your target systems.

Shadows

Shadow volumes, which allow an arbitrarily shaped object to cast a shadow onto another arbitrarily shaped object, can produce some incredibly realistic effects. To create shadows with stencil buffers, take an object you want to cast a shadow. Using this object and the light source, build a set of polygonal faces (a shadow volume) to represent the shadow.

You can compute the shadow volume by projecting the vertices of the shadow-casting object onto a plane that's perpendicular to the direction of light from the light source, finding the 2D convex hull of the projected vertices (that is, a polygon that "wraps around" all the projected vertices), and extruding the 2D convex hull in the light direction to form the 3D shadow volume. The shadow volume must extend far enough so that it covers any objects that will be shadowed. To simplify computation, you might want the shadow caster to be a convex object.

To render a shadow, you must first render the geometry and then render the shadow volume without writing to the depth buffer or the color buffer. Use alpha blending to avoid having to write to the color buffer. Each place that the shadow volume appears will be marked in the stencil buffer. You can then reverse the cull and render the backfaces of the shadow volume, unmarking all the pixels that are covered in the stencil buffer. All these pixels will have passed the z-test, so they'll be visible behind the shadow volume. Therefore, they won't be in shadow. The pixels that are still marked are the ones lying inside the front and back boundaries of the shadow volume—these pixels will be in shadow. You can blend these pixels with a large black rectangle that covers the viewport to generate the shadow.

The ShadowVol and ShadowVol2 Demos

The ShadowVol sample on the companion CD in the \mssdk\Samples\Multimedia\ D3dim\Src\ShadowVol directory contains a project that shows how to create and use stencil buffers to implement shadow volumes. The code illustrates how to use shadow volumes to cast the shadow of an arbitrarily shaped object onto another arbitrarily shaped object. The ShadowVol2 sample, which the Microsoft DirectX 7 SDK setup program on the companion CD installs in the \mssdk\Samples\Multimedia\D3dim\ Src\ShadowVol2 directory on your hard disk, provides some additional capabilities for producing shadows with stencils.

The sample application provides these features in its Shadow Modes menu:

- **Draw Shadows**   Allows you to turn on and off shadow rendering.

- **Show Shadow Volumes**   Draws the shadow volumes used to compute the shadows rather than drawing the shadows themselves.

- **Draw Shadow Volume Caps**   When you turn this item off, some "extra" shadows might become visible where the far caps of the cylindrical shadow volumes happen to be visible.

- **1-Bit Stencil Buffer Mode**   Tells the code to use a different algorithm that uses only 1 bit of stencil buffer, which won't allow overlapping shadows. If the device supports only 1-bit stencils, you'll be forced to use this mode.

■ **Z-Order Shadow Vols in 1-Bit Stencil Buffer Mode** The shadow volumes must be rendered front to back, which means that if you don't check this option, rendering might be incorrect.

Figure 12-1, Figure 12-2, and Figure 12-3 show three views of the scene generated by the ShadowVol2 sample application. You can see the shadows in Figures 12-1 and 12-3; Figure 12-2 illustrates the shadow volumes.

Figure 12-1
Shadow cast

Figure 12-2
Shadow volumes

Figure 12-3
Another view of the rendered shadows

The Code So Far

In this chapter, we didn't add any new code to the RoadRage project. To see these effects in action, refer to the ShadowVol and ShadowVol2 demo projects included in the DirectX samples.

Conclusion

In this chapter, you learned about stencil buffers and the exciting effects they can produce. In today's market, making your code stand out is a requisite if you want it to sell your applications and keep your users coming back for more. Incorporating strategic stencil-buffer effects into the introduction and into the body of a 3D real-time game might help you win over even the most discriminating game players.

In Chapter 13, we'll discuss how to load and animate 3D models. Creating animated, lifelike characters that your users can interact with is one of the most powerful capabilities you can add to any game.

CHAPTER THIRTEEN

Loading and Animating 3D Models

If you intend to develop games or simulations with high-quality graphics and animation, you should know how to load 3D model files generated by external tools. You also need to be able to animate these models, especially those representing the characters that will be in your program. In this chapter, we'll examine techniques for adding 3D objects and animated characters to a 3D world.

Animated Characters

Character animation is another area of 3D programming that's critical to game development. Nothing makes a game more exciting—to the point that it draws you in and makes you feel like you're there—than being able to interact with animated, lifelike characters. Even better, you can use the Microsoft DirectPlay API to add network capabilities to your game (as you'll see in Chapter 15) so that users can play an immersive, head-to-head game with friends. Animated characters can represent real people that are playing on remote computers, animals in your 3D world, and so on.

You can create animated characters to add to your 3D world in several ways. Here are two of the most popular methods:

- Using segmented, 3D characters that are animated with motion capture data. Motion capture generally consists of the recording of human body movement for delayed playback. Because the data is generated from real people, 3D characters animated with motion capture data look incredibly lifelike. The body parts are each separate, however, so sometimes you can see *seams* at the joints that make the character appear less realistic than if it were rendered as a single mesh.

■ Using single-mesh characters that are animated with one of the numerous 3D tools for motion, including 3D Studio Max and its many plug-ins. (The plug-ins I use most are LifeForms, Motion Manager, HyperMatter, and Character Studio.) These models are very realistic, but Microsoft DirectX doesn't provide a facility to load and animate them. The code we'll cover shortly implements this capability for you.

On the CD accompanying this book are two characters—an animated horse model and an animated human model—provided by Credo Interactive, the makers of the LifeForms series of character animation software. These characters have been animated using LifeForms and then exported as animated 3D studio (.3ds) file format objects. I have also converted them to DirectX file format. These are in the \models\credo directory on the CD.

Segmented Characters

A segmented character is a 3D model with separate components for all the articulated body parts (such as the head, upper arms, lower arms, hands, and torso). Segmented characters work wonderfully with Microsoft Direct3D because you can directly manipulate their body parts using the transformations (rotation, translation, and so on) that Direct3D supplies. For example, you can move a character's arm up and down by rotating the shoulder joint the desired number of degrees. All the attached body parts (the lower arm, the hand, and so on) will move with the upper arm as expected because of the hierarchical nature of the transformations in Direct3D.

The ability to apply motion capture data to 3D characters is particularly thrilling. I often use LifeForms, a piece of character animation software by Credo Interactive. This package is not only powerful, it's easy to use. The folks at Credo have supplied a demo copy of LifeForms for this book's companion CD that allows you to experience all its power and convenience. Credo has also supplied two 3D character models whose body parts will accept the motion capture data you create with the LifeForms software. In addition, Credo has supplied several motions that you can apply to your own 3D characters.

Single-Mesh Characters

Single-mesh characters are very popular in 3D games and simulations. To use this technique, you create a set of single-mesh models that, when played in a 3D sequence, produce an animation. Each step of the animation is stored as a mesh representation of the shape of the body. Therefore, to replicate the motion of walking, you store a set of 3D models that represent each movement made in a complete walking sequence. You have models that represent the body starting to take a step, models in the various positions that the body assumes as it's progressing through the step, and finally models representing the body after the step is complete.

Packages such as the HyperMatter and Character Studio plug-ins for 3D Studio Max enable you to animate single-mesh characters. In Character Studio, you can animate a character by attaching a skeleton to the character's single-mesh skin in a way that allows the skin's vertices to move convincingly with the bones. Using this technique, you can attach motion capture (or hand-generated) data to the skeleton components, causing the mesh to move accordingly.

The ability to animate the mesh itself using tools such as HyperMatter is even more exciting because the mesh represents the character's flesh or clothing. With HyperMatter, you can make clothing look like it's made of fabric and flex realistically as the character moves.

One key feature that Immediate Mode neglects to provide developers is the ability to load either the segmented or the single-mesh characters or objects you might want to use in your games. Although you can always create 3D objects on the fly using the vertices (such as vertex buffers) with DrawPrimitive, it's often much more logical to create and animate an object in advance. The main reason Immediate Mode doesn't support this capability is that developers have a variety of methods they use to create their applications' objects and characters. Because these methods often require different file formats and animation techniques, attempting to provide a standard format for all developers using Immediate Mode wasn't practical. In addition, the complexity of the file formats, such as 3D Studio (.3ds), makes it difficult to import the files correctly.

The RoadRage application on the companion CD allows you to load static 3D models (furniture, buildings, and so on) stored in the 3D Studio format (.3ds). The code that implements this capability is in the import3ds.cpp file. The CD also contains a program called RoadRage Map Editor (rr_editor.exe) that allows you to generate your own 3D environment for RoadRage. Using RoadRage Map Editor, you can create your own 3D world and place objects such as roads, buildings, lights, and signs in it, from a top-down view. See the readme.txt file on the companion CD for more details on RoadRage Map Editor.

Although discovering how to write code to load and animate 3D characters can be a great learning experience, it's one of the most difficult tasks game developers face. The difficulty lies in the fact that understanding Direct3D in detail is only the first step—you must also understand character animation and 3D modeling and the multitude of file formats the various rendering tools use. This depth of knowledge isn't something I'd expect from every developer interested in using Direct3D. Many of you are no doubt familiar with the game Quake II, which uses models constructed with single-mesh characters. Each movement the models in this game make consists of a sequence of frames that produces an animation. The following table shows the models' movements and the frames represented by the various positions of each mesh.

Motion	Frames
Stand	0 through 39
Run	40 through 45
Attack	46 through 53
Pain1	54 through 57
Pain2	58 through 61
Pain3	62 through 65
Jump	66 through 71
Flip	72 through 83
Salute	84 through 94
Taunt	95 through 111
Wave	112 through 122
Point	123 through 134

The RoadRage code on the companion CD lets you load an animated 3D model (in Quake II MD2 format) and "play" the various motions you want to use in a complete, real-time 3D game. In addition, you can play the various motion sequences of the model through keyboard or code control.

The companion CD also includes a number of excellent shareware applications (written by a variety of authors) that allow you to create your own models for use in Direct3D (or in Quake if you want). These tools also enable you to "paint" a character so that you can apply details such as clothing and facial features. Once you're equipped with these tools, you'll be well on your way to creating incredible animated characters for your games and simulations. For more information on these programs, see the readme.txt file on the companion CD.

Loading and Handling RoadRage Models

The remainder of this chapter consists of a description of the code that's necessary for loading and using 3D Studio Max–animated and Quake II–animated models in your Direct3D Immediate Mode applications. I'll give step-by-step descriptions of the functionality of the render loop, which renders the scene for each frame in the animation process.

I'll mention the key routines for loading the 3D Studio and Quake character files so that you can visualize the code necessary for loading a file format and converting it to DrawPrimitive data. You should be able to understand this code on your own because the code simply performs a step-by-step load of the data in these files and stores the data in a format that Direct3D can use to render 3D objects. Describing all the nuances of the .3ds file format would take an entire book! If you want more details on the 3D Studio and Quake file formats, look at the files in the Quake II Utilities and 3D Studio Max Utilities directories on the companion CD. These directories also contain a number of utilities, links to various Web sites that have information on these formats, and files containing descriptions of these formats.

The first routines you need to modify so that you can implement character animation are the *CD3DApplication::Render3DEnvironment* and *CD3DApplication::MovePlayer* routines. These routines handle all input from the keyboard and other input devices.

Each Quake character model has a weapon model associated with it. The weapon model contains frames defining motion sequences just as the character model does. You can load these motions and use them in the same manner as you would load and use the movement of characters.

The *CD3DApplication::Render3DEnvironment* member function checks whether the user has selected the joystick as the input device. (The user makes this selection by pulling down the Control menu item from the main menu on the main screen.) If the joystick is in use, you acquire the joystick information (and reacquire the joystick if you lost it).

```
else if( g_bUseJoystick )
{
    g_pD3DApp->CreateInputDevice( GetParent(hWnd),
                                  g_guidJoystick, &c_dfDIJoystick,
                                  DISCL_EXCLUSIVE|DISCL_FOREGROUND );
    g_pdidDevice2->Acquire();
```

Once you have the joystick (indicated if you have a valid pointer), you need to determine whether the character is walking or driving. In RoadRage, characters can either walk or drive around the 3D world. If the character is walking, set the field of view to the appropriate value, as the following code shows:

```
if(walk_mode_enabled == TRUE)
{
    // JOYSTICK WALK MODE
    car_speed = (float)0;
```

Now that you know you have a joystick in use, start checking the status of the input device's buttons. (Recall that in DirectX the term *joystick* includes steering wheels, yokes, and so on.) The user switches to driving mode by hitting the second joystick button, as this code segment shows:

```
if(delay_key_press_flag == FALSE)
{
    if (dijs.rgbButtons[JOY_BUTTON_2] & 0x80)
    {
        walk_mode_enabled = FALSE;
        delay_key_press_flag = TRUE;
        SetTimer(m_hWnd, 3, KEY_DELAY,NULL);
    }
}
```

The user presses the third button to switch to the previous gun in the weapon inventory, but switching to the previous gun has no effect if the first gun in the list of guns available to the user is currently selected. Selecting the previous gun causes the gun to switch its 3D model in this loop, using the animation sequence for switching weapons that's stored in the weapon model. The following code illustrates this switch:

```
if (dijs.rgbButtons[JOY_BUTTON_3] & 0x80)
{
    current_gun--;
    if (current_gun < 0)
        current_gun++;
    delay_key_press_flag = TRUE;
    SetTimer(m_hWnd,3, KEY_DELAY,NULL);
}
```

The user presses the fourth button to switch to the next gun in the weapon inventory. Pressing the fourth button has no effect if the currently selected weapon is the last one on the list. Switching to the next weapon in the list causes the gun to switch its 3D model in this loop, using the animation sequence for switching weapons that's stored in the weapon model. The next code segment, in the *CD3DApplication::Render3DEnvironment* function, shows how to program this switch:

```
if (dijs.rgbButtons[JOY_BUTTON_4] & 0x80)
    {
        current_gun++;
        if (current_gun > MAX_NUM_WEAPONS)
            current_gun--;
        delay_key_press_flag = TRUE;
        SetTimer(m_hWnd,3, KEY_DELAY,NULL);
    }
}
```

Next you need to determine the *x* value of the joystick. If the user moves the joystick to the left, rotate the view of the scene to the left. If the user pushes the joystick to the right, rotate the view to the right. Now you also check the *y* value of the joystick. If the user pushes the stick forward, increase the speed of the user. If the user pushes the joystick backward, slow down the user. This next code segment shows you how to control an object's speed. To handle the motion, you call the *MovePlayer* routine with the axis and button information as follows:

```
MovePlayer( dijs.lX<0, dijs.lX>0, dijs.lY<0, dijs.lY>0,
            dijs.rgbButtons[0] & 0x80, 0, 0 );

VOID CD3DApplication::MovePlayer( BOOL bLeft, BOOL bRight,
    BOOL bForward, BOOL bBackward, BOOL bUp, BOOL bDown,  BOOL bFire )
{
    ⋮
    if( bForward  == TRUE )
    {
        m_vEyePt.x += speed * sinf(angy * k);
        m_vEyePt.z += speed * cosf(angy * k);
    }

    if( bBackward  == TRUE)
    {
        m_vEyePt.x += -speed * sinf(angy * k);
        m_vEyePt.z += -speed * cosf(angy * k);
    }
    ⋮
```

You also need to check the current camera angle. If you've pushed the angle below 0 degrees, add 360 degrees to the angle value to make it a valid setting. If you've pushed the camera angle past 360 degrees, subtract 360 degrees from its value. Here's the code for this technique:

```
if(angle >= 360)
    angle = angle - 360;
if(angle < 0)
    angle += 360;
```

If the game is in joystick driving mode rather than in joystick walking mode, check whether the user has pressed the second button. If the user has, switch to walking mode. This code works the same as the code above for walking mode does, but it places the eyepoint closer to the ground.

If the user presses the third or fourth button on the joystick, set the speed and gear of the car:

```
if (dijs.rgbButtons[JOY_BUTTON_3] & 0x80)
{
    if((car_speed > 0) && (car_gear == -1))
        car_speed-=(float).2;
    else
        car_gear = 1;
}
if (dijs.rgbButtons[JOY_BUTTON_4] & 0x80)
{
    if((car_speed > 0) && (car_gear == 1))
        car_speed-=(float).2;
    else
        car_gear = -1;
}
```

If the user moves the joystick to the left or the right, you need to rotate the view of the scene accordingly as long as the user is moving, as we did with the keyboard handling code. If the user moves the joystick backward or forward, you set the speed and gear of the car accordingly. You can also set the speed to a maximum of 64 mph and a minimum of 0 mph, as shown in this next code segment:

```
if(dijs.lY < -200) // Accelerate
{
    frequency = 12000 + (int)((float)car_speed * (float)250.0);
    car_speed+=(float).1;
}
```

```
if(dijs.lY > 200) // Brake
{
    frequency = 12000 + (int)((float)car_speed * (float)187.5);
    car_speed-=(float).2;
}

if(car_speed<0)
    car_speed=(float)0;

if(car_speed>64)
    car_speed=(float)64;
```

If the user is running in keyboard mode (meaning that all control comes from keyboard input), you need to check the keyboard status. If the user presses the Flip key, you need to play the sequence that makes the character gesture. ("Flip" is Quake terminology for "gesture.") To make this action visible, the RoadRage code causes this button to make the main character stand by the corner of the main buildings at the end of the town when you start the game gesture—for example, by waving, taunting, and so on.

If the user presses the Salute, Taunt, Wave, or Point key, we play the appropriate sequence to make the character perform the desired action in a similar manner. Refer to the *CD3DApplication::Render3DEnvironment* function to see all the key states that are handled. This code will also handle switching weapons, entering or exiting a car, rotating, speeding up, or slowing down.

To position the weapon the user has selected, you must offset it from the viewpoint. You also need to set the gun angle and make sure to restrict it to between 0 and 360 degrees so that it returns to 0 after passing 360 degrees. The next routine you need to create will set the frame sequences that animate the actions of the gun: fire, idle, put away, reload, burst fire, and last round. Here's the routine:

```
void LoadYourGunAnimationSequenceList(int model_id, world_ptr wptr)
{
    int i;

    i = model_id;

    wptr->your_gun[0].current_sequence = 2;
    wptr->your_gun[0].current_frame = 13;
    wptr->your_gun[1].current_sequence = 2;
    wptr->your_gun[1].current_frame = 13;
```

(continued)

```
wptr->your_gun[2].current_sequence = 0;
wptr->your_gun[2].current_frame = 0;

wptr->pmdata[i].sequence_start_frame[0] =0;   // Active1
wptr->pmdata[i].sequence_stop_frame [0] =10;

wptr->pmdata[i].sequence_start_frame[1] =11; // Fire
wptr->pmdata[i].sequence_stop_frame [1] =12;

wptr->pmdata[i].sequence_start_frame[2] =13; // Idle
wptr->pmdata[i].sequence_stop_frame [2] =39;

wptr->pmdata[i].sequence_start_frame[3] =40; // Put away
wptr->pmdata[i].sequence_stop_frame [3] =44;

wptr->pmdata[i].sequence_start_frame[4] =45; // Reload
wptr->pmdata[i].sequence_stop_frame [4] =63;

wptr->pmdata[i].sequence_start_frame[5] =64; // Burst fire
wptr->pmdata[i].sequence_stop_frame [5] =69;

wptr->pmdata[i].sequence_start_frame[6] =70; // Last round
wptr->pmdata[i].sequence_stop_frame [6] =71;

}
```

To load all the models you import from 3D Studio or Quake format, use the *LoadImportedModelList* routine in the file loadworld.cpp. This routine loads the player, car, gun, and debug models from the requested file so that you can use them in your game.

The routine *ImportMD2* in the file importMD2.cpp loads the Quake character models. The *ImportMD2* routine loads a Quake character model in MD2 format and converts it into a triangle strip or a triangle fan. William Chin created a third routine to load Quake models and directly animate them in Direct3D. This routine allows you to load any of the thousands of characters available on the Internet or ones you create yourself using Quake Modeller, included on the companion CD. You can then render this object using DrawPrimitive. You'll find the Quake file format that's used to create this routine described in a number of places on the Internet. Also, the companion CD contains utilities for creating and texturing Quake models that should help you greatly in understanding this format if you want to investigate it further. Be aware that the term *skin*, which appears in the following code comments, defines each of the meshes that represent one step in the animation sequence.

The other key code to look at is the *Import3ds* routine and several auxiliary routines that *Import3ds* uses (look in the file import3DS.cpp). William Chin also created this code. The 3D Studio (.3ds) file format is complex, but you can use this routine to load any .3ds files containing nonanimated objects. This code doesn't handle many of the .3ds file data types, but the case statement lists each data type not handled so that you can add code to handle the ones you want to use.

This code creates data structures that hold and load the data from a 3D Studio .3ds file. Describing the format of the .3ds files would fill an entire book. If you want to learn more about this file format, consult one of the many books discussing this topic.

The Code So Far

At this point, you should build the Chap13 subproject and run it. If you walk around the 3D world, you'll come across an animated character. Figure 13-1 shows a screen shot of the 3D character that has been added to the world for this chapter's project. Far more intriguing is the ability to interact with 3D characters controlled by other human players. In Chapter 15, I'll show you how to add the capability to support networked game play. As you move about in a networked game, you'll see animated 3D characters as described in this chapter, but the characters will be controlled by other human players who will be able to make them walk, drive, and shoot at you.

Figure 13-1
An animated character

Conclusion

In this chapter, you learned about several advanced Direct3D concepts. You saw how to load and utilize static and animated 3D characters in a DrawPrimitive-based Immediate Mode application. You also learned how to load and use both 3D Studio Max and Quake II models and had a chance to read about or view all the necessary code. Using this code, you can create applications that are far more powerful than you could normally produce using the built-in Direct3D functionality.

In Chapter 14, you'll find a variety of hints for optimizing your 3D applications. If you use these tips when designing your applications, you'll greatly boost the performance of your games and simulations.

CHAPTER FOURTEEN

Optimizing a Direct3D Application

Before you set off to develop your own 3D games and simulations, I want to supply you with some techniques that can help you optimize your applications. This chapter will list each of the areas that I and many of the 3D developers at Microsoft have found to be essential for producing the most efficient applications possible. The more of these suggestions you use, the faster your programs will be. I covered several of these topics earlier in this book but have reiterated them here to help make sure that you have a handy list of the key items you need to consider when writing Microsoft Direct3D Immediate Mode applications.

The Direct3D Framework

Microsoft DirectX 7 provides a framework, the *CD3DFramework7* class. This class is used in the Immediate Mode examples that the DirectX 7 setup program copies to the \mssdk\samples\multimedia\D3dim\src\ directory. Although this framework doesn't necessarily speed up your applications, it's a great starting point that can help speed up your development process.

In conjunction with this class, a series of routines prefixed with *D3DEnum* are provided to enumerate and select devices. The *CD3DApplication* class provides an application class you can use to create applications that use the Direct3D Framework library. Another series of helper functions are provided to work with the Direct3D Framework. These routines use the prefix *D3DUtil*. These routines supply a set of utilities that provide all the functions for getting the DirectX SDK media path; building a DDSURFACEDESC2 structure; initializing a D3DMATERIAL7 and a D3DLIGHT7 structure; setting up a view matrix, a projection matrix, and a rotation matrix; and handling error messages sent to the output stream.

All the RoadRage code in this book is built on the Direct3D Framework. I suggest that you use the Direct3D Framework for any of your future applications.

Conserving Texture Memory

The suggestions in this section will help you make optimal use of memory when working with Direct3D textures.

AGP Memory

Accelerated Graphics Port (AGP) memory is an excellent tool for texturing applications. You can achieve excellent performance using AGP memory, and it's your best option for using multiple, high-resolution textures. The following code shows how you can use AGP memory like video memory:

```
//
// Use the IDirect3DDevice7::GetCaps method to check the
// D3DDEVCAPS_TEXTURENONLOCALVIDMEM flag to determine whether the
// device can retrieve textures from nonlocal video (AGP) memory.
//
if (D3DHWDesc.dwDevCaps & D3DDEVCAPS_TEXTURENONLOCALVIDMEM != 0)
{
    //
    // The card supports AGP texturing.
    // You should use the IDirectDraw7::GetCaps method to check that the
    // flags used for blt operations are the same for nonlocal and local
    // video memory.
    //
    :
    //
    // You can now treat AGP memory like video memory.
    //
    // Create a surface in AGP memory.
    //
    DDSURFACEDESC2 ddsd2;

    ZeroMemory(&ddsd2, sizeof(ddsd2));
    ddsd2.dwSize = sizeof(ddsd2);
    ddsd2.dwFlags = DDSD_CAPS | DDSD_HEIGHT | DDSD_WIDTH;
    ddsd2.dwWidth = width;
    ddsd2.dwHeight = height;
    ddsd2.ddsCaps.dwCaps = DDSCAPS_VIDEOMEMORY |
                           DDSCAPS_NONLOCALVIDMEM |
                           DDSCAPS_TEXTURE |
                           DDSCAPS_ALLOCONLOAD;
```

```
    lpDD7->CreateSurface(&ddsd2, &lpDDSurface7, NULL);
}
⋮
//
// Perform an AGP write here.
//
lpDDSurface7->Blt(&ScreenCoords0, BackBuffer, &ScreenCoords1,
                  NULL, NULL);
```

Note that if you use Direct3D's automatic texture management, it will automatically take advantage of AGP memory when appropriate.

Texture Map Compression

A high-quality texture map often is 512 × 512 pixels and at least 16-bit-per-pixel color. Therefore, its image takes up over 500 KB. Using more than seven of these textures on a 4-MB video card would make the card run out of memory. To address this problem, many cards now have 16 to 64 MB of dedicated video memory. Other video cards use the AGP video slot and often can use system memory as video memory when needed.

Applications that have a lot of visual detail might need even more video memory. You might not want to grab a large amount of system memory, and you won't have to because DirectX 7 supports texture compression. Using the S3TC algorithm licensed from S3 Inc., DirectX 7 supports a number of different compression formats. This algorithm allows you to compress textures by 400 percent or more. The format you use is based on image attributes such as whether the image contains transparency information, color-keyed transparency, or color-masking information, as well as whether it's opaque. More and more new 3D accelerators support drivers that allow you to directly pass the compressed data to the card, which saves a great deal of bus transfer time spent getting the data to the card's video memory.

To use compressed textures on the hardware supporting them, simply create a compressed-texture surface and load the texture image into it. You must create this surface by specifying the compressed-texture format you want to use in the *dwFlags* member of the DDPIXELFORMAT structure. You can load an uncompressed texture to this surface by using the *Blt* method, or you can load a compressed image that is already in the correct format.

Be aware that DirectX allows you to load and store compressed textures on software and hardware renderers that don't directly support compressed textures. These compressed surfaces need to be blitted to uncompressed surfaces before the textures can be used.

Enhancing Your 3D Effects

Now let's look at some ways that you can get the most out of the special effects you use in your Direct3D applications.

Multitexturing

You should always use multitexturing (discussed in Chapter 8) for your applications. The more textures you use and the higher their resolution, the better your applications will look. You should use single-pass multitexturing (also called multiple-texture blending) when you can rather than multipass texturing (also called multipass texture blending). Keep in mind, however, that many cards don't support single-pass multitexturing for more than a few texture stages. The following code checks for multitexturing support by determining the maximum number of textures that can be simultaneously bound to the texture blending stages.

```
//
// Fill pD3D with an IID_IDirect3D7 interface.
// Create a LPD3DDEVICEDESC7 variable: m_d3dDeviceDesc.
//
{
    ⋮
    pD3D->GetCaps(m_d3dDeviceDesc);
    ⋮
    if (m_d3dDeviceDesc->wMaxSimultaneousTextures >= 2)
        return S_OK;
}
```

Once you know that the system supports single-pass multitexturing, you can use the *IDirect3DDevice7::ValidateDevice* method to verify that the device can render, in a single pass, the texture-blending operations and arguments you've set. Here's the call for this method:

```
pD3D->ValidateDevice(&dwExtraPasses);
```

Triple Buffering

Triple buffering, which works like double buffering (but with three buffers), allows you to avoid the problems that occur when you attempt to wait for vsync (a video-stream signal indicating that the display device is about to draw a new screen). With double buffering, waiting for vsync results in frame-rate dependencies. If you try to avoid frame-rate dependencies by not waiting for vsync, the redraw appears as though it's tearing because you see it while it's updating. Here's the code for creating the primary surface and two back buffers:

```
DDSURFACEDESC2 ddsd2;
ZeroMemory(&ddsd2, sizeof(ddsd2));
//
// Create the primary surface with two back buffers.
//
ddsd2.dwSize = sizeof(ddsd2);
ddsd2.dwFlags = DSD_CAPS | DDSD_BACKBUFFERCOUNT;
ddsd2.ddsCaps.dwCaps = DDSCAPS_PRIMARYSURFACE | DDSCAPS_FLIP |
                       DDSCAPS_COMPLEX;
ddsd2.dwBackBufferCount = 2;
hr = lpDD7->CreateSurface(&ddsd2, &lpDDSPrimary, NULL);
//
// If CreateSurface fails here, use double buffering instead.
//
```

Triple buffering uses more video memory than double buffering, of course, but in some configurations the performance gain can be worthwhile.

True-Color Rendering

True-color rendering, which requires 24 or 32 bits per pixel (bpp), provides the most realistic visuals because it allows you to produce photo-quality color. When you use multiple alpha layers in lower color modes (for example, 16 bpp), you often get a number of undesirable artifacts because rounding errors are more severe. When enumerating devices, you should try to obtain a device that supports true-color rendering if the capability exists.

Optimizing Your Geometry Handling

In this section, I'll cover some key issues you need to consider when you're designing the geometry and rendering features of your 3D world.

ComputeSphereVisibility

You should use *IDirect3DDevice7::ComputeSphereVisibility* to check the visibility of objects. This method calculates the visibility (complete, partial, or none) of an array of spheres within the current viewport of a device. If an object is not visible, there's no need to waste time submitting it to Direct3D for rendering. Direct3D computes sphere visibility by back-transforming the viewing frustum to the model space. This technique is performed using the inverse of the combined world, view, or projection matrices. If the combined matrix can't be inverted (if the determinant is 0), the method will fail, returning D3DERR_INVALIDMATRIX.

Vertex Buffers

By using *DrawPrimitiveVB* and *DrawIndexedPrimitiveVB* rather than their non–vertex buffer counterparts, you can minimize data copying and speed up rendering, especially when multitexturing or using a Direct3D device that supports transformation and lighting in hardware. You should also use vertex indexing, triangle strips, and triangle fans where appropriate to share vertices and therefore save time in the T&L pipeline.

Batching *DrawPrimitive* Calls

To reduce CPU overhead, use efficient batching by reducing the number of primitive-drawing calls you make. Calling DrawPrimitive once for each triangle in your scene is the *worst* thing you can do for performance! You can improve performance by sending all the triangles with the same attributes (texture and render state) in one call. If the lists are too large, however, you won't always see improvements in speed by sending lists of triangles together.

You should usually break your rendering jobs into chunks of about 100 triangles at a time because you need to consider the bus, processor, and multiple pipelines. For example, if the 3D pipelines are forced to wait idly while the processor transforms thousands of vertices and then transfers them over, when the 3D processor acts on the data, the CPU will be finished and will be idle while the accelerator works.

Floating-Point Precision and Multithread *SetCooperativeLevel* Flags

In DirectX 7, using the floating-point unit (FPU) control and multithread *SetCooperativeLevel* flags will reduce internal overhead. If your program never changes the floating-point precision level, set the DDSCL_FPUSETUP flag when calling *SetCooperativeLevel* so that Direct3D doesn't have to check the precision level every time it uses the FPU. If your program uses multiple threads, set the DDSCL_MULTITHREADED flag. If you have a single-threaded program, don't set this flag, and Direct3D will reduce its thread-synchronization overhead.

Guard-Band Clipping

Guard-band clipping helps increase performance by offloading clipping from software. When your code checks the boundaries to clip primitives to, it doesn't need to send primitives that are outside the viewport for rendering. The D3DDEVICE-DESC7 structure queries the current device with methods such as *IDirect3DDevice7:: GetCaps*. The members applicable to guard-band clipping are *dvGuardBandLeft*, *dvGuardBandTop*, *dvGuardBandRight*, and *dvGuardBandBottom*. These members define the screen-space coordinates of the guard-band clipping region. Direct3D will automatically clip any coordinates inside this rectangle but outside the viewport rectangle.

Texture-Type Hints

DirectX 7 offers the STATIC, DYNAMIC, and OPAQUE texture-type hints. Using these texture-type hints when creating textures will allow the renderer to make the most efficient possible use of textures.

Minimizing Resources

The tips in this section will help you cut down on resources so that your application runs more smoothly and quickly.

High-Cost State Changes

You should draw all non-alpha polygons before drawing all alpha polygons so that you have to toggle alpha (call *SetRenderState* with D3DRENDERSTATE_ALPHABLENDENABLE for the first parameter and TRUE or FALSE for the second) only twice per frame. Also remember that if you always render something over every pixel, you won't need to clear the back buffer at the start of each frame.

Polygons

By splitting the number of triangles you pass to Direct3D at a time into smaller chunks, you might have a bit more calling overhead, but the transfer is almost the same. However, the 3D engine will be kept busy, most likely finishing a few machine cycles after the processor passes the last polygon, meaning that rendering is much more efficient. Experiment with different batch sizes to see what works best for your program.

Texture Changes

You should always sort your objects by texture and render them in batches to minimize your texture changes. You should limit yourself to fewer than 100 texture changes per frame.

Texture Memory

You should always work toward intelligent texture memory usage. Avoid over-committing memory whenever possible. If you have to overcommit memory, try to keep the level of overcommitment below 30 percent. For example, if there isn't enough video memory to hold all the textures you need at once, consider dropping the highest mip level. The image quality will be lower, but the graphics will render much faster.

Visibility Grids

You should always design your 3D worlds so that you only submit to Direct3D the data that's currently visible. For example, in an outdoor simulation, you would break the 3D world into a grid and load the objects and triangles for the neighboring grid elements that are visible. As the user moves through the simulation, unload the grid elements that the user can't see and load the ones that become visible.

Conclusion

In this chapter, you saw a number of techniques and tricks that can help you optimize your real-time 3D applications. You should now feel comfortable enough with Direct3D Immediate Mode to begin considering ways to optimize your own 3D applications. Once you incorporate the hints discussed in this chapter into your own code, you'll be well on your way to producing commercial-quality applications!

Chapter 15 will discuss how to integrate the DirectPlay component of DirectX. DirectPlay allows you to integrate multiple player support. These multiple players can be connected to a gaming session using a variety of connection methods, including modems, networks, direct-cable connections, and so on.

CHAPTER FIFTEEN

Integrating DirectPlay

The integration of network, modem, or serial-linked game play is essential for developing top-quality 3D games. The most popular games on the market enable users to connect other players to their gaming sessions so that they can play head-to-head or as a team. If you want to develop a game that can compete in today's cut-throat software market, you must incorporate these capabilities.

The Microsoft DirectPlay API provides a powerful set of communication capabilities, which keeps you from having to deal with the variety of connectivity approaches out there. DirectPlay is implemented as a network abstraction and distributed object system. As with all the DirectX APIs, if the system your code runs on doesn't support the functionality you need (such as group or guaranteed messaging), DirectPlay will emulate it. DirectPlay integrates seamlessly with your Microsoft Direct3D applications, as do the other APIs such as DirectDraw and DirectInput. With DirectPlay's capabilities added to your program, you'll have all the tools you need to build a top-notch game.

DirectPlay Concepts

There are a few key terms and concepts in DirectPlay that you should be aware of before you start using it. Once you understand these terms, it will be easier to follow what the DirectPlay methods are used for.

DirectPlay allows players to connect to each other for multiplayer games in several ways: via serial cable, modem, or some sort of network connection. Each kind of connection is referred to as a *service provider* or *connection type*. It is possible for game developers or network companies to provide custom service providers for DirectPlay, but most of the time your choice of connection type will be between the standard types that DirectPlay provides: TCP/IP, IPX, modem, and serial. DirectPlay provides a method to enumerate the currently available service providers. Once the user has selected one, a *connection* can be initialized. Initialization of a connection often involves specifying information such as the phone number (for a modem connection) or the Internet address (for a TCP/IP connection).

Once a connection is initialized, it is possible to enumerate the available sessions. A *session* is a particular game being played by multiple players. A *player,* not surprisingly, is a participant in a session. Each player has a name and a numeric *player ID.* There is a special, "virtual" player in every session that is known as the *host.* The host doesn't represent a human player but rather manages system-level messages and operations for the session.

After everyone has joined the session, the game itself can begin. Players can all send DirectPlay *messages* to each other to indicate their status and actions. The structure of most messages is determined by the needs of the game, but there are some predefined messages, called *system messages,* that indicate game-level operations such as players entering or leaving the session.

DirectPlay also provides support for *lobbies,* which are places where users can launch applications, arrange game sessions, and exchange messages. Lobbies make it easy for users to create a session with other players. Because lobbies dictate the service provider that players must use, they enable users to easily find available opponents. In addition, lobbies provide the network address or configure the network if necessary, pass the name of the player (entered by the user upon connecting) so that he or she can join the game, and maintain a list of sessions in progress that users can join. Furthermore, lobbies can acquire final scores and maintain player-ranking information for tournaments. If the game isn't started from a lobby, the game itself needs to determine the connection type, enumerate available sessions (games in progress), and either join an existing session or create a new session.

If you like analogies, you might find a restaurant metaphor useful for understanding all these DirectPlay terms. Picking a service provider is like deciding what kind of restaurant to eat at or perhaps what neighborhood you want to eat in. After enumerating the available types, you can choose a particular restaurant and go there, which is like initializing a connection. Inside the restaurant, there are several eating "sessions" going on at different tables. You can either create a new session by sitting down at an empty table and waiting for people to join you, or you can join an existing session where people are already eating (or waiting for you). The host is like the waiter, who directs the process and disseminates information that is useful to all the players. Using a lobby is a bit like getting some friends on a conference call in advance and deciding on where exactly to meet, right down to the table number in the restaurant. Once you've all agreed, you can all head straight for that restaurant and table without making any further decisions. DirectPlay messages are comparable to conversations between those who are eating. Without them, you might as well be eating alone!

Getting Started

Setting up your project to be able to use the DirectPlay API is easy. As with other DirectX APIs, to use DirectPlay, you must link the dxguid.lib library into your application or define the INITGUID symbol before all your other #*include* and #*define* statements. You'll also need to link your program to the dplayx.lib library.

Once you've integrated DirectPlay into your project, you're ready to write the code to add DirectPlay support to your Direct3D application. Just as the DirectX SDK provides the Direct3D Framework code to do some common Direct3D tasks, it also provides a file named dpconnect.cpp, which performs the basic tasks involved in getting into a DirectPlay session. RoadRage uses this code, and I recommend that you try it as well because the initial steps in using DirectPlay are nearly identical for all multiplayer programs.

You'll insert the first piece of code you need to add to the application into the *WinMain* function. The following code block (from roadrage.cpp) walks through the steps that *WinMain* takes and lists the other routines you need to create to enable multiplayer game play:

```
INT WINAPI WinMain( HINSTANCE hInst, HINSTANCE,
                    LPSTR strCmdLine, INT )
{
    HRESULT hr;

    ⋮

    // STEP 1
    // Read information from the registry.
    ReadDpInfoFromRegistry();

    // STEP 2
    g_hDPMessageEvent = CreateEvent( NULL, FALSE, FALSE, NULL );

    // STEP 3
    if( FAILED( hr = CoInitialize( NULL ) ) )
        return FALSE;

    ⋮

    // STEP 4
    // Determine whether the application was launched from a
    // lobby server.
    hr = DPConnect_CheckForLobbyLaunch( &bLaunchedByLobby );
```

(continued)

353

```
    if( FAILED(hr) )
    {
        if( hr == DPERR_USERCANCEL )
            return S_OK;

        return hr;
    }

    // STEP 5
    if( !bLaunchedByLobby )
    {
        // If not, the first step is to prompt the user about the
        // network connection and ask which session he would like to
        // join or whether he wants to create a new session.
        nExitCode = DPConnect_StartDirectPlayConnect( hInst, FALSE );

        // See the above EXITCODE #defines for what nExitCode
        // could be.
        if( nExitCode == EXITCODE_QUIT )
        {
            // The user canceled the multiplayer connect.
            // The sample will now quit.
            return E_ABORT;
        }

        if( nExitCode == EXITCODE_ERROR || g_pDP == NULL )
        {
            MessageBox( NULL, TEXT("Multiplayer connect failed. "
                        "The sample will now quit."),
                        TEXT("DirectPlay Sample"),
                        MB_OK | MB_ICONERROR );

            return E_FAIL;
        }
    }

    ⋮

    // STEP 6
    // The next step is to start the game.
    return d3dApp.Run();
    if( SUCCEEDED( hr ) )
    {
        // Write information to the registry.
        WriteRegisteryInfo();
    }
```

```
// STEP 7
// Clean up DirectPlay.
if( g_pDP )
{
    PrintMessage(NULL, "Cleanup DirectPlay FAILED", NULL,
                LOGFILE_ONLY);

    // STEP 8
    g_pDP->DestroyPlayer( g_LocalPlayerDPID );
    g_pDP->Close();

    SAFE_DELETE_ARRAY( g_pDPLConnection );
    SAFE_RELEASE( g_pDPLobby );
    SAFE_RELEASE( g_pDP );
}

// STEP 9
CoUninitialize();

// STEP 10
CloseHandle( g_hDPlaySampleRegKey );
CloseHandle( g_hDPMessageEvent );
    ⋮
}
```

In STEP 1, the code calls the *ReadDpInfoFromRegistry* routine. This function acquires the default player, session, and preferred service provider name from the registry.

STEP 2 of the *WinMain* code calls *CreateEvent*. The *CreateEvent* function creates an event object. This object will be used to detect when DirectPlay messages have arrived. The handle returned by this routine has EVENT_ALL_ACCESS access to the new event object and can be used in any function that requires a handle to an event object. You can have any thread for the calling process specify the event-object handle using a call to one of the *wait functions*. Each of the single-object wait functions will return when the state of the object specified is signaled. Each of the multiple-object wait functions can be requested to return when one or all of the objects specified are signaled. When the wait function returns, the waiting thread is released so that it can continue executing.

STEP 3 of the code for the *WinMain* function calls the *CoInitialize* function. This function initializes the COM library for use. You will typically pass NULL as the parameter to *CoInitialize*.

With the COM library initialized, you're now ready to call to the first DirectPlay-related routine (STEP 4 in the code for the *WinMain* function). The *DPConnect_CheckForLobbyLaunch* routine determines whether the DirectPlay session was launched by a lobby. If it was, the routine retrieves the information for starting and connecting an application and then calls *DPConnect_DoLobbyLaunch* to create the session or to join it.

If this is not a lobby launch, RoadRage calls the *DPConnect_StartDirectPlayConnect* routine (STEP 5) to prompt the user for the DirectPlay connection and the DirectPlay session he or she wants to join or create. The *DPConnect_StartDirectPlayConnect* routine first determines whether the user has already been through the connection process and has backtracked from the main game. If the user hasn't yet gone through the connection process, it uses the *DPConnect_ConnectionsDlgProc* routine to display the Multiplayer Connect dialog box, which is shown in Figure 15-1. If the user has already connected, it creates the Multiplayer Games dialog box (shown in Figure 15-2) by using the *DPConnect_SessionsDlgProc* routine.

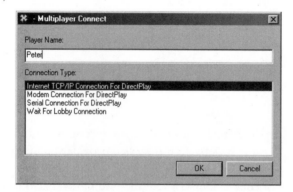

Figure 15-1
The Multiplayer Connect dialog box

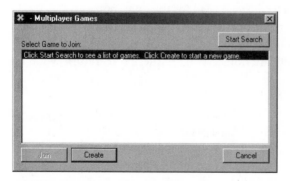

Figure 15-2
The Multiplayer Games dialog box

The Multiplayer Connect Dialog Box

In the Multiplayer Connect dialog box (shown in Figure 15-1), the user enters his name and selects a connection type: Internet, modem, or serial. The user can also choose Wait For Lobby Connection and wait for a connection via a lobby.

Although it's not part of the connection initialization process, this dialog box allows the user to enter a player name. This name is stored in the *g_strLocalPlayerName* global variable. The actual enumeration of connection types happens in the *DPConnect_ConnectionsDlgFillListBox* routine, which has the following definition:

```
//----------------------------------------------------------------
// Name: DPConnect_ConnectionsDlgFillListBox
// Desc: Fills the DirectPlay connection list box and adds
//       a Wait For Lobby Connection option
//----------------------------------------------------------------
HRESULT DPConnect_ConnectionsDlgFillListBox( HWND hDlg )
{
    HRESULT       hr;
    HWND          hWndListBox = GetDlgItem( hDlg,
                                            IDC_CONNECTION_LIST );
    LPDIRECTPLAY4 pDP = NULL;
    int           nIndex;

    // Create an IDirectPlay object.
    if( FAILED( hr = CoCreateInstance( CLSID_DirectPlay, NULL,
                                       CLSCTX_ALL,
                                       IID_IDirectPlay4A,
                                       (VOID**)&pDP)))
    {
        if( hr == E_NOINTERFACE )
        {
            MessageBox( NULL,
              TEXT("This application requires DirectPlay 6 or later. "
                   "The sample will now quit."),
              TEXT("DirectPlay Sample"), MB_OK | MB_ICONERROR );
        }

        return hr;
    }
```

(continued)

```
    // Enumerate all DirectPlay connections, and store them in the
    // list box.
    if( FAILED( hr = pDP->EnumConnections( &g_AppGUID,
                           DPConnect_EnumConnectionsCallback,
                           hWndListBox, 0 ) ) )
    {
        SAFE_RELEASE( pDP );
        return hr;
    }

    SAFE_RELEASE( pDP );

    // Add Wait For Lobby Connection selection to the list box.
    SendMessage( hWndListBox, LB_ADDSTRING, 0,
                 (LPARAM)"Wait for Lobby Connection" );

    SetFocus( hWndListBox );
    nIndex = SendMessage( hWndListBox, LB_FINDSTRINGEXACT,
                          (WPARAM)-1,
                          (LPARAM)g_strPreferredProvider );
    if( nIndex != LB_ERR )
        SendMessage( hWndListBox, LB_SETCURSEL, nIndex, 0 );
    else
        SendMessage( hWndListBox, LB_SETCURSEL, 0, 0 );

}
```

This routine fills the DirectPlay connection list box with all the possible connection options. To do so, it calls *CoCreateInstance* to create a *IDirectPlay* object, requesting the *IID_IDirectPlay4A* interface (the newest DirectPlay interface). *CoCreateInstance* creates an instance of the class defined in the *clsid* parameter, requesting the interface specified in the *iid* parameter using the execution contents defined in the *grfContext* parameter.

Once it has created the interface, *DPConnect_ConnectionsDlgFillListBox* calls the *IDirectPlay4::EnumConnections* method with the *DPConnect_EnumConnectionsCallback* callback function. Here's the declaration for *EnumConnections*:

```
HRESULT EnumConnections(
    LPCGUID lpguidApplication,
    LPDPENUMCONNECTIONSCALLBACK lpEnumCallback,
    LPVOID lpContext,
    DWORD dwFlags
);
```

Parameter	Description
lpguidApplication	Pointer to an application's globally unique identifier (GUID). Only service providers and lobby providers that this application can use will be returned. If this parameter is set to a NULL pointer, a list of all the connections is enumerated regardless of the application GUID.
lpEnumCallback	Pointer to a user-supplied *EnumConnectionsCallback* function that will be called for each available connection.
lpContext	Pointer to a user-defined context that is passed to the callback function.
dwFlags	Flags that specify the type of connections to be enumerated. The default (0) will enumerate DirectPlay service providers only. Here are two possible values for this parameter: **DPCONNECTION_DIRECTPLAY** Enumerates DirectPlay service providers to communicate in an application session **DPCONNECTION_DIRECTPLAYLOBBY** Enumerates DirectPlay lobby providers to communicate with a lobby server

The routine then adds the Wait For Lobby Connection option to the list box using the *SendMessage* function. Then it tries to find an entry in the list box that exactly matches the value in the *g_strPreferredProvider* global variable. (This value is the preferred provider you've stored in this variable.) If this entry appears in the list box, the code selects it. Otherwise, it selects the first entry.

The *DPConnect_EnumConnectionsCallback* function used to enumerate the DirectPlay connections follows.

```
//-----------------------------------------------------------------
// Name: DPConnect_EnumConnectionsCallback
// Desc: Enumerates through all DirectPlay connection types
//       and stores them in the list box
//-----------------------------------------------------------------
BOOL FAR PASCAL DPConnect_EnumConnectionsCallback( LPCGUID    pguidSP,
                                       VOID*      pConnection,
                                       DWORD      dwConnectionSize,
                                       LPCDPNAME  pName,
                                       DWORD      dwFlags,
                                       VOID*      pvContext )
```

(continued)

359

```
{
    HRESULT         hr;
    LPDIRECTPLAY4 pDP = NULL;
    VOID*           pConnectionBuffer = NULL;
    HWND            hWndListBox = (HWND)pvContext;
    LRESULT         iIndex;

    // Create an IDirectPlay object.
    if( FAILED( hr = CoCreateInstance( CLSID_DirectPlay, NULL,
                                        CLSCTX_ALL,
                                        IID_IDirectPlay4A,
                                        (VOID**)&pDP )))
        return FALSE; // Error; stop enumerating

    // Test whether the connection is available by attempting to
    // initialize it.
    if( FAILED( hr = pDP->InitializeConnection( pConnection, 0 ) ) )
    {
        SAFE_RELEASE( pDP );
        return TRUE; // Unavailable connection; keep enumerating.
    }

    // Don't need the IDirectPlay interface anymore, so release it.
    SAFE_RELEASE( pDP );

    // Found a good connection, so put it in the list box.
    iIndex = SendMessage( hWndListBox, LB_ADDSTRING, 0,
                        (LPARAM)pName->lpszShortNameA );
    if( iIndex == CB_ERR )
        return FALSE; // Error; stop enumerating

    pConnectionBuffer = new BYTE[ dwConnectionSize ];
    if( pConnectionBuffer == NULL )
        return FALSE; // Error; stop enumerating

    // Store pointer to GUID in list box.
    memcpy( pConnectionBuffer, pConnection, dwConnectionSize );
    SendMessage( hWndListBox, LB_SETITEMDATA, iIndex,
                (LPARAM)pConnectionBuffer );

    return TRUE; // Keep enumerating
}
```

This enumeration callback is similar to the other enumeration callbacks you've seen throughout this book. For each connection type, the function creates a temporary *IDirectPlay4A* interface and then calls *IDirectPlay4::InitializeConnection* using the connection data passed to the callback function. If this fails, the connection type might not be available for some reason, so it won't be added to the dialog box's list of connection types. Here's the declaration for the *IDirectPlay4:: InitializeConnection* routine:

```
HRESULT InitializeConnection (
    LPVOID lpConnection
    DWORD dwFlags
);
```

Parameter	Description
lpConnection	Pointer to a buffer that contains all the information about the connection to be initialized as a DirectPlay address
dwFlags	Not used; must be 0

You're now done with the *IDirectPlay4* interface, so you can release it using the SAFE_RELEASE macro, shown here:

```
#define SAFE_RELEASE(p)        { if(p) { (p)->Release(); (p)=NULL; } }
```

The Multiplayer Games Dialog Box

Once the user has chosen a connection type, the next dialog box is shown. In this dialog box, you can either create a new game session or enumerate the existing game sessions and join one of them. This dialog box is controlled by the *DPConnect_ SessionsDlgProc* function.

If the user indicates that he wants to see the available sessions (by clicking the Start Search button), *DPConnect_SessionsDlgProc* uses the function *DPConnect_ SessionsDlgShowGames* to enumerate the available sessions (via *IDirectPlay4:: EnumSessions*) and to add their names to the list box in the Multiplayer Games dialog box. The list is recomputed continuously to account for sessions being created, so a timer is used to periodically call *DPConnect_SessionsDlgShowGames* and update the list. Here's the declaration for *EnumSessions*:

```
HRESULT EnumSessions (
    LPDPSESSIONDESC2 lpsd,
    DWORD dwTimeout,
    LPDPENUMSESSIONSCALLBACK2 lpEnumSessionsCallback2,
    LPVOID lpContext,
    DWORD dwFlags
);
```

Parameter	Description
lpsd	Pointer to the DPSESSIONDESC2 structure describing the sessions to be enumerated. Only sessions that meet the criteria set in this structure will be enumerated. You can set the *guidApplication* member to the GUID of an application that interests you if you know it, or you can set this member to GUID_NULL to obtain all sessions. You need the *lpszPassword* member only if you want private sessions. All data members other than *guidApplication* and *lpszPassword* are ignored.
dwTimeout	In the asynchronous case, *dwTimeout* is the interval (in milliseconds) by which DirectPlay will broadcast enumeration requests to update the internal sessions list. If the time-out is set to 0, a default time-out appropriate for the service provider and connection type will be used. I recommend that you set this value to 0. The application can determine this time-out by calling *IDirectPlay4::GetCaps* and examining the *dwTimeout* data member of the DPCAPS structure.
lpEnumSessionsCallback2	Pointer to the application-supplied *EnumSessionsCallback2* function to be called for each DirectPlay session that's responding.
lpContext	Pointer to a user-defined context that's passed to each enumeration callback.
dwFlags	The default is 0, which is equivalent to DPENUMSESSIONS_AVAILABLE. When enumerating sessions with DPENUMSESSIONS_ALL or DPENUMSESSIONS_PASSWORDREQUIRED, the application must know which sessions cannot be joined and which sessions are password protected so that it can warn the user or prompt for a password.
	The possible values for the *dwFlags* parameter are:
	DPENUMSESSIONS_ALL Enumerates all active sessions, whether or not they're accepting new players. Sessions in which the player limit has been reached, new players have been disabled, or joining has been disabled will be enumerated. Password-protected sessions won't be enumerated unless the DPENUMSESSIONS_PASSWORDREQUIRED flag is also specified. If DPENUMSESSIONS_ALL isn't specified, DPENUMSESSIONS_AVAILABLE is assumed.

362

Parameter	Description
	DPENUMSESSIONS_ASYNC Enumerates the current sessions in the session cache and returns immediately. Starts the asynchronous enumeration process if it hasn't already begun. Updates to the session list continue until canceled by calling *EnumSessions* with the DPENUMSESSIONS_ STOPASYNC flag, or by calling Open or Release. If this flag isn't specified, the enumeration is performed synchronously.
	DPENUMSESSIONS_AVAILABLE Enumerates all sessions that are accepting new players to join. Sessions that have reached their maximum number of players, have disabled new players, or have disabled joining won't be enumerated. Password-protected sessions won't be enumerated unless the DPENUMSESSIONS_PASSWORD-REQUIRED flag is also specified.
	DPENUMSESSIONS_PASSWORD-REQUIRED When combined with either the DPENUMSESSIONS_AVAILABLE or DPENUM-SESSIONS_ALL flag, this flag allows password-protected sessions as well as sessions without password protection to be enumerated. If this flag isn't specified, no password-protected sessions will be returned.
	DPENUMSESSIONS_RETURNSTATUS If this flag is specified, the enumeration won't display any dialog boxes showing the connection progress status. If the connection cannot be made immediately, the method will return with the DPERR_CONNECTING error. The application must keep calling *EnumSessions* until DP_OK returns, indicating successful completion, or until another error code returns, indicating an error.
	DPENUMSESSIONS_STOPASYNC Enumerates all the current sessions in the session cache and cancels the asynchronous enumeration process.

When *IDirectPlay4::EnumSessions* is called for the first time, the Locate Session dialog box (shown in Figure 15-3) appears. The appearance of this dialog box varies based on the connection type. For the TCP/IP connection type, users can type the computer name or the IP address of the session host they want in the Locate Session dialog box; otherwise, they can leave this dialog box blank and search for other sessions to join.

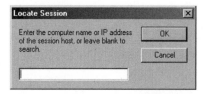

Figure 15-3
The Locate Session dialog box

If the user selects a session in the list box, the code attempts to keep the session selected (if one was selected previously) unless it ends and therefore disappears.

If the user selects a session and clicks the Join button, the *DPConnect_ SessionsDlgJoinGame* function is called. Here's the definition of this routine:

```
//------------------------------------------------------------------
// Name: DPConnect_SessionsDlgJoinGame
// Desc: Joins the selected DirectPlay session
//------------------------------------------------------------------
HRESULT DPConnect_SessionsDlgJoinGame( HWND hDlg )
{
    DPSESSIONDESC2 dpsd;
    DPNAME         dpname;
    HRESULT        hr;
    HWND           hWndListBox = GetDlgItem( hDlg, IDC_GAMES_LIST );
    DPSessionInfo* pDPSISelected = NULL;
    int            nItemSelected;
    char           buffer[256];


    nItemSelected = SendMessage( hWndListBox, LB_GETCURSEL, 0, 0 );

    // Add status text in the list box.
    pDPSISelected = (DPSessionInfo*) SendMessage( hWndListBox,
                                                  LB_GETITEMDATA,
                                                  nItemSelected, 0 );

    if( NULL == pDPSISelected )
    {
```

```
            MessageBox( hDlg, TEXT("There are no games to join."),
                    TEXT("DirectPlay Sample"), MB_OK );
        return S_OK;
    }


    // Set up the DPSESSIONDESC2 and get the session GUID from
    // the selected list box item.
    ZeroMemory( &dpsd, sizeof(dpsd) );
    dpsd.dwSize          = sizeof(dpsd);
    dpsd.guidInstance    = pDPSISelected->guidSession;
    dpsd.guidApplication = g_AppGUID;


    // Join the session.
    g_bHostPlayer = FALSE;
    if( FAILED( hr = g_pDP->Open( &dpsd, DPOPEN_JOIN ) ) )
        return hr;


    // Create player based on g_strLocalPlayerName.
    // Store the player's DPID in g_LocalPlayerDPID.
    // All DirectPlay messages for this player will signal
    // g_hDPMessageEvent.
    ZeroMemory( &dpname, sizeof(DPNAME) );
    dpname.dwSize         = sizeof(DPNAME);
    dpname.lpszShortNameA = g_strLocalPlayerName;


    if( FAILED( hr = g_pDP->CreatePlayer( &g_LocalPlayerDPID,
                                          &dpname,
                                          g_hDPMessageEvent, NULL,
                                          0, 0)))
        return hr;


    pCMyApp->MyRRnetID = g_LocalPlayerDPID;
    itoa((int)pCMyApp->MyRRnetID, buffer, 10);
    PrintMessage(NULL, "Direct Play : Joined game", NULL, NULL);
    PrintMessage(NULL, "Player's dpid : ",
                dpname.lpszShortNameA, NULL);
    PrintMessage(NULL, "MyRRnetID    : ", buffer, NULL);


    pCMyApp->multiplay_flag = TRUE;

    // DirectPlay connect successful, so end dialog.
    EndDialog( hDlg, EXITCODE_FORWARD );

    return S_OK;
}
```

In this routine, as long as there's a game to join, you can set up a DPSES-SIONDESC2 structure and get the session GUID the user selected from the list. You can then call the *IDirectPlay4::Open* method with the DPOPEN_JOIN flag to join a session that was enumerated by your previous call to *IDirectPlay4:: EnumSessions*. Here's the declaration for the *IDirectPlay4::Open* method:

```
HRESULT  Open(
    LPDPSESSIONDESC2 lpsd
    DWORD dwFlags
);
```

The Open method has the following parameters.

lpsd   Pointer to the DPSESSIONDESC2 structure that describes the session the user is creating or joining. If the user is joining a session, you need to specify only the *dwSize*, *guidInstance*, and *lpszPassword* data members. You need to supply a password only if the enumerated session had the DPSESSION_PASSWORD flag set.

If the user is creating a session, the application must completely fill the DPSES-SIONDESC2 structure with the properties of the sessions to be created. DirectPlay will generate the *guidInstance* data member.

dwFlags   You can use only one of the following flags:

- **DPOPEN_CREATE**   Create a new instance of an application session. The local computer will be the name server and host of the session.

- **DPOPEN_JOIN**   Join an existing instance of an application session for the purpose of participating. The application will be able to create players and send and receive messages.

- **DPOPEN_RETURNSTATUS**   If this flag is specified, the method won't display any dialog boxes showing the connection progress status. If the connection cannot be made immediately, the method will return with the DPERR_CONNECTING error. The application must keep calling *Open* until either DP_OK returns, indicating successful completion, or an error code returns.

Finally, *DPConnect_SessionsDlgJoinGame* creates a local player for the current session based on the name in the *g_strLocalPlayerName* variable. By passing the *g_hDPMessageEvent* value as the third argument to *IDirectPlay::CreatePlayer*, it indicates that all the DirectPlay messages for this player will signal *g_hDPMessage-Event*. Here's the declaration for the *IDirectPlay4::CreatePlayer* routine:

```
HRESULT CreatePlayer(
    LPDPID lpidPlayer,
    LPDPNAME lpPlayerName,
    HANDLE hEvent,
    LPVOID lpData,
    DWORD dwDataSize,
    DWORD dwFlags
);
```

Parameter	Description
lpidPlayer	Pointer to a variable that the DirectPlay player ID will fill. DirectPlay defines this value.
lpPlayerName	Pointer to a DPNAME structure that holds the name of the player. NULL indicates that the player has no initial name information. The name in *lpPlayerName* is provided for the player's use only; it isn't used internally and doesn't need to be unique.
hEvent	An event object created by the application that DirectPlay will signal when it receives a message addressed to the player.
lpData	Pointer to a block of application-defined data to associate with the player ID. NULL indicates that the player has no initial data. The data specified in this parameter is assumed to be remote data that will be propagated to all the other applications in the session, as if *IDirectPlay4::SetPlayerData* had been called.
dwDataSize	Size, in bytes, of the data block that *lpData* points to.
dwFlags	Flags indicating what type of player is currently using the game. The default (0) is a nonspectator, nonserver player. These flags are available: **DPPLAYER_SERVERPLAYER** The player is a server player for client/server communications. Only the host can create a server player. Only one server player can exist in a session. If this flag is specified, *CreatePlayer* will always return a player ID of DPID_SERVERPLAYER. **DPPLAYER_SPECTATOR** The player is created as a spectator. A spectator player behaves exactly as a normal player except that the player is flagged as a spectator. The application can then limit what a spectator player can do. The application completely defines the behavior of a spectator player. DirectPlay simply propagates this flag.

If the user clicks the Create Game button, the code calls the *DPConnect_SessionsDlgCreateGame* routine to attempt to create a new game and initialize the player data. Here's the code for this routine:

```
//-------------------------------------------------------------------
// Name: DPConnect_SessionsDlgCreateGame
// Desc: Asks the user the session name and creates a new DirectPlay
//       session
//-------------------------------------------------------------------
HRESULT DPConnect_SessionsDlgCreateGame( HWND hDlg )
{
    DPSESSIONDESC2 dpsd;
    DPNAME         dpname;
    HRESULT        hr;
    int            nResult;
    HINSTANCE      hInst;
    FILE *fp;

    hInst = (HINSTANCE) GetWindowLong( hDlg, GWL_HINSTANCE );

    // Display a modal Multiplayer Connect dialog box.
    EnableWindow( hDlg, FALSE );
    nResult = DialogBox( hInst,
                         MAKEINTRESOURCE(IDD_MULTIPLAYER_CREATE),
                         hDlg, DPConnect_CreateSessionDlgProc );
    EnableWindow( hDlg, TRUE );

    if( nResult == IDCANCEL )
        return S_OK;

    // Set up the DPSESSIONDESC2 based on g_AppGUID, and
    // g_strSessionName. The DPSESSION_KEEPALIVE flag keeps
    // the session alive if players exit abnormally.
    ZeroMemory( &dpsd, sizeof(dpsd) );
    dpsd.dwSize          = sizeof(dpsd);
    dpsd.guidApplication = g_AppGUID;
    dpsd.lpszSessionNameA = g_strSessionName;
    dpsd.dwMaxPlayers    = 10;
    dpsd.dwFlags         = DPSESSION_KEEPALIVE |
                           DPSESSION_MIGRATEHOST;
    if( g_bUseProtocol )
        dpsd.dwFlags |= DPSESSION_DIRECTPLAYPROTOCOL;

    // Create a new session.
    g_bHostPlayer = TRUE;
    if( FAILED( hr = g_pDP->Open( &dpsd, DPOPEN_CREATE ) ) )
        return hr;
```

```
// Create a player based on g_strLocalPlayerName.
// Store the player's DPID in g_LocalPlayerDPID.
// All DirectPlay messages for this player will signal
// g_hDPMessageEvent.
ZeroMemory( &dpname, sizeof(DPNAME) );
dpname.dwSize         = sizeof(DPNAME);
dpname.lpszShortNameA = g_strLocalPlayerName;

 // Create the player.
 if( FAILED( hr = g_pDP->CreatePlayer( &g_LocalPlayerDPID,
                                       &dpname,
                                       g_hDPMessageEvent, NULL, 0,
                                       DPPLAYER_SERVERPLAYER ) ) )
    return hr;

// Initialize the player data.
pCMyApp->num_players = 0;
pCMyApp->MyRRnetID = g_LocalPlayerDPID;

pCMyApp->player_list[pCMyApp->num_players].x = 600;
pCMyApp->player_list[pCMyApp->num_players].y = 12;
pCMyApp->player_list[pCMyApp->num_players].z = 500;
pCMyApp->player_list[pCMyApp->num_players].rot_angle = 0;
pCMyApp->player_list[pCMyApp->num_players].model_id = 0;
pCMyApp->player_list[pCMyApp->num_players].skin_tex_id = 0;
pCMyApp->player_list[pCMyApp->num_players].current_weapon = 0;
pCMyApp->player_list[pCMyApp->num_players].current_car = 0;
pCMyApp->player_list[pCMyApp->num_players].current_frame = 0;
pCMyApp->player_list[pCMyApp->num_players].current_sequence = 0;
pCMyApp->
    player_list[pCMyApp->num_players].bIsPlayerInWalkMode = TRUE;
pCMyApp->
    player_list[pCMyApp->num_players].RRnetID = g_LocalPlayerDPID;
pCMyApp->player_list[pCMyApp->num_players].bIsPlayerValid = TRUE;
pCMyApp->num_players++;


if(dpname.lpszShortNameA == NULL)
    strcpy(pCMyApp->player_list[0].name, "no name");
else
    strcpy(pCMyApp->player_list[0].name, dpname.lpszShortNameA);

// Enter information into the log file.
fp = fopen("rrlogfile.txt","a");
fprintf( fp, "Direct Play : Created game\n");
fprintf( fp, "Player's name : %s\n",
         pCMyApp->player_list[0].name);
```

(continued)

369

```
        fprintf( fp, "Player's dpid  : %d\n",
                 pCMyApp->player_list[0].RRnetID);
        fprintf( fp, "MyRRnetID      : %d\n", pCMyApp->MyRRnetID);
        fprintf( fp, "--------------\n\n");
        fclose(fp);

        pCMyApp->multiplay_flag = TRUE;

        // DirectPlay connect successful, so end dialog.
        EndDialog( hDlg, EXITCODE_FORWARD );

        return S_OK;
}
```

This code presents a dialog box in which the user enters a name for the session and specifies whether or not to use the DirectPlay protocol, which provides guaranteed messaging even if the service provider is designed for unguaranteed messaging. The dialog box is shown in Figure 15-4.

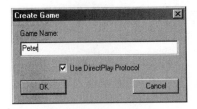

Figure 15-4
The Create Game dialog box

Once this dialog box has been dismissed, *IDirectPlay4::Open* is called with the DPOPEN_CREATE flag to create the session. And finally, a player is created, just as it was in the *DPConnect_SessionsDlgJoinGame* function.

As you can see, getting into a DirectPlay session takes several steps and can involve a lot of interaction with the user. The code in dpconnect.cpp is great either to use in your program or just to study to understand how this process works.

DirectPlay Messages

You're now ready to start creating all the game-specific DirectPlay code. You'll handle all Microsoft Windows messages in your program, but you also need to handle any DirectPlay messages received from other players. The *MsgWaitForMultipleObjects* routine, called at the top of the message-processing loop, handles player notifications received in the form of signaled events in the message loop that the *WinMain* function handles.

All you need to do is handle these messages when they are received. Often this consists of updating the other players' positions and verifying whether they've interacted with you somehow—for instance, checking that they didn't shoot or talk to your character. In the RoadRage code, you'll handle these types of messages as well as position messages sent so that each player's system can render the other players as they move through the virtual world.

The key issue here is understanding how to make the custom messages (message structures) required for your application, fill them with your data, and pass them to others connected to your game. You also need to know the counterpart to this, which is how to receive these messages, along with DirectPlay system messages, and what to do with them once you receive them. After all, although setting up your connection type and making the connection takes a great deal of code, a potentially more challenging (but fun) part is producing the code for passing the actual game-related messages to the other players connected to your session.

Passing Game Messages to Players

In your code, you need to define a player for each person connected to the gaming session. This PLAYER structure holds the player position and the rotational information so that the player can face in the desired direction. The structure also contains the *RRnetID* variable, which identifies the player when you create a message to pass to all the other players using the *SendActionFlagMessage*, *SendActionWord-Message*, or *SendPositionMessage* routine. (We'll cover these routines shortly.)

Here is the PLAYER structure:

```
typedef struct player_typ
{
    float x;
    float y;
    float z;
    float rot_angle;
    int model_id;
    int skin_tex_id;
    BOOL walk_or_drive_mode;
    int current_weapon;
    int current_car;
    int current_frame;
    int current_sequence;
    int health;
    int armour;
    int frags;
    int ping;
    DWORD RRnetID;
    char name[256];
} PLAYER, *player_ptr;
```

After creating the routines to handle the DirectPlay-based messaging you need to perform, along with setting up the *CMyD3DApplication::MsgProc* message handler routine to handle the user connecting, disconnecting, and respawning a character after it dies, you also need to add routines to handle messages for the DirectPlay control of the characters as well as the general motions for when the characters are *at rest*. Because the characters we've created for our game are Quake II–style characters, even when they are at rest, they move—for example, they breathe, shuffle their feet, or do some other basic repetitive action.

To handle DirectPlay messaging, we'll insert new case statements into the message-handling switch statement of *CMyD3DApplication::MsgProc*. The first item to check for is a WM_TIMER message. If the timer is the animation timer, loop through each player and animate it as well as its weapon (by using the *Animate-Characters* routine). If the timer is the RESPAWN_TIMER, the player was killed, so it's regenerated with full health and at its starting position.

Finally, we need to add code to handle DirectPlay messages generated when a player disconnects from the game (ID_MULTIPLAYER_DISCONNECT) or connects to the game (ID_MULTIPLAYER_CONNECT).

```
LRESULT CMyD3DApplication::MsgProc( HWND hWnd, UINT uMsg,
                                    WPARAM wParam,
                                    LPARAM lParam )
{
    int MyPlayerNum;
    int     nExitCode;
    BOOL    bLaunchedByLobby;
    ⋮
    switch( uMsg )
    {
        ⋮
        case WM_TIMER:

            if(wParam == ANIMATION_TIMER)
            {
                if( GetFramework() && GetbActive() &&
                    GetbReady() && m_bWindowed )
                {
                    if(IsRenderingOk == TRUE)
                        AnimateCharacters();
                }
            }

            if(wParam == RESPAWN_TIMER)
            {
                m_vEyePt.x = 700;
                m_vEyePt.y = 22;
                m_vEyePt.z = 700;
```

```
            MyHealth = 100;

            MyPlayerNum = GetPlayerNumber(MyRRnetID);

            player_list[MyPlayerNum].x = m_vEyePt.x;
            player_list[MyPlayerNum].y = m_vEyePt.y;
            player_list[MyPlayerNum].z = m_vEyePt.z;
            player_list[MyPlayerNum].rot_angle = 0;
            player_list[MyPlayerNum].bIsPlayerAlive = TRUE;
            player_list[MyPlayerNum].bStopAnimating = FALSE;
            player_list[MyPlayerNum].current_weapon = 0;
            player_list[MyPlayerNum].current_car = 0;
            player_list[MyPlayerNum].current_frame = 0;
            player_list[MyPlayerNum].current_sequence = 0;
            player_list[MyPlayerNum].bIsPlayerInWalkMode = TRUE;
            player_list[MyPlayerNum].health = 100;

            SendActionFlagMessage(MyRRnetID, TRUE,
                            APPMSG_RESPAWN);

            KillTimer(hWnd, RESPAWN_TIMER);
        }
        break;
        :
    case WM_COMMAND:
        switch( LOWORD(wParam) )
        {
            case MENU_ABOUT:
                Pause(TRUE);
                DialogBox(hInstApp, MAKEINTRESOURCE(IDD_ABOUT),
                            hWnd, (DLGPROC)AppAbout);
                Pause(FALSE);
                break;

            case ID_MULTIPLAYER_DISCONNECT:
                PrintMessage(NULL,
                    "MsgProc - ID_MULTIPLAYER_DISCONNECT",
                    NULL, LOGFILE_ONLY);
                RrDestroyPlayer();
                break;

            case ID_MULTIPLAYER_CONNECT:

            if(multiplay_flag == TRUE)
                break;

            // See whether the session was launched from a
            // lobby server.
            hr = DPConnect_CheckForLobbyLaunch(&bLaunchedByLobby);
```

(continued)

```
                    if( FAILED(hr) )
                    {
                        if( hr == DPERR_USERCANCEL )
                            return S_OK;
                        return hr;
                    }

                    if( !bLaunchedByLobby )
                    {
                        // If not, the first step is to prompt the user
                        // about the network connection and ask which
                        // session he would like to join or whether he
                        // wants to create a new session.
                        nExitCode = DPConnect_StartDirectPlayConnect(
                                                hInstApp, FALSE );
                        // See the above EXITCODE #defines for what
                        // nExitCode can be.
                        if( nExitCode == EXITCODE_QUIT )
                        {
                            // The user canceled the multiplayer
                            // connect.
                            // The sample will now quit.
                            return E_ABORT;
                        }

                        if(nExitCode == EXITCODE_ERROR || g_pDP == NULL)
                        {
                            MessageBox( NULL,
                                    "Multiplayer connect failed. ",
                                    "You might need to reboot",
                                    MB_OK | MB_ICONERROR );
                            return E_FAIL;
                        }
                    }
                    break;
                    :
        }
```

To create a routine to handle all of the application-specific DirectPlay messages, we call the *IDirectPlay4::Receive* method. This method is defined as:

```
HRESULT Receive(
    LPDPID lpidFrom,
    LPDPID lpidTo,
    DWORD dwFlags,
    LPVOID lpData,
    LPDWORD lpdwDataSize
);
```

Parameter	Description
lpidFrom	Address of a variable to receive the sender's player ID. If the DPRECEIVE_FROMPLAYER flag is specified, this variable must be initialized with the player ID before calling this method.
lpidTo	Address of a variable to receive the receiver's player ID. If the DPRECEIVE_TOPLAYER flag is specified, this variable must be initialized with the player ID before calling this method.
dwFlags	One or more of the following control flags can be set. By default (*dwFlags* = 0), the first available message will be retrieved.
	DPRECEIVE_ALL Returns the first available message. This is the default.
	DPRECEIVE_PEEK Returns a message as specified by the other flags but doesn't remove it from the message queue. This flag must be specified if *lpData* is NULL.
	DPRECEIVE_TOPLAYER and DPRECEIVE_FROMPLAYER If both DPRECEIVE_TOPLAYER and DPRECEIVE_FROMPLAYER are specified, *Receive* will only return messages that are (1) sent to the player specified by *lpidTo* and (2) sent from the player specified by *lpidFrom*. Both conditions must be met. If only DPRECEIVE_TOPLAYER is specified, *Receive* will only return messages sent to the player specified by *lpidTo*. If only DPRECEIVE_FROMPLAYER is specified, *Receive* will only return messages sent from the player specified by *lpidFrom*. If neither DPRECEIVE_TOPLAYER nor DPRECEIVE_FROMPLAYER is set, *Receive* will return the first available message.
lpData	Pointer to a buffer where the message data is to be written. Set this parameter to NULL to request only the size of data. The *lpdwDataSize* parameter will be set to the size required to hold the data. If the message came from player ID DPID_SYSMSG, the application should cast *lpData* to DPMSG_GENERIC and check the *dwType* member to see what type of system message it is before processing it.
lpdwDataSize	Pointer to a DWORD that is initialized to the size of the buffer before calling this method. After the method returns, this parameter will be set to the number of bytes copied into the buffer. If the buffer was too small (DPERR_BUFFERTOOSMALL), this parameter will be set to the buffer size required.

This method is used to get a DPLCONNECTION structure holding the information necessary to start and connect the application to a gaming session.

Once a message is received by the *ProcessDirectPlayMessage* routine, pass it (stored in the *puMsgBuffer* variable) to *HandleSystemMessages*, if the message is a system message (indicated by the DPID_SYSMSG ID) or *HandleAppMessages*, if the message is an application-specific (in our case, RoadRage) message.

This routine is defined as follows:

```
HRESULT ProcessDirectPlayMessages( HWND hDlg )
{
    DPID    idFrom;
    DPID    idTo;
    LPVOID  pvMsgBuffer;
    DWORD   dwMsgBufferSize;
    HRESULT hr;


    if(g_pDP == NULL)
        return FALSE;

    // Read all messages in the queue.
    dwMsgBufferSize = g_dwDPMsgBufferSize;
    pvMsgBuffer     = g_pvDPMsgBuffer;

    while( TRUE )
    {
        // See what's out there.
        idFrom = 0;
        idTo   = 0;

        hr = g_pDP->Receive( &idFrom, &idTo, DPRECEIVE_ALL,
                             pvMsgBuffer, &dwMsgBufferSize );

        if( hr == DPERR_BUFFERTOOSMALL )
        {
            // The current buffer was too small,
            // so reallocate it and try again.
            SAFE_DELETE_ARRAY( pvMsgBuffer );

            pvMsgBuffer = new BYTE[ dwMsgBufferSize ];
            if( pvMsgBuffer == NULL )
                return E_OUTOFMEMORY;

            // Save new buffer in global variables.
            g_pvDPMsgBuffer     = pvMsgBuffer;
            g_dwDPMsgBufferSize = dwMsgBufferSize;

            continue; // Now that the buffer is bigger, try again.
        }
```

```
if( DPERR_NOMESSAGES == hr )
    return S_OK;

if( FAILED(hr) )
    return hr;

// Handle the messages. Messages from DPID_SYSMSG are system
// messages; messages from elsewhere are application messages.
if( idFrom == DPID_SYSMSG )
{
    hr = HandleSystemMessages( hDlg,
                        (DPMSG_GENERIC*)pvMsgBuffer,
                        dwMsgBufferSize, idFrom, idTo );
    if( FAILED(hr) )
        return hr;
}
else
{
    hr = HandleAppMessages( hDlg,
                        (GAMEMSG_GENERIC*)pvMsgBuffer,
                        dwMsgBufferSize, idFrom, idTo );
    if( FAILED(hr) )
        return hr;
}
}

return S_OK;
}
```

The *SendPlayerInfoMessage* routine verifies that the mode is multiplayer mode. If it is, the routine creates a message containing the message type, the player number, the number of players in the gaming session, the player ID, and the player name. It then sends the message to all the other players (indicated by the DPID_ALLPLAYERS flag) by using the *IDirectPlay4::SendEx* method. This method is defined as follows:

```
HRESULT SendEx(
    DPID idFrom,
    DPID idTo,
    DWORD dwFlags,
    LPVOID lpData,
    DWORD dwDataSize,
    DWORD dwPriority,
    DWORD dwTimeout,
    LPVOID lpContext,
    LPDWORD lpdwMsgID
);
```

Parameter	Description
idFrom	ID of the sending player. The player ID must correspond to one of the local players on the computer from which the message is sent.
idTo	The destination ID of the message. To send a message to another player, specify the ID of the player. To send a message to all the players in a group, specify the ID of the group. To send a message to all the players in the session, use the constant symbol DPID_ALLPLAYERS. To send a message to the server player, specify the constant symbol DPID_SERVERPLAYER. A player can't send a message to himself or herself.
dwFlags	Indicates how the message should be sent. By default (*dwFlags* = 0), the message is sent nonguaranteed.
	DPSEND_ASYNC Sends the message asynchronously. The function returns immediately and fills in the *lpdwMsgID* parameter. If this flag isn't specified, the function doesn't return until the message has been sent (and acknowledged, if sent guaranteed). A DPMSG_SENDCOMPLETE system message is posted when the send has completed. When this flag is used, the return value will be DPERR_PENDING if the message is put in the send queue. This is not a fatal error but rather a return value that lets you know the message didn't get sent immediately.
	DPSEND_ENCRYPTED Sends the messages encrypted. This can be done only in a secure session. This flag can be used only if the DPSEND_GUARANTEED flag is also set. The message will be sent as a DPMSG_SECUREMESSAGE system message.
	DPSEND_GUARANTEED Sends the message by using a guaranteed method of delivery if it is available.
	DPSEND_NOSENDCOMPLETEMSG If this flag is set, no completion message is posted. This flag can be used only if the DPSEND_ASYNC flag is also set.
	DPSEND_SIGNED Sends the message with a digital signature. This can be done only in a secure session. This flag can be used only if the DPSEND_GUARANTEED flag is also set. The message will be sent as a DPMSG_SECUREMESSAGE system message.
lpData	Pointer to the data being sent.
dwDataSize	Length of the data being sent.

Parameter	Description
dwPriority	Priority of the message in the range from 0 through 65535. Zero is the lowest priority message. A larger number indicates a message with a higher priority. A message with a given priority will be sent only when there are no messages in the queue with a higher priority.
	Not all service providers support this option. If it isn't supported, specifying a nonzero priority will return a DPERR_ UNSUPPORTED error. Call *GetCaps* to determine whether this option is supported.
dwTimeout	Optional application-supplied time-out, in milliseconds, that specifies a time limit for delivering the message. If the message can't be delivered within this time, it is automatically canceled and a DPMSG_SENDCOMPLETE message is posted. Zero indicates that no time-out should be used.
	Not all service providers support this option. If it isn't supported, specifying a nonzero time-out will return a DPERR_ UNSUPPORTED error. Call *GetCaps* to determine whether this option is supported.
lpContext	An application-defined context that is returned to the application as part of the completion message when the send has been completed. Can be NULL.
lpdwMsgID	Pointer to a DWORD that will be filled in with a DirectPlay-generated ID for the message. Use this ID to check the status of the message or to cancel it. Pass NULL if no message ID is needed. This parameter is returned only for asynchronous messages.

The *SendPlayerInfoMessage* routine follows:

```
HRESULT SendPlayerInfoMessage(DWORD player_id, BYTE player_num,
               char *player_name, BYTE num_players, DWORD dwType)
{
    LPMSG_PLAYER_INFO lpPIMessage = NULL;
    DWORD dwPIMessageSize = NULL;
    HRESULT    hr;
    FILE *fp;
    DWORD player_name_length;

    if(pCMyApp->multiplay_flag == FALSE)
        return NULL;
```

(continued)

```
    player_name_length = lstrlen(player_name);

    // Create space for message and player's name.
    dwPIMessageSize = sizeof(MSG_PLAYER_INFO) + player_name_length;
    lpPIMessage = (LPMSG_PLAYER_INFO) GlobalAllocPtr(GHND,
                                                    dwPIMessageSize);
    if (lpPIMessage == NULL)
    {
        hr = DPERR_OUTOFMEMORY;
        goto FAILURE;
    }

    // Build message.
    lpPIMessage->dwType   = dwType;
    lpPIMessage->player_number = player_num;
    lpPIMessage->num_players = num_players;
    lpPIMessage->RRnetID = player_id;
    lstrcpy(lpPIMessage->name, player_name);

    fp = fopen("rrlogfile.txt","a");

    fprintf( fp, "\n Send APPMSG_PLAYER_LIST -----\n");
    fprintf( fp, "player_id      : %d\n", player_id);
    fprintf( fp, "player_number : %d\n", player_num);
    fprintf( fp, "num_players    : %d\n", num_players);
    fprintf( fp, "-------------------\n\n");

    fclose(fp);


    // Send this string to all other players if you are the server.
    hr = g_pDP->SendEx(pCMyApp->MyRRnetID, DPID_ALLPLAYERS,
                    DPSEND_GUARANTEED,
                    lpPIMessage, dwPIMessageSize , 1,
                    time_out_period,
                    NULL, NULL);


    if(hr == DP_OK || DPERR_PENDING)
        pCMyApp->num_packets_sent++;
    else
        goto FAILURE;

    return (hr);

FAILURE:
```

```
    if (lpPIMessage)
        GlobalFreePtr(lpPIMessage);

    return (hr);
}
```

The next routine, *SendActionDWordMessage*, is similar to the *SendPlayer-InfoMessage* routine, but it creates a message containing a DWORD for player actions (such as the APPMSG_HIT message when a player is hit) rather than player information:

```
HRESULT SendActionDWordMessage(DWORD RRnetID, DWORD action_dword,
                               DWORD dwType, DWORD SendTo)
{
    LPMSG_ACTIONDWORDINFO lpADWMessage = NULL;
    DWORD dwADWMessageSize = 0;
    HRESULT    hr;

    if(pCMyApp->multiplay_flag == FALSE)
        return NULL;

    // Create space for message.
    dwADWMessageSize = sizeof(MSG_ACTIONDWORDINFO);
    lpADWMessage = (LPMSG_ACTIONDWORDINFO) GlobalAllocPtr(GHND,
                                             dwADWMessageSize);
    if (lpADWMessage == NULL)
    {
        hr = DPERR_OUTOFMEMORY;
        goto FAILURE;
    }

    // Build message.
    lpADWMessage->dwType   = dwType;
    lpADWMessage->RRnetID = pCMyApp->MyRRnetID;
    lpADWMessage->action_dword = action_dword;

    // Send this string to all other players.

    hr = g_pDP->SendEx(RRnetID, SendTo, DPSEND_GUARANTEED,
                       lpADWMessage, sizeof(MSG_ACTIONDWORDINFO),
                       1, 0, NULL, NULL);

    if(hr == DP_OK || DPERR_PENDING)
        pCMyApp->num_packets_sent++;
    else
        goto FAILURE;
```

(continued)

```
        return (hr);

FAILURE:

    if (lpADWMessage)
        GlobalFreePtr(lpADWMessage);

    return (hr);
}
```

The next routine, *SendActionFloatMessage*, is again similar to the *SendPlayer-InfoMessage* routine, but it creates a message-handling server and client messages (such as APPMSG_PING_TO_SERVER) rather than player information:

```
HRESULT SendActionFloatMessage(DWORD RRnetID, float action_float,
                               DWORD dwType, DWORD SendTo)
{
    LPMSG_ACTIONFLOATINFO lpADWMessage = NULL;
    DWORD dwADWMessageSize = 0;
    HRESULT    hr;

    if(pCMyApp->multiplay_flag == FALSE)
        return NULL;

    // Create space for message.
    dwADWMessageSize = sizeof(MSG_ACTIONFLOATINFO);
    lpADWMessage = (LPMSG_ACTIONFLOATINFO) GlobalAllocPtr(GHND,
                                                dwADWMessageSize);
    if (lpADWMessage == NULL)
    {
        hr = DPERR_OUTOFMEMORY;
        goto FAILURE;
    }

    // Build message.
    lpADWMessage->dwType  = dwType;
    lpADWMessage->RRnetID = RRnetID;
    lpADWMessage->action_float = action_float;

    // Send this message to all other players.

    hr = g_pDP->SendEx(RRnetID, SendTo, DPSEND_ASYNC, lpADWMessage,
                    sizeof(MSG_ACTIONFLOATINFO) , 1,
                    time_out_period, NULL, NULL);

    if(hr == DP_OK || DPERR_PENDING)
        pCMyApp->num_packets_sent++;
    else
```

```
            goto FAILURE;

        return (hr);

FAILURE:

        if (lpADWMessage)
            GlobalFreePtr(lpADWMessage);

        PrintMessage(NULL, "SendActionFloatMessage : FAILED", NULL,
                    LOGFILE_ONLY);
        return (hr);
}
```

Another routine we need to create is *SendChatMessage*. RoadRage provides the capability to send chat-style messages to other players in a gaming session (triggered by pressing the Tab key during a multiplayer gaming session). Once the user has typed a message, pressing Enter sends it to the other players. This capability adds to the fun when you're playing long distance because you can talk back and forth with the other players as the game progresses.

```
HRESULT SendChatMessage(DWORD RRnetID, char *pChatStr)
{
    LPMSG_CHATSTRING    lpChatMessage     = NULL;
    DWORD               dwChatMessageSize;
    HRESULT             hr;

    if(pCMyApp->multiplay_flag == FALSE)
        return NULL;

    // Create space for message plus string (string length included
    // in message header).
    dwChatMessageSize = sizeof(MSG_CHATSTRING) + lstrlen(pChatStr);
    lpChatMessage = (LPMSG_CHATSTRING) GlobalAllocPtr(GHND,
                                                    dwChatMessageSize);

    if (lpChatMessage == NULL)
    {
        hr = DPERR_OUTOFMEMORY;
        goto FAILURE;
    }

    // Build message.
    lpChatMessage->dwType = APPMSG_CHATSTRING;
    lstrcpy(lpChatMessage->szMsg, pChatStr);
```

(continued)

```
        // Send this string to all other players.
        hr = g_pDP->SendEx(RRnetID, DPID_ALLPLAYERS, DPSEND_ASYNC,
                            lpChatMessage, dwChatMessageSize, 1,
                            time_out_period, NULL, NULL);

        if(hr == DP_OK || DPERR_PENDING)
            pCMyApp->num_packets_sent++;
        else
            goto FAILURE;

        return (hr);

FAILURE:

        if (lpChatMessage)
            GlobalFreePtr(lpChatMessage);

        return (hr);
}
```

If a player has fired her character's gun, the first call is to *StopDSound*. This routine verifies that DirectSound is initialized, and if it is, calls *SndObjStop*.

The *PlayDSound* routine is then called. This routine calls *SndObjPlay*, which plays the sound by using the *IDirectSoundBuffer_Play* routine as long as DirectPlay is initialized.

Now that the sound associated with the character's action has been played, the DirectPlay task associated with this action can be performed. In this case, we need to send a message to the other players indicating we are firing our weapon.

To do this, we call the *SendActionWordMessage* routine indicating which gun is firing and specifying the *APPMSG_FIRE* message. This routine is one of three routines we define for the three message types we'll be sending or receiving.

The *SendActionWordMessage* routine is defined as follows:

```
HRESULT SendActionWordMessage(DWORD RRnetID, int action_word,
                              DWORD dwType)
{
    LPMSG_ACTIONWORDINFO lpAWMessage = NULL;
    DWORD dwAWMessageSize = 0;
    HRESULT    hr;

    if(pCMyApp->multiplay_flag == FALSE)
        return NULL;

    // Create space for message.
    dwAWMessageSize = sizeof(MSG_ACTIONWORDINFO);
    lpAWMessage = (LPMSG_ACTIONWORDINFO) GlobalAllocPtr(GHND,
                                            dwAWMessageSize);
```

```
    if (lpAWMessage == NULL)
    {
        hr = DPERR_OUTOFMEMORY;
        goto FAILURE;
    }

    // Build message.
    lpAWMessage->dwType  = dwType;
    lpAWMessage->RRnetID = pCMyApp->MyRRnetID;
    lpAWMessage->action_word = action_word;

    // Send this string to all other players.

    hr = g_pDP->SendEx(RRnetID, DPID_ALLPLAYERS, DPSEND_ASYNC,
                       lpAWMessage, sizeof(MSG_ACTIONWORDINFO), 2,
                       time_out_period, NULL, NULL);

    if(hr == DP_OK || DPERR_PENDING)
        pCMyApp->num_packets_sent++;
    else
        goto FAILURE;

    return (hr);

FAILURE:

    if (lpAWMessage)
        GlobalFreePtr(lpAWMessage);

    return (hr);
}
```

The *SendActionWordMessage* routine verifies that we're in a multiplayer game. If we are, it allocates space for our message and then constructs it. The three parameters we specify for this message are *dwType*, *RRnetID*, and *action_word*. These parameters define the type of message we are sending, who is sending it (defined by our ID), and the action word that specifies which action our character is performing. In this case, we have passed APPMSG_FIRE to this routine, so we're indicating that we're firing our weapon.

The *UpdatePosCallBack* routine, used to update our position in the 3D world, first calls *ReceiveMessage*, which loops until it successfully reads a message. Once a message is read, *ReceiveMessage* determines whether the message is a system message or an application message. Finally, we call the *SendPositionMessage* routine to send out a message telling the other players where we are. (We'll go over this routine shortly.)

The *UpdatePosCallBack* routine is defined as follows:

```
BOOL CALLBACK UpdatePosCallBack(UINT uTimerID,
        UINT uMsg, DWORD dwUser, DWORD dw1, DWORD dw2)

{

    int player_num;


    if(pCMyApp->multiplay_flag == FALSE)
        return FALSE;

    ProcessDirectPlayMessages( NULL );

    player_num = GetPlayerNumber(pCMyApp->MyRRnetID);
    if(player_num == RRnetID_ERROR)
    {
        PrintMessage(NULL,"IsPlayerHit - UpdatePosCallBack FAILED",
                    NULL, LOGFILE_ONLY);
        return FALSE;
    }

    SendPositionMessage(pCMyApp->MyRRnetID,
                    pCMyApp->m_vEyePt.x,
                    pCMyApp->m_vEyePt.y,
                    pCMyApp->m_vEyePt.z,
                    pCMyApp->angy,
                    pCMyApp->have_i_moved_flag );

    return TRUE;
}
```

The *SendPositionMessage* routine takes the (x, y, z) location and view angle of the player. As long as we're in multiplayer mode, this routine allocates space for our position message and fills it with the position and the view angle, our player's ID, and the APPMSG_POSITION message type to indicate that the new message is a position message. By passing this message, we tell the other systems connected to the gaming session our newest position so that their 3D representations of our character can be rendered and animated.

```
HRESULT SendPositionMessage(DWORD RRnetID, float x, float y, float z,
                        float view_angle, BOOL IsRunning)
{
    LPMSG_POS lpPosMessage    = NULL;
    DWORD     dwPosMessageSize = NULL;
    HRESULT   hr;
```

```
        if(pCMyApp->multiplay_flag == FALSE)
            return NULL;

        // Create space for message.
        dwPosMessageSize = sizeof(MSG_POS);
        lpPosMessage = (LPMSG_POS) GlobalAllocPtr(GHND,
                                            dwPosMessageSize);
        if (lpPosMessage == NULL)
        {
            hr = DPERR_OUTOFMEMORY;
            goto FAILURE;
        }

        // Build message.
        lpPosMessage->dwType    = APPMSG_POSITION;
        lpPosMessage->x_pos = x;
        lpPosMessage->y_pos = 0;
        lpPosMessage->z_pos = z;
        lpPosMessage->view_angle = (WORD)view_angle;
        lpPosMessage->IsRunning  = IsRunning;

        hr = g_pDP->SendEx(RRnetID, DPID_ALLPLAYERS, DPSEND_ASYNC,
                        lpPosMessage, sizeof(MSG_POS) , 1,
                        time_out_period, NULL, NULL);

        if(hr == DP_OK || DPERR_PENDING)
            pCMyApp->num_packets_sent++;
        else
            goto FAILURE;

        return (hr);

FAILURE:

        if (lpPosMessage)
            GlobalFreePtr(lpPosMessage);

        return (hr);
}
```

The *HandleSystemMessage* we called in the *ReceiveMessage* routine earlier checks the message type of any system message we receive. If the message type is DPSYS_CREATEPLAYERORGROUP, we create a new player, getting the player name and initializing the player data for this new player. The data passed via this message includes the player position, name, weapon number, and so on.

```
//-------------------------------------------------------------------
// Name: HandleSystemMessages
// Desc: Evaluates system messages and performs appropriate actions
//-------------------------------------------------------------------
HRESULT HandleSystemMessages( HWND hDlg, DPMSG_GENERIC* pMsg,
                              DWORD dwMsgSize,
                              DPID idFrom, DPID idTo )
{
    LPSTR    lpszStr = NULL;
    LPDPMSG_CREATEPLAYERORGROUP
             lp = (LPDPMSG_CREATEPLAYERORGROUP) pMsg;
    LPSTR    lpszPlayerName;
    LPSTR    szDisplayFormat = "%s has joined";

    FILE *fp;
    int i;
    int player;


    switch( pMsg->dwType )
    {
        case DPSYS_SESSIONLOST:
            // Non-host message. This message is sent to all
            // players when the host exits the game.

            PrintMessage(NULL, "DPSYS_SESSIONLOST - host has quit",
                        NULL, LOGFILE_ONLY);
            if( g_bHostPlayer )
                return E_FAIL; // Sanity check
            AddDpChatMessageToDisplay( "Host has quit the game" );
            PostQuitMessage( DPERR_SESSIONLOST );
            break;

        case DPSYS_HOST:
            PrintMessage(NULL, "DPSYS_HOST - you are now the host",
                        NULL, LOGFILE_ONLY);
            g_bHostPlayer = TRUE;
            pCMyApp->MyPing = 0;
            AddDpChatMessageToDisplay( "You are now the host" );
            break;

        case DPSYS_CREATEPLAYERORGROUP:
            DPMSG_CREATEPLAYERORGROUP* pCreateMsg;
            pCreateMsg = (DPMSG_CREATEPLAYERORGROUP*) pMsg;
```

```
// Update the number of active players.
g_dwNumberOfActivePlayers++;

// Get pointer to player name.
if (lp->dpnName.lpszShortNameA)
    lpszPlayerName = lp->dpnName.lpszShortNameA;
else
    lpszPlayerName = "unknown";

for(i = 0; i < MAX_NUM_PLAYERS; i++)
{
    if( pCMyApp->player_list[i].bIsPlayerValid == FALSE )
    {
        player = i;
        pCMyApp->player_list[i].bIsPlayerValid = TRUE;
        break;
    }
}

fp = fopen("rrlogfile.txt","a");
fprintf( fp, "\n receive DPSYS_CREATEPLAYERORGROUP \n");
fprintf( fp, "player_id     : %d\n", lp->dpId);
fprintf( fp, "player_number : %d\n", player);
fprintf( fp, "------------------\n\n");
fclose(fp);

pCMyApp->player_list[player].x = 500;
pCMyApp->player_list[player].y = 12;
pCMyApp->player_list[player].z = 500;
pCMyApp->player_list[player].rot_angle = 0;
pCMyApp->player_list[player].model_id = 0;
pCMyApp->player_list[player].skin_tex_id = 27;
pCMyApp->player_list[player].ping = 0;
pCMyApp->player_list[player].health = 100;
pCMyApp->player_list[player].bIsPlayerAlive = TRUE;
pCMyApp->player_list[player].bStopAnimating = FALSE;
pCMyApp->player_list[player].current_weapon = 0;
pCMyApp->player_list[player].current_car = 0;
pCMyApp->player_list[player].current_frame = 0;
pCMyApp->player_list[player].current_sequence = 0;
pCMyApp->player_list[player].bIsPlayerInWalkMode = TRUE;
pCMyApp->player_list[player].RRnetID = lp->dpId;
pCMyApp->num_players++;
```

(continued)

```
strcpy(pCMyApp->player_list[player].name,
       lpszPlayerName);

if(g_bHostPlayer == TRUE)
{
    for(i = 0; i < MAX_NUM_PLAYERS; i++)
    {
        if(pCMyApp->player_list[i].bIsPlayerValid ==
           TRUE)
        {
            SendPlayerInfoMessage(
                pCMyApp->player_list[i].RRnetID,
                i,
                pCMyApp->player_list[i].name,
                pCMyApp->num_players,
                APPMSG_PLAYER_LIST );
        }
    }

    strcpy(buffer, lpszPlayerName);
    strcat(buffer, " has joined the game");
    AddDpChatMessageToDisplay( buffer );
}

DisplayNumberPlayersInGame( hDlg );
break;
```

If the message type is DPSYS_DESTROYPLAYERORGROUP, indicating a player or group is leaving the gaming session, we call *GetPlayerNumber*, which determines which player has the *RRnetID* value we're looking for. We then call *AddDpChatMessageToDisplay* to create and post the message "Player [player name] has left the game" to all the other players to notify them that we're exiting the game. Next we decrement the global variable *g_dwNumberOfActivePlayers*, which defines the number of players in the game, and call *DisplayNumberPlayersInGame* to display this information.

```
case DPSYS_DESTROYPLAYERORGROUP:
    DPMSG_DESTROYPLAYERORGROUP* pDeleteMsg;
    pDeleteMsg = (DPMSG_DESTROYPLAYERORGROUP*) pMsg;
```

```
            fp = fopen("rrlogfile.txt","a");
            fprintf( fp, "\n receive DPSYS_DESTROYPLAYERORGROUP \n");

            player = GetPlayerNumber(pDeleteMsg->dpId);
            if(player == RRnetID_ERROR)
            {
                PrintMessage(NULL,
                    "IsPlayerHit - DPSYS_DESTROYPLAYERORGROUP FAILED",
                    NULL, LOGFILE_ONLY);
                break;
            }
            pCMyApp->player_list[player].bIsPlayerValid = FALSE;

            fprintf( fp, "player_id       : %d\n", pDeleteMsg->dpId);
            fprintf( fp, "player_number : %d\n", player);
            fprintf( fp, "------------------\n\n");
            fclose(fp);

            strcpy(buffer, pCMyApp->player_list[player].name);
            strcat(buffer, " has left the game");
            AddDpChatMessageToDisplay( buffer );

            // Update the number of active players.
            g_dwNumberOfActivePlayers--;

            DisplayNumberPlayersInGame( hDlg );
            break;
    }

    return S_OK;
}
```

If the message type is DPSYS_HOST, we know that the current session host has exited the session. This means that we now need to become the host to allow everyone else to continue playing if the person who initiated the session decides to exit. To indicate that we are now the host, we set our *bIsHost* flag to TRUE.

```
case DPSYS_HOST:
    PrintMessage(NULL, "DPSYS_HOST - you are now the host",
                NULL, LOGFILE_ONLY);
    g_bHostPlayer = TRUE;
    pCMyApp->MyPing = 0;
    AddDpChatMessageToDisplay( "You are now the host" );
    break;
```

Besides handling the system messages, we need to handle the application-specific messages. Application-specific messages are those that we create for our application rather than those that are generated by DirectPlay when certain events occur. We handle any application-specific messages with *HandleApplicationMessage*, which we call in the *ReceiveMessage* routine (discussed earlier) whenever an application-specific message is received.

The *HandleAppMessage* routine is rather long, so I won't show it all here. You can find it in the file dpmessages.cpp on the companion CD.

The first application-specific message we receive in the RoadRage code (and handled by the *HandleApplicationMessage* routine) is the APPMSG_GESTURE message. When this message is received, we determine which player made this gesture by calling *GetPlayerNumber*. This simple routine finds the player that matches the net ID (*RRnetID*) that was passed in.

GetPlayerNumber is defined as follows:

```
int GetPlayerNumber(DWORD dpid)
{
    int i;

    for(i = 0; i < pCMyApp->num_players; i++)
    {
        if(pCMyApp->player_list[i].bIsPlayerValid == TRUE)
        {
            if(pCMyApp->player_list[i].RRnetID == dpid)
                return i;

        }
    }

    PrintMessage(NULL, "GetPlayerNumber: Failed to get player ID",
                NULL, LOGFILE_ONLY);
    return RRnetID_ERROR;
}
```

We then set the current animation sequence to the starting frame of the animation sequence for the gesture sequence so that this motion can be played.

NOTE In Quake terminology, a *gesture* is a specific motion made by the 3D virtual character. When creating your own Quake character (using a tool such as the Quake 2 Modeller contained on this book's CD), you can decide what you want this motion to look like.

The next RoadRage application message we can receive is the APPMSG_ CHANGE_WEAPON_TO message. When this message is received, we determine which player is switching weapons. We then set the weapon of that player to the new weapon so that the player will be rendered and animated with the correct weapon.

```
case APPMSG_CHANGE_WEAPON_TO:
    lpActionWord = (LPMSG_ACTIONWORDINFO)pMsg;
    player_num = GetPlayerNumber(idFrom);
    //lpActionWord->RRnetID);
    if(player_num == RRnetID_ERROR)
    {
        PrintMessage(NULL,
            "IsPlayerHit - APPMSG_CHANGE_WEAPON_TO FAILED",
            NULL, LOGFILE_ONLY);
        break;
    }
    pCMyApp->player_list[player_num].current_weapon =
        lpActionWord->action_word;
    pCMyApp->num_packets_received++;
    break;
```

The next application message we can receive is the APPMSG_FIRE message, which indicates that someone is firing a weapon using the *GetPlayerNumber* routine. When this message is received, we determine which player is firing and what weapon she has. We then set up the sequence of frames for firing this weapon so that the player model is animated correctly for firing the current weapon. Finally, we play the DirectSound sound associated with the firing of this weapon.

```
case APPMSG_FIRE:
    lpActionWord = (LPMSG_ACTIONWORDINFO)pMsg;
    player_num   = GetPlayerNumber(lpActionWord->RRnetID);
    if(player_num == RRnetID_ERROR)
    {
        PrintMessage(NULL,"IsPlayerHit - APPMSG_FIRE FAILED",
                    NULL, LOGFILE_ONLY);
```

(continued)

393

```
            break;
        }
        curr_wep = lpActionWord->action_word;

        pCMyApp->player_list[player_num].bIsFiring = TRUE;

        if(pCMyApp->player_list[player_num].current_sequence != 2)
        {
            if(pCMyApp->player_list[player_num].bIsPlayerAlive ==
                TRUE)
                pCMyApp->SetPlayerAnimationSequence(player_num, 2);

        }
        pCMyApp->StopBuffer(TRUE, 0);
        pCMyApp->PlaySound(0, NULL);

        pCMyApp->num_packets_received++;
        break;
```

We can also receive the APPMSG_WALK_OR_DRIVE application message, which is sent when we switch between driving and walking mode in RoadRage. This code block sets the flag for the player switching modes so that it is rendered properly. Two other messages we can receive are APPMSG_JUMP and APPMSG_ CROUCH. These messages will trigger the character to perform the walk or jump motions in the same manner as the APPMSG_GESTURE message. For details on this code, see the code for this chapter on the companion CD.

```
    case APPMSG_WALK_OR_DRIVE:
        lpActionFlag = (LPMSG_ACTIONFLAGINFO)pMsg;
        player_num = GetPlayerNumber(lpActionFlag->RRnetID);
        if(player_num == RRnetID_ERROR)
        {
            PrintMessage(NULL,
                "IsPlayerHit - APPMSG_WALK_OR_DRIVE FAILED",
                NULL, LOGFILE_ONLY);
            break;
        }
        pCMyApp->player_list[player_num].bIsPlayerInWalkMode =
            lpActionFlag->action_flag;
        pCMyApp->num_packets_received++;
        break;

    case APPMSG_RESPAWN:
        lpActionFlag = (LPMSG_ACTIONFLAGINFO)pMsg;
        player_num = GetPlayerNumber(lpActionFlag->RRnetID);
        if(player_num == RRnetID_ERROR)
        {
            PrintMessage(NULL,
                "IsPlayerHit - APPMSG_RESPAWN FAILED", NULL,
                LOGFILE_ONLY);
```

```
        break;
    }
    pCMyApp->player_list[player_num].bIsPlayerAlive = TRUE;
    pCMyApp->player_list[player_num].bStopAnimating = FALSE;
    pCMyApp->player_list[player_num].current_weapon = 0;
    pCMyApp->player_list[player_num].current_car = 0;
    pCMyApp->player_list[player_num].current_frame = 0;
    pCMyApp->player_list[player_num].current_sequence = 0;
    pCMyApp->player_list[player_num].bIsPlayerInWalkMode =
        TRUE;
    pCMyApp->player_list[player_num].health = 100;
    pCMyApp->num_packets_received++;
    break;

case APPMSG_JUMP:
    pCMyApp->num_packets_received++;
    break;

case APPMSG_CROUCH:
    pCMyApp->num_packets_received++;
    break;
```

We can also receive the APPMSG_POSITION RoadRage application message, which is sent whenever a player moves. We first determine which player this message is from by calling the *GetPlayerName* routine and passing it the players network ID (*RRnetID*).

The APPMSG_POSITION message also contains the (*x*, *y*, *z*) position information in the *x_pos*, *y_pos*, and *z_pos* members. Additionally, the *view_angle* member is used to determine the direction the player is facing. Finally, if the *IsRunning* member is set to TRUE, we set up the character animation to play the running motion so that the character runs through our virtual world as we reposition him according to the player's selection of motion via the keyboard or joystick.

```
case APPMSG_POSITION:
    lpPos = (LPMSG_POS)pMsg;
    player_num = GetPlayerNumber(idFrom);
    //lpPos->RRnetID);
    if(player_num == RRnetID_ERROR)
    {
        PrintMessage(NULL,
            "IsPlayerHit - APPMSG_POSITION FAILED", NULL,
            LOGFILE_ONLY);
        break;
    }
    pCMyApp->player_list[player_num].x = lpPos->x_pos;
    pCMyApp->player_list[player_num].y = lpPos->y_pos+12;
```

(continued)

```
pCMyApp->player_list[player_num].z = lpPos->z_pos;
pCMyApp->player_list[player_num].rot_angle =
    lpPos->view_angle;
pCMyApp->player_list[player_num].bIsRunning =
    lpPos->IsRunning;

if(lpPos->IsRunning == TRUE)
{
    if(pCMyApp->player_list[player_num].current_sequence
       != 1)
    {
        if(pCMyApp->player_list[player_num].bIsPlayerAlive
           == TRUE)
            pCMyApp->SetPlayerAnimationSequence(
                player_num, 1);
    }
}
pCMyApp->num_packets_received++;
break;
```

The final message we need to handle for the RoadRage program is the APPMSG_CHATSTRING message. This message allows us to pass textual messages to other players so that we can talk to them during a multiplayer session.

The code to handle a chat string message follows:

```
case APPMSG_CHATSTRING:
    LPMSG_CHATSTRING   lpszStr = (LPMSG_CHATSTRING) pMsg;

    // Post string to chat window.
    if (lpszStr)
    {
        if (lpszStr->szMsg[0] != 13 )
        {
            AddDpChatMessageToDisplay(lpszStr->szMsg);
            pCMyApp->num_packets_received++;
        }
    }
    break;
```

To create the chat string, call the *AddDpChatMessageToDisplay* routine. This routine copies the message string passed into the routine into the next line of the chat message we are readying to display to the other players.

```
void AddDpChatMessageToDisplay(char *msg)
{
    int i;

    if(DpChatMessage_counter < 4)
```

```
    {
        strcpy(DpChatMessages[DpChatMessage_counter], msg);
        DpChatMessage_counter++;
    }
    else
    {
        for(i = 0; i < 3; i++)
            strcpy(DpChatMessages[i], DpChatMessages[i+1] );

        strcpy(DpChatMessages[3], msg);

    }
}
```

The routine to display the message is *DisplayIncomingDpChatMessages*. It displays the lines of the chat message (up to four) by outputting the lines to the screen.

```
void DisplayIncomingDpChatMessages()
{
    int i;

    for(i = 0; i < 4; i++)
    {
        if(DpChatMessages[i])
            pCMyApp->OutputText(20,60+i*20, DpChatMessages[i]);
    }
}
```

The *SendActionFlagMessage* routine is the final routine for handling the RoadRage application-specific messages. This message is used when we enter or exit the car as we switch between walking and driving mode. As with the other message-handling routines, this routine first verifies that we are connected to a multiplayer session. If we are, it allocates space for a new message, and as long as the allocation is successful, it fills the message. The slots we fill are the *dwType*, *MyRRnetID*, and the *action_flag* slots. Once constructed, this message is sent to all the players in the gaming session.

```
HRESULT SendActionFlagMessage(DWORD RRnetID, BOOL action_flag,
                                DWORD dwType)
{
    LPMSG_ACTIONFLAGINFO lpAFMessage = NULL;
    DWORD dwAFMessageSize = NULL;
    HRESULT    hr;


    if(pCMyApp->multiplay_flag == FALSE)
        return NULL;
```

(continued)

```
        // Create space for message plus.
        dwAFMessageSize = sizeof(MSG_ACTIONFLAGINFO);

        lpAFMessage = (LPMSG_ACTIONFLAGINFO) GlobalAllocPtr(GHND,
                                                   dwAFMessageSize);
        if (lpAFMessage == NULL)
        {
            hr = DPERR_OUTOFMEMORY;
            goto FAILURE;
        }

        // Build message.
        lpAFMessage->dwType = dwType;
        lpAFMessage->RRnetID = pCMyApp->MyRRnetID;
        lpAFMessage->action_flag = action_flag;


        // Send this string to all other players if you are the server.

        hr = g_pDP->SendEx(RRnetID, DPID_ALLPLAYERS, DPSEND_GUARANTEED,
                           lpAFMessage, sizeof(MSG_ACTIONFLAGINFO) , 3,
                           time_out_period, NULL, NULL);

        if(hr == DP_OK || DPERR_PENDING)
            pCMyApp->num_packets_sent++;
        else
            goto FAILURE;

        return (hr);

FAILURE:

        if (lpAFMessage)
            GlobalFreePtr(lpAFMessage);

        return (hr);
}
```

We've now covered all the messages, both system and application, that we need to handle for RoadRage. Remember that the *SendActionWordMessage* routine supports messages indicating a gun is firing using the *APPMSG_FIRE* message. Once the calls are made to generate the animated sequence for firing the weapon, this routine calls the *IsPlayerHit* routine as the final step.

The *IsPlayerHit* routine determines whether the person firing hit a player. If a player is hit, a pop-up message is displayed. *IsPlayerHit* then calls *SendAction-WordMessage* to send an APPMSG_HIT message indicating that a player was hit. Although this routine is fairly long, it's pretty basic. The majority of the body just determines whether or not a character has been hit.

This routine is defined as follows:

```
//----------------------------------------------------------------
// Name: CMyD3DApplication::IsPlayerHit
// Desc: Determines whether one of the network players
//       is hit when you fire your weapon
//----------------------------------------------------------------
void CMyD3DApplication::IsPlayerHit()
{
    int i;
    int player_num;
    DWORD player_id;


    if(num_players == 0)
        return;

    for(i = 0; i < num_players; i++)
    {
        player_id = player_list[i].RRnetID;

        if( (player_list[i].RRnetID != MyRRnetID) &&
            (player_list[i].bIsPlayerValid == TRUE) &&
            (player_id > 0) )
        {
            gv_dx = player_list[i].x -m_vEyePt.x;
            gv_dz = player_list[i].z -m_vEyePt.z;

            gv_gradient    = gv_dz / gv_dx;
            gv_target_angle = -1 * ((float)180 / (float)3.14159) *
                                    (float)atan(gv_gradient);
            gv_distance    = (float)sqrt(gv_dx * gv_dx +
                                         gv_dz * gv_dz);

            gv_temp_angle   = (float)angy;

            if((gv_dx >= 0) && (gv_dz >= 0))
            {
                gv_quadrant = 0; //quadrant 1    0 to 90
                gv_target_angle = 90 + gv_target_angle;
            }

            if((gv_dx >= 0) && (gv_dz < 0))
                gv_quadrant = 90; //quadrant 2   90 to 180

            if((gv_dx < 0) && (gv_dz < 0))
            {
```

(continued)

```
            gv_quadrant = 180; //quadrant 3  180 to 270
            gv_target_angle = 90 + gv_target_angle;
        }

    if((gv_dx < 0) && (gv_dz >= 0))
            gv_quadrant = 270; //quadrant 4  270 to 360

    gv_target_angle += gv_quadrant;

    if (gv_temp_angle >= 360)
            gv_temp_angle = gv_temp_angle - 360;

    if (gv_temp_angle < 0)
            gv_temp_angle = gv_temp_angle + 360;

    if (gv_target_angle >= 360)
            gv_target_angle = gv_target_angle - 360;

    if (gv_target_angle < 0)
            gv_target_angle = gv_target_angle + 360;

    gv_da           = gv_temp_angle - gv_target_angle;
    gv_hit_width  = (float)(abs((int)((float)tan(k * gv_da) *
                                    gv_distance)));

    if(gv_hit_width < 10)
    {
        player_list[i].health -= 20;

        if(player_list[i].health >= 0)
        {
            player_num = GetPlayerNumber(MyRRnetID);
            if((player_num >= 0) &&
               (player_num < MAX_NUM_PLAYERS))
            {
                SendActionDWordMessage(MyRRnetID,
                        player_list[i].RRnetID,
                        APPMSG_HIT,
                        DPID_ALLPLAYERS);
            }
            else
                PrintMessage(NULL,
                    "IsPlayerHit - GetPlayerNumber FAILED",
                    NULL, LOGFILE_ONLY);
        }

        if(player_list[i].health <= 0)
        {
            if(player_list[i].bIsPlayerAlive == TRUE)
            {
```

```
                    SetPlayerAnimationSequence(i, 6);
                    player_list[i].bIsPlayerAlive = FALSE;
                    player_list[player_num].frags++;
                }
            }
        else
            SetPlayerAnimationSequence(i, 4);
        }
    }

    } // end for i loop
}
```

The final routine we need to create is the *CMyD3DApplication::SetPlayer-AnimationSequence* routine. This member function is used to set the current animation sequence we want to have a particular player's model use. The *sequence_number* variable specifies which of the motions we want to have the animated character perform (based on our input—or someone else's, depending on the player number).

The *start_frame,* which is the first frame in the animation sequence, is stored in the *current_frame* of the desired player so that we can play this sequence. Remember that *play* means to load each model and render it sequentially to create an animated motion.

```
void CMyD3DApplication::SetPlayerAnimationSequence(int player_number,
                                                    int sequence_number)
{
    int model_id;
    int start_frame;

    if(player_number >= num_players)
    {
        PrintMessage(NULL,
                    "SetPlayerAnimationSequence player_"
                    "number too large FAILED",
                    NULL, LOGFILE_ONLY);
        return;
    }
    player_list[player_number].current_sequence = sequence_number;

    if(sequence_number > 6)
    {
        PrintMessage(NULL,
                    "SetPlayerAnimationSequence - sequence_number "
                    "too large FAILED", NULL, LOGFILE_ONLY);
        return;
    }
```

(continued)

```
model_id = player_list[player_number].model_id;

if(model_id > MAX_NUM_PLAYERS)
{
    PrintMessage(NULL,
                 "SetPlayerAnimationSequence - model_id "
                 "too large FAILED",
                 NULL, LOGFILE_ONLY);
    return;
}

start_frame =
    pmdata[model_id].sequence_start_frame[sequence_number];
player_list[player_number].current_frame = start_frame;
}
```

With that, we've implemented nearly all the code necessary to turn RoadRage into a multiplayer game that supports all the available connection techniques (network, modem, and so on). A final necessary step is to create the code for allowing a character to exit from a multiplayer gaming session.

Ending the Game

When the game is complete (for example, if the user exits), you need to clean up. Simply destroy your player using the *IDirectPlay4::DestroyPlayer* method, which deletes a local player from the session. This method also removes any pending messages from the message queue that were intended for this player and removes the player from any groups she belonged to. Both the application that created the player and the session host can destroy the player. Here's the declaration for the *IDirectPlay4::DestroyPlayer* method:

```
HRESULT DestroyPlayer (
    DPID idPlayer
);
```

This function has only one parameter, *idPlayer*, which is the player ID of the locally owned player to remove from the session. When the session host calls *Destroy-Player*, the DPID can be that of any player, including the local player and any remote players.

You can then call *IDirectPlay4::Close* to close your DirectPlay connection. This method will move any groups that were created locally so that the session host owns them. *IDirectPlay4::Close* also will destroy any locally created players and send the DPMSG_DELETEPLAYERFROMGROUP and DPMSG_DESTROYPLAYER-ORGROUP system messages to the other players in the session. The definition of the DPMSG_DELETEPLAYERFROMGROUP structure follows:

```
typedef struct{
    DWORD dwType;
    DPID dpIdGroup;
    DPID dpIdPlayer;
} DPMSG_ADDPLAYERTOGROUP, FAR *LPDPMSG_ADDPLAYERTOGROUP;
typedef DPMSG_ADDPLAYERTOGROUP DPMSG_DELETEPLAYERFROMGROUP;
```

Parameter	Description
dwType	Identifies the message; this member is DPSYS_DELETEPLAYERFROMGROUP
dpIdGroup	ID of the group from which the player was removed
dpIdPlayer	ID of the player that was removed from the group

And here's the definition of the DPMSG_DESTROYPLAYERORGROUP structure:

```
typedef struct{
    DWORD   dwType;
    DWORD   dwPlayerType;
    DPID    dpId;
    LPVOID  lpLocalData;
    DWORD   dwLocalDataSize;
    LPVOID  lpRemoteDate;
    DWORD   dwRemoteDataSize;
    DPNAME  dpnName;
    DPID    dpIdParent;
    DWORD   dwFlags;
} DPMSG_DESTROYPLAYERORGROUP, FAR *LPDPMSG_DESTROYPLAYERORGROUP;
```

Parameter	Description
dwType	A DWORD that identifies the message. This member is DPSYS_DESTROYPLAYERORGROUP.
dwPlayerType	A DWORD that identifies whether the message applies to a player (DPPLAYERTYPE_PLAYER) or a group (DPPLAYERTYPE_GROUP).
dpId	ID of a player or group that's been destroyed.
lpLocalData	Pointer to the local data associated with this player or group.

(continued)

continued

Parameter	Description
dwLocalDataSize	Size, in bytes, of the local data.
lpRemoteData	Pointer to the remote data associated with this player or group.
dwRemoteDataSize	Size, in bytes, of the remote data.
dpnName	Structure containing the name of the player or group.
dpIdParent	ID of the parent group if the group being destroyed is a subgroup. (The group being destroyed was created by a call to *IDirectPlay4::CreateGroupInGroup*; otherwise, the value is 0.)
dwFlags	Player or group flags. This parameter takes one or more of the following values:
	DPGROUP_HIDDEN Set when a hidden group is destroyed
	DPGROUP_STAGINGAREA Set when a group that is a staging area is destroyed
	DPPLAYER_SERVERPLAYER Set when the player being destroyed is a server player for client/server communications
	DPPLAYER_SPECTATOR Set when the player destroyed is a spectator; a spectator player behaves exactly like a normal player except that the player is flagged as a spectator

The following code shows how to handle this:

```
void RrDestroyPlayer()
{
    if(pCMyApp->multiplay_flag == FALSE)
        return;

    timeKillEvent(pCMyApp->UpdatePosTimer);
    timeKillEvent(pCMyApp->FireWeaponTimer);

    if(g_pDP == NULL)
    {
        PrintMessage(NULL, "RrDestroyPlayer FAILED - g_pDP = NULL",
                    NULL, LOGFILE_ONLY);
        return;
    }
    else
        PrintMessage(NULL, "RrDestroyPlayer  - g_pDP ok ",
                    NULL, LOGFILE_ONLY);
```

```
    if(g_pDP->DestroyPlayer( g_LocalPlayerDPID ) != DP_OK)
    {
        PrintMessage(NULL, "RrDestroyPlayer FAILED - DestroyPlayer",
                    NULL, LOGFILE_ONLY);
        return;
    }
    else
        PrintMessage(NULL, "RrDestroyPlayer - DestroyPlayer ok",
                    NULL, LOGFILE_ONLY);

    if(g_pDP->Close() != DP_OK)
    {
        PrintMessage(NULL, "RrDestroyPlayer FAILED - Close",
                    NULL, LOGFILE_ONLY);
        return;
    }
    else
        PrintMessage(NULL, "RrDestroyPlayer - Close ok",
                    NULL, LOGFILE_ONLY);


    SAFE_DELETE_ARRAY( g_pDPLConnection );
    SAFE_RELEASE( g_pDPLobby );

    PrintMessage(NULL, "RrDestroyPlayer - disconnected ok",
                NULL, LOGFILE_ONLY);

    pCMyApp->multiplay_flag = FALSE;
    pCMyApp->num_players = 0;
}
```

As the final steps of the *WinMain* routine (and thus the program), we call the *CoUninitialize* function as well as *CloseHandle* for the registry key and message event that we created at the beginning of the game. The *CoUninitialize* function closes the COM library.

Finally, the calls to *CloseHandle*, passing the registry key and message event handle, will invalidate the object handles you pass and decrement each object's handle count. When the last handle of the object is closed, the object is removed from the system.

The Code So Far

Build and execute the code for this chapter. When you run the code, you'll see a dialog box like the one shown in Figure 15-5.

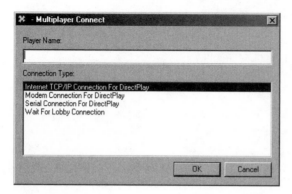

Figure 15-5
The Multiplayer Connect dialog box

Try selecting the type of connection you want to use (modem, network, and so forth), and then choose whether you want to join an existing session or create a new session. Once you've successfully created a new game or connected with another player's game (using a network connection, a modem, and so on), you'll see the other players if they are in your area of the 3D world. Try shooting at the other player's character. If you hit the character, it will react and you'll probably start to feel the thrill of playing head to head in a networked game.

You might want to add the ability to maintain *hit points* for the players in a better manner so that you can keep track of the status of each one. You can add hit points to the screen using a heads-up display (HUD) so that players can continuously see this information as they wander around the 3D world.

Conclusion

This chapter covered all the aspects of DirectPlay needed to completely support multiplayer gaming using any of the available connection approaches (modem, network, and so on). With this code integrated into your application, you're guaranteed to catapult players to the next level of gaming excitement.

You can use the code presented in this chapter for any game you create. All you need to do to make the code work with your applications is define the messages that you want to pass between players. These messages can include those that broadcast when a player is moving, when a player's hit points change, and when a player fires a weapon and the projectile hits an object. With a little imagination, I'm certain you'll find a great deal of ways to use the message-passing abilities of DirectPlay!

CHAPTER SIXTEEN

Conclusion

That's it! You're now ready to start developing your first Microsoft Direct3D Immediate Mode application. As you've no doubt seen, Immediate Mode is an API that provides a powerful library of commands to help you produce real-time 3D games and simulations. Before you finish this book, I'd like to help you start thinking about the possibilities for application development using Immediate Mode.

Games

By far the most popular use of Direct3D is for game development. Throughout this book, you've seen portions of the code for the RoadRage game included on the companion CD. This game provides dynamic loading and unloading of segments of the 3D world to provide the fastest rendering possible. RoadRage also provides multiple textures, DirectInput-based joystick and steering wheel input, DirectPlay-based network gaming, and animated 3D characters. (For details on these features, see the "Using the Companion CD" section at the beginning of this book.). An editor for building new worlds using a 2D map editor is also provided so that you can build custom 3D worlds.

With the RoadRage game as a basis for your development, you should be well on your way to developing a powerful 3D application. I'd greatly appreciate it if you kept me abreast of any games you produce based on the code from this book and its companion CD. Feel free to e-mail me anytime at *kovach@ imageman.com* or *kovach@headtappersoftware.com* (the Web site for our game development company, Head Tapper Software). I'll be happy to post anything you want on the Web site *www.headtappersoftware.com* (such as code or 3D objects) to help everyone gain the most they can from the efforts of others in Direct3D development.

Most commercial games today at least provide support for Direct3D hardware acceleration. Many of the newer games have been developed using the Immediate Mode API. These games, which are among the top sellers in the industry, show off the capabilities of the Direct3D Immediate Mode API. With the integration of other Microsoft DirectX capabilities for network and input device support, these products offer some incredible game play! Using this book and the RoadRage code together with a new, imaginative storyline, you should be able to create a high-quality 3D game that competes quite well in this market.

Simulation and Virtual Reality

Although game development is by far the most prevalent use of Direct3D, this product is applicable to other 3D development arenas. The two I see the most potential in are simulation and virtual reality (VR). Many uses for 3D simulation exist, including driving and flight simulations and architectural visualization. Using the techniques covered in this book, you should be able to produce some excellent commercial-quality systems for these markets.

VR is another area that Direct3D is applicable to. I've been involved in the VR market for a number of years and find that Direct3D, in conjunction with the new PC-based 3D accelerator boards, has great potential for this arena. Only a few years ago, you needed to purchase a system that cost well over $50,000 to even consider developing a visually compelling VR environment.

Today, 3D accelerator boards that provide multiple 3D processors sell for well under $1000. Using one or two of these boards in a PC-based system, you can drive a VR headset with incredibly detailed, 3D graphic worlds. Combining these boards with a 3D head-tracking system (which have dropped greatly in price during the last few years) and some unique input devices, you can produce a full VR system. With a proper delivery format to the customer (such as site-based gaming or downloadable, networked software that runs on the Internet), it's possible to produce a revolutionary system. The market is ready to explode for the person who develops an application that captures the population's attention.

Remember, the RoadRage code on the companion CD provides the framework for stereo vision output, so you can support 3D VR headsets with very little additional effort on your part.

Good Luck and Enjoy!

On that note, I'll say goodbye. I hope you find Direct3D Immediate Mode (and DirectX in general) as enjoyable, useful, and powerful as I do. More important, I hope I've been helpful in teaching you how to use Direct3D Immediate Mode effectively in your development efforts. Have fun with Direct3D!

INDEX

Note: Italicized page references indicate figures, tables, or code listings.

3D acceleration hardware
    Direct3D support, 5
    and DirectDraw devices, 37
    and DXT surfaces, 227
    game support, 407, 408
    HAL and TnLHAL device support, 85
    transformation and lighting support, 79
3DNow!, 79
.3ds files, 332, 333
3D Studio, 332, 333

A

Accelerated Graphics Port (AGP) architecture
    DMA model, 81
    execute model, 81
    support for, 81–82
    and texture memory, 344–45
acceleration, 3D. *See* 3D acceleration hardware
accelerator tables, 21–22, 23
acquiring DirectInput devices, 185
AddAttachedSurface method,
    IDirectDrawSurface7 interface, 100
AddDpChatMessageToDisplay routine, 396–97
AddRef method, *IUnknown* COM interface, 7
AGP memory, 344–45
alpha, defined, 283
alpha blending
    code compilation, 297–98
    vs. color-key transparency, 291–93
    and frame buffer, 283–86
    legacy modes, 295–96
    overview, 283–86
    and palettized textures, 293–94

alpha blending, *continued*
    premultiplied vs. nonpremultiplied alpha,
        296–97
    setting states, 163
    special effects, 287–89
    and texture stages, 294
alpha testing, 163–64, 289–91, 293
ambient light
    controlling color, 164
    defined, 129
    vs. direct light, 128, 130
    setting level, 129
AMD 3DNow!, 79
animated characters
    loading and handling models in RoadRage
        application, 335–41
    methods of creating, 331–34
    overview, 331
    segmented, 331, 332
    single-mesh, 332–34
anisotropic texture filtering, 241
antialiasing, 165
applications, 3D. *See* Direct3D applications
application-specific messages vs. system
    messages, 392
attenuation. *See* light attenuation
autocentering spring, 201
axis data, 190

B

back buffers
    creating, 64–69, 78
    defined, 35
    and page flipping, 72–75

Peter J. Kovach

Peter Kovach has been involved in computer software and hardware development since the mid-1970s. Early on—after becoming intrigued with the initial Colossal Cave text adventure—Peter began developing text-based adventures. When the first home computers were introduced, he was hooked. He bought every type of computer that came out—several Tandy computers, a Color Computer, a Commodore Pet, an Ohio Scientific, an Apple, and the Exidy Sorcerer. Most of these machines had between 4 KB and 16 KB of memory, so developing graphics games on them was a challenge—but the Exidy Sorcerer, with its S-100 bus and 800 × 600 resolution, made the challenge fun.

Peter received his interdisciplinary degree in 1983 in computer science and business, with a focus on artificial intelligence and robotics. During college, he created a robot (that looked a little like R2-D2 from *Star Wars*) that had two unique arms: one with a rotating end effecter and articulated shoulder and elbow, and the other with a multifingered hand. The fun part was using an acoustic sensor for mapping the room and the planning program for determining the best path to a target location, replanning as new obstacles were located.

His first paying job was as an engineer developing robotic driverless vehicles, 3D simulators for military air (such as F15, F16, and Apache helicopter), land, and sea vehicles (submarines), and expert/learning systems (using Symbolics machines running Lisp and Silicon Graphics machines running GL). After 11 years in various levels of development and project management, he was eager to begin pushing the envelope in 3D virtual world development. After starting a company with a partner to develop 3D product prototyping using OpenGL on various Silicon Graphics platforms, he became vice president of R&D at Virtual Express, Inc. This company designed a series of virtual reality exercise equipment platforms (including a stair climber, a ski machine, and an exercise bike) that presented users a 3D view of the virtual world using head tracking. He currently works at Medtronic, where he is the project lead developing programmable, implantable medical devices that use a next-generation graphical user interface.

Peter has continued to work on 3D simulations and game development. He began writing articles and books on 3D game development a few years ago, focusing on DirectX from the time it was introduced because it was such an excellent choice for PC-based game development. He is also a partner in the company Head Tapper Software (*www.headtappersoftware.com*), a company focusing on state-of-the-art game engine development and founded by William Chin. In addition, Peter teaches classes on DirectX to help spread the word of its power and ease of use.

Peter enjoys woodworking, the outdoors, scuba diving, trapshooting, and a multitude of other hobbies he never has time to do anymore. He lives in Fridley, Minnesota, with his wife, Monica, and his daughter, Shannon.

The manuscript for this book was prepared and submitted to Microsoft Press in electronic form. Text files were prepared using Microsoft Word 2000. Pages were composed by Microsoft Press using Adobe PageMaker 6.52 for Windows, with text in Galliard and display type in Helvetica bold. Composed pages were delivered to the printer as electronic prepress files.

Cover Graphic Designer
Girvin | Strategic Branding & Design

Cover Illustrator
Glenn Mitsui

Interior Graphic Artists
Joel Panchot, Rob Nance

Principal Compositor
Gina Cassill

Principal Proofreader/Copy Editor
Patricia Masserman

Indexer
Julie Kawabata

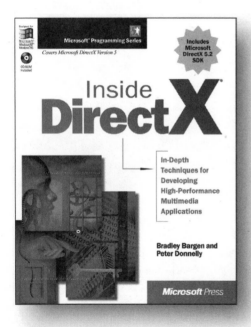

Masterful instruction.
Your pace.
Your place.

Master the tools of your trade with in-depth developer training—straight from the source. The award-winning MICROSOFT MASTERING series is now available in ready-anywhere book format. Work at your own pace through the practical, print-based lessons to master essential development concepts, and advance your technique through the interactive labs on CD-ROM. It's professional-level instruction—when and where you need it—for building real-world skills and real-world solutions.

Learn how to deliver *live data analysis* to your *Web and intranet pages.*

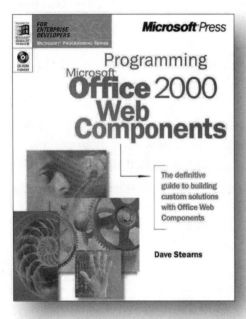

FOR ENTERPRISE DEVELOPERS

MICROSOFT PROGRAMMING SERIES

CD-ROM Included

Microsoft Press

Programming

Microsoft

Office **2000**
Web
Components

The definitive
guide to building
custom solutions
with Office Web
Components

Dave Stearns

U.S.A.	**$49.99**
U.K.	£32.99 [V.A.T. included]
Canada	$74.99

ISBN 0-7356-0794-X

Microsoft® Office 2000 features a powerful new set of ActiveX® controls called Office Web Components (OWC) that can help you build and distribute data analysis and reporting solutions. PROGRAMMING MICROSOFT OFFICE 2000 WEB COMPONENTS comes directly from the leader of the team that created OWC. It shows how to use these components, both in traditional containers and in Web browsers, for online analytical processing and transactional systems. The book begins with a complete overview of the Spreadsheet, Chart, PivotTable®, and Data Source components. Then it presents hands-on, step-by-step examples of how to use the components to build solutions for common business tasks such as reporting sales, processing timesheets, and charting business metrics. It includes complete, adaptable code samples plus extensive insider tips and tricks for enterprise developers.

Microsoft®

mspress.microsoft.com

Build *dynamic*
Web solutions
where databases
drive the action.

Build, debug, and deploy Web-based applications faster than ever before with PROGRAMMING MICROSOFT® VISUAL INTERDEV® 6.0. This essential resource takes you under the hood of the version 6.0 development environment, explaining how to capitalize on integrated functionality with Microsoft Internet Information Server (IIS) 4.0, Microsoft Transaction Server (MTS), and other business-tier services to architect a powerful new class of transactional Web solutions.

MICROSOFT LICENSE AGREEMENT
Book Companion CD

IMPORTANT—READ CAREFULLY: This Microsoft End-User License Agreement ("EULA") is a legal agreement between you (either an individual or an entity) and Microsoft Corporation for the Microsoft product identified above, which includes computer software and may include associated media, printed materials, and "online" or electronic documentation ("SOFTWARE PRODUCT"). Any component included within the SOFTWARE PRODUCT that is accompanied by a separate End-User License Agreement shall be governed by such agreement and not the terms set forth below. By installing, copying, or otherwise using the SOFTWARE PRODUCT, you agree to be bound by the terms of this EULA. If you do not agree to the terms of this EULA, you are not authorized to install, copy, or otherwise use the SOFTWARE PRODUCT; you may, however, return the SOFTWARE PRODUCT, along with all printed materials and other items that form a part of the Microsoft product that includes the SOFTWARE PRODUCT, to the place you obtained them for a full refund.

SOFTWARE PRODUCT LICENSE

The SOFTWARE PRODUCT is protected by United States copyright laws and international copyright treaties, as well as other intellectual property laws and treaties. The SOFTWARE PRODUCT is licensed, not sold.

1. **GRANT OF LICENSE.** This EULA grants you the following rights:

    a. **Software Product.** You may install and use one copy of the SOFTWARE PRODUCT on a single computer. The primary user of the computer on which the SOFTWARE PRODUCT is installed may make a second copy for his or her exclusive use on a portable computer.

    b. **Storage/Network Use.** You may also store or install a copy of the SOFTWARE PRODUCT on a storage device, such as a network server, used only to install or run the SOFTWARE PRODUCT on your other computers over an internal network; however, you must acquire and dedicate a license for each separate computer on which the SOFTWARE PRODUCT is installed or run from the storage device. A license for the SOFTWARE PRODUCT may not be shared or used concurrently on different computers.

    c. **License Pak.** If you have acquired this EULA in a Microsoft License Pak, you may make the number of additional copies of the computer software portion of the SOFTWARE PRODUCT authorized on the printed copy of this EULA, and you may use each copy in the manner specified above. You are also entitled to make a corresponding number of secondary copies for portable computer use as specified above.

    d. **Sample Code.** Solely with respect to portions, if any, of the SOFTWARE PRODUCT that are identified within the SOFTWARE PRODUCT as sample code (the "SAMPLE CODE"):

        i. **Use and Modification.** Microsoft grants you the right to use and modify the source code version of the SAMPLE CODE, *provided* you comply with subsection (d)(iii) below. You may not distribute the SAMPLE CODE, or any modified version of the SAMPLE CODE, in source code form.

        ii. **Redistributable Files.** Provided you comply with subsection (d)(iii) below, Microsoft grants you a nonexclusive, royalty-free right to reproduce and distribute the object code version of the SAMPLE CODE and of any modified SAMPLE CODE, other than SAMPLE CODE, or any modified version thereof, designated as not redistributable in the Readme file that forms a part of the SOFTWARE PRODUCT (the "Non-Redistributable Sample Code"). All SAMPLE CODE other than the Non-Redistributable Sample Code is collectively referred to as the "REDISTRIBUTABLES."

        iii. **Redistribution Requirements.** If you redistribute the REDISTRIBUTABLES, you agree to: (i) distribute the REDISTRIBUTABLES in object code form only in conjunction with and as a part of your software application product; (ii) not use Microsoft's name, logo, or trademarks to market your software application product; (iii) include a valid copyright notice on your software application product; (iv) indemnify, hold harmless, and defend Microsoft from and against any claims or lawsuits, including attorney's fees, that arise or result from the use or distribution of your software application product; and (v) not permit further distribution of the REDISTRIBUTABLES by your end user. Contact Microsoft for the applicable royalties due and other licensing terms for all other uses and/or distribution of the REDISTRIBUTABLES.

2. **DESCRIPTION OF OTHER RIGHTS AND LIMITATIONS.**

    - **Limitations on Reverse Engineering, Decompilation, and Disassembly.** You may not reverse engineer, decompile, or disassemble the SOFTWARE PRODUCT, except and only to the extent that such activity is expressly permitted by applicable law notwithstanding this limitation.

    - **Separation of Components.** The SOFTWARE PRODUCT is licensed as a single product. Its component parts may not be separated for use on more than one computer.

    - **Rental.** You may not rent, lease, or lend the SOFTWARE PRODUCT.

    - **Support Services.** Microsoft may, but is not obligated to, provide you with support services related to the SOFTWARE PRODUCT ("Support Services"). Use of Support Services is governed by the Microsoft policies and programs described in the user manual, in "online" documentation, and/or in other Microsoft-provided materials. Any supplemental software code provided to you as part of the Support Services shall be considered part of the SOFTWARE PRODUCT and subject to the terms and conditions of this EULA. With respect to technical information you provide to Microsoft as part of the Support Services, Microsoft may use such information for its business purposes, including for product support and development. Microsoft will not utilize such technical information in a form that personally identifies you.

- **Software Transfer.** You may permanently transfer all of your rights under this EULA, provided you retain no copies, you transfer all of the SOFTWARE PRODUCT (including all component parts, the media and printed materials, any upgrades, this EULA, and, if applicable, the Certificate of Authenticity), **and** the recipient agrees to the terms of this EULA.

- **Termination.** Without prejudice to any other rights, Microsoft may terminate this EULA if you fail to comply with the terms and conditions of this EULA. In such event, you must destroy all copies of the SOFTWARE PRODUCT and all of its component parts.

3. **COPYRIGHT.** All title and copyrights in and to the SOFTWARE PRODUCT (including but not limited to any images, photographs, animations, video, audio, music, text, SAMPLE CODE, REDISTRIBUTABLES, and "applets" incorporated into the SOFTWARE PRODUCT) and any copies of the SOFTWARE PRODUCT are owned by Microsoft or its suppliers. The SOFTWARE PRODUCT is protected by copyright laws and international treaty provisions. Therefore, you must treat the SOFTWARE PRODUCT like any other copyrighted material **except** that you may install the SOFTWARE PRODUCT on a single computer provided you keep the original solely for backup or archival purposes. You may not copy the printed materials accompanying the SOFTWARE PRODUCT.

4. **U.S. GOVERNMENT RESTRICTED RIGHTS.** The SOFTWARE PRODUCT and documentation are provided with RESTRICTED RIGHTS. Use, duplication, or disclosure by the Government is subject to restrictions as set forth in subparagraph (c)(1)(ii) of the Rights in Technical Data and Computer Software clause at DFARS 252.227-7013 or subparagraphs (c)(1) and (2) of the Commercial Computer Software—Restricted Rights at 48 CFR 52.227-19, as applicable. Manufacturer is Microsoft Corporation/One Microsoft Way/Redmond, WA 98052-6399.

5. **EXPORT RESTRICTIONS.** You agree that you will not export or re-export the SOFTWARE PRODUCT, any part thereof, or any process or service that is the direct product of the SOFTWARE PRODUCT (the foregoing collectively referred to as the "Restricted Components"), to any country, person, entity, or end user subject to U.S. export restrictions. You specifically agree not to export or re-export any of the Restricted Components (i) to any country to which the U.S. has embargoed or restricted the export of goods or services, which currently include, but are not necessarily limited to, Cuba, Iran, Iraq, Libya, North Korea, Sudan, and Syria, or to any national of any such country, wherever located, who intends to transmit or transport the Restricted Components back to such country; (ii) to any end user who you know or have reason to know will utilize the Restricted Components in the design, development, or production of nuclear, chemical, or biological weapons; or (iii) to any end user who has been prohibited from participating in U.S. export transactions by any federal agency of the U.S. government. You warrant and represent that neither the BXA nor any other U.S. federal agency has suspended, revoked, or denied your export privileges.

DISCLAIMER OF WARRANTY

NO WARRANTIES OR CONDITIONS. MICROSOFT EXPRESSLY DISCLAIMS ANY WARRANTY OR CONDITION FOR THE SOFTWARE PRODUCT. THE SOFTWARE PRODUCT AND ANY RELATED DOCUMENTATION ARE PROVIDED "AS IS" WITHOUT WARRANTY OR CONDITION OF ANY KIND, EITHER EXPRESS OR IMPLIED, INCLUDING, WITHOUT LIMITATION, THE IMPLIED WARRANTIES OF MERCHANTABILITY, FITNESS FOR A PARTICULAR PURPOSE, OR NONINFRINGEMENT. THE ENTIRE RISK ARISING OUT OF USE OR PERFORMANCE OF THE SOFTWARE PRODUCT REMAINS WITH YOU.

LIMITATION OF LIABILITY. TO THE MAXIMUM EXTENT PERMITTED BY APPLICABLE LAW, IN NO EVENT SHALL MICROSOFT OR ITS SUPPLIERS BE LIABLE FOR ANY SPECIAL, INCIDENTAL, INDIRECT, OR CONSEQUENTIAL DAMAGES WHATSOEVER (INCLUDING, WITHOUT LIMITATION, DAMAGES FOR LOSS OF BUSINESS PROFITS, BUSINESS INTERRUPTION, LOSS OF BUSINESS INFORMATION, OR ANY OTHER PECUNIARY LOSS) ARISING OUT OF THE USE OF OR INABILITY TO USE THE SOFTWARE PRODUCT OR THE PROVISION OF OR FAILURE TO PROVIDE SUPPORT SERVICES, EVEN IF MICROSOFT HAS BEEN ADVISED OF THE POSSIBILITY OF SUCH DAMAGES. IN ANY CASE, MICROSOFT'S ENTIRE LIABILITY UNDER ANY PROVISION OF THIS EULA SHALL BE LIMITED TO THE GREATER OF THE AMOUNT ACTUALLY PAID BY YOU FOR THE SOFTWARE PRODUCT OR US$5.00; PROVIDED, HOWEVER, IF YOU HAVE ENTERED INTO A MICROSOFT SUPPORT SERVICES AGREEMENT, MICROSOFT'S ENTIRE LIABILITY REGARDING SUPPORT SERVICES SHALL BE GOVERNED BY THE TERMS OF THAT AGREEMENT. BECAUSE SOME STATES AND JURISDICTIONS DO NOT ALLOW THE EXCLUSION OR LIMITATION OF LIABILITY, THE ABOVE LIMITATION MAY NOT APPLY TO YOU.

MISCELLANEOUS

This EULA is governed by the laws of the State of Washington USA, except and only to the extent that applicable law mandates governing law of a different jurisdiction.

Should you have any questions concerning this EULA, or if you desire to contact Microsoft for any reason, please contact the Microsoft subsidiary serving your country, or write: Microsoft Sales Information Center/One Microsoft Way/Redmond, WA 98052-6399.

OWNER REGISTRATION CARD

0-7356-0613-7

Register Today!

Return the bottom portion of this card to register today.

Inside Direct3D®

FIRST NAME | MIDDLE INITIAL | LAST NAME

INSTITUTION OR COMPANY NAME

ADDRESS

CITY | STATE | ZIP

(   )

E-MAIL ADDRESS | PHONE NUMBER

U.S. and Canada addresses only. Fill in information above and mail postage-free.
Please mail only the bottom half of this page.

For information about Microsoft Press®
products, visit our Web site at
mspress.microsoft.com

Microsoft®